ALSO BY HELMUT SCHMIDT

A Grand Strategy for the West
Perspectives on Politics

MEN AND POWERS

HELMUT SCHMIDT

MEN AND POWERS

A Political Retrospective

Translated from the German by Ruth Hein

Random House   New York

Library of Congress Cataloging-in-Publication Data

Schmidt, Helmut.
[Menschen und Mächte. English]
Men and powers: a political retrospective / by Helmut Schmidt;
translated from the German by Ruth Hein
p. cm.
Translation of: Menschen und Mächte.
Includes index.
ISBN 0-394-56994-6
1. Schmidt, Helmut. 2. Germany (West)—Foreign
relations. 3. Germany (West)—Politics and government—1982–
4. Heads of state—Germany (West)—Biography. I. Title.
DD260.85.S3613 1989
943.087'7'092—dc20   88-43219

Manufactured in the United States of America

3 5 7 9 8 6 4 2

FIRST AMERICAN EDITION

Book design by Carole Lowenstein

Note to the American Reader

This book was originally meant to address German readers; it was written and first published in the German language. Nevertheless, Americans may also find my experiences with other nations and their leaders as well as my analyses and evaluations to be illustrative examples of how the political class in Germany views the great powers of the world in general and the United States in particular.

My personal experiences with four American presidents may differ somewhat from the experiences of my French or British colleagues and of other European leaders, but—generally speaking—my evaluations may not differ too much from theirs. All of us in Western Europe regard the United States as our most important ally; and American interests, goals, and attitudes are of overriding importance to us. Although we share our basic values and the basic principles of our constitutions with America, we are sometimes taken aback by what we perceive as misunderstandings of our European interests, goals, and attitudes by American leaders.

In international relations—between citizens, enterprises, or governments—we must try to understand our friends or partners, competitors, and adversaries alike. Otherwise they themselves will not show understanding, and friendship may collapse, deals may fail, competition may turn into enmity, conflicts may turn into hatred. Compromises over conflicts may turn into sources of misunderstanding and differing interpretations, and therefore into suspicion, mistrust, and new conflicts. It was this lesson, which I learned from my political life, that has moved me to write down what I seem to have understood about the Soviets, the Chinese, and the Americans—or, in other words, about the three world powers and the men at their helms.

Only two years after this book was finished we witnessed the sad events in Beijing's Tienanmen Square as well as the rapprochement between the two Communist giants, crowned by the visit of Mikhail Gorbachev with Deng Xiaoping. While the latter development was foreseen in this book as a possibility, the bloody repression of the Chinese students came as a surprise to most observers in the West, and certainly to me. It seems unclear as yet whether and why Deng himself ordered the troops to shoot. He may have been motivated by his terrifying memories of the so-called Red Guards and of the turmoil and atrocities that were brought about by a former generation of youngsters during the Maoist Cultural Revolution. The role of Prime Minister Li Peng and of other leaders is as yet also not easily analyzed. But I wonder whether we really need a thorough scrutiny of the actions of current Chinese leaders, who will not live forever. What matters more is the necessary effort to understand the possible and also the probable developments of the huge Chinese state and its future role within the global strategic and economic fabric.

In this global aspect the underlying thesis of this book still is likely to be proved right by future events. I assume that China's role as a strategic superpower will basically not be suspended by domestic Chinese developments. It also seems highly probable that the rapprochement between Beijing and Moscow will be maintained, increasing China's capabilities to become a dominating regional power in East and Southeast Asia. At the same time China will remain a developing country for decades to come, regardless of whether Deng Xiaoping's process of economic reforms will be undercut by recent political events—maybe even interrupted for a longer period of time—or be continued. Whatever happens, China will not become a major factor in the world economy for the next twenty or thirty years.

These expectations lead me to the conclusion that, however strongly we must and will condemn Chinese violations of the basic rights of the individual, we must also carefully avoid interference with, or intervention into, Chinese sovereignty, and violations of Chinese self-esteem and sensitivity, be it by ourselves or by friendly or allied states and their leaders.

The economic situation of the People's Republic of China may signal weakness for some time to come, but we could precipitate dangerous developments if we were to interpret Chinese economic weakness and vulnerability as an invitation or a chance for interference from the outside. Instead we need to maintain our connections with China as far as possible and keep open our various channels of communication. We are dealing with a nuclear-strategic power, the population of which amounts to one fifth of the world's population and the governing political party of which has proven its capacity for brutal action over four decades. At the same time we are dealing with a nation with a cultural heritage older than that of any European or American nation. There is no need to abandon our hopes for a revival of the presently subjugated cultural values of that heritage.

The political developments inside the other Communist superpower during the last couple of years have in no way been instigated or propelled by the use of force but on the contrary by the abandonment of traditional police state practices. The process of *glasnost* and *perestroika* inside the Soviet Union is nevertheless even more dramatic than the repression in China. Mikhail Gorbachev has established himself as an energetic, pragmatic leader in both economic reform and freedom of speech and other basic rights of the individual. He is a courageous man, and he may need all his courage to overcome both the enormous objective difficulties and the subjective inertia of the Soviet bureaucracies and of the masses of the Soviet citizens.

He has curtailed the costly international operations in Afghanistan, Kampuchea, Angola, and elsewhere that were launched during the Brezhnev era. He is obviously aware of the necessity of cutting down the enormous military budget, which consumes about 15 percent of the Soviet gross national product (his ministers speak of "only" around 9 percent, but there are some Western estimates on the order of 20 percent or even more). At the same time the military-industrial complex absorbs the qualitatively best research, development, and production capacities. By my assessment no tangible improvement of the standard of living for 290 million citizens is attainable within a politically acceptable time frame if *perestroika* is not accompanied by a considerable armaments reduction. Gorbachev's freedom to reduce Soviet armaments unilaterally is politically limited. He urgently needs additional treaties with the West—and with the United States in particular—for arms reduction and disarmament the strategic result of which can be presented vis-à-vis his adversaries at home as establishing an equilibrium of forces with the West. The INF treaty ought to serve as a useful precedent because it has diminished the old rigid attitudes on both sides and has installed numerous bilateral verification inspections.

Today there does exist an open window of opportunity for East-West arms treaties, but only as long as *perestroika* is pursued. In case *perestroika* fails and Gorbachev is replaced by a more conservative leadership, that window will probably close. It is possible that time is running out faster than the West seems to realize, because at the end of the 1980s the food and consumer-goods supplies are obviously sparser in the Soviet Union than at the beginning of the decade. Today the old economic system is no longer functioning, but a new system is not in place yet, either. The Soviet masses have been led to hope for a rather quick success of *perestroika* and now—under the new freedom of *glasnost*—voices of disappointment and impatience become louder and stronger.

Glasnost has brought about an amazing freedom of expression not only compared with the Brezhnev era, but also in comparison with almost all the other Communist states in the world; the only parallel cases are Hungary and Poland. Basket Three of the Helsinki Final Act is rapidly becoming reality in the Soviet Union. Ironically enough, the recently established human rights might endanger the success of the whole reform process. The quest for national identity in the three Baltic republics, in Armenia, and in a number of republics with an Islamic cultural background could undermine the powers exercised by Moscow and precipitate intervention by force. The spillover into East European member states of the Soviet-led Warsaw Pact could create a loss of cohesion in that pact and endanger the Soviet Union's strategic power position even in Central Europe. If Moscow reacts with military force or even the threat of it, such actions may spell the end of the reform and put an end to the Gorbachev era and to *perestroika*. In such a case a return to the old Russian strategies that have been followed for almost the entire lifetime of Soviet rule cannot be excluded.

At this moment, however, the breathtaking political developments in Poland and Hungary hold our attention. Both countries are clearly on the path toward democracy and pluralism, but they and their new governments find themselves in dire economic straits. The same may soon occur in East Germany and—possibly—in Czechoslovakia. In the autumn of 1989 the mass exodus of East German citizens to West Germany has led to the replacement of Erich Honecker, head of the one-party state for nearly two decades, and, even more sensationally, to the opening of the Berlin Wall and of all the GDR borders. Political pluralism and economic reforms are being called for, but as yet the agenda for the immediate future has not been set.

Any newly reformist Eastern European state needs economic assistance from the West: Poland, Hungary, and—hopefully in the near future—East Germany and Czechoslovakia. In providing it, the West must not forget that the Soviet Union maintains considerable numbers of its armed forces in each of these four countries. Consequently, further arms-reduction agreements are necessary, for which Gorbachev appears accessible. It is high time that a reduction toward an agreed-upon equilibrium of the existing forces in Europe is undertaken.

The vast majority of the people living in both halves of the European continent and I myself have placed their hopes in Gorbachev's success. They also hope that their governments will avail themselves of this window of opportunity. It is natural for the West Europeans, including the Germans, to look to Washington for prudent guidance in this situation.

HELMUT SCHMIDT
Hamburg, November 1989

Preface

This book contains recollections and analyses of my relations with the three superpowers: the Soviet Union, the United States, and China. It is not an attempt at an autobiography, since I have always had my suspicions of political narcissism. Of necessity such life stories tempt the author to present himself as flawless or at least to put himself in a better light than history's judgment will justify. Nevertheless I have always been fascinated by the memoirs of both politicians and artists; I find that they stimulate me to think, to critically review, to supplement or amend the opinions I had previously formed.

In the three major sections of this book I describe my personal impressions of the Russians, Americans, and Chinese, and in particular my encounters with their statesmen. I try to present their views, as well as my own, on the problems that concerned my country and myself and that in part continue to be relevant. Occasionally I cannot prevent a repetition or a second treatment of a topic, when the subject was of equal importance in, say, Washington and Moscow.

During the years I was a member of the government of the Federal Republic of Germany, I took part in a fascinating kaleidoscope of human and political encounters: with heads of state, with government leaders and ministers, with artists and scientists, as well as with people who were never in the limelight. Much has been written about the isolation of leading politicians and statesmen, but that truism tells only half the truth. In reality my years in government were the source of many friendships, and even more frequently I was granted genuine partnerships.

At the present time profound and sometimes shocking changes are occurring in all three superpowers. They justify an effort to present and evaluate, from a German viewpoint, the epochs that came to an end—or are about to come to an end—in the 1980s in Moscow, Washington, and Beijing. Whether the changes within the three powers will also cause crucial changes in the world cannot be predicted. To me it is still unclear whether Mikhail Gorbachev will succeed in permanently altering the Soviet landscape.

As for George Bush, he will have to address, along with unresolved problems of foreign policy, those resulting from the United States' enormous foreign debt in particular. And it is not Japan, the economic giant, that will carry increasing weight in international politics but the People's Republic of China, which at present is fairly insignificant as far as the world economy is concerned—but whose future course cannot be plainly envisioned. Before we can judge opportunities for the future, we must be familiar with the factors that have determined the present; of course we can only guess whether and to what extent they will affect the future.

I do not claim to offer a history of the contemporary world as I lived it. Rather, I want to pass on some of what I believe I learned or came to understand in the conversations I held with people from other nations. I am not basing these pages on official documents or archives that have since been opened nor on the published works of the leaders I met with. I am not a historian. The dialogues and analyses described here are based on the notes I kept. They are meant to reflect not an objective view of history but the impressions I started out with or thought I should start out with, as well as the impressions and opinions I arrived at.

To deny my own subjectivity or to suppress my identity as a German and a Social Democrat would be unnatural. This is the personal report of a man who was born at the end of the First World War, who as a young man did not—thanks to his family upbringing—become a Nazi but who, being drafted during the Second World War, believed his patriotic obligations were overriding. This book reflects the insights and experiences of a man who, as a twenty-six-year-old prisoner of war, was guided by much older prisoners to become a Social Democrat and who relatively late in his life—thanks to the Western allies, especially Great Britain and the United States—for the first time experienced democracy for himself.

I am more deeply marked by Kant's categorical imperative and Marcus Aurelius' *Meditations* than by Lassalle, Engels, or Marx; but the greatest influences on me were my older Social Democratic contemporaries and friends. The experienced mayors Max Brauer, Wilhelm Kaisen, Ernst Reuter, and Herbert Weichmann and the Bundestag Social Democratic delegation leaders Fritz Erler, Carlo Schmid, and Herbert Wehner gave me my education in foreign affairs; and whatever I learned in the realm of economics I owe most of all to Heinrich Deist, Karl Klasen, Alex Möller, and Karl Schiller. I must add, however, that many men and women in industrial and union management, in the sciences, and in public relations, many civil servants and soldiers, as well as people in the other parliamentary parties—the CDU (Christian Democratic Union of Germany), the CSU (Christian Socialist Union of Bavaria), and the FDP (Free Democratic Party)—have influenced my judgment and my actions.

Foreign models and examples also influenced me profoundly. I took my place on the international stage in the second half of the 1950s as a young and insignificant member of parliament—an Anglophile, as was Hamburg, the district that elected me. As the 1950s came to an end, I realized more and more clearly how closely the fate of Germany is entwined with that of the United States. In the 1960s I recognized German-French friendship as an essential precondition of European peace. Throughout the years keeping this peace has seemed to me the overriding political consideration.

During the first millennium of the Christian era the German people settled and flourished in the center of Europe. Unlike many of the other European peoples, Germans live neither on an island nor on a peninsula, nor have they been shielded by natural barriers; they exist in an open, flat land that is comparatively densely populated. We Germans have more foreign neighbors than any other people in Europe. Of all the world's nations, only Russia and China are surrounded by a similar number of countries; but Russia and China are huge. Germany, on the other hand, is small and, as a result of Hitler's totally controlled and totally lost war, is divided in two. Auschwitz and the Holocaust will long cast their shadow on our neighbors' minds—and on everything the younger Germans do.

I have always believed in each nation's right to self-determination. If ever in the course of the next century we Germans are to be reunited, such an event will not come about against our neighbor's will, nor without his assurance that he can trust Germany to be a dependable, constant, peaceful neighbor.

If Germans and Russians still have a long way to go before becoming good, trusting neighbors, we alone are not to blame. Many European nations, not only Germany, feel threatened by the Soviet occupation of Eastern Europe, most especially the Eastern European nations. The Soviet Union's expansionist strivings for security as well as its efforts toward the international spread of Communist ideology have brought about a feeling of insecurity and fear. This situation motivated Western Europe and North America to join in the North Atlantic Treaty Organization. But many Russians feel equally threatened—without justification, at least inasmuch as they see Germany as a potential source of danger. Nevertheless I understand the Soviet Russians completely; they lost twenty million people in Hitler's war. The people of the Soviet Union want peace just as we do. Their Communist leaders share the same desire.

Because of the latent threat of war, we Germans need alliances with other democratically ruled nations, with the United States of America, and with our Western European friends. At the same time, however, we must make every effort to achieve friendly relations with the Soviets, with the Poles, and with the other bordering nations in the eastern half of the Continent. This twofold task is enormously difficult: Pursuing it relentlessly occasionally triggers a mistrust of Germany—now by the East, now by the West. This state of affairs will also be addressed in these pages.

In the early 1970s the Federal Republic of Germany ceased to be a political midget. Not only did our nation of sixty million people develop one of the greatest, most efficient economies in the world, but during the 1970s it also learned to play a political role commensurate with its importance and its geographic and historical position. This was no simple process. The leaders of many nations, even outside our immediate geographic area, have helped us in our effort—and, in return, have asked us for help.

In more than thirty years of parliamentary activity—thirteen years as a member of the German government, more than eight years as chancellor, and ever since—I have made every effort to contribute to an understanding among nations. The problem remains monumental and is posed anew for each generation. Peace cannot be created once and for all; it must be brought about over and over. I considered it my primary duty to serve it in my generation. I know my counterparts beyond our borders felt much the same about their obligation. Nonetheless international conflicts of interest, misunderstanding of one's own and others' interests, and domestic pressures time and again have led to situations of the utmost gravity. We must therefore remember to recognize the interests, fears, and hopes of other nations and their governments. Anyone who pictures others as enemies cannot bring about peace. Anyone who refuses to sit down and talk with others and who will not listen to them cannot understand them. This book is first of all the result of conversations with the statesmen of the superpowers. I am beholden to them.

Furthermore, I would like to express my thanks for suggestions and corrections to those who helped me in revising the manuscript: Kurt Becker, Willi Berkhan, Klaus Bölling, Gerd Bucerius, Jens Fischer, Manfred Lahnstein, Ruth Loah, Hans Matthöfer, Lothar Rühl, Eugen Selbmann, Manfred Schüler, Horst Schulmann, Walter Stützle, and my wife. I did not accept every suggestion; the responsibility for errors, lapses of memory, and opinions is mine alone.

I began the manuscript in 1984 and, because of other work, have been able to finish it only now. I hope to have enough time left for another book, in which I will present my impressions of dealing with the European nations and their heads, especially France and Europe as a whole.

HELMUT SCHMIDT
Hamburg, April 1987

Contents

I

Living
with the
Russians

I FIRST MET Soviet General Secretary Leonid Brezhnev in May 1973 at the official residence of German Federal Chancellor Willy Brandt. It was the beginning of a very special and personal relationship between a Russian who, while emotional, was politically calculating and a north German who, though cooler, was by no means devoid of emotion.

Brandt gave a small, rather private dinner for perhaps ten or twelve guests. Since Brandt and Brezhnev—as well as the two foreign ministers, Walter Scheel and Andrei Gromyko—had met several times in previous years, the conversation was loose and informal, although of course it had to be interpreted paragraph by paragraph and was therefore frequently interrupted. Of necessity consecutive translation creates pauses that give the speaker and listener time to sort out their thoughts. Thus what the conversation loses in spontaneity it gains in clarity.

In the course of the evening—I was never sure whether the move was premeditated or grew out of a momentary mood—Brezhnev became caught up in a monologue on the sufferings of the people of the Soviet Union during the Second World War. The Ukrainians, he said, had endured unspeakable suffering; he himself had served in the Ukraine as a major general and political commissar of the Eighteenth Army. Brezhnev worked himself up into a troubled and troubling description, increasingly detailed, of the losses, the horror of the war, and the Germans' criminal outrages, their violations of international law. He always referred to the enemy as "the fascist soldiers" and "the fascist invaders."

I had lived through the same war. I knew he was right. I also knew he was right to speak as he did—though at times I thought he exaggerated somewhat. Willy Brandt and the other Germans present must have felt the same way; all of us listened respectfully to Brezhnev for a long time. We understood clearly that it mattered to him to make his hosts aware of the great turn of events, the great strength of mind required of him and the Russians in agreeing to collaborate with the Federal Republic of Germany, to the Moscow nonaggression treaty, and to the Four Power Agreement on the governance of Berlin—and to the visit to Bonn, the capital of the former enemy.

As Brezhnev spoke, I thought about my own wartime experiences, now more than thirty years in the past. I recalled the smell in the burning town of Sychevka, the corpses along the sides of the road—my battery had repeatedly received orders to set the villages and towns on fire with two-centimeter antiaircraft guns in order to smoke out nests of enemy resistance on the outskirts. I recalled my uncomprehending horror the time I witnessed the inhuman conditions of a prisoner transport at a supply base behind the lines. And I recalled the so-called commissar order; though we ourselves did not have to watch it being carried out, we did know that its aim—the execution of all captured commissars—had been achieved. I thought about our nervousness at any personal contact with Russian prisoners of war; I remembered the mutual fear German soldiers and Russian civilians had of each other when, in the winter of 1941, we finally took refuge in houses to get some sleep—the Germans on the floor and the Russians on the stove. I remembered our own fears: my profound horror at the dreadful screams of another soldier dying of a serious abdominal wound. I remembered my panic and fear when, in December 1941, we were cut off and trapped near Klin, with possible imprisonment staring us in the face. Brezhnev was right: the war had indeed been terrible, and we Germans were the ones who had brought it to his country.

But at the same time he was wrong in his one-sided view. It was not only German soldiers, but Russian ones as well, who had committed atrocities against their then enemies. And he was wrong to think of all German soldiers as fascists. The great mass of German soldiers, the noncommissioned officers, the officers, and the generals had not been Nazis any more than the great mass of the Soviets were Communists. Both sides believed in the necessity of serving and defending their countries. It had been known for a long time that the commanders in chief on both sides were ruthless. Brezhnev accused Hitler alone; did he not know, or did he not want to know, that Stalin too had had many of his enemies executed? I had no intention of comparing the two; nor did Brezhnev have any reason to mention Soviet war crimes.

Nevertheless, I decided to contradict him. No, not actually to contradict, but to make the other side of the war tangible to him and his entourage. Brezhnev must have spoken for twenty minutes or so. I began softly and with some hesitancy, but I spoke for nearly the same length of time. Willy Brandt did not stop the former German soldier, who had so recently exercised a command over the Bundeswehr.

I conceded that Brezhnev was right to a large degree, but I objected to the phrase "fascist soldiers." I described my generation's situation: Only a few of us, I said, had been Nazis and believed in the "Führer"; they were the exception. Most of us had felt it our duty to follow the orders issued by our military commanders; like us, only a small number of them had been Nazis. During my eight years in the army I had never, in fact, served under a single committed Nazi. But I had been raised to be a patriot.

I reminded Brezhnev of those officers who, as patriots, had fought both against the enemy and against Hitler, prepared to commit high treason but not to betray their country. I spoke about the deaths in the bombed-out cities, of the misery during retreat and rout; I noted that those of us who were on the front lines often did not know for weeks whether our parents, wives, and children at home were still alive. While at night we cursed Hitler and the war, during the day we did our duty as soldiers. I described to our Russian guests the schizophrenia of the young German soldiers who endured and withstood the ravages of war.

Whether any of this was news to Brezhnev I could not tell, but I could see that he was listening attentively. It is probable that this exchange of bitter war memories contributed substantially to the respect that characterized our relationship in the years from 1974, when I first visited Moscow, to 1982, the year of his death and my retirement from the chancellorship. During those eight years we returned two or three times to the topic we discussed in May 1973. In the summer of 1980, during a fairly dramatic confrontation in the Kremlin, I remarked, "General Secretary, I have never lied to you"; impulsively, Brezhnev interjected, "That is the truth."

At the time of our 1973 conversation I had been involved in national politics for twenty years. As a representative to the Bundestag, as head of the Social Democratic Party (SPD), and as minister of defense, I had worked out a picture of the world that included Russia's historical development as well as the current role of the Soviet Union in power politics. The double overall strategy of the West à la Pierre Harmel concluded by the Atlantic alliance in 1967, Richard Nixon's policy of arms limitation vis-à-vis the Soviet Union after 1968, and Willy Brandt's policy toward Russia and the Warsaw Pact countries—what Germans call *Ostpolitik*—from the outset of his chancellorship were not new considerations for me. On the contrary: I had long advocated similar ideas—in speeches in the Bundestag and at party congresses, in two books on strategy, and as a member of the NATO North Atlantic Council.

I had long been a staunch supporter of the necessity both to check the Soviet Union's further expansion with a joint Western defense capability and, on the basis of the security thus brought about, to cooperate with the Soviet Union. This cooperation would be exercised not only in the area of arms limitations and economic exchange but, it was to be hoped, on the cultural level as well. In short, I supported an overall strategy of balance and accommodation of interests between East and West.

When in October 1974, by an agreement previously made by Willy Brandt and Brezhnev, I visited the capital of the Soviet Union for the first time as chancellor of West Germany, I am sure that carefully compiled dossiers concerning the attitudes of the new chancellor were being consulted in Moscow. Surely the researchers looked into where and when the young officer had been assigned to the unit of the First Panzer Division in 1941 and 1942 and whether he might possibly have committed war crimes or other offenses. Surely there were notes on a private vacation I—along with my wife, Loki, my daughter, and my coworker Wolfgang Schulz—had spent in Moscow and Leningrad in the summer of 1966.

It had been an interesting trip: With me at the wheel of my Opel Rekord, equipped with expensive Intourist vouchers, we had traveled from Nürnberg via Prague, Wroclaw, and Warsaw to the two Russian metropolises and back by way of Helsinki, 5,000 kilometers in all. All along our route the Soviet police took note of our arrival times and promptly made telephone reports, a procedure that was not kept from us. Surely they also reported on the sights that attracted us and the people we spoke with. I have a particularly vivid memory of the bronze portals of the cathedral in the citadel of Novgorod and especially the beauty of Leningrad enhanced by city planning: the clear midsummer nights in the very European city on the Gulf of Finland, its handsome

canals and quays—and of course the almost incomparable artistic richness of the Hermitage.

At the time I was deputy parliamentary leader of the SPD, and the
Soviet Foreign Ministry sounded me out by assigning some carefully
selected journalists to conduct long interviews with me. Finally I had
a three-hour conversation with the then assistant foreign minister,
Vladimir S. Zemyanov. Subsequently Zemyanov was ambassador to
Bonn while I was chancellor; he knows a great deal about German art,
German history, and German interests. In 1966 he repeatedly brought
the conversation back to his country's economic development and the
idea of economic collaboration with the West. I went along with him
but placed the emphasis on stabilizing a strategic balance and on developing nonaggression treaties between the Federal Republic and the
Soviet Union and the various Eastern European states, including the
boundaries of the German Democratic Republic. It was especially on
this point that Zemyanov showed interest, but he would not be drawn
into any comment.

In 1974 there must therefore have been enough reliable sources
about my views on matters of mutual interest. I am sure that relevant
reports existed from 1969, when my close friends Alex Möller and Egon
Franke and I, at the time leading personalities of the Social Democratic
parliamentary group, had paid a quasi-official visit to Moscow. In Germany 1969 was an election year. The Grand Coalition in Bonn was
about to come to an end as the differences of opinion on foreign policy
between Chancellor Kurt Georg Kiesinger and Foreign Minister Willy
Brandt became increasingly unbridgeable. We believed that a change of
government and Brandt's assuming the chancellorship were entirely
possible, and we were eager to explore whether this change would allow
normalized relations between Bonn and Moscow.

In Moscow in 1969 the people who spoke to us were on a higher level
than those we had talked with three years before. Several important
members of the Central Committee as well as Politburo and foreign
ministry staff, including Valentin Falin, were included. Falin, who was
later to be ambassador to Bonn, had a talent for conceiving new ideas.
But most important, Andrei Gromyko received us in Spiridov Palace for
a lengthy interview. Since at the time Gromyko was not yet a member
of the Politburo, we also met with Dmitri S. Polyanski, who was a
member.

During our talk with Gromyko I outlined the subsequent *Ostpolitik*
of the Brandt-Scheel government, without having any idea whether
such a government would ever become actuality. In my opening re-

marks I made it clear that the Germans would never give up hope of living in *one* house. They were convinced, I said, that history gave them this right. But in the light of the actual situation we were prepared to sign treaties with the German Democratic Republic based on equal rights. Among them would be a nonaggression treaty that would respect all the GDR's boundaries according to international law. Gromyko expressed no opinion on this topic; instead he spoke about West Berlin. In this respect, he said, our viewpoints were radically different.

Our talk touched on many factual and abstract questions of international politics. At the end Gromyko asked for greater elasticity and flexibility on the part of West Germany. I replied, "Elasticity can be a virtue if it is coupled with firm moral principles. But it leads to political advantages only when both partners display elasticity." The talk with Polyanski took a similar course, though a more cursory one.

Both sides took careful notes on all remarks, and our words were surely analyzed for the "Schmidt dossier." Leonid Brezhnev must have studied it before my first official visit five years later. The dossier will certainly have included my book, *Die Strategie des Gleichgewichts (A Grand Strategy for the West),* published in 1969. In it I analyzed the power and military role of the Soviet Union in relation to its own allies, to the West, and specifically to Germany. I drew conclusions from my analysis that might affect my own nation's defense and foreign policies. Finally, I am convinced, the Soviet military studied my stated objectives, actions, and utterances during the three years I had served as defense minister.

I had resolutely advocated confirmation of the Western alliance and internal reform and strengthening of the Bundeswehr. For the first time I had published a "defense white paper," which was available to anyone. It had been worked up by my friend Theo Sommer, who headed the defense ministry planning staff on the Hardthöhe, after many conferences to gain information and hold discussions with representatives of the ranks as well as the military leadership.

Finally, during the turbulent Bundestag debates in the spring of 1972 concerning the treaties negotiated by the Brandt-Scheel government with the Eastern bloc, I had vehemently advocated ratification, justifying its necessity by my overall view of the Soviet Union. Presumably in 1974 the advisory staffs in Moscow could not fit me into the mold of alleged German "militarism" or "retaliation." At the same time I can hardly have given them the impression of a man advocating "appeasement" or accommodation. Probably their analysis of my opinions was more or less accurate.

Presumably the Soviets had even more detailed profiles of my predecessor in office, Willy Brandt; his foreign minister, Walter Scheel; and
his negotiator, Egon Bahr, who held the office of undersecretary of
state. The fact that Scheel moved up to the office of president and Bahr
became federal minister in my first cabinet may have appeared to the
Russians as a sign of German continuity. Brandt's resignation may,
however, have faced them with a political riddle, especially as the new
foreign minister, Hans-Dietrich Genscher, was an almost unknown
quantity.

One of the crucial factors in developing Bonn's *Ostpolitik* after 1969
was the parliamentary head of the SDP, Herbert Wehner. For thirteen
years, working with his counterpart in the Free Democratic Party
(FDP), Wolfgang Mischnick, and closely assisted by his colleague in the
Foreign Office, my friend Eugen Selbman, he promoted the steady
progress of German *Ostpolitik*. Wehner had a major influence especially
on our policies toward Moscow and East Berlin; unfortunately neither
Soviet nor German public opinion was able to recognize his full importance to this process.

Herbert Wehner was hugely talented in every area of politics. Jean
Monnet, Henry Kissinger, later Erich Honecker, and many other observers of German politics understood as much. A former German
Communist, he had suffered a great deal in Moscow after 1933, during
the Stalin era. He had renounced his allegiance to Communism, and
after 1945 he had become a Social Democrat and returned to Germany,
where he was received with great confidence by the SPD's Kurt Schumacher. I first met him in 1949, when he was editor of the *Hamburger
Echo*, and starting in 1953 I ran into him daily in the Bonn parliament.
It was Wehner who in June 1960—after Fritz Erler, Carlo Schmid,
himself, and others had planted the ideological seeds—once and for all
anchored the foreign policy intentions of my party in the realities
already established: NATO, European Community, Bundeswehr.

No fair-minded observer can doubt Wehner's inner ties to Western
values, the values of democratic society and individual freedom—although a few domestic critics tried repeatedly to disparage his credibility. Wehner's temperament and his occasional bluntness did at times
supply occasion for such criticism; the right wing especially mistrusted
his steadfast support for accommodation with the Soviet Union and his
unwavering commitment to steps in the direction of a reunification of
all Germans. Konrad Adenauer treated him with respect; in spite of a
few vehement confrontations, I loved the man. He seemed to me the
guarantor of a vigorous synthesis of a social, democratic domestic policy
and an *Ostpolitik* based on the close Western alliance. When in 1969 I

was asked to serve as minister of defense, I made it a condition of my acceptance that Wehner—who until then had been federal minister— would take over my office as head of the Social Democratic Party in the Bundestag. I wanted to make sure I had backing. I was not disappointed.

When expedient, Herbert Wehner could wield a sledgehammer with the best of them; but he was also extremely sensitive to others, especially people in need. He is said to have remarked that he loved Russia because that country had suffered so much. In 1969 and even in 1974, during my first visit as chancellor to Moscow, the Soviet leadership may still have been suspicious of him, an apostate. Probably Moscow and East Berlin both needed longer to understand his importance to our *Ost- politik*. I, on the other hand, knew that Wehner's conceptions of an Eastern policy had been firmed up before Willy Brandt developed his own and before Brandt's associate at the time, Egon Bahr, spoke of "change through accommodation" in the first half of the 1960s. In all the years of my chancellorship I made Herbert Wehner the sounding board for my policies once a week, most especially my Eastern policy— and I could always depend on him.

Russian-Soviet Continuity

MY IDEAS about the Soviet Union in the 1960s and 1970s differed from the views I hold now only in details but not in principle. I have always considered the foreign policy and overall strategy of the Soviet Union in many respects to be a direct continuation and extension of the policies of old Russia from the sixteenth and seventeenth centuries to the eighteenth and nineteenth. To put it roughly and simply, I felt that three fourths of the strategy hatched in Moscow was traditionally Russian, while one fourth was Communist.

Lenin—and Stalin as well—was probably right to see Ivan the Terrible as the real founder of the absolutist Greater Russian state with a centralized government. Ivan IV, born in 1530, assumed the title of czar in 1547 and led the first Russian war of conquest across the old boundary of the Kiev state, ending in victory over the Tatar Volga dukedoms of Kazan and Astrakhan. This was the beginning of the Russian history of land expansion resulting in extensive Russification of foreign peoples, as well as occasional forced resettlement, which secured Russian domination of Novgorod, Tver, and Pskov. Stalin did not invent the brutal weapon of forced resettlement; Peter I and Catherine II had used the same tool before him. Russian expansion was directed at the Baltic; Constantinople, the Bosphorus, and the Dardanelles were also frequent focal points. At the same time Russian eyes turned to the Caucasus, the lower Volga, the Caspian Sea, Tashkent, Samarkand, Turkestan, and Afghanistan. On the horizon the immeasurable expanse of northern Asia all the way to the Pacific and, beyond the Bering Strait, Alaska beckoned. And these led to Mongolian, Chinese, eventually Japanese, and finally German territories. More recently political strong points in the Near East, Africa, and Latin America have been added to the list.

In spite of many setbacks, and whether the state was headed by Ivan IV, Catherine II, Stalin, Nikita Khrushchev, or Brezhnev, the Russian expansionist drive never really died out. It is based on a Moscow-centered messianism that has remained inherent in the Russian idea of nationhood. When Constantinople was conquered by the Turks in 1453 and the eastern Roman center of Christianity was lost, Moscow declared itself to be a "third Rome . . . and there will never be a fourth." This firm faith in salvation took different forms in the second half of the nineteenth century, manifesting itself as Moscow-centric pan-Slavism and again in the twentieth century as Moscow-centric international revolutionary Communism.

A turn toward the humanistic and liberal spirit of Western Europe or the conscious embrace of Russian messianism, with all its attendant dangers—that would be one way to describe Russia's choices during the nineteenth century. In literature Turgenev supports the first position, while Dostoyevski supports the second, which represents the mainstream of Russian opinion—although the authorities first condemned Dostoyevski to death and then exiled him to Siberia.

Today dissidents in the Soviet Union face a comparable question. But all Russians who have opted for individual freedom and the inviolability of human dignity, for a government of law and an open society that would refuse to subordinate the individual to the collective will and would assign a higher value to basic rights than to the claims of the state or its rulers—these Russians have until now always been in the minority and for the most part a politically insignificant, marginal group. It is highly questionable whether this situation can be significantly changed under Gorbachev—much as I myself might wish it.

The European Enlightenment, the ideas of a constitutional state and of democracy, had little influence on Russia's political development. Peter the Great—like the Meiji emperor in Japan during the second half of the nineteenth century—had purposely opened his country to European science and technology; but—again like the Meiji emperor—he did not materially alter the spirit of his people. He wanted to use the European example in order to grow equal to the then European great powers.

The Russian-Soviet expansionary drive can be understood as imperialism; the justification for it is the same as in all other parts of the world, whether it be a matter of the Portuguese, Spanish, or British empires, ancient Rome, or the United States, all of which were established chiefly by means of hostile land seizure. Whenever the West speaks of Soviet imperialism, it is impossible to ignore the moral condemnation implicit in the phrase. At the time the earlier empires were put together, there were few such moral judgments. The subjugation of alien peoples and the dissolution of their nations were considered less a sin on the part of the conqueror than an inevitable destiny. When my generation learned in school of Alexander the Great, Caesar, Charlemagne, and Napoleon, it never occurred to our teachers to tell us these legendary conquerors had committed crimes against humanity. On the contrary, they were accorded the status of heroes. The same was true for the white man's conquest of the North American continent, originally settled by Indians. And no one would ever have thought to call the Athenian statesman Pericles and the philosopher-king Marcus Aurelius to account for heading states that were unthinkable without conquest and slavery. The philosophical, moral, and legal condemnation of the conquest of foreign lands and their peoples is of relatively recent date. The short-lived dreams of a world empire harbored by the Japanese, Mussolini, and Hitler would not—if it were not for the fact that unimaginable crimes were involved—have been condemned so absolutely a century and a half ago as they were in the 1930s and 1940s. Since that time open claims to global domination have been considered unlawful, even criminal, the world over.

After the pact between Hitler and Stalin was broken, the Russian Communists also adopted this view. But they seemed incapable of measuring their own territorial conquests by the same criteria. Sometimes Moscow legitimized its expansionism as a necessary historical element, citing the doctrine of Communist world revolution and the limitation on international law within the socialist camp. Of course not all Soviet politicians and strategists share the conviction that they are fulfilling Lenin's vision of making Moscow the center of a worldwide historical-materialist upheaval—which, by the way, would stand Marxist philosophy on its head. Many of Moscow's politicians and diplomats may well think very pragmatically, even cynically, when it comes to world revolution and look on the self-understanding of the USSR's and other countries' Communist parties as more desirable instruments of Soviet foreign policy. It is difficult to imagine these Soviet diplomats, who are often very well educated and sensitive lovers of Western art, as devout believers in world revolution. But they are conscientious servants of their state and its interests.

In 1974 I did not doubt Mikhail Suslov's conviction that it was his mission to bring the revolution to the rest of the world, nor the orthodoxy of less prominent assistants, such as Boris Ponomaryov. Given the heavy load of their daily obligations, such men as Brezhnev, Alexei Kosygin, and Nikolai Tikhonov probably had little time to spare for historical or philosophical reflections. But they were convinced of the legitimacy of expanding their domain—a conviction that had become a matter of course to Russians in the course of their history. Of course the centuries of foreign rule by Tatars and Mongols played a large part in shaping this attitude. Since Ivan III destroyed the city-states, such as Novgorod, Russia has become familiar with absolutism in all its forms and consequences, from the murder of successors to the throne through serfdom to exile in Siberia. Historically most Russians hardly ever lived in conditions of personal freedom; underprivileged groups and classes existed at most times. That is why to a hard-working man such as Gromyko his country's present system probably seems completely normal, even though he is very familiar with, for example, the fundamentally and categorically freer American social system.

In short, it makes little sense to keep on measuring the policies of the Russians—or the Soviets—by today's French, British, or American standards. This is surely not a way to influence them. Even less influence will be exerted by moralistic accusations and indictments. Quite the opposite: Such attitudes may force Moscow into a dogged retreat into Russian messianism. Close relations with Western social and political culture over many generations must take place before the Russians can acquire an understanding of the basic values of people raised and educated in Western cultures. In the meantime it is essential that the West protect itself against a further expansion of Russian-Soviet power. Because today Russia is not only, as that brilliant French thinker Alexis de Tocqueville predicted as early as the 1830s, one of the two superpowers—along with the United States—to emerge from the Second World War; it is also the only remaining expansionist world power. The West must adhere to the sum and substance of the overall strategy formulated by George F. Kennan in 1947 for the United States: ". . . the main element of any United States policy toward the Soviet Union must be that of a long-term, patient, but firm and vigilant containment of

Russian expansive tendencies." If the West does not lose sight of this overall strategy, it will enjoy an advantage, namely that of being able to calculate Soviet strategy—if not entirely, at least to a large extent.

The original directions of Russian expansionism have not changed, but new ones have been added since the early 1960s, as a result of the economic and political needs of the Third World countries relinquished by or freed from colonial rule. To put it more precisely, this new situation presented opportunities for the Soviets to exert their influence. The development of the Soviet merchant fleet and the unusually single-minded construction of a powerful deep-sea navy on all the world's oceans by Admiral Sergei G. Gorchkov, who took his bearing from Alfred T. Mahan's doctrines of naval warfare as well as the naval policies of admirals Alfred von Tirpitz and Paul Nimitz, were both precondition and consequence. On the whole the arms limitation treaties between Washington and Moscow at the time were restricted to intercontinental nuclear warfare; therefore even in an age in which both sides proclaimed their desire for peaceful coexistence, large areas of the ideological and power-political contest were excluded. In any case, enough elbow room remained for a single-minded buildup of armaments.

Soviet expansion and intervention usually occur in quiet ways. Direct military operations using Soviet armies have been rare; in general they have been limited to the German Democratic Republic (1953), Hungary (1956), Czechoslovakia (1968), and Afghanistan (1979)—that is, mainly countries within the Warsaw Pact. Only once after 1945 did the Soviet Union depart from this cautious limitation that avoided the risk of war—when Nikita Khrushchev attempted to install Soviet nuclear missiles in Cuba in 1962. That was, as it were, a step onto the threshold of the United States, and the missiles were intended to have a threatening effect on America. But in the end Khrushchev had to pay for this foray with the loss of his power.

Brezhnev and the Politburo he headed returned to the cautious expansion strategy of a carefully calculated limited risk. Military intervention in Afghanistan after late 1979 has been kept within the framework of the concept of limited risk, as was the continued indirect support, provided for more than twenty years, of North Vietnam and later of Vietnamese conquests. The Soviets are chess masters; they are not good at poker and are in no way inclined to stake everything on one bet.

The caution displayed by the Soviet leadership has its roots in part in the outcome of the Cuban missile crisis. Moscow is determined that

in any international crisis it will never again be in the position where
it is forced to back down because it is strategically inferior. It is this idea
that stands behind the idée fixe of catching up with the United States
on the level of global strategy, whatever the economic cost. The Soviet
view is: "An event such as Cuba will never occur again."

But long before Cuba there were other bitter experiences: the humiliating outcome of the Russo-Japanese War of 1904–1905 and the lost
sea battle of Tsushima; the First World War with the enforced peace
of Brest-Litovsk in 1918 and the Peace of Riga in 1921, after the West
had intervened in the Russian civil war on the side of the "Whites" and
again during the war against Poland. But the real nightmare was Hitler's
advance on Stalingrad, on the peaks of the Caucasus, and to the suburbs
of Leningrad and Moscow; only after years of bloody battles and only
with American help could his forces be repelled. In the end the victory
over Hitler cost twenty million lives.

The leaders of the Soviet Union suffer from a typically Russian phobia
about security and safety that first manifested itself in 1856, after the
defeat in the Crimean War. "Russia's borders are secure only when
Russian soldiers stand on both sides of the frontier," a czarist minister
is said to have stated. Stalin's policy of creating a circle of satellite states
just beyond the Soviet Union resulted in an American system of alliances erected by John Foster Dulles in Europe as well as in the Middle
and Far East, essentially as a *cordon sanitaire*. This step, in turn, was seen
by Moscow as a menacing encirclement, and the break with Mao Zedong's China, provoked by Khrushchev in the late 1950s and subsequently seriously aggravated by Mao, only served to reinforce this
understandable phobia.

And there was another element as well. The Soviet Union's striving
for equality in the global strategic sphere and for "equal security" with
the other superpower was not merely a defensive posture. It was also
compensation for the inferiority complex in the face of the country's
obvious inability to achieve economic equality with the Western industrial societies.

From a military standpoint the Soviet security phobia is an expression
of the fear of potential foes, which—in historical sequence—Germany,
the United States, and China are seen to be. In spite of Germany's
division into two states, and in spite of formidable Soviet troop stationing in central Europe, the fear of Germany remains. Since it also serves
as an instrument to discipline the Poles, it has been artificially kept alive.
If the opportunity should arise to isolate the Federal Republic of Germany, the artificial threat of Germany can also be used to keep the
French and other Western European countries on edge.

The deep concern about possible inferiority to the United States remains one of the principal driving forces behind the Soviet Union's massive buildup of missiles and naval forces. The country's concern about China is less serious, but it too has been clearly felt since the evolution, at first inconceivable to Moscow, of a communist state to political independence, countrary to all doctrine. But probably the fact of China's four-times-greater population weighs heavier in the scales than Beijing's ideological independence. A subliminal prejudice against the yellow race is an added factor. Covert aggression against the foreign colossus could not be ignored even in the era of apparent harmony. Moscow regards the People's Republic of China as a future world power, as attested to by the Soviet deployment of conventional and nuclear forces along the 7,000 kilometers of their joint border.

Acknowledgment of the historical continuity of Russian expansion does not require a belief in geopolitical determination. This continuity seems rather to be a matter of a political-cultural tradition that has always seen itself to have a mission, originating in the Russian Orthodox Church and subsequently adopted and continued by the Communist Party of the Soviet Union. It is too soon to tell whether under Gorbachev a basic, lasting alteration of this old tradition can be achieved.

Soviet Strategy and German Interests

A NY WEST GERMAN statesman committed to pursuing the interests of the German nation must have a clear picture of the interests and directions of our neighbors to both the West and the East. He must put himself in their place and see the situation through their eyes. It is the only way he can realistically assess his own options.

In 1974, having just been elected chancellor, I was facing my first visit to Moscow. At the time there was hardly a European government that genuinely regretted the partition of Germany. A different opinion may have prevailed in Washington or faraway Beijing, but Washington could not translate its understanding of the German situation into a policy directed straightforwardly at reunification of the two Germanys, and Beijing had no chance to act anyway—not even theoretically.

Thus the world seemed largely satisfied with the division of Germany; paradoxically, it was far less content with the division of Europe. In Germany, after decades of vain hopes for reunification, we had finally learned to live with the partition of Germany without complaining too much and without indulging in embarrassing self-pity; but neither did we make it a primary issue. I must admit that neither then nor now have we abandoned hope of living under one roof someday, even though we are aware that such a day lies in a far distant, unforeseeable future and that until then it is important to preserve the cohesiveness of the nation.

We knew then, and we know now, that given the partition of Europe, this unity cannot be maintained by the German nation against the Soviet Union. We must direct our Soviet policy to winning Moscow's acceptance of our desire to maintain our national identity and to ease the destiny of those Germans who have been forcibly confined in a Communist state.

But the means available to the Federal Republic are severely limited. Bonn cannot accommodate the Soviet Union to such an extent that its social order comes under Russian-Soviet influence. The liberty and dignity of the individual on the one hand, the social and governmental order based on the principle of freedom on the other—to preserve these must, in the end, be the predominant objective of any West German government. This order is jeopardized by the threat posed by Soviet military power and by the expansionism, evident throughout Europe, that underlies that threat.

Other democratic states in Western, Northern, and Southern Europe also feel threatened. Though most of them lie farther away from the boundary that separates East and West, some of these nations contain strong Communist minority parties that cooperate with Moscow. Awareness of the potential threat is what has driven the Western European states into NATO, led to the establishment of the European Community, and created increasingly close ties between the free countries of Europe on the military, political, and economic levels. Nor should we forget that even the neutral states—Sweden, Finland, Austria, and Yugoslavia—indirectly base their liberty on the common self-determination of the states united in the European Community and NATO. Thus, because of the threats emanating from the Soviet Union, the most important objectives for Western Europe are the preservation of its freedom and the maintenance of peace.

Unlike Italy, France, England, Holland, and Denmark, the Federal Republic of Germany is not a national state but merely a part of the nation. This circumstance underlies the Germans' particular desire to forge a modus vivendi with the Soviet Union, in order at least to make the living conditions of those east of the dividing line as bearable as possible. Elsewhere in Western Europe, of course, a deep wish also exists for improved living conditions for all Eastern Europeans and for greater individual, cultural, and political freedom for the Poles, Hungarians, and Czechs. The consciousness of the historical and cultural unity of all of Europe is deeply ingrained in people's thoughts and feelings; it was most strongly exemplified on the political level by Charles de Gaulle. But of course the ties that unite Germans on both sides of the border by family, friendship, home, history—in short, sociocultural ties—are incomparably stronger than, for example, the ties uniting Frenchmen and Hungarians or Italians and Poles.

The Federal Republic's territory forms a geostrategic barrier blocking the Soviet Union from any expansion in the direction of Western Europe along the narrow land strip from the Baltic to the Alps that leads through Central Europe. Since the earliest migration of peoples, Central Europe—a small, geographically confined area—has over and over again served as a battleground for foreign conquerors.

Because of today's confrontation of the two military alliances, the territory of the Federal Republic cannot be renounced. The loss of this entity—or even its withdrawal from the continental NATO area, which can be defended only by joint efforts—would be irreplaceable; it would also mean an almost total isolation of Scandinavia and Southern Europe.

If it came down to it, NATO could stand France's departure, though it would be painful; it might survive a possible elimination of one of the smaller members without endangering its ability to act defensively; but the withdrawal of the Federal Republic would be something of a catastrophe. It could be balanced only by a considerable retreat on the part of the Soviets. But at present—unlike the situation that prevailed thirty years ago, at the time of the Rapacki plan (a proposal for the denuclearization of Central Europe made by a Polish foreign minister)—there is absolutely no basis for speculation that this might occur. For the Soviet Union to withdraw to such an extent would mean that Moscow would have to give up its power clamp around East Germany, Poland, and Czechoslovakia.

All this leads to the following conclusion: In the interests of strategic balance in Europe and therefore the defense capabilities of the West, West Germany cannot relinquish or loosen its ties to the West, not even though it may desire to work toward concessions on the part of the Soviet Union. Any attempt of this sort would provoke deep suspicion and political reactions by its Western allies, while at the same time disquieting Poland, Czechoslovakia, Hungary, Sweden, Finland, Austria, *and* the eastern sector of its own nation—because such a change could lead to a corresponding aggravation of Soviet pressure on these countries.

But these are not all the limitations on the Federal Republic's options. West Germany's blocking position, it must be noted, makes it the most important European deployment zone for Western land and tactical air forces. Thus, in the military theory of both sides, it is potentially the most important battleground. On the Warsaw Pact side, the same is true of East Germany. Thus for Germans in both German states, the presence on their soil of foreign forces in addition to their own—a situation completely unprecedented during peacetime, especially as it includes a considerable number of "tactical" nuclear weapons—is a constant reminder of the precarious nature of European peace. Whenever there is public discussion of military plans and the deployment of weapons, great waves of fear naturally begin to swell. The awareness in both West and East Germany of living in one of the most important nuclear targets of the world is not, after all, the stuff of nightmares but is a very realistic assessment of the situation. At the same time this awareness is the source of the desire for mutual arms reduction worked out in treaty negotiations—a desire we Germans feel with special fervor.

These feelings hold true, as I have said, for the citizens of the other German state as well. No doubt it applies to Erich Honecker, the current East German head of government, as well as to future leaders of East Germany. It must be pointed out, however, that the government of the German Democratic Republic is in a significantly worse starting position than West Germany in one respect: It recognizes that its political existence depends on the presence of Soviet troops on its territory. For West German citizens, by contrast, democracy—though originally imposed on them by the victorious Western powers—has by now become so natural and practical that they have long ago ceased to rely on outside support.

And yet the government of the Federal Republic, even if it must remain unpersuaded of the legitimacy of the East German government, can do nothing to destabilize that government, much less to undermine it. Such actions would elicit Soviet countermeasures, which would additionally aggravate the situation of the Germans and their relations with each other.

On the other hand, the Federal Republic is at one disadvantage compared with the Democratic Republic. The troops commanded by the East Berlin government—the Nationale Volksarmee (National People's Army)—hardly matter in comparison to the troop strength available to the Soviet leadership in Eastern Europe; they are more properly seen as auxiliary forces. The Federal Republic's forces, on the other hand, are the nucleus of all the Western forces in Europe. The number of United States and British troops stationed in Europe or available in case of mobilization is relatively minor, and France withdrew its troops from NATO in 1966. French troops cooperate in joint defense but are not required to. Because of the Bundeswehr's key role, the government of the Federal Republic is under constant pressure from its Western allies to strengthen its troops and arsenal. Thus little room exists for unilateral military concessions on the part of the Federal Republic to the Soviet leadership. On the contrary, the numerical superiority of the Soviet Union's troops and the reserves it can mobilize in Europe—a situation that has not changed in forty years—precludes any unilateral reduction of forces, which would swing the already precarious balance of power against the West.

Finally, the government of the Federal Republic must always take account of its human, economic, cultural, and political relations with West Berlin, the geographically and militarily isolated western section of the former German capital. In addition, when it comes to Berlin—even with full compliance with the Four Power Agreement—the Soviet Union or East Germany could interfere in various ways. Some troublesome questions therefore arise: Where, and with what actions and offers, can Bonn persuade the Soviet Union to participate in normalizing relations in Central Europe? What would make at least the maintenance of a feeling of communality and an easing of relations between the two parts of the German nation acceptable? There are only two areas in which Soviet interests, on the one hand, and German negotiating options, on the other, are significant enough to bring about progress. For one, there has been a decrease in Soviet concern about the Germans, especially with regard to the East-West border established in 1945. There is also the area of economic relations between the Federal Republic and the Soviet Union. In the light of Russian-Soviet suspiciousness, both areas, however, also require reciprocity: mutual renunciation of political-military violence and mutual advantages in the exchange of German capital goods for Soviet raw materials.

These were the realizations we Social Democrats built on when, in 1969, we established a social-liberal coalition to run the government and began to make it work. The agreements we finally arrived at were not easily achieved either bilaterally, in relation to Moscow—especially in view of our determination not to allow ourselves to be maneuvered into bargaining away the objective of German unity—or multilaterally, in relation to Moscow as well as to Washington, Paris, and London. Here we had many misgivings about abolishing the Four Power Agreement on Berlin; without it we could not have accepted the agreements.

In the 1960s, and later as a cabinet member, I had taken part in the intellectual preparations for the new *Ostpolitik*. As chancellor I was fully determined to continue and elaborate on these policies, as the Soviets well knew. They could hardly be aware, however, how much my education in history, literature, and music helped me in this regard.

Those of us who were raised in the old Hanseatic cities of Hamburg and Lübeck are very conscious of the centuries-long trade with Novgorod, Pleskau, Tartu, and Reval. These economic relations go back to Ivan IV; even after the Hanseatic cities had lost their original significance, the relationship was repeatedly revived, not last by Peter the Great. Russian troops freed Hamburg from the harsh Napoleonic despotism; when I was a little boy, my grandfather still told stories "from the time of the French." In school I had been introduced to Turgenev and Dostoyevski, as well as Pushkin, Tolstoy, Chekhov, and Lermontov; after the war I read Mayakovski, Sholokhov, and Solzhenitsyn. I was attracted by the "Russian soul" as I encountered it in the works of these writers and as it was celebrated by Gerhart Hauptmann and Thomas Mann.

The war in Russia had let me experience the boundless expanse of the Russian steppes, where those novels and tales were set. During the 1960s I had noticed the crowds in the Tretyakov Gallery in Moscow, as well as in the Hermitage in Leningrad, thronging in front of European paintings. I could not imagine European music without the Russian masters—without Tchaikovsky and Mussorgsky, without Shostakovich and Prokofiev. I had been the recipient of heartwarming hospitality in Russia; but I had also seen the deep scars Hitler's war had left on the cities of the country and the hearts of the Russians.

Of course I knew what Russia owed to Western Europe as far as philosophy, science, and architecture were concerned. In spite of the country's quite different "political culture," which repelled me, the Russians, the White Russians, and the Ukrainians seemed to me—and continue to seem—part of the continuum of Europe's cultural evolution.

Feelings and reflection led me to believe that it was correct to tie Russians as much as possible to Europe and European culture—a task to which we in Germany bring more historical qualifications and experience than the peoples of Western Europe or the United States. For centuries, even though at times we were not aware of what was happening, we functioned as a bridge between Russia—though it was also under Asian influence—and Europe, a function not like that performed by German-speaking Austria for the Hungarians and the people of the

Balkans. The Finns, the Balts, the Poles, the Polish and Galician Jews, the Czechs, and the Slovaks also reaped many benefits from this bridging function of the Germans and Austrians; and they have also contributed a great deal to the mutual exchange.

The bridges must be restored and made strong. For the Russians it has always been difficult—and will be no less difficult in future—to understand the West; it has always been difficult for the West to understand Russia and Russian politics—but the Germans can bring about understanding. They have done it often throughout their history. I was conscious of this fact when, in 1974, I traveled to Moscow for the third time in my life, to speak with the most powerful man in the huge Soviet nation.

I was the third German chancellor to go to Moscow to meet with the leadership. In September 1955 Konrad Adenauer had paid a visit and, contrary to the advice of his foreign minister, Heinrich von Brentano, had realistically assessed the German situation and established diplomatic relations with the Soviet Union. That was the beginning, the striking up of a protracted process of coming to terms with the situation created by Hitler's war. It was through Adenauer's mediation that Moscow released the last ten thousand German prisoners of war who were still detained in the Soviet Union—ten years after the end of the war. Germany had believed the number to be far higher; now the Germans had to become resigned to the fact that hundreds of thousands of missing soldiers had died either during the fighting or in prisoner-of-war camps. Nevertheless, the Soviet leadership, by releasing these prisoners, had made a gesture toward Germany—though it was hardly a page of glory in the annals of history. But the German leaders continued to refuse to admit that the partition of Germany ratified at Potsdam was a fact and that there was no getting around it.

The Hallstein doctrine thus continued to prevail. According to this doctrine (named for Walter Hallstein), the government of the Federal Republic represented all of Germany and Bonn was therefore not allowed to have diplomatic relations with nations that had recognized the German Democratic Republic as being a state and therefore subject to international law. Of course within the framework of the doctrine, West German relations with East Germany were quite unthinkable. Small remnants of the doctrine survive to this day, especially in the ideology of many of the Christian Democratic Union–Christian Socialist Union (CDU-CSU) politicians as well as some of the leaders of the FDP. Another remnant of that period is the form in which our authorized representatives to the other German government are still addressed:

They may not be called ambassadors because, the argument goes, that title signifies diplomatic relations, and such relations can exist only with foreign nations, not with the German Democratic Republic.

Although these are pseudolegalistic formal arguments that annoy the leadership of East Germany, I did nothing to change this peculiarity of protocol during my eight years as chancellor. For one thing, I wished to avoid unnecessary controversy with sections of the FDP, which was a partner in our coalition. Another—and most important—reason was that I wished relations with the German Democratic Republic to continue to be handled from the chancellor's office. I did not want to see them fall to Foreign Minister Hans-Dietrich Genscher who, though tactically gifted, had a strong legalistic orientation. In addition there were considerations of expediency concerning my friend Egon Franke; at Herbert Wehner's advice, I allowed his ministry for domestic affairs, which had become insignificant for all practical purposes, to remain in existence.

However, during my time in office the Hallstein doctrine no longer played a limiting role in our pursuit of our interests toward the East. This relief we owed especially to Willy Brandt, his foreign minister, Walter Scheel, and Egon Bahr.

Brandt was the second chancellor to visit Moscow. His meeting with Brezhnev in August 1970, inspired by the desire "finally to get beyond empty talk and determined to make a new beginning," marked the breakthrough. Though his nonaggression treaty with Moscow did not lend legitimacy to the borders established after the war in Eastern Europe—something the subsequent nonaggression treaties with Warsaw and Prague and the friendship treaty with the German Democratic Republic also did not do—it nevertheless included a promise not to violate them. This was the basis for Moscow's new attitude toward Bonn.

As well as a change of Soviet attitude toward the West, Brandt's visit of August 1970 brought about the beginning of Moscow's *Öffnungspolitik,* or "opening policy," which was marked a little while later by meetings with Nixon in mid-May 1972 in Moscow and mid-June 1973 in Washington, as well as the SALT I agreement and the ABM treaty, and which would be crowned in 1975 by the Helsinki Conference on Security and Cooperation in Europe and the Helsinki Accord.

Many Western observers were puzzled by the Soviet policy of détente. I never doubted Brezhnev's concern with the possibility of war; there was no denying his love of peace. But his feeling was countered by the equally obvious Soviet desire to consolidate the empire won in

the Second World War and the following twenty-five years, as well as
Soviet sovereignty over the eastern part of Central Europe, and to
achieve its recognition by the West. Moscow sought to stabilize the
partition of the world into Soviet and American spheres of influence,
with the exclusion of large segments of the Third World, where competition with the United States was expected to occur at some future date.
At that time, the Kremlin's new *Öffnungspolitik* probably was the ideal
fulfillment of the Soviet objective of consolidating its possessions.

Presumably a third motive weighed just as heavily. Strategic parity
with the United States had in fact been achieved; Moscow was now
eager for Washington officially to acknowledge this state of affairs to the
world. This was also a motive for the internal politics of Greater
Russia—and was surely essential to restoring consensus within the Politburo.

Fourth, those members of the Politburo—headed by Alexei Kosygin—who were responsible for the Soviet economy may have been
influenced by the idea that an arrangement with the West would furnish
the Soviet Union with breathing space in which the nonmilitary part
of the domestic economy, which had obviously been constrained by the
forced arms buildup, could flourish. Much later, under Mikhail Gorbachev, the economic motive took on much greater importance.

At the time I was not sure whether these four motives, or even one
of them, were shared or sanctioned by the ideologues surrounding
Mikhail Suslov and the military. It was also hard to measure what effect
the Soviet Union's undeniably increasing irritation at the independent
course, including nuclear armament, taken by Mao had on its policy of
détente with the United States. However the motives of the Politburo
are linked, Chancellor Brandt recognized the opportunity they represented for Bonn, and together with Brezhnev he shaped a viable framework for future German-Soviet relations. It would be up to his successor
to fill in this framework during years of spadework.

As for the West, the resolution of the NATO Council of Ministers
concerning the recommendations of the Harmel report had already
envisaged détente in general terms, and Germany had had an active part
in its formulation. On the part of the Soviets, Leonid Brezhnev had
been the driving force; Richard Nixon, Georges Pompidou, and Willy
Brandt had been his most important allies in this effort. Now all three
had left the world stage within a few months of each other—Brandt
being forced to retire when a foolish, provocative East German espionage attempt was discovered.

Brezhnev could not help but be disturbed by the loss of his most important allies, especially as from time to time he met with difficulties in the Politburo when he attempted to advance various steps in his policy. Because Brezhnev's prestige was at risk, he was determined that this visit by the new German chancellor should be a success. Although my objective was the same, our negotiations would nevertheless turn out to be difficult. That was obvious from the very first day.

My First Visit
to Brezhnev

T HE red carpet treatment laid on for us in Moscow was especially lavish. When our Boeing, decorated with the emblems of the Bundeswehr, rolled down the runway at Vnukovo airport, we were received not only by Prime Minister Kosygin and Foreign Minister Andrei Gromyko, which would have been more than enough to satisfy protocol, but also by the general secretary himself. Such had not been the case when either Nixon or Brandt had visited Moscow. I took it as a very special gesture.

Equally special was Brezhnev's effusive, almost excessive cordiality; the television lens saw the very martial military ceremony merely as a background to the general secretary's demeanor. Hundreds of Muscovites, waving little flags, and all the members of the city's German colony stood on the tarmac. The wives of our hosts—Kosygin had brought his daughter instead—presented flowers to my wife, Mrs. Genscher, and Mrs. Schlei. Kosygin and Gromyko stayed in the background.

Our cortege drove to the guest houses in the Lenin Hills, already prepared for us. Brezhnev himself showed me the rooms that were to be my home for the next three days, sat down in my living room for several welcoming vodkas, and urged Kosygin and Gromyko to join us.

A number of toasts were drunk, and the conversation was friendly. Clearly I was to be impressed—and I was. Of course I knew quite well that the exuberant Russian hospitality did not mean there would not be hard and, if necessary, rough discussions. I was no less impressed by the prominence of Brezhnev's role in comparison to those of his colleagues. He was the one who cared most about getting to know his German guest better and luring him out of his reserve. I was perfectly willing to comply.

We met again a little while later in the Kremlin, after I had shown my respect by placing a wreath at the monument to Soviet soldiers at the outer wall of the Kremlin. I had been inside the Kremlin once before, years earlier, but until this time I had had no idea of the splendor of the inner buildings, to which we were now taken. Huge entrance rooms, luxurious staircases, corridors, and halls, the George Room, the Vladimir Room. Led from one room to another, we finally found ourselves in the Catherine Room, where we were to have our discussions. Four years earlier, in 1970, my predecessor in office had signed the German-Soviet treaty in that same room. It was a baroque symphony in white, gold, and green; the pillars and columns were sheathed in malachite—a green Russian marble, as I later learned—and there were three or four magnificent crystal chandeliers hanging overhead. I am familiar with the Elysée Palace, the White House, the palaces of Rome; but the Kremlin palaces, restored to their authentic historical splendor at enormous expense and great care, beggar all comparisons with the government residences of the Western world. And presumably the men of the Politburo perceived their role as hosts as a foregone conclusion, just as their autocratic predecessors had done during the time of the czars. The splendor was impressive—almost blinding.

Brezhnev began by letting the photographers have their moment. With exaggerated dramatic distaste he referred to them as "our tormentors"; the German photographers and television cameramen took no umbrage. A Western statesman must use kid gloves in dealing with the princes of the mass media; an Eastern head of state is himself a prince.

The ascendancy of the media gave me an unexpected opportunity. During my visit Brezhnev allowed me to speak on television to the Soviet public. I made full use of the occasion. "We must make sure," I said in my speech, "that the bridge is long enough to cross the river." I used another image as well: "If you want to make a forest, you must plant trees"; and I added the Russian saying "Sober calculation does no harm to friendship." But in the main I clearly and simply stated my support of the German-Soviet treaty, its political objectives, and its full application. But just as clearly I told the millions of television viewers, "The German people have not abandoned hope that one day we will live together in peace under one roof." Presumably it was the first time Soviet citizens heard this sentiment from German lips, whereas the danger of German "revanchism" must have been suggested hundreds of times.

Brezhnev opened the official talks with a lengthy prepared declaration that contained little that was new in view of previously exchanged official and private letters. He stated that the Moscow treaty, which had gone into effect a year and a half before, was for him one of the major historical events of the last twenty years (a period that went far beyond his time in office as general secretary); now it was important to make certain that Soviet-German relations would continue to evolve steadily, even if such development could be carried out only one small step at a time. Brezhnev placed the friendship treaty between the Federal Republic of Germany and the German Democratic Republic and the admission of both to the United Nations—long blocked by Bonn on the basis of the Hallstein doctrine—in the same context. He did not refer either to Brandt's resignation, caused by the espionage scandal, or to the recent lowering of the GDR's minimum exchange requirement for tourists visiting East Germany, no doubt in response to pressure from Moscow; it had been arbitrarily raised to frighten citizens of West Germany and West Berlin out of visiting East Germany.

There were signs that there had been differences of opinion between Moscow and East Berlin concerning East Germany's attitude to West Germany and that such conflicts might still be alive. Brezhnev balanced his silent but unignorable criticism of the German Democratic Republic with a warning hint at certain "martial speeches" given in the Federal Republic, specifically naming Franz Josef Strauss. He ended his statement with a vision of the possibilities inherent in the development of economic cooperation between the Soviet Union and the Federal Republic; speaking of the "transition from traditional trade to larger projects," he envisioned a period of twenty to thirty years.

Brezhnev's tone and choice of words were firm but friendly. The demeanor of Kosygin, Gromyko, Ivan Archipov, Nikolai Patolitchev, and the other members of the Soviet delegation made it clear that Brezhnev's statement had been approved in the Politburo; obviously they were hearing nothing new to them.

Nor was it likely that my reply surprised our hosts in any way. I called our relationship with Moscow a "cornerstone in our policy of détente"; I said that the Moscow treaty was a turning point that had penetrated deeply into German consciousness—not in spite of the fact, but precisely because it had given rise to a lively debate in the Bundestag and finally new elections. But it was these confrontations that had persuaded a large majority of the German people that the treaty was right. Brezhnev, I said, must not look at different opinions in Germany through a magnifying glass.

We Germans, I continued, saw the Soviet Union as a great power. The Federal Republic was no more than a medium-sized state, unable "if attacked from without to defend itself alone" but requiring others to come to its aid and protection. I welcomed the fact that Brezhnev had expressed concern about revanchism—it was good to speak openly to each other about our feelings and thoughts.

At this point Brezhnev interrupted me. If at times he was carried away by emotion, he said, that had its natural causes in the loss of millions to war and the destruction of great parts of his country. "The war was not an easy matter! I saw too much in the war! That is why this problem [of revanchism] touches my feelings deeply."

I agreed with Brezhnev but noted that millions of Germans had also lost their lives, that we too had experienced extraordinary destruction, and that as a result of the war our country had been divided. Brezhnev's mention of the problem of revanchism gave me an opening to mention publicly that too many among us were filled with suspicion and fear of the Soviet Union's great power. "I myself, though, am afraid neither of revanchism nor of the Soviet Union."

Once again Brezhnev interrupted me. "Your words have given us a very important message in principle, which fills me and my colleagues with satisfaction." I had earlier stood up for Strauss: "I am not his friend; but we do him an injustice if we accuse him of revanchism." Brezhnev had not responded, but clearly my simple solidarity had made an impression on him—even if he perhaps did not understand it entirely.

I seconded Brezhnev's remarks on future economic cooperation and elaborated on it. Two states, I said, that depended on each other economically would not go to war with each other. Economic collaboration, which I repeatedly advocated at home, would therefore advance peace. Of course it could function only when it was based on mutual benefit. (Here Brezhnev interrupted to express agreement.) I pointed out the difficulties resulting from the different structures of the two economies—on the one side public ownership, on the other a huge number of large and medium-sized private enterprises. Working out the mechanics of cooperation between such different partners would require the utmost care.

I concluded with the remark that alongside the economic questions there were still other bilateral topics, and it seemed to me difficult to make successful economic advances if other areas were deadlocked. This observation was, of course, aimed at the differences of interpretation of the Four Power Agreement on Berlin.

They understood me. Not an hour later, Brezhnev returned to the same theme in his after-dinner speech. "Strict observance—that is precisely what we need to stop the question of West Berlin from poisoning the political atmosphere in Central Europe."

This short statement seemed to me an attempt to take the editors of Brezhnev's manuscript by surprise, and I was forced to improvise my reply. "A year and a half ago you and Willy Brandt, meeting in Bonn, agreed on strict observance *and full application* of the Berlin Four Power Agreement. This continues to be our intention." Brezhnev's phrase "strict observance" formulated only Soviet interests, while the missing words—"full application"—represented German interests.

The following day both the conference of the two foreign ministers and the economic and political discussion between Prime Minister Kosygin and myself revealed that Moscow was balking at the legally binding resolution of the Bundestag to establish an agency for environmental protection in West Berlin. Not only did they see this resolution as a violation of "strict observance" and therefore of the agreement itself, but they were also unwilling to tolerate this commitment. In fact, for years Moscow had delayed the conclusion of several fully worked out agreements because the wording concerning the inclusion of West Berlin was in dispute.

The history of the establishment of the environmental protection agency had, in fact, run an unfortunate course. My predecessor in office, Willy Brandt, had allowed the proposal in the honest belief that it was consonant with the terms of the Four Power Agreement; in addition, the three Western signatories had given him assurances to that effect. Brandt did, however, foresee protests by Moscow. When I followed him into office in mid-May 1974, I might still, technically, have been able to revise the decision that Berlin was to be the site of the agency; but if I had done so, the Bundestag, public opinion, and the diplomats of the three Western signatories, as well as the other party in our coalition government, whose head was also the foreign minister, would inevitably have reproached me for being more submissive to Moscow than Brandt had been; most especially, I would have had to disavow Brandt. More than once he had already faced the accusation of being too soft on Moscow. Was I supposed to invite even stronger accusations? Finally Genscher, who until mid-May had been minister for domestic affairs, had placed his full authority behind the establishment of the agency. Since after long deliberation I had come to believe that we were in the right, I let the draft law pass—even though I felt uneasy about the Soviet reaction.

In late summer of 1974 Bonn received a visit by then Deputy Prime Minister Nikolai Tikhonov and Foreign Minister Gromyko. It revealed that my instincts had not betrayed me. Before our departure for Moscow, furthermore, Genscher had initiated some publicity on the question of Berlin that could not help but anger Moscow. As a result, the *Rheinische Post* had called him "the German marrow in Schmidt's backbone"—a characterization I had accepted without comment. But now we had to take the consequences in Moscow—and Genscher was not up to it; Gromyko could be even more fussy than his German counterpart.

The fruitless attempt at accord between the two foreign ministers had been preceded on the morning of the second day of negotiations by a discussion by a group of five—Brezhnev, Kosygin, Gromyko, Genscher, and myself—that turned mainly on Berlin. Brezhnev seemed unwilling to deal with the subject of Berlin and wanted to pass it on to the foreign ministers. But I insisted on sticking to the topic, saying that after assuming the chancellor's office, I had studied the prehistory of the Four Power Agreement even more thoroughly than I had done as a cabinet member. Today the agreement seemed to me even more artful than I had originally believed. The art of the agreement consisted primarily in what was omitted. For example, the title did not specify what was actually being discussed. The text of the agreement also left many questions open.

Thus the agreement, which had indeed represented a major step forward, could also be a source of misunderstanding if we were not careful. As an example, the establishment of the federal environmental protection agency had given rise to such a misunderstanding. Bonn believed it had acted in full accord with the agreement, while Moscow—following its own interpretation—accused us of wanting to use the new agency to expand or transgress the agreement. But that was by no means the case.

Gromyko, I went on, had recently said in Bonn that Berlin was not seen by Moscow as either the center of the universe or its most serious problem. There was no contradicting such a statement, but for us Berlin and our ties to Berlin remained a central concern. Now I confidently hoped both sides would be able to agree to long-term economic collaboration. But this outcome required approval from our citizens, and they were seriously disconcerted by such tiny psychological pinpricks as unnecessary complications involving visits of retirees living in one part of the city whose children and grandchildren lived in the other part. In addition, the investigation of Günther Guillaume's espionage attempt was still making daily headlines.

Unless the Four Power Agreement and the friendship treaty with the German Democratic Republic were made productive, the Moscow pact could not bear fruit. German public opinion saw all three agreements as a unified complex, under the inclusive name of *Ostpolitik.* "We are proceeding," I said, "with a firm resolve to observe all three agreements strictly, but also to apply what has been agreed upon. If it appears that there is suspicion on the part of the Soviets that we are trying to stretch the terms of the agreements illegitimately—"

"Yes, extensively apply and overstep," Gromyko interrupted.

I continued. "I can understand such suspicion, but I cannot feel that it is justified. We, too, harbor some suspicions—namely, that the Soviet Union wishes to curtail the agreements." I gave examples, such as the fact that the Soviets demanded that our tourism agency in the Soviet Union was not to represent Berliners.

I pointed to earlier agreements on scientific and technical collaboration, cultural exchange, and legal aid that had been worked out in detail but blocked for a year by the question of whether West Berlin should be included or not. Genscher and I, I noted, had publicly said at home that we did not expect these agreements to be signed during our visit because we had no use for disappointment. Nor would it be a tragedy if the current positions remained unchanged. But any progress would strengthen confidence in the agreements' viability. "Herr Genscher and I have not come here to beg for anything," I stressed. But, I said, we were hoping the Soviets would understand that though a fundamental widening and deepening of mutual economic relations were desirable, the situation in Berlin and the mood in West Germany could make it either easier or more difficult. "The decision is yours."

Brezhnev responded in lapidary fashion. It was not, he said, a matter of details; surely it was simple to arrive at sensible agreement on those. "What matters is the principle. If the negotiations of the Federal Republic of Germany are directed at correcting the Four Power Agreement to achieve the aim of transforming West Berlin into a province of the Federal Republic, then friction and increasing tension are inevitable. The Soviet Union has never attempted to aggravate the question of West Berlin; nor does it wish to use the Four Power Agreement to introduce any changes." Once again he proposed that the two foreign ministers be charged with making further clarifications. But they should not, he cautioned, begin by revising the agreement.

I expressed my satisfaction with this proposal and pointed out that though the Four Power Agreement did not prescribe a binding solution to the question of the part Berlin was to play in the three negotiated bilateral agreements, it did facilitate such a solution. Brezhnev explained that he had understood the exchange of letters to date to say that the economic, scientific-technical, cultural, and other questions would be viewed bilaterally and were not linked with the problem of Berlin.

I am repeating the differences of opinion about the Four Power Agreement on West Berlin in such detail, to the best of my recollection, because even at the time it seemed to me that for a long time they would place difficulties in the path of progress. I was not surprised when that same afternoon the foreign ministers did not arrive at any result on the question of the three bilateral agreements because of Berlin. I did not consider that outcome unfortunate; for months I had expected nothing else, especially as I was aware of Gromyko's doggedness.

But that evening in the guest house Genscher and I discussed whether, given the serious disagreements, we should cut short our visit in Moscow unless the controversy could be smoothed over. We spoke loudly and clearly so that our discussion would be picked up by the KGB tape recorders; we were quite certain that they were concealed and turning.

The following day the conflict was blunted in a private conversation between Brezhnev and myself. I had said, "General Secretary, one of your messages sent after I became chancellor contained a statement that was important to me in connection with the establishment of the environmental protection agency. You wrote that you understood that a new man must take on a sizable heritage. You certainly hit the nail on the head. I wish to assure you that my predecessor, Willy Brandt, when he approved the draft law and submitted it to the parliament, was convinced—and is convinced to this day—that he had acted in full legal compliance with the Four Power Agreement; he acted in good conscience. I myself share Brandt's point of view about the law; I discussed the matter with him several times. But let me add this: I know that sometimes in life we must make a distinction between defending the legal point of view and political expediency. I assure you that as far as my influence goes, I will prevent similar conflicts from arising in future."

Brezhnev took his time before replying; first he spoke on other topics. He said he understood the difficulties made for us by the Bonn opposition. Many of the questions we were debating today, he noted, could be easily resolved if the Conference on Security and Cooperation in Europe (CSCE) came to a successful conclusion. The element of trust would outweigh everything else.

Then Brezhnev accepted my invitation to visit the Federal Republic again, using this change of subject to come back to the subject of Berlin. He said, "Perhaps you, Chancellor, or Mr. Brandt were hasty. Possibly you took too much for granted in establishing the federal environmental protection agency and have therefore created a difficult situation. But there's no point in crying over spilled milk. In general, I believe that haste can be as damaging to a policy as unnecessary delay."

This statement removed the obstacle to a political settlement. Now Brezhnev had to instruct Kosygin and Gromyko accordingly; surely the foreign minister was less than delighted. In any case, in our final talks on the following day Berlin was no longer an obstacle. Rather, a positive approach was taken in discussing a project, already on the table, for a nuclear power plant on Soviet soil whose power was to be fed to the West German power grid as well (a project that, in the end, came to nothing). For the first time Kosygin confirmed that it would be possible to set up the switches and transformers in West Berlin. This concession met our condition that these plants must not be situated in any territory controlled by the East German government.

Gromyko, too, used a new formulation concerning the inclusion of West Berlin in the pending draft agreements; persons residing in West Berlin were not to be eliminated from the collaboration between the Soviet Union and the Federal Republic because of their professions. This phrasing seemed to allow the collaboration of the officials of the environmental protection agency in joint scientific projects.

For the time being, Kosygin's and Gromyko's statements blunted the disagreement about the interpretation of the Four Power Agreement that hinged on the federal environmental protection agency. But months later it would turn out that Moscow could be flexible even when that was a drawback. In both areas—long-distance electricity transmission and collaboration agreements—the old positions were resumed.

During this visit Brezhnev and I spent about twelve to fifteen hours talking together. Of these the most interesting—and most significant—were the four and a half hours we spent in private. It became clear that Brezhnev was taking the controversy caused by the federal environmental agency far less seriously than he took progress in the CSCE and the expansion of economic collaboration between our two countries.

We began with the latter. Illustrating his points with the use of a map, Brezhnev described in detail the sources and reserves of raw materials in Siberia, Soviet plans for developing them, the transportation problems involved, and the railroad link from Lake Baikal to the Amur River and on to the ice-free port of Komsomolsk. In discussing this subject, which was clearly close to his heart, he grew animated. The Soviets, he assured me, could in future deliver great amounts of raw materials—that was the nub of his statement. In subsequent years Brezhnev frequently returned to this topic. Kosygin shared his vision but concentrated fully on the most imminent projects, especially those that could be considered for joint ventures with Germany.

In all my talks with Brezhnev and Kosygin I had the impression that both the general secretary and the premier basically saw economic expansion of their country as their chief task. Their thinking in this area was always couched in terms of production and quantities, not of finance and budget. In discussing each separate large-scale project, the final consideration was always financial quantification. But the interest rate for the loans we were expected to advance also played an ideologically determined role.

For example, Kosygin raised no objections—he even agreed—when in a large meeting I told him that of course it was possible to think about a 6.5 percent interest rate, even one of only 4 percent. However, the consortium responsible for the financing would have to pay practically 11 percent. Since the West German government would not bridge the interest differential, the difference would have to be covered by the delivery price. Kosygin's concern focused more on the question of whether our banks could handle the size of the financing. He was satisfied with my reference to the openness of our financial markets, which made a practically unlimited capacity possible. He nodded in agreement when I remarked that so far no major transaction had been aborted because of financing. In fact, while we were still in Moscow, leading industrialists and bankers signed a third agreement on a natural gas pipeline. At home in Munich Franz Josef Strauss saw himself justified in remarking that in Moscow the German chancellor was promoting the interests of heavy industry—as if it were not also a matter of German workers' interests and, from a political point of view, of German interests in general!

Brezhnev also spoke about the other large-scale projects that were being negotiated between Moscow and Bonn. He proudly pointed to his country's economic and technical achievements—for example, the technology behind a Soviet-made quartz watch, which he gave to me. (Unfortunately it worked for only a few days.)

The most important point of discussion for Brezhnev was the continuation of détente. The CSCE negotiations, he said, were taking too long for his taste. He mentioned his discussions with Nixon on the subject, and he expressed concern that the bureaucracies were inventing ever new difficulties, both in the so-called confidence-building measures and in the human rights portion of the Helsinki Accord. Apparently many people were eager to use these tactics to prevent a conclusion to the conference negotiations. I replied that the Federal Republic would not contribute to such difficulties. As far as the confidence-building measures were concerned, Bonn was absolutely ready to make contributions if all parties contributed proportionally. We had only *one* vital interest—that the basic principle of the possibility of a peaceful change in the borders would be given the same ranking as all the other principles.

On the whole I came away with the impression that Brezhnev had invested considerable personal prestige in the CSCE negotiations as far as his relations with his colleagues in the Politburo and the leaders of the other Communist states in East Europe were concerned. I also felt he wanted me to know this without his actually saying so. Perhaps the wish for a balance with the so-called Brezhnev doctrine—that is, the theory proclaimed after the invasion of Czechoslovakia in 1968 to the effect that none of the Socialist countries could rely on its national sovereignty in questions affecting the common security of all Socialist countries—played a role. This doctrine was a clear violation of the principle of nonintervention enunciated in Article 2 of the United Nations constitution.

A year later, in fact, all of Moscow's European allies took part in the concluding CSCE session in Helsinki, holding the same rank by protocol as Moscow itself. But it was evident that for Brezhnev the CSCE final conference was also to be a confirmation that the Soviet Union held the same rank as the United States and that it was thus legitimized in its predominant position in Europe.

Equal status as a world power also played an important though tacit role in Brezhnev's presentation of the status of the SALT II deliberations. Two days earlier Henry Kissinger had come to Moscow for this purpose; Brezhnev reported with a trace of pride that his summary on the status of the SALT II negotiations had been called a "very good basis for a treaty" by Kissinger. Of course the question of removing

American bombers and strategic missiles from the Federal Republic (by which he meant the fighter planes and intermediate-range rockets, which have a relatively short range) was still open. Brezhnev spoke of Nixon and Kissinger with evident respect—he seemed to regret Nixon's resignation—and referred with some satisfaction to SALT I and the antiballistic missile (ABM) treaty. "The people of the United States are clever, they know what atomic war would mean. If anyone were to attack us first, or if the Soviet Union were ever to commit such foolishness, all Europeans would perish—perhaps something of Latin America might be left. That is why I refuse to let the thought of the viability of nuclear war arise in the first place!"

Brezhnev spoke with great animation; he was both convinced and convincing. I replied that in my opinion the political elite in none of the world's major states would deliberately accept a nuclear war, regardless of who headed the government in Washington or Moscow. The danger of nuclear war was not, I said, located in Washington or Moscow; but it could not be considered out of the question in small states, as long as there were terrorists willing to die for their cause. However, even threats were dangerous; that was why West Germany was supporting the nonproliferation treaty for SALT I and SALT II. It would be in our own interest and that of Europe for a long-range SALT II agreement to be concluded, extending beyond 1977.

Brezhnev threw in, "I'm certain of it." But in fact his meeting with Gerald Ford a few weeks later in Vladivostok did not lead to a breakthrough—in part because of the Soviet long-range Backfire bomber and the Soviet SS-20 rockets. Only in 1979, when Jimmy Carter was prepared to eliminate nuclear weapons with a Eurostrategic range (therefore including the Soviet SS-20), was SALT II enacted—much too late to advance détente.

I could not know this at the time; but I did see the Soviet nuclear arms pointed at Europe and the Federal Republic. I therefore steered the discussion to balance in Europe. To maintain it, I noted, American troops in Europe were necessary; but on the whole, fewer forces on both sides would surely be sufficient. The key to Europe's security was parity not only with Soviet troops but also with its missiles.

To the best of my knowledge this was the first time Bonn had pointed to the specific imbalance created by the large number of Soviet intermediate-range missiles aimed at European targets and the Federal Republic. I would have raised the threat posed by the Soviet Union's Eurostrategic weapons if only because Brezhnev had at one time mentioned that the Soviet Union was threatened by American missiles stationed in the Federal Republic. That statement had been a wild exaggeration, since the Soviet territories were beyond the range of the American weapons stationed in Germany at the time—a fact Brezhnev was well aware of.

However, I thought it necessary to stress balance because I was made uneasy about the new Soviet SS-20 intermediate-range missiles then being tested. To me they represented an additional threat to my country. I wanted the general secretary and his staff to know that a problem was being created and that we were aware of it. In fact the new SS-20s and the new Soviet Backfire bombers began to play a significant role in the SALT negotiations from November 1974 on.

The buildup of SS-20s beginning in 1976 later turned into one of the most important factors in the breakdown of détente between West and East. But neither Brezhnev nor I anticipated this breakdown at the time. Quite the contrary: I felt Brezhnev's unmistakable personal desire for further détente, and he recognized mine. Each of us understood that the other was ready to compromise, but not to the extent of disadvantaging his own country—nor his allies and friends.

Even in subsequent years Brezhnev always avoided expressing to me his dissatisfaction with the leaders of Communist countries other than by veiled allusions. In spite of his sanguine temperament, his self-discipline on this point never broke down. If need be, he would let me know his opinion or criticism indirectly, through a third person's spoken remarks.

Only the People's Republic of China and Mao Zedong were exempt from this reserve. In passing I had mentioned my intention to visit Beijing, a plan that could hardly please Brezhnev. He immediately asked me what I thought of China. I said that I viewed the tension between the Soviet Union and China with a certain concern, since on an international scale it could have only an adverse effect on the process of détente. My opinion clearly opened the floodgates. For almost half an hour Brezhnev talked about China, interrupted only by an occasional drawing of breath caused by my questions.

Brezhnev told in detail about the help rendered by the Soviet Union to the People's Republic of China over many years and in many fields. Why had the relationship between Moscow and Beijing been so bad for more than ten years? To put it bluntly, he did not know the reason either. Perhaps the estrangement had come about after a visit to China by Khrushchev; he did not know. "Perhaps the reason lies in China's great-power chauvinism. The Chinese have innumerable internal conflicts, but they try to sow dissension abroad wherever they can. They will give you, Chancellor, a great reception. They will tell you, 'You cannot trust the Russians, the Russians want to conquer all of Germany and all of Europe, and put you, Chancellor, in jail.' "

This prognosis turned out to be not entirely wrong when I visited China a year later. A deeply rooted mutual mistrust between Moscow and Beijing predominated. I cannot judge whether Brezhnev was aware of the errors committed by Stalin in being Mao's patron and later by Khrushchev in abruptly terminating all Soviet aid programs to China. What was clear to me, however, was that the mutual aversion deriving from history and the geostrategic situation was only superficially explained by ideological differences.

Brezhnev devoted long passages to the conflict with China. "Every month they take a new direction. At the moment the teachings of Confucius are the predominant theme. I am trying to describe to you what I understand. Mao has said that every Chinese must look within himself for the errors that go back to Confucius. What mischief! I believe that ninety-nine out of a hundred Chinese haven't the slightest idea who Confucius is. Once I witnessed a purification campaign in Beijing—it was at a time when we still enjoyed cordial relations. At that time the 'personality' of all Chinese was being examined. They themselves had to decide whether they were enemies or not. I observed Chinese standing at the wall of a pagoda to find out whether they had been exposed to Confucius' pernicious influence. . . .

"At one time, at a conference of the Communist and Workers' parties, Mao said, 'We must wage war on imperialism; even if three hundred million people die in the struggle, we shall finally triumph over imperialism.' Now the Chinese say that I, Leonid Brezhnev, have restored imperialism one hundred percent. At the time [Palmiro] Togliatti and our other friends were shocked by Mao's words, though he was still highly respected then.

"At a later conference in Moscow, Liu Shaoji was the spokesman. The conference went on for two or three months. Liu Shaoji was very authoritarian. He spent the nights sending long reports to Beijing, which is why he could not attend the sessions until midday. Then he suddenly disappeared; he simply stopped existing. I don't know what happened to Liu Shaoji. Lin Biao was elected to be Liu's successor; but he perished in an airplane accident. After that they fought his followers. . . . All the Chinese know is intrigue. Even now there are new internal struggles. Their cadres suffer unimaginable attrition; new faces keep appearing on the stage. The military and civilians battle each other. . . . The Chinese people have a lot of discipline; it's probably based on fear. The Red Guards openly executed people. When people see other people's heads being cut off, it's only natural that they become afraid. And anybody who is afraid is very careful what he says."

At this last sentence I thought, "A Russian doesn't need the Chinese example to arrive at this conclusion." Brezhnev did not mention that the conflicts between Moscow and Beijing had only been papered over, not removed, by the verbal compromises of 1960, arrived at by a council of the world's eighty-one Communist parties. Of course he must have been remembering the fight about the claim to hegemony by the Soviet Communist Party; his description was not wrong, but it was extremely one-sided. By the way, neither Zhou Enlai nor Deng Xiaoping was included in his condemnation; their names went unmentioned.

In conclusion Brezhnev spoke at length on the development of the Chinese atomic forces. It would be a long time, he said, before theirs would rival the Soviets'. The same was true of the Chinese air and tank forces; it would be a mistake to overestimate them. It was clear that Brezhnev was eager to create the impression that the Soviet Union was not worried about Chinese armament. So he claimed that the Chinese reports of a Soviet million-man army along the border were nothing but propaganda. I knew he was exaggerating; I felt the Soviet leaders were seriously disturbed by China. Brezhnev repeated several times that the Soviets were eager for friendly relations with China, "without any kind of military temptations."

A year later it became clear that the American-Soviet SALT talks were being seriously influenced by Soviet concern over Chinese nuclear power. From Moscow's point of view—as a Russian told me in 1975—future Chinese strength might be a problem for tomorrow, but its effects were already evident today. For Washington, he added, the whole matter was merely a problem to be addressed the day after tomorrow. It was this situation that had led to misunderstandings between Moscow and Washington.

In the autumn of 1975, immediately before I left for China, Brezhnev suddenly sent me a message that Chinese nuclear power, which he had dismissed so offhandedly, had made great progress, especially in the area of rockets and nuclear warheads. Now Moscow was within China's range. Once the Chinese achieved a comparative strength of 1 to 10—that is, 10 percent of Soviet nuclear power—the danger of a conflict would exist. At present the ratio was still 1 to 60. But Beijing seemed to be feeling its own strength, an overestimation typical of a new atomic power. Moscow had therefore decided to transfer additional forces to the East and to rearm in the West. Stalin's error—being caught by surprise by Hitler's attack in 1941—would not be repeated.

My visit to Beijing, Brezhnev further stated, was of extreme importance to the Chinese; from their point of view Germany was just as important as the United States in relation to the Soviet Union. Beijing would surely try to influence me along anti-Soviet lines and to talk me out of détente.

Such an approach was, in fact, to be expected, and Mao did make attempts in that direction. When I returned from China, Brezhnev inquired urgently about my impressions. I was happy to pass them on to him. Moscow's interest in the developments along its eastern borders was obvious. It seemed only natural to me that the two Communist great powers did not understand each other. Each mistrusted the other—with one crucial difference: Beijing believed that it was possible to calculate Moscow's behavior, while Moscow felt that it was faced with an equation containing too many unknowns.

The Kremlin was eager to know why I had gone to Urumqi, the capital of Xinjiang. I truthfully explained that I had seen no reason not to accept this suggestion made by the Chinese. After all, President Scheel would soon be visiting Tashkent in response to a Soviet invitation. Both cities symbolized Chinese-Soviet competition for territories in Central Asia that are settled by neither Chinese nor Russians.

The Moscow talks of October 1974 ended harmoniously. My visit had not been planned with any immediate operative objectives in mind. But I did have two general purposes. First, I wanted to get to know the Soviet leaders better in order to acquire a feel for their way of thinking, their future policies, and their possible reactions to the policies of the West and of Bonn. Second, I wanted to present the views of the new West German government and myself to my Soviet negotiating partners. I wanted Moscow to know we were willing to continue Brandt's Eastern policies and to flesh them out in the economic area; but I wanted them also to realize that we would not lose sight of our German security interests in the process; that we were in a position to negotiate the necessary compromises soberly but in a binding fashion; and that we would not be swayed by our awareness of the Soviet Union's superior power into giving up positions without an appropriate quid pro quo.

In this regard we were satisfied with the outcome of our visit. The German-Soviet agreements we concluded concerning further steps in our economic collaboration and the final statement signed by Brezhnev and myself were icing on the cake.

The hundred or so German journalists who had come with us to Moscow took a similar view of the situation. The *Frankfurter Allgemeine Zeitung,* for example, wrote, "Guest and host met openly. . . . This situation, it is true, did not preclude opinions from colliding sharply. But again and again all parties stressed an objective tone. . . . Each side was able to express its opinions clearly without the other's misunderstanding. Such a state of affairs was . . . by no means to be taken for granted." The *Stuttgarter Zeitung* reported, "Perhaps no German statesman before this has been so unambiguous in making it clear to the gentlemen of the Kremlin that the Federal Republic is not prepared to pay a supplementary price for business with the East, either in the form of subsidized loans or in the form of political concessions." The *Süddeutsche Zeitung* noted, "Schmidt harbors . . . no illusions; the way he conducted all negotiations in Moscow revealed that he has not abandoned the fundamentals of realizable business." The Norddeutsche Rundfunk (North German Radio) mentioned the "deep-seated and genuine irritation on the part of the Soviets about situating the federal environmental protection agency in Berlin. . . . The resulting suspicion [is] now the chief obstacle to progress in the question of Berlin." And finally, the *Rheinische Post* remarked, "Since the difference of opinion concerning West Berlin is built into the Four Power Agreement, it will be difficult to bury the different interpretations in the small print."

Altogether German press reaction was positive. But even *Pravda* and *Izvestia* specifically emphasized mutual relations. The commentaries in the Soviet newspapers stressed on the one hand the pipeline agreement (intended to be valid until the year 2000) and on the other the realistic nature of the talks. Overall, the Soviet reaction was positive.

In Moscow there had, of course, been several press conferences, among them a joint appearance by Klaus Bölling and Leonid Zamyatin. Another time Foreign Minister Genscher and I had met the press in the splendid Vladimir Room of the Kremlin. Mrs. Brezhnev, Mrs. Gromyko, and my wife also wished to attend. As my wife told me later, during our return flight, the episode furnished a tragicomic illustration of the Soviet social order. Though the wives had been invited to the two large banquets, they were otherwise kept completely in the shadows (this situation did not change until the accession of Gorbachev, Brezhnev's third successor). Now they were eager to be part of a press conference at least once. When the chief of protocol came for them, someone whispered to Mrs. Brezhnev; she remained seated and announced that she would, after all, prefer to stay away. Mrs. Genscher politely remained with her, while the other ladies started on their way down long corridors. A few of the Soviet officials who accompanied them spoke urgently to Mrs. Gromyko; abruptly she apologized to some of the women and turned back. Shortly before the party got to the door of the Vladimir Room, Kosygin's daughter was also persuaded to turn back. Furious but feeling the need to show solidarity, my wife went with her. A few minutes later the ladies were once more gathered around the tea table, but all were silent as the grave.

There were, however, some friendly gestures acknowledging the women. Thus a young KGB major in plainclothes, who accompanied my wife for the whole of our visit, noticed Loki's interest in the trees and bushes in the Moscow parks. The following morning an autumn-red maple leaf lay on the seat of her car.

Of course the KGB security officers had official duties to attend to. At a small dinner in the Kremlin the German security officers were sitting with their Russian counterparts and some senior officers. Russian students who were attending schools in East Berlin served as interpreters. The highest-ranking general present assured them that they were eating "at least" as well as the official delegations in the next room. The quantity of dishes and the many glasses seemed to confirm his claim. During the meal the Russian general drank several toasts to German-Russian friendship, and the Germans replied in kind. Every toast ended with an exhortation to empty the glass of vodka. When the general noticed that one of the Germans drank only half of what was in his glass, he rose to his feet and announced dramatically that genuine friendship demanded that all glasses be emptied to the dregs. But one of our men had noticed that the Russians refilled their glasses with water rather than vodka. When he raised this objection to the general, the latter replied with a smile that one did not examine a good friend's glass. Amid hearty laughter vodka was now poured into all the glasses.

The entire Soviet leadership attended Brezhnev's dinner in the colorful Hall of Mirrors. In spite of the obvious differences of interpretation in the passages of the two after-dinner speeches that referred to Berlin, and in spite of the controversy during the afternoon talks, the mood was cheerful. Hans Ulrich Kempski of the *Süddeutsche Zeitung* later wrote that the mutual frankness had not darkened the atmosphere. Rather, "all the guests are cheerful and chirpy, like people at a party who are happy to have left a bothersome topic behind, who are happy that everything is to be considered settled. . . . Leonid Brezhnev radiates charm, makes massive advances to the Chancellor, and finally grabs all the flowers in the centerpieces so as to present a rose to each of the German ladies." This description was accurate. Even if the act was motivated by a calculated intention to spread cordiality, his naive pleasure and his emotion at the German-Russian meeting were nevertheless genuine.

Without a doubt, when Brezhnev mentioned the sacrifices and suffering of the people of the Soviet Union during the Second World War, it was not simply a negotiating tactic; he was clearly speaking from the heart when he said that it was not so simple to make a clean break with the tragic past. But I realized with increasing clarity, especially at our final meeting, that in the course of our long discussions he had also come to understand that I was serious when I said that the memory of the past could be softened only by the view of a peaceful future.

Before we left for Kiev, there was another very formal military ceremony at the airport. Tears came to Brezhnev's eyes—memories of the awful past or hope for a peaceful future had moved this powerful man strongly. I was deeply touched.

Marie Schlei, secretary of state in the federal chancellery, was a member of our delegation. Marie had lost her husband during the Russian campaign; she was a great reader of Russian literature, especially of the postrevolutionary period; and most of all, she was persuaded to the depth of her soul of the necessity of reconciliation between Russians and Germans. She was especially grateful for the cordiality and humanity of our host.

Though I met with Brezhnev several more times, I never had occasion to alter the deep impression I brought away from Moscow. Leonid Brezhnev was a Russian, and he had all the traits we commonly associate with Russians: strength, the ability to hold his liquor, sentimentality, warmth, generosity—and at the same time suspicion of enigmatic strangers, tactical caution and calculating cunning, consciousness of power, even brutality when that seemed called for. And yet, all in all, he was less a prince in the Machiavellian sense than the kind of man who might have been portrayed by Maxim Gorki and many other Russian writers.

During the moments when the Russian military band was playing our national anthem, I too was moved. I thought of the twenty million Soviet victims of the Second World War, of the seven million German dead. I recalled my own time as a soldier in Russia.

Flying back to Hamburg, I felt relief. During my four days in Moscow I had never lost sight of my analyses of Soviet strategy. I had represented the interests of my people calmly but clearly and decisively; to that extent everything was fine. But this visit to Moscow was such a major event in my life that I did not fully take in two occurrences late on the day I returned to Germany.

The first was the news, deeply saddening to me, of the retirement of my friend Peter Schulz as mayor of Hamburg. That same evening I gave a speech in the Jacobi church in Hamburg; youthful enthusiasts were trying to interrupt it noisily. My thoughts were still so much engaged with the Moscow talks that I can recall only the organist's striking up "A Mighty Fortress" while the congregation spontaneously intoned, "And though this world, with devils filled . . ." and the young people made their intimidated way out of the church—but I have forgotten what I talked about.

Entr'acte

IN THE YEARS that followed, our discussions with the Soviet leaders basically continued to focus on the same principal topics: economic exchange and the status of Berlin. Negotiations with the German Democratic Republic played a lesser role. Increasingly, however, multilateral topics also moved to the foreground: the Conference for Security and Cooperation in Europe (CSCE) in Helsinki and the follow-up conferences, the Viennese negotiations about mutually balanced force reduction in Central Europe (MBFR), and of course the American-Soviet strategic arms limitation talks (SALT II). My personal contact with Leonid Brezhnev grew closer in proportion to his increasing difficulty, after the American presidential election of 1976, in understanding the motives and objectives of the new president, Jimmy Carter.

A retrospective view of the 1970s shows the Helsinki Conference of the summer of 1975 to have been the high point of détente between East and West. This policy began very slowly and at first hesitantly during the second half of the 1960s. A gradual decline began in 1976, and the Soviet invasion of Afghanistan in December 1979 together with the Western reaction in 1980 killed it. These developments limited the German government's chances of continuing to work toward maintaining and safeguarding cohesiveness among the citizens of East Germany, the Federal Republic, and West Berlin. It had always been my goal to ease the situation of the Germans in the Democratic Republic; I now saw this effort being increasingly jeopardized. I realized that the growing confrontation of the two world powers would significantly diminish the influence of my government as well as my own foreign and domestic political arena. I would not dream of Bonn's adopting any kind of quasi-neutral position; I was all too aware of the Soviet Union's long-standing strategic objectives.

The German Democratic Republic continued for a long time in its attempt on the one hand to impair our relations with the Soviet Union and to blacken our name in Moscow and on the other to barter trivial political concessions for significant economic advantages. On one point, though, I was pleasantly surprised. Erich Honecker, Chairman of the German Democratic Republic's Council of State, seemed to see with increasing clarity that the hardening of the situation endangered his own international opportunities—which in any case had become more limited—and the economic development of his state. As the years passed, Honecker turned into a supporter of détente. It even seemed to me that as he grew older, his feelings as a German became stronger than his ideological positions as an orthodox Communist. During my last years in office, 1981 and 1982, Honecker made an effort to salvage as much as possible of the latitude he had only just gained for negotiating an inter-German policy.

The first time I met Honecker was at the Helsinki Conference in 1975. The fact that the seating in the general assembly was alphabetically by nation allowed us to have some preliminary informal contacts that led to long conversations then and there. Our first meeting, however, took place in an atmosphere determined by both our chiefs of protocol, which was almost ridiculously stiff. A tense choreography steered us toward each other in the cafeteria of the conference center. But it did not take us long to discover a way to be normal and easy together.

In Helsinki I also had conversations with Yugoslav president Josip Broz Tito, Hungarian party secretary János Kádár, Bulgarian head of state Todor Zhivkov, Romanian president Nicolae Ceauşescu, and even Czechoslovakian president Gustav Husák and Head of State Lubomir Štrougal. I spent an entire evening and half the night with the head of the Polish Communist Party, Edward Gierek. This conversation was the most important one for me, since it led to the second German-Polish agreement.

Of course the Helsinki Conference also provided an opportunity to talk with Western heads of state and heads of government. The strangest conversation I had was with Archbishop Makarios of Cyprus. The Turkish occupation of part of his island had ended a year before, and he spoke about it with pugnacious fervor. I interrupted him to say that I had always assumed that what bishops cared about most was reconciliation; but he taught me otherwise. As a rule these useful dialogues at the edge of the conference lasted for an hour or two.

My talk with Brezhnev—some of it in private—did not take much longer. It was once again devoted to discussing our economic collaboration. I had come to the conclusion that only a dynamic expansion of the German-Soviet economic relationship could help us resolve our conflicts over Berlin and the Four Power Agreement, which were troublesome to both of us. I therefore made every effort to get various large projects going. But in spite of both sides' basic willingness, it was always difficult because as a rule a number of major German industrial firms and even more banks were involved in each separate project. On the Soviet side, a number of ministries and other authorities had to be involved, and apparently they tended to drag their heels when it came to working together. In some cases Moscow was forced to ask for a vote from interested member states of the Council for Mutual Economic Assistance (COMECON) and their bureaucracies. All that took time, and as a result a project might temporarily have to be raised to a high political level. Where approval by the Communist states was essential—for example, where pipelines and electric circuits were concerned—the immediate political interests of these states were brought into play. For a long time the German Democratic Republic was far from helpful.

Within the Politburo total responsibility for the domestic economy seemed to lie with Kosygin. Negotiations on international economics were usually supervised—or conducted—by Tikhonov, who later became Kosygin's successor. Both were pleasant to deal with because they were objective, always well informed, and, most important of all, more concerned with success than with prestige.

Alexei N. Kosygin, born in 1904, had served in the Red Army until 1921 and taken part in the Civil War. He had been trained as an engineer and had enormous administrative experience. At the age of only thirty-four he had headed the municipal soviet in his native city of Leningrad—which, for all practical purposes, made him mayor; at forty-four he was called to the Politburo. At times I compared him to the top people among our own officials: dutiful, meticulous, reliable. At the same time, he had a great conceptual ability.

I do not know the accuracy of the rumors that Kosygin spoke in the

Politburo against the invasions of both Czechoslovakia and Afghanistan. I consider such behavior quite possible; Kosygin had considerable knowledge of the world, he had a grasp of international politics, and he was a moderate. It was easy to carry on a discussion with him, though such talks never became cordial. Actually Kosygin always made a somewhat sad impression, which was all the odder considering that he could be very witty.

Kosygin always looked melancholy, and this impression was heightened by a large dark birthmark; I sometimes explained this effect to myself by speculating that someone with his economic acumen would have to understand not only the inefficiency of the Soviet economy but also its causes. In the end he may have grown resigned to the fact that his attempts to establish reforms invariably failed. As general manager of the Soviet economy Kosygin seemed to me like a good chairman of the board at the head of a badly structured concern, almost beyond directing. When I met Kosygin for the first time in 1974, he was seventy years old. Perhaps even then his health was worse than we knew.

Nikolai Tikhonov was only a year younger. Like his boss, he too had had a managerial career—Kosygin in the textile industry, Tikhonov in steel. As far as their competence in economics and administration went, I could detect no difference between the two. Tikhonov was also very knowledgeable about the world, though he seemed reluctant to engage in any discussions of foreign policy. It seemed he was personally closer to Brezhnev than Kosygin was. I was present on two occasions when Brezhnev gave signs of impatience with Kosygin; it was not clear to me whether this was an expression of Brezhnev's general temperament or was based on tension between the two of them. I never observed such signs of tension between Brezhnev and Tikhonov.

Incidentally, it was always a pleasure to talk with Tikhonov; Hans Friderichs, the minister of commerce, and Finance Minister Count Otto Lambsdorff, as well as the heads of the large German concerns and banks, felt the same way. Tikhonov was a relaxed, friendly man who cared about expanding and deepening the economic relationship with West Germany in order to enhance the Soviet domestic economy. When he rose to the Politburo in late 1979 and became premier a year later as successor to his former boss, I took it as a sign that Brezhnev would not alter his course. Tikhonov was older by a year than even the general secretary. So gerontocracy—rule by the old—would be continued for as long as humanly possible. Probably the fear of the uncertain consequences of a change of generations was only one of several motives; reciprocal personal familiarity may have been another. Not even Tikhonov could alter the clumsiness of his country's foreign policy machinery.

In the mid-1970s, considering the enormous and ever-growing foreign exchange reserves in the Bundesbank, I toyed with the idea of assigning a small portion of the foreign currency—which would in any case be invested abroad in interest-bearing accounts—to the Soviet central bank against the prevailing interest rate. But the idea did not prove viable. Today such ideas may cause conservative noses to turn up. I mention the episode because it demonstrates how hard I worked to create economic inducements for the Soviet leadership; all the same, there can be no doubt that the USSR was a first-rate debtor.

On the other hand, in 1978 a different idea fell on fertile soil. In May another visit by Brezhnev to Bonn was imminent. It was important to me to give our guest an awareness of success and the public of both states a perspective of long-range economic cooperation. In the autumn of 1977 I told the Soviet ambassador, Valentin Falin, that for reasons of foreign policy I was proposing an economic treaty that would be binding for twenty-five years; such a contract, extending into the next century, could become a basis for growing political trust. Of course the agreement would be merely an outline, with details to be added at regular intervals. Both sides could make long-range financing instruments, sureties, or credit available; it was, of course, clear that for all practical purposes only the Soviet Union would use German bank credits. Brezhnev immediately responded positively. And the agreement did come about when he visited Bonn.

On the whole, in spite of some disappointments, the German-Soviet economic relationship worked well, with our imports from the Soviet Union always lagging slightly behind our exports. Two remarks should be added for the benefit of concerned Americans. First, to the best of my knowledge we never gave a state subsidy unless it was a direct one, by way of taxes or interest rates. Second, the Soviet share of total German imports usually did not exceed 3 percent—less than our imports from our small neighbor, Austria, a country of 7.5 million inhabitants.

Thus to speak of the Federal Republic's economic dependence on Moscow to a degree large enough to affect foreign policy indicates either ignorance or malice. This is especially true of our imports of natural gas from the Soviet Union; from the outset I limited them to a maximum of 30 percent of our total natural gas imports—that is, a maximum of 6 percent of our total energy imports. Our other, substantially larger, shares of energy imports from the Mideast countries, on the other hand, unfortunately carry much higher political risks.

The question of the three agreements on scientific-technical collaboration, judicial aid, and cultural exchange, which were ready to be signed as early as 1973, during Willy Brandt's chancellorship, was not solved during my time in office. The solution failed because of a lack of flexibility in the two foreign ministries in applying the Four Power Agreement on Berlin.

Domestic conditions kept both Brezhnev and myself from risking an attempt at a political agreement; both in the Politburo and in the Bundestag there were mistrustful champions of each side's doctrine of purity; Argus-eyed, now engaging in subtle hairsplitting, now using the crude weapon of polemical accusation, they saw to it that every compromise proposed became impossible. In 1977 I became convinced it would be best to put the matter on ice for a few years; in the meantime practice would teach us how to circumvent the legal traps even without an agreement.

Although on one occasion I clashed vehemently with him, I always felt great respect for Andrei Gromyko, the Soviet foreign minister. He was a tireless, persevering advocate of his country's interests as they were defined by whatever leadership was in power. Henry Kissinger is supposed to have said about him that his eyes were alert and melancholy, like those of a hunting dog who must put up with his master's inscrutable moods but who in the end imposes his own will on his master. If this quotation is correct, it is true of many a foreign minister of many a country at many times. What is true in any case is that Gromyko had to go along with many changes of course as well as the changing moods of the Soviet heads of state. Khrushchev openly made fun of him as an *apparatchik* who would carry out any order, and, as I myself had occasion to witness in 1974, Brezhnev could treat his foreign minister with great anger and without a trace of politeness. But presumably it is equally true that in the last part of his period as foreign minister Gromyko became an increasingly serious factor in determining Soviet foreign policy.

Gromyko was born in 1909. At thirty-four he was ambassador to Washington, at thirty-six permanent representative of his country in the United Nations Security Council. At forty-five he was named foreign minister, a post he held from early 1957 to 1985, almost thirty years, after which he became the formal head of state. The last twelve years he was also a member of the Politburo, thus belonging to the decision-making center of the state. But even earlier he spoke on many foreign policy questions in the Politburo; the premier might have been his superior in a formal sense, but hardly in fact.

Gromyko was a good tactician; he had an impressive memory for details and could call these into play in any discussion. Whoever was involved in talks with him had to formulate his position very carefully to avoid being cornered. Secretly he probably considered most of his professional colleagues to be lightweights. In personal encounters Gromyko remained equally correct. And yet he could be thoroughly sarcastic, provocative on any subject, at times even witty. But he was never insulting and was always controlled.

Whatever the occasion, his expression was somewhat glum, even sad and wry. I cannot remember ever having seen him drink vodka. He may well have felt silent contempt for Brezhnev's drinking habits. There was one occasion in 1978, in the guest house in Hamburg, when Gromyko was not present. Brezhnev, his entourage, and I had already downed at least two welcoming vodkas, and I presented a boisterous toast to Andrei Andreyevich. The entire company burst into rollicking laughter. At home, because of Gromyko's abstemiousness, it is unlikely that toasts were exchanged with him.

With all his sobriety and modesty, Gromyko was nevertheless a man who employed theatrical gestures when he felt them to be appropriate. Later he could silently pass over earlier threats as if he had never uttered them. From Khrushchev's Berlin ultimatum and the Cuba crisis through the Soviet occupations of Prague and Kabul to the ABM treaty and SALT II, Gromyko justified and worked out every foreign operation of the Soviet Union—or helped it to be forgotten. He was a man of great flexibility at the same time that he was a great patriot.

During our bilateral talks in Helsinki in 1975, Brezhnev said about Gerald Ford, "The poor man has to take criticism from every side."

I replied, "He is a man who inspires confidence. I hope he is reelected next year."

"Yes," said Brezhnev, "but he hasn't got an easy job of it."

"Who does?" I asked. "Herr Genscher and I also want to be reelected in 1976. Some of our chances depend on the quality and specificity of our Eastern policy. The more amiable Mr. Gromyko is, the better are our chances for reelection. But Mr. Gromyko is a very cautious chess player. I wish he had more of the generous Russian nature."

Brezhnev objected roguishly, "But he's not a Russian—he's a White Russian."

To which Gromyko drily remarked, "White Russians are the best Russians."

The same discussion brought us once again to the troublesome questions arising from the Four Power Agreement on West Berlin. We had an endless exchange of words, led by Gromyko alone for the Soviet side, while Hans-Dietrich Genscher and I took turns. I remember one of my examples: Would it really mean anything if the Soviet Embassy were to inform us that on a visit to Moscow, Herbert von Karajan, conductor of the Berlin Philharmonic, could not be led to the VIP lounge by our ambassador?

Of course Gromyko did not reply to this example; he stuck to fundamentals instead. Then he cited examples of alleged violations on our part. He had heard, he said, of our intention to establish international agencies in West Berlin.

Genscher objected, "There is no truth to these rumors."

I added, "Mr. Gromyko, you shouldn't read *Pravda* so much."

Gromyko grew angry. "But I do read *Pravda*. It's a good paper!"

Both of us moderated our tone, but the conversation continued to go in circles. For a long time Brezhnev remained purely a spectator to the dispute, supporting Gromyko by not so much as a word, although at one point Gromyko called out to him, "You see, that's what Germans are like!"

Very much later Brezhnev said, "What bothers me is your explosive mood, Chancellor. One could almost believe you no longer want cooperation. But even if that turns out to be true, the Soviet Union won't go under."

My answer was terse. "The same is true for us."

By dealing with a number of details, we managed to continue the useless conversation. Brezhnev either was not familiar with the problems of the Four Power Agreement—at one point he mentioned that he had, after all, not taken part in the talks between Genscher and Gromyko in Moscow in 1974—or wanted us to feel how distanced he was. In any case he continued to keep quiet.

Finally the talk turned to more pleasant topics. At the end of the discussion Brezhnev turned to me. "You mustn't feel offended. It is always good to speak the truth openly. We are in favor of improvements. As far as West Berlin is concerned, what Gromyko said is right. Rapprochement is possible to the extent that the basic principles are not violated." Then we agreed on a statement for the press in which we spoke of our mutual determination to advance and deepen our countries' agreement and cooperation.

I doubted that my harshness had been to much avail. It was good to have shown that if need be, we could be inflexible and that we would not let the Soviet Union bully us. Whether that attitude helped Berlin in any way is another question, since Gromyko would not forget the incident. But neither he nor I referred to it at our subsequent meetings. One thing was clear: each of us respected the other.

When Brezhnev died in November 1982—I had left office six weeks earlier—Gromyko sent me a message that he would be happy to receive me in Moscow for the funeral. Since Chancellor Kohl was already being represented, I was reluctant to accept the foreign minister's invitation, though I considered it entirely appropriate. I have honestly regretted this decision, not only for the sake of Brezhnev, of whom I was fond, but also because of Gromyko himself, since—as I realized to my surprise—I felt equally attached to him.

During the first three years after the Helsinki Conference it became clear that some of the Soviets had hoped for greater things from Moscow's nonaggression pact with the Federal Republic than we were willing and able to offer. Obviously Nikolai Podgorny was suspicious, as presumably was Suslov; whether Gromyko had stirred up distrust—as had been hinted to me—I can't say. In any case Brezhnev had become more and more interested in direct mutual contact—that is, bypassing his ambassador and his foreign minister. I was used to this sort of behavior from my dealings with other Communist states—in the United States they called this sort of thing "back channel," meaning that contact is made through the back door. Our techniques and methods often changed; for me each instance created the minor problem of informing my own foreign minister without exposing anyone.

Brezhnev's overwhelming motive in continuing to keep the direct line open could be explained by a desire to have an information advantage over his colleagues in the Politburo. He could use it, for example, to predict foreign reactions or developments that his colleagues could not fully see yet. Aside from Prague and Bucharest, I had such channels to the heads of all the Communist states—just as, of course, I frequently had telephone conversations with the presidents in Washington and Paris and with the prime minister at 10 Downing Street. The least complicated was my connection with Honecker, because we spoke the same language. When Brezhnev and I exchanged views, both of us had to rely on interpreters, thus eliminating the telephone for practical reasons. That was why we communicated by way of written messages that we had read to each other by others.

Because of his position in the Politburo, it was also important for Brezhnev to understand the motives and objectives of the West German government in individual cases. He was therefore grateful both for personal interpretations of events and for preliminary hints that saved him from surprises. Of course the same held true in the opposite direction. I was especially interested in intimations of imminent or current agreements between Moscow and East Berlin.

In the summer of 1977 Brezhnev complained to me that he was unable to make out Jimmy Carter's plans. I suggested to both statesmen that I establish a direct line between them. In Gerald Ford's time the White House's old "back channel" had presumably gone through the Soviet ambassador in Washington, with the result that Gromyko had a chance to read the news before Brezhnev did. I do not remember whether a new channel with Carter was actually established.

Of course such channels in no way take the place of official diplomatic relations, most especially the negotiations of the foreign ministers; nor do they give any reliable guarantee against errors, false estimations, and surprises. But they can create a great deal of confidence between individuals—which is all the more valuable the more disagreement there is on particular issues. A marginal bonus was the fact that I always knew which of our opposition politicians were dancing attendance on Moscow just then (for national reasons I always supported such requests for visits).

Brezhnev's irritation with Carter had two causes. One, the Russian did not understand what had persuaded the Americans to discard the SALT II framework worked out by Brezhnev and Ford in Vladivostok in November 1974; Brezhnev at least had a vague feeling that he was being defrauded. I was not surprised. I had predicted as much to Cyrus Vance when he had informed the European governments about his president's intentions. I had tried in vain to warn the Carter administration of the unforeseeable psychological consequences. To suggest to the Soviets in March 1977, two and a half years after the agreement made in Vladivostok, that they come down from the joint upper limit for strategic weapons systems from 2,400 each to one fourth of that amount, and to urge a special limitation on the heavy Soviet intercontinental missiles, as Vance did in Moscow, must have seemed to the Russians to be a provocation and an abrogation of the agreement. In the press Gromyko curtly called this behavior on the part of the Americans "illegal."

Second, Moscow understood Jimmy Carter's human rights campaign as an attempt to undermine the domestic policies of the Soviet government. Carter, the idealistic preacher, had not really had this purpose in mind; rather, he was acting on the hope of somewhat improving individual freedom in the Soviet sphere of power by mobilizing world opinion. Europeans more familiar with Russian history and the Soviet present knew this attempt would not succeed. They also knew that such an attempt could negate all efforts devoted to arms limitation negotiations, because it robbed the Soviet partners of trust. Therefore the Europeans—Valéry Giscard d'Estaing and myself among them—put a damper on Carter's human rights campaign. But in such a situation there is always the danger of being completely misunderstood from a moral standpoint.

When, some years later, Reagan, François Mitterrand, and other leaders boycotted commercial deliveries to Poland, they believed they were in the moral right. I, on the other hand, knew that the Polish people were suffering from want; an increase in this misery might lead to an aggravation of the domestic crisis but would not result in freeing the Polish people. More probably the opposite would ensue. It was therefore foolish to deprive the famished Polish people of additional food. I called for donations, and at Christmas 1981 the citizens of West Germany sent packages in the amount of several hundred million marks to Poland. This was a victory of compassionate and neighborly solidarity over a well-intentioned but harmful propaganda action. Of course in the Western world, even in the German Roman Catholic Church, there were a great many people who criticized our action as self-serving. The Reagan administration had the least understanding. But I was proud of this thousandfold sign of solidarity with the Polish people.

The missionary zeal of the American administration after 1976 made it hard for us to get Germans in jeopardy out of the Soviet Union and other Eastern European states. As a rule such efforts proceeded silently; as soon as *public* pressure turned them into prestige matters, willing helpers on the other side had a difficult time asserting themselves against their adversaries. During my time in office we managed to bring a total of 424,000 people from the Eastern states to the Federal Republic. We used a number of criteria, among them the reuniting of families; many of those we brought out had been released from prison.

For Brezhnev this point was not, in general, a question of principle; but it could always become one if the West put him under public pressure or even ultimatums by worldwide campaigns or by the Jackson Amendment in favor of allowing Jewish Soviet citizens to emigrate. That is why in many individual cases I advised working for release in covert ways, as we invariably did. Once, when I pleaded with Brezhnev in a private talk in favor of an imprisoned intellectual well known in the West, he clearly was not immediately familiar with the name; my interpreter heard Brezhnev asking who the man was and what the facts about him were. This was a firsthand object lesson in the selective knowledge of a Communist head of state concerning public opinion in the rest of the world.

It never became entirely clear to me to what extent Marxist-Leninist ideology actually affected the Soviet Union's foreign policy. Karl Marx's life had ended a full century before; his thoughts and writings had not been composed under the living conditions of a hegemonistic Communist state or the existence of nuclear arms. The case is different for Lenin—as it is for Stalin, with his "socialism in one country"—who died more than fifty years ago, and his theoretical works do not apply to the situation in the last quarter of a century that underwent a radical break in the middle.

I always imagined it would be very difficult to insert retroactively the experiences of the Second World War or the rational and irrational effects of nuclear arms into the ideological structure of Marxism-Leninism. Of course we read the great manifestos of the Communist Party of the Soviet Union and the international statements of its allied parties and states. But I was very uncertain about whether those who had proclaimed or sanctioned these resolutions were really convinced. By comparison Mao Zedong's world political–ideological conclusions drawn from the Marxist-Leninist system seemed to me much more logical—and also much more dangerous. None of the leading Russians or other Communist heads of state of Eastern Europe ever justified the foreign and security policies of his state to me with Marxist, Leninist, or any other Communist ideological doctrines; all of them invariably made use of arguments based on their own reasons of state and their own national interests.

The situation was no different in the area of European security policies. The principle of international coexistence—an abstract principle that appeared to be as practical as it was unassailable—can be deduced in one way or another from the doctrines of the early thinkers—Marx, Engels, and Lenin. But the principle of military balance, to the extent that it means a prohibition on placing the other in danger, and the use of the word coexistence in this sense are new formulations of the general precept of peace or the law of nations as they are stated in, for example, the constitution of the United Nations. If, however, the word "coexistence" is to be given lesser significance, it can be a psychological trick.

What do the members of the Politburo think about these matters? What do they say to each other? I have never been able to discover any signs that the Moscow Politburo differs from the earlier governments of Greater Russia in its approach to world politics. In the meantime, however, a strong wish for peace has been added—a sensible change in the atomic age. For the rest, perhaps brandishing the slogans of military parity or "security balance," they seek diligently and with tactical cleverness to gain advantages and territory in every area.

This was apparently true of the SALT negotiations. It was certainly true of the Vienna MBFR negotiations, in which the Federal Republic participated. Since the Rapacki plan of the 1950s—for twenty years, that is—I had participated in and contributed my own opinions to the discussions on mutual limitation and reduction of the troops stationed in Central Europe. From the outset the theoretical considerations presented difficulties, since the Continent's landmasses and marshaling areas differ in size on the east and west sides of the dividing line at the Elbe and the Werra. Furthermore—again from the angle of geography—the Eastern world power has a great advantage over the Western one in that it can quickly deploy troops and reserves from its own country's territory to Central Europe. But I never felt, and still do not feel, that these are insurmountable problems. I continue to believe that troop limitation in Europe would bring great psychological relief and even greater political freedom for all European nations and people.

In the military sphere troop limitation could also have the effect of the West's relinquishing the military strategy and planning based on the early first use of nuclear weapons. Until now the West has based its position on the numerical superiority of Eastern conventional troops and weapons, believing that adequate defense requires it to be ready to launch so-called tactical nuclear weapons relatively quickly—that is, within a few days—and ahead of the other side. Such planning envisages destroying parts of whatever it is that is to be defended. In the long run these plans will not be acceptable to the peoples of the West; in an actual defense situation these tactics would extinguish not only German cities but also our soldiers' willingness to fight.

If, however, a numerical balance of conventional troops, air power, and weapons were to be established in Europe by agreement, the West could reasonably hope to defend itself for a long time without employing nuclear arms. Under such circumstances only the approach of Soviet reserves from deep in the Russian area would disturb the balance, and even this could be countered for some time by the West's bringing in the French—and the relatively small American and British—reserves. This would mean not "making war viable again" but turning from nuclear deterrence toward conventional deterrence.

It was obvious that the Soviet leadership did not desire a significant reduction of Soviet troops stationed in Central Europe for reasons relating to Eastern-bloc politics. In the same way, France has shown no readiness to throw the reserves it can mobilize into the joint defense of Western Europe. When Valéry Giscard d'Estaing began to take an interest in the problem—the only French statesman to do so thus far—he was (of course for different political reasons) replaced by François Mitterrand; the latter adopted de Gaulle's exclusive nuclear strategy, which was designed to serve the protection of France alone and assigned to Germany the role of battle area for Western "tactical" nuclear weapons. But neither has the United States promoted MBFR with any great vigor, especially since an East-West agreement would curtail its own military role in Europe. As a consequence, Eastern and Western bookkeepers ("nitpickers") sit across the table from each other in Vienna, questioning each other's numbers—and nothing is accomplished.

Brezhnev assured us that he would support the effort to reduce both sides' armed forces by the same percentage. For, he said, "for a long time an approximate balance of forces has developed anyway; neither side is noticeably superior to the other." That remark was inaccurate— though not as inaccurate as the West was determined to believe. A sensible answer on the part of the West would have been: Allow both sides the same maximum numbers of soldiers, tanks, guns, airplanes, and so forth; anything else that is actually in place must simultaneously be reduced by the same percentage, step by step, so that with the last step any deviation from the established top limit is eliminated.

The West, too, has not acted productively in the Vienna MBFR negotiations in the years since 1973. To the extent that Brezhnev really wished for a solution, as he always assured me he did, either he had been inadequately informed or deceived at home by the interested authorities (such as the military) or he had been unable to recognize the grand scheme because of the diplomats' endless disputing of details.

For me an important basic condition was that the Bundeswehr must not be given any special status, perhaps by making it the only one on the side of the West subject to controls and objections. For reasons of political psychology I was always opposed to singling out the Federal Republic and the Bundeswehr.

Brezhnev and I had a number of discussions on the problems of MBFR. But beginning in the autumn of 1977, the topic was dwarfed by new problems: the rapid Soviet buildup of the SS-20 intermediate-range missiles pointed at Western Europe, the inevitable Western reaction, and the Americans' newly developed neutron weapons (enhanced radiation, or ER, weapons), which they intended to station in Europe. The subject of neutron weapons was removed from the agenda relatively quickly because Carter, on his own initiative, abandoned them. The topic of the SS-20s, on the other hand, gained in strategic significance, troubling me exceedingly. The atomic intermediate-range missiles formed a "gray zone" in that they were included neither in the SALT discussions nor in the MBFR negotiations but remained outside all arms reduction talks. In consequence, the Soviets had a completely free hand. During Brezhnev's second visit in 1978, as well as at our last meetings in Moscow in 1980 and in Bonn in 1981, these questions again played a predominant role.

Brezhnev
in Langenhorn

I T WAS time for Brezhnev's return visit. More than once it had almost been set, but time and again it had had to be postponed—first for international reasons, then to accommodate the West German election campaign of 1976, and finally because of Brezhnev's health. Ever since I had known him, Brezhnev had suffered from various debilities that had often disrupted and interrupted the course of the political process in Moscow as well—including the setting of Soviet policies on Germany.

Immediately on Brezhnev's arrival at the Cologne-Bonn airport on May 4, 1978, I saw that he had aged greatly and was clearly ill. His retirement seemed merely a matter of time. I felt a personal compassion for this powerful man, who seemed to consider a reliable relationship with Germany so important that he was willing to take on the exertions of an exhausting state visit. It was Brezhnev's second visit to Bonn, and I thought it might well be his last. As it turned out, three years later, in 1981, he came to Bonn once more.

The year 1978 had begun with a great commotion caused by President Carter's intention to station neutron weapons on German soil. Some of Brezhnev's officials in the international arena—and later he himself—were seriously disturbed by this plan because it would initiate a new arms race. There were, however, signs that in reality the Soviet military had no worries on this score; as I understood the matter, they would have been happy to have similar weapons. In no way would the neutron bomb give the West a significant advantage—that became more and more apparent to me. In fact, Moscow was more concerned with the slow progress in the SALT negotiations.

I myself had a different worry in early 1978—Moscow's production of SS-20s. I first spoke publicly about this concern in London in November 1977, and I made sure that Brezhnev's attention was called to the relevant passage of my address. In the meantime production of the Soviet SS-20s was running to capacity; we had a fairly accurate picture of what was happening through United States satellite observations. The number of SS-20s stationed in Eastern Europe was still small, but each month about eight were added. Each SS-20 could carry three atomic warheads, each of which could be aimed at a different target. This meant that each SS-20 rocket could destroy three different targets at the same time—three air bases or three cities.

Clearly the SS-20 had originally been intended to replace the old SS-4s and SS-5s, which had single warheads. In addition, the old SS-4 and SS-5 emplacements (more precisely, launchers) could send up only one missile, while the SS-20 launcher could be reloaded and could therefore launch additional rockets. Another important aspect was that in contrast to the old SS-4 and SS-5 emplacements, which were fixed, the SS-20 launchers were motorized and therefore movable, making them elusive targets for Western weapons.

Finally, the ranges of the SS-4s and SS-5s were only about 2,000 and 4,800 kilometers respectively. The SS-20s were estimated to have a range of 5,500 kilometers. Thus, when pointed in a western direction, they would hardly reach across the Atlantic. They could, however, be placed much farther east than the SS-4s and SS-5s, putting all targets on Western European soil within their range even if they were stationed beyond the Urals. Such an eastward shift would place the SS-20s out of reach of the American, British, and French nuclear weapons stationed in Europe. They would be vulnerable only to American intercontinental ballistic missiles (ICBMs). But since SALT I, there has been parity in ICBMs between the Americans and the Russians. We could not, therefore, count on the United States' being in a position to deploy its ICBMs against Soviet SS-20s. (Five years later, Reagan's SDI arguments made it clear that in future the two world powers should no longer be able to threaten each other with ICBMs!)

My perceptions in the mid-1970s forced me to the conclusion that the SS-20 fleet then being produced was many times more dangerous to Western Europe than the old fleets of SS-4s and SS-5s. Furthermore, the majority of the targets of the new as well as the old missiles were on German soil: Germany was becoming a threatened pawn. The possibility of future political duress of the Germans was looming on the horizon.

I was not certain whether Brezhnev knew that the Soviet Union's military leadership was in the process of arming his country with such instruments of extortion. It was possible that the military had talked him and the Politburo into authorizing the SS-20s by arguing that nothing more than routine modernization was involved, and the leaders had never imagined the political consequences. But it might be equally true that when the Politburo had made its decision—an extremely expensive one, by the way—it was only too well aware of the burden it was imposing on all of Western Europe and most especially on Germany. In either case I felt it necessary to discuss the matter with Brezhnev, especially as Carter was reluctant to do so himself for fear of jeopardizing the SALT negotiations.

On May 5 we had a long private talk in Gymnich Castle. Our officials had prepared a "joint communiqué" as well as—at my instigation—the agreement I mentioned before, which was to extend over twenty-five years and to cover industrial and general economic cooperation. Both documents were on the table in draft form; there were only a few points where, as usual, questions of formulation remained. Brezhnev and I spoke almost entirely about other topics: first there were the old, still unresolved controversies concerning the full application of the Four Power Agreement and the place of West Berlin in German-Soviet relations; finally we touched superficially on some critical aspects of the international situation. The principal topic of our meeting, however, was the intermediate-range weapons, that gray zone that had been bypassed by every arms limitations talk then being conducted.

Brezhnev began with a long, general statement prepared in writing ahead of time; he also had some complaints. I improvised my answers to each of his points before expressing my concerns in detail: "I am not worried that the Soviet Union might exploit its superiority, much less that it will attack us, as long as the leadership is in your hands. But I must give some thought to the future, when another generation will take over the leadership—perhaps a generation that has no firsthand experience of the Second World War. . . . I must contradict you if you believe we are reinforcing the Bundeswehr. That is not the case, nor do we have any such intention. We respect the borders that have been set for us in part internationally and in part by ourselves and that have been openly proclaimed. I am glad that we have finally exchanged military attachés, as we discussed doing in Moscow four years ago. Now you can observe our maneuvers; this opportunity allows your specialists to assure themselves at first hand that I am telling the truth. . . . However, I do worry about your numerical superiority of tanks and airplanes in Europe, and most of all about your intermediate-range missiles."

Brezhnev contradicted me. It was absurd, he said, to justify strategic considerations with an alleged threat by the Soviet Union. The Soviet Union had no wish to attack the Federal Republic with either conventional arms or nuclear weapons. He assured me he took no pleasure in speaking of such things. But if we were to create an atmosphere of trust between us, we would have to discuss strategic questions. He listed all the components of the United States' nuclear strategic potential and complained about the cruise missiles the Americans were developing. It was the Americans, he insisted, who were trying for superiority and seeking to gain unilateral advantages through SALT II. Finally, the Soviet Union also had to keep its long border with China in mind. But as far as the gray zone was concerned, the Soviet Union was prepared to reduce every kind of weapon: "Of course only in agreement with all nations; security must not be compromised on either side. Of course only with complete reciprocity. . . . After all, in Europe we do in fact enjoy an approximate balance of security!"

I was not entirely sure whether Brezhnev felt that this statement was to the point. It was not beyond the realm of possibility that this was his true view of matters. I had always wondered whether the old complex of the Russians, feeling threatened at all times, might possibly have led the Politburo to overestimate the West, with the result that they believed their evaluation of the balance of power to be "objective," though it was in fact distorted.

Fortunately before our meeting I had let Brezhnev know that I would be bringing military maps to explain my concern to him, and I suggested that he might want to do the same. I came back to this procedure now, spreading out a large map of Europe that extended beyond the Urals. It reflected the state of our knowledge about all Soviet and Western nuclear weapons with a range beyond the actual battle area. Next to the approximate positions and the respective number of the various weapons systems their ranges were indicated.

Brezhnev had seized on my suggestion; now he had his colleague Anatoli P. Alexandrov spread out an equally large map of Europe. Both maps were—to no one's great surprise—quite similar in their overall structure, though probably not in every detail. Both maps were stamped with red and blue secrecy marks. The impression of extreme importance and absolute secrecy, specifically for military documents, had been carefully fashioned by the military on both sides. It is true that these maps were and continue to be of the greatest importance; the stringent secrecy that has surrounded them on both sides for decades, on the other hand, is politically pointless and harmful. Secrecy only makes arms limitations negotiations, which are complicated at the best of times, unnecessarily difficult and nourishes mistrust. The only positive outcome of secrecy in this area is a kind of job program: Each side provides a livelihood for an espionage apparatus employing thousands of people. All of it is highly superfluous, especially since the countless reconnaissance satellites of both world powers are now able to take precise readings of the weapons systems the other side has in place.

I sensed that the Soviet map might confirm my argument. It was difficult, however, to understand all the data entered on the map, both because of the Cyrillic alphabet and because of the different systems of symbols. Nor did I have enough time to study the map closely, since my guest grew annoyed when I used his map to demonstrate to him my concern about the SS-20s. Whether the details overtaxed him, whether his anger was because he had allowed himself to become enmeshed to this extent, or whether there was another reason—whatever the case, with a sweep of the hand and a few rough words Brezhnev swept the map from the table. Alexandrov picked it up and laid it aside. I surrendered my own map, which had been drawn up expressly for this meeting, to Brezhnev, suggesting that he have the numbers entered on it checked back in Moscow.

The atmosphere of our talk had remained amiable, even though we had been unable to come to an agreement. Driving to Godesberg from Gymnich, we came back to the question of parity; it was still unresolved in the prepared joint communiqué. The Soviet side wanted it specifically to say that approximate equality and security existed in Europe. I had given orders to reject this language and instead to formulate the statement so as to express the intention of bringing about equality of security and parity of defense efforts through negotiations and agreements. Brezhnev came back to this controversy; I remained adamant.

Finally, that night, both parties were able to agree on a text that allowed each to save face. "Both sides consider it important that there be no striving for military superiority. They rely on the belief that approximate balance and parity are sufficient to guarantee defense." These words were sufficient unto the day; in the following years I repeatedly used the same formulation in my arguments against the persistently growing SS-20 fleet. In view of the differences in numbers cited by each side in the Vienna MBFR negotiations, and in view of the growing disparity in intermediate-range missiles, however, the problem was by no means solved.

The banquet President Scheel gave in Augustusburg Castle in Brühl, as well as the "counterbanquet" Brezhnev hosted in the Godesberg Redoubt, were gala opportunities for German guests to view the Soviet head of state and his foreign minister in person. They followed Brezhnev's two after-dinner speeches with curiosity and interest, and at least once they were able to witness Scheel—who before his election to the presidency had been a successful and experienced foreign minister—and myself react to the self-assured Soviet guests. They did not attend any major event, but they did see a degree of normality in relations between Russians and Germans that no one could have dreamed of ten years earlier. But there was also a degree of soberness far from the euphoria that some of my party friends had connected with our Eastern policy five years earlier.

My friend Kurt Becker, writing in *Die Zeit* at the beginning of Brezhnev's visit, called the meeting a "fragile hope," since détente was "on the edge" of failing. The West German public probably had a similar view. As it turned out, nothing slipped over the edge—but then nothing moved very much at all. The facts that a larger number of German and Soviet leaders—as well as the entire West German public—gained a greater understanding of the political aims, hopes, and fears of the other side, that the Russians learned they would not be able to bully the Germans, that the Germans had met the Russians as very human counterparts, in spite of their great power: All these meant little to the press. But the press, after all, could observe only parts of the encounter and only from a distance.

Those of us who were closer could perceive interesting human traits. For one thing, there was Brezhnev's drinking. Even at meals he drank vodka from tumblers; a minuscule sign summoned his personal servant (I believe Brezhnev addressed him as Alyosha), who refilled the glass from a flask he carried in his pocket. For another, there was Brezhnev's self-discipline about the ban on smoking that had been imposed on him; he had become a passive smoker who begged me repeatedly to light a cigarette so that he could enjoy the smell. For still another, there was Brezhnev's undisguised curiosity to learn more about the reasons why both our agriculture and our small towns and cities were in such good health, a condition he had seen clearly during his long car trips. Those who understood Russian could also hear the remarks Brezhnev and Gromyko occasionally exchanged. When Brezhnev expressed satisfaction at my statement that we did not plan to establish any new federal agencies in Berlin, Gromyko whispered back, "That's what the Germans always say; and then they do the opposite."

On his final day in Hamburg Brezhnev appeared the most relaxed. I had invited him to a private luncheon at my home in Langenhorn. Brezhnev's staff had been opposed to this side trip, perhaps for reasons of security. They had also refused the suggestion that Brezhnev and I fly together in a Bundeswehr plane from Bonn to Hamburg, perhaps for fear of losing radio contact with the high command in Moscow. But Brezhnev, who was not only an extremely gregarious host but also a trusting guest, happily accepted both invitations. As a result both of us, as well as Gromyko and Genscher, gained many additional hours for very private conversation.

Of course, hardly had we arrived in the living room, than the party began with vodka—in this case Polish Zubrowka, a gift to me from Edward Gierek, which seemed to agree with Brezhnev particularly well. My apartment is crammed with books; suddenly someone noticed that Brezhnev had sat down in an armchair directly under the forty volumes of the collected works of Marx and Engels. There was much laughter— even Gromyko smiled.

Then we got down to business. Our guests wanted to talk politics even before lunch. They wanted to discuss our relations with the German Democratic Republic, they wanted to talk in detail about China, and finally they wanted to return one more time to MBFR. We therefore left our other guests in the living room with my wife, and we retired to my very small den. There are only three seats in the room; I think Genscher squatted on the library ladder, and the two interpreters stood. By now the mood was very cordial, but neither side made any concessions. An hour later we went back down the stairs for asparagus and ham.

In the meantime Brandt, Lambsdorff, and Bahr had joined us; we made a pretty cheerful group. Our guests had looked around at my books and discovered the many Russian writers up to Gorki, Sholokhov, Pasternak, and Solzhenitsyn, and a conversation about Russian literature ensued. The Soviet visitors could see that we were not speaking on the basis of notes prepared for us by the Foreign Ministry but from our own knowledge—and that we knew a great deal about Russian literature.

Of course we also talked about Hamburg, about shared aspects of Hanseatic-Russian history since the Middle Ages. Then the conversation turned to Ernst Thälmann, the Hamburg native and onetime head of the German Communist Party, whom the National Socialists had killed; that morning Brezhnev had visited his memorial in Eppendorf. Hamburg interested our Soviet visitors. Brezhnev had been lodged in the senate guest house along the Aussenalster—a handsome introduction to the city. The morning had begun with a visit to the Rathaus. Though there had been a few right-wing demonstrators, most of the faces lining the streets had been friendly and inquisitive. As often happened when foreign dignitaries came to visit, many of my neighbors in Langenhorn had gathered at my little front yard to take snapshots.

Brezhnev had great difficulty believing that the Neue Heimat housing development, to which my row house belonged, was predominantly inhabited by ordinary people; he probably thought that the privately owned houses with garages and little gardens out front were too luxurious for ordinary skilled workers and salaried employees. But he clearly felt at ease, and there was much joking, much vodka, much laughter. At one point Brezhnev's physician needed to give him an injection, a procedure for which the gentlemen retired to our bathroom.

The visit of the Soviet statesman thus ended in harmony in Hamburg, though the day before, in Bonn, the official ending—the signing of the joint communiqué—had been less than overwhelming, given the outcome. The following day the newspapers summed up the visit. The Soviet press had a very positive view of the event. This reaction surely had domestic as well as international reasons: In view of Brezhnev's— exaggerated—worries about China, and considering his murky relations with Jimmy Carter, he was eager to consolidate his European policy. The German and Western press were rightly more cautious; they did, however, note quite correctly that though our fundamentally divergent positions had come closer together, the opposing lines had by no means been blurred. One commentator went too far in praise: Franz Josef Strauss spoke publicly of a "milestone in the historical process" of German-Soviet development. I wondered what he might have said if he had known that only three days earlier Brezhnev had wanted to cancel a meeting with Strauss; during a motor tour I had talked him out of his resolution. "But what am I to say to him?" he objected, and I told him, "The same things you have said to me, of course, only in less detail."

As 1978 continued, it became clear that the Soviets were continuing

to deploy SS-20s at an undiminished pace. During the SALT II discussions, however, the Americans made no serious attempt to stop their
deployment or include it in SALT II. My concern increased, and I
continued to assail the ears of both world powers with this problem—
but without being heard.

The Politburo
Changes Its Mind

L ATE in 1978 the White House had a change of opinion on the question of the SS-20s. The new evaluation of the situation led to a meeting in early 1979 among Jimmy Carter, James Callaghan of Great Britain, Valéry Giscard d'Estaing, and myself on the island of Guadeloupe in the French West Indies. I immediately conveyed the two elements of the resolution we formulated—which later became known as the TNF resolution and was adopted in more precise form by NATO in December 1979—to the Soviet general secretary. I also told him that I, for one, was determined to pursue this policy—in other words, that I would emphatically support negotiations about intermediate-range missiles; but should such negotiations fail, I would agree to stationing American intermediate-range missiles on German soil.

On the other hand, all through 1979 demonstrations in the principal cities of the NATO countries clearly showed Moscow how controversial this resolution would be. So the Kremlin, resting its hopes on the fact that opposition was developing in so many places, took great pains to nourish this opposition. The Soviets clearly trusted that by the end of the four-year negotiation process—that is, by the end of 1983—they would attain a huge lead in intermediate-range missiles in Europe. Only then would the West be able to take the first steps toward its own preparations for war. Guadeloupe thus did not seem to trouble Brezhnev; he calmly continued with the policies he had already set. For him, the principal topics of our correspondence remained first of all China, then MBFR, and finally the German Democratic Republic and West Berlin. Of course our bilateral economic relations also remained on the agenda. For me, the intermediate-range missiles were always important.

My flight to the economic summit in Tokyo on June 25, 1979, allowed me to meet for three hours at the Moscow airport with Kosygin, Gromyko, and Tikhonov. I was accompanied by Ministers Hans Matthöfer and Volker Hauff. I quickly brought the conversation around to my principal concern. Kosygin and Gromyko reported in detail on the meeting between Brezhnev and Carter that had taken place in Vienna on June 16–19, only a few days earlier, at which the SALT II agreement had been signed. The three Moscow dignitaries praised SALT II enthusiastically, as well as the plans for the SALT III discussions to follow; France, Great Britain, and China, all nuclear powers, were to participate in these as well. Of course the preparations for SALT III would have to deal with the American nuclear forward-based systems (FBS) deployed in Europe.

Here I took over. "When it comes to SALT III, the Federal Republic has three principal interests. First, the number of intercontinental strategic nuclear weapons and warheads must be reduced further. Second, SALT III must also take into account Eurostrategic [intermediate-range] weapons. Third, the same principle of equality must be applied to these weapons that was agreed upon in SALT II." Since the early 1960s, I went on, there had been no intermediate-range weapons on European soil that could have threatened Soviet territory (aside from a few—more precisely, eighteen—French missile systems). Conversely, the Soviet Union had always had SS-4 and SS-5 missiles at their disposal. "But now you are adding your new SS-20 missiles in steadily growing numbers. Even now the SS-20s carry a considerable military weight. In the 1980s they will also gain considerable political weight. The West sees two possibilities for arriving at parity here."

Here Gromyko interrupted me. He tried to persuade Kosygin to end this part of the conversation. Kosygin did try, but because he was a courteous man, he did not get beyond a feeble attempt. I continued. "If the Eurostrategic weapons are not included in SALT III, I believe the Western alliance will be forced to rearm even more. . . ." After that, our conversation turned to other subjects.

During the meal one of our Russian hosts played his trump card. "Chancellor, we do not understand you. In Vienna neither President

Carter nor any other American so much as mentioned the intermediate-range weapons!"

I had to swallow this and hold my peace; inwardly I was deeply dismayed. I had not thought such an omission possible immediately after the Guadeloupe meeting. But the following day in Tokyo, Cyrus Vance largely confirmed the Soviet claim: The intermediate-range weapons had been mentioned only once—and only in passing.

A few days later Moscow informed me that Brezhnev and Carter had in fact touched on the topic in Vienna, though only during a shared elevator ride in the Soviet Embassy; Carter had brought up the SS-20s. I was told that he had raised no objections of any kind to Brezhnev's reply that there were still not enough SS-20s. Brezhnev had fully expected the SS-20s to play an important part at the Vienna meeting. So insult was added to injury as far as I was concerned.

It seemed to me that the episode encouraged several persons in both Moscow and East Berlin to sow mistrust of the Federal Republic and myself, as if I had exaggerated Western concerns. But within the East bloc there was also internal misunderstanding. Certain circles in Moscow were suspicious of Honecker and, for different reasons, of Gierek. Others thought it suspicious that apparently both Kosygin and Suslov had spoken out firmly on international questions in the Politburo. Moscow sensed that Brezhnev's power was declining; he himself seemed to favor Konstantin Chernenko (a preference Brezhnev himself hinted to me a year later). But none of this consoled me. On October 6 Brezhnev gave an important speech in which he spoke out against the impending TNF resolution of the Western alliance. Stationing new American missiles in Europe, he warned, would lead to a fundamental change in the strategic situation in Europe. If that happened, the Soviet Union would have to take additional steps to assure its own security. The effect of Brezhnev's speech on public opinion in the Federal Republic and in Western Europe in general was impressive.

His speech contained both threats and inducements. On the one hand NATO was accused of trying to bring about Western military superiority in Europe—"but matters will turn out differently than they think!" On the other hand Brezhnev announced that 20,000 troops would be withdrawn from the German Democratic Republic. He also promised to decrease the number of Soviet intermediate-range missiles in the western part of the Soviet Union, provided that "no additional intermediate-range missiles are stationed" in Western Europe. Of course he did not mention that the Soviet Union was in the process of tripling its potential by placing three warheads on each SS-20 rocket. And there was not a word about the fact that, given their longer range, the SS-20s would be able to zero in on the old targets in Western Europe even from the other side of the Urals. But—unlike Gromyko three months earlier at the airport—Brezhnev did announce that the Soviet Union was prepared, within the framework of SALT III, to discuss "limitation not only of intercontinental missiles but also of other weapons." This statement seemed to mean that the Russians were prepared to negotiate on intermediate-range weapons.

I immediately and publicly welcomed this willingness to negotiate; I deliberately ignored the threats. In any case, the latter turned out, on careful examination of the text, to apply only to actual deployment, not to adoption of the TNF resolution. But I reminded Brezhnev of the text of our joint communiqué of May 1978: "Both sides are convinced that approximate balance and parity are sufficient to guarantee defense." Then I factually demonstrated that Soviet deployment of SS-20s—even if the number of launchers did not increase from the number previously emplaced for the SS-4s and SS-5s—would cause a substantial power shift in Europe to the detriment of the West because of their three warheads, mobility, greater range, and reloading capability. For the rest, the impending TNF resolution was intended to open negotiations; these would show where the military might be carrying their responsibility for security too far.

The Soviet leadership seemed unsure of how to evaluate subsequent developments. Letters, messengers, envoys, and reconnaissance agents on several levels were sent to take soundings. Perhaps the situation, which was to achieve worldwide significance during October and November and arouse the citizenry in both parts of Europe, would turn into a test of Brezhnev's position in Moscow. In Bonn we were not certain to what extent Brezhnev himself had accelerated the deployment of SS-20s; whether he might have underestimated their military significance to NATO and their political effect on the West; or whether he might have attempted—though unsuccessfully—to slow down the process. Whatever the case, he seemed to have grown unsure of himself. This did not surprise me, since I too was having difficulties at home. Such was the situation when Gromyko arrived for a meeting with me on November 23, 1979.

At the beginning of his visit to Bonn, Gromyko invited Hans-Dietrich Genscher to visit the Soviet Union; Genscher willingly accepted. I myself announced that I would fulfill the invitation Brezhnev had extended to me, possibly as soon as the spring of 1980, since in October 1980 our elections would be held. It seemed to me extremely important in the months to come to keep up not only close political contacts but also personal ones.

It was almost inevitable that our first several hours were once again devoted to the topic of China. Hua Guofeng had just paid a visit to Bonn, and we had had some long talks. I described him as a self-assured man with a modest manner, a representative of a great but not at all aggressive power. Gromyko replied that according to Soviet opinion the Chinese leadership was far from having abandoned its idea of the inevitability of war; it was now believed that the Chinese wanted to postpone the war, but not that it could be avoided. Therefore he could not share my "optimistic" opinion. Furthermore, China was strongly against SALT II, and its aggression, which I was denying, was obvious in its attitude toward Vietnam.

Our discussion focused on Asia for a long time. I suggested that the Soviet Union consider helping the United States in the Teheran hostage crisis. Gromyko was evasive, replying only that the United States must not lose its nerve. This led to a normal political world tour—from the Persian Gulf through Arab oil to the European energy crisis; we barely touched on Europe, Germany, and Berlin. Only at the end did Gromyko address the burning problem of the intermediate-range missiles, which he had already discussed with Genscher that morning. On this topic, too, he remained vague; it was reasonable, he argued, to negotiate on the intermediate-range missiles now, before NATO voted on its resolution and before SALT III became a reality.

I reminded him of the three to four years NATO had set aside for the negotiations; this time frame was the reason I was not pessimistic. In any case, we would use our influence to see that these negotiations came to a successful conclusion.

That evening, in a private discussion in my Bonn apartment, we came back to the missiles. On a map Gromyko pointed out to me the Soviet territories which, according to Moscow's analyses, could be reached by Western advanced nuclear systems. He argued that NATO's December resolution, with its offer to negotiate, would in reality destroy the foundation of the negotiations offered by the Soviet Union on October 6. I showed him my map, which correctly indicated that the Pershing 2 missiles, to be stationed in four years should negotiations fail, could reach approximately as far as Moscow; therefore the range of the American missiles marked on his map was exaggerated. "But," I added, "the actual ranges, and especially the short flight times, are bad enough." The reverse, I went on, was true for us; to illustrate, I showed Gromyko my second map, which indicated that the SS-20s stationed in

Siberia and aimed at the West covered the entire Federal Republic—with equally short flight times.

We then had a long, very objective conversation about all related topics. Gromyko seemed to me to be seriously disquieted. I had the impression, however, that he also took my deep concern seriously. He continued to insist that the impending NATO resolution would destroy the basis for negotiations. But it almost seemed as if he was not inwardly happy about clinging to a line that had obviously been determined in Moscow; for the first time he seemed to me a little helpless. Finally he asked me what he might tell the general secretary.

I replied that since May 1978 I had repeatedly tried to tell him and the other Soviet leaders as plainly as the Western alliance allowed what the almost inevitable outcome of deploying SS-20s would be. I had made every effort to avoid surprises. But as far as the nuclear problem was concerned, I could not speak for the entire West. Germany was not a nuclear power. Nor should any attempt be made to separate me from the Western alliance and the American leadership. My government would do everything it could to take the impending negotiations to a successful conclusion; I did not believe that a resolution on counter-measures would destroy the basis for negotiation. I would be happy to visit Moscow in the spring, I said, and I was eager to maintain and expand German-Soviet relations.

As we parted, I realized that the Soviet leadership still did not comprehend the situation it had created in Western Europe and Germany. Acutely conscious of the Soviet Union's vulnerability, it had made improvements in its own security system the sole criterion of its armament policy and its overall strategy. Perhaps the Soviets did not understand that their excessive security complex must arouse fear in their Western neighbors, or else they had decided to put up with that effect. They seemed adamant in their belief that the White House was playing a similar—and absolutely dominant—role in the Western alliance as the Kremlin was playing in the Warsaw Pact and that therefore the only thing that mattered was to negotiate on equal terms with the United States as the only important counterfactor. The Soviet leadership had been confirmed in its neglect of Western European concerns by Carter's failure to bring the interests of his European allies into play in the SALT negotiations. Now the Soviet Union realized it had been mistaken in its belief, following the Vienna conference, that the deployment of SS-20s had no great significance for the West. On October 6 the Soviet general secretary had risked his personal prestige. What freedom of action was left to the Soviets?

On December 12, 1979, in Brussels, the foreign and defense ministers of the Western alliance issued a communiqué adopting the long-proclaimed TNF resolution on the modernization of the long-range theater nuclear forces (LRTNF) and on arms control. On December 14 TASS declared that the NATO resolutions had destroyed the basis for discussions on intermediate-range weapons.

I was still certain that the Soviets would eventually agree to negotiate, although they would make every effort to save face. But on December 27 the Soviet army invaded Afghanistan, resulting in a storm of world protest. It was only natural for the American president to place himself at the head of the wave of outrage. The Soviet leadership locked itself into its position and insisted on sanctimoniously justifying its intervention. Of course under these conditions arms limitation talks were out of the question; the prospect of ratifying SALT II sank below the horizon as well.

I too was shocked and outraged by Afghanistan. And yet I should have known better; after all, I had never doubted the continuing expansionist drive of Russia and the Russian-led Soviet Union. True, there is a difference between abstract knowledge and concrete realization. The chasm between illusion and the disillusionment caused by brutal experience is even greater. Jimmy Carter, who no more than six months previously had embraced Leonid Brezhnev and kissed him on the cheek in Vienna, now called him a liar.

American public opinion, confident at all times in the face of international crises, and Jimmy Carter's equally confident temperament were also deeply affected by the drama of the American failure in Teheran. The vain attempt to free the hostages by force openly demonstrated the same helplessness of the Western world power that had been evident in the face of Soviet aggression in Afghanistan. The American trade embargo of the Soviet Union followed and, on April 3, 1980, the American decision to boycott the Olympic summer games, which were to be held in Moscow in July.

The Western European governments have never held a high opinion of trade embargoes; in this case they were also unwilling to follow the American example and refused Carter's request. Their attitude toward boycotting the Olympic Games was different. Most heads of states emphatically agreed with Carter as a matter of morality, Margaret Thatcher first of all. But in democratically constituted societies athletics are a private concern, and governments cannot give orders. As it turned out, a few months later almost all Western European nations participated in the Olympic Games in Moscow. Norway, the Federal Republic, and Turkey were the exceptions—not coincidentally, they are three states that have Soviet fighting forces on their immediate borders and therefore feel more heavily dependent on American public opinion.

Persuading the German athletic associations and their governing bodies of the political necessity of Germany's staying away—in spite of the fact that our athletes could be expected to take a number of medals—was a costly domestic effort that was insufficiently appreciated in Washington. The American election campaign had already started; the clever secretary of state, Cyrus Vance, who had always been given to moderation, had resigned, and the Americans' tone grew more shrill.

The Western European governments were displeased by the shortsightedness in foreign policy that seemed to characterize Washington's actions. This was especially true of Paris and Bonn. We knew, after all, that even after the American presidential election we would be unable to manage if we did not have a modus vivendi with the Russians. I therefore held to my intention to visit Moscow again, and I kept my friend in the Elysée Palace informed of my plans.

Valéry Giscard d'Estaing took the first step, meeting with Leonid Brezhnev on May 21, 1980, in Warsaw, halfway between their two capitals. Of course the United States sharply criticized Giscard for breaking through the sham quarantine laid on Moscow. But in my view it was to his credit that he demonstrated to the world that even—and especially—in acute international crises it was important to keep communication open if escalation were to be avoided.

Of course the head of a nuclear power could afford to offend the White House with such a meeting more easily than could the German chancellor. But the German head of government could follow Giscard's example. And that is what I did, in spite of harsh reproaches from Jimmy Carter, who had been persuaded by his all-knowing national security adviser, Zbigniew Brzezinski, that I was about to embrace neutrality. I responded with some vehemence. I thought I completely understood Carter's psychological makeup—he was, in fact, a man who never stopped searching his soul and tended repeatedly to change his mind—and it seemed necessary to be firm with him.

When I left for Moscow on June 30, the Soviets knew, of course, that we were just as unlikely to deviate from our ties, obligations, and decisions as was Giscard d'Estaing. Gromyko and Brezhnev were more familiar with our firm though relaxed and calculable consistency than were Brzezinski and Carter. The Russians knew that Genscher and I would not let ourselves be seduced or intimidated; we would certainly not submit. They themselves, by the way, never tried anything along those lines, even during this extremely precarious encounter. Instead, the Soviets always tried to circumvent Bonn, to blacken our name with third parties, to place the West German government under domestic pressure—for example with disinformation, disguised as confidential leaks, to people in my party and in religious organizations, to writers and journalists, to the peace movement, and the like.

None of these efforts by the Kremlin influenced my opinions or purposes in the international arena; the Soviets managed merely to make my domestic policy more difficult to carry out. Perhaps some people in Moscow believed that they would get along better with Strauss or Helmut Kohl. To nip such illusions in the bud, I made it clear more than once—both before the election campaign of 1976 and in 1980—that *any* West German government would continue our foreign policy and overall strategy vis-à-vis the Soviet Union. In these statements I specifically mentioned the TNF resolution Moscow hated so deeply.

I therefore knew that Brezhnev and Gromyko had no expectation of persuading me to give up the principles I had previously sent in draft form to the general secretary by way of Ambassador Zemyanov. The contents of this communiqué were as follows:

Though in Moscow I would be speaking for my country alone, I would be basing myself on positions that had been discussed with the American president and other Western leaders (the Venice summit had taken place on June 22 and 23). Neither this year nor in the future would there be any change in German loyalty to the Western alliance, the European Community, and France. Every German government would adhere to the principle of military parity. We would continue to make our military contribution to it, but we would also continue our efforts to bring about parity through mutual arms limitation on lower levels. The problem of intermediate-range weapons came under that heading. My views were known to Brezhnev; they had not changed in any respect, nor would they change in future. Furthermore, in Moscow I would speak about Afghanistan in detail. I closed the memorandum by noting that nothing would keep us from fulfilling our contracts with the Soviet Union, including the long-range economic agreement, and our other contracts with the East, the Four Power Agreement, and the Helsinki Final Act just as meticulously as we honored our agreements with our Western friends and allies.

I added that though it was to our mutual economic advantage for West Germany to collaborate with the Soviets, our main motive was a political one. This was also true for our coming meeting, where the substance of our talks would be the most important aspect; it was therefore desirable to avoid any ceremonial pomp and pageantry. I did, however, emphatically insist on two things. First, I wanted an opportunity for a talk with Dmitri F. Ustinov, the minister of defense; second, I asked for an opportunity to meet with the other leading personalities of the Soviet Union. Brezhnev and I were unlikely to be in our offices twenty-five years hence, and thus it was important to make German political ideas clear to the other members of the Soviet leadership.

As it turned out, both the externals and the substance of my visit conformed to my suggestions. Nevertheless I was taking a major risk—though nothing as drastic as a suicide mission. On the one hand, I was not sure how the majority of the Politburo would respond. On the other, many in the Federal Republic, as well as in the United States, were watching me with great suspicion and following everything I did with sharp eyes, always ready to make the spiteful criticism that the Russians would make mincemeat of the German chancellor. Finally, Germany, like the United States, was approaching an election campaign, and secretly Genscher was prepared to come to an arrangement with the CDU-CSU. But by the time of my flight home I was certain of one thing: The gamble had paid off.

Driving to Moscow from the airport, past the Lenin Hills, Brezhnev pointed to one side: There was the Olympic Village, he said. This was the only mention of the games in which we had just refused to participate.

Our opening session was a long one; it consisted basically of two monologues—a long opening statement by the general secretary, which he read, and an equally long improvised answer from me. Neither statement held any real surprises for the other side. Brezhnev condemned any pressure on Khomeini's Iran. Camp David, he declared, was a dead end. The Palestinians must be given their own state. Pol Pot's bloodbath in Kampuchea had to be laid at China's doorstep, demonstrating that its policies had not changed, even under its new leadership.

On the subject of Afghanistan, Brezhnev was fairly calm. "We know your opinion. It is probably unnecessary to emphasize that we reject it. Your estimate of the situation is based on prejudice about the actual events. We could not refuse to help a friendly neighboring country. Its independence was threatened, and there was a danger it would be transformed into a military staging area that would have been hostile to the Soviet Union. . . . We will not abandon our friends there. The revolution of 1978 was the result of Afghanistan's internal evolution. Without outside interference there would have been no disturbances in that country. We cannot deny the Afghans the right to self-determination, to decide for themselves what kind of government they want and whom they ask for help. . . . We are in favor of a political solution. It must include treaties with Pakistan and Iran on the cessation of outside interference and aggression. . . . In the framework of the political solution, the question of withdrawing our troops will be solved when the reasons for our aid are gone."

A full hour went by before I could speak on this subject. I focused my argument on the fact that I was not persuaded by the reasoning cited to justify Soviet intervention. We could not see any signs of outside interference that would justify intervention. "On the contrary, it seems to us, General Secretary, that the population is rising against an intellectual minority intent on imposing on the country a system that violates the rules of Islam and is foreign to the country. But what interests us is not casting blame but finding ways out of the situation."

It was our view, I went on, that a number of simultaneous measures must be enacted that would equally guarantee the retreat of all Soviet troops, the self-determination of the Afghan people, international controls, and the return of Afghan refugees as well as Soviet security interests. "As Giscard has already told you, we fear that confidence in your policies will be jeopardized—and without confidence, arms limitations cannot proceed. We in the West are not the only ones to be disturbed, as was shown by the conferences in Islamabad [an international meeting of Islamic states] and the resolutions of the United Nations. The presence of your airborne troops and your fighter-bombers in Afghanistan is an especially disturbing factor, they should be withdrawn as soon as possible." I closed by saying that we welcomed the idea of a political solution. Talks with the tripartite commission established in Islamabad would be appropriate to this end; but Moscow and Washington would also have to have direct communication on the new conflict. "The red telephone was not set up to exchange Christmas greetings; it is there for direct communication in crisis situations."

Brezhnev had mentioned the intermediate-range missiles in only very general terms. As early as October 6—nine months previously—he said, he had submitted a number of suggestions to which he had received no response. Unfortunately the government of the Federal Republic had also actively supported the NATO resolution. "But what was the result? The conditions for negotiations on intermediate-range missiles are destroyed, and the ratification of SALT II is blocked!"

I had intended to reserve my answer on the topic of the Eurostrategic intermediate-range missiles for the following day's negotiations. But I emphasized that as far as I could see, Carter had suspended the ratification process the previous winter because that had been the only possible way of saving SALT II from defeat in Congress. The American president was as determined as his Western allies, however, to honor the treaty even without ratification. I closed with an unmistakable, fairly comprehensive description of our loyal adherence to treaties as far as our alliance with the United States was concerned. This alliance, I stated, was unrenounceable; because of it we would continue to contribute our share to maintaining the military balance. But we also had an unconditional determination to uphold the bilateral German-Soviet treaties and to continue our collaboration based on them.

I too spoke for about an hour. Occasionally, as I made specific points, we thought we detected signs of understanding from Brezhnev but gestures of displeasure from Kosygin and Gromyko. I had spoken fairly softly and insistently, articulating my words slowly and with great earnestness. The three gentlemen had sensed my serious intent; they were respectful of their guest, from whom they had not expected anything different but whose visit had all the same been important to them. So far this meeting had changed nothing. The catharsis occurred during dinner.

As we walked from the Catherine Room to the equally splendid old Palace of the Czars, we passed a historical painting depicting both secular and clerical dignitaries. I joked to Kosygin that these must be members of the Politburo. He responded with a dry, understated wit that he found this supposition unlikely, "since none of them has a halo!"

In the lobby the members of the Politburo were waiting for us. Since I had seen photographs, I recognized Suslov; Ustinov, who was in uniform; Chernenko; and Yuri Andropov. Later I heard that, remarkably, only those Politburo members who were away from Moscow were absent. I had already met some of the ministers and leading officials. Almost the entire national leadership of the huge nation was present—Brezhnev had heeded my request.

All the men seemed overworked and gray. It was noticeable how well and tastefully they were dressed. Hardly a one seemed to me younger than I was. On the contrary, almost all had passed their sixty-fifth birthday. Furthermore, there was not a single woman in the group. My idea that I would explain our policies to the younger members of the Politburo as well had been silly—clearly there *were* no younger members. But my hope of speaking to Brezhnev's presumptive successor had come true. As it turned out, Brezhnev was followed only a few years later in quick succession first by Andropov, then by Chernenko (that night I was only fleetingly and subconsciously aware of Gorbachev).

All those present had started at the bottom and worked their way up through the ranks of functionaries and officials. Brezhnev had been a metalworker, Suslov and Kosygin—and probably Gromyko as well— were the sons of small farmers. Almost all of them had later attended various training institutes. Their paths were like a delayed and belated "second education." Their final examinations had surely been prerequisites to further advancement. But they owed the actual advancement to their successes in practical life—and presumably also to their ability to adapt. Finally, they had already held high offices under Stalin and had advanced to the gerontocratic Areopagus of the Politburo in the era of Khrushchev or—most of them—of Brezhnev.

They had hard faces, clearly marked by their lifelong struggle for power; at the same time they behaved with dignity and great self-control. It was unlikely that, except for Gromyko, any of them knew the West. None spoke a Western language. Since only Brezhnev and I had interpreters standing behind our chairs, the rest of the Russians and Germans, seated at a long table, could barely carry on the simplest conversations with each other. (Some of the members of my delegation did speak a little Russian.)

Because we had anticipated this situation, I did not leave my after-dinner speech to the vagaries of oral interpretation but had it printed and placed at the side of the Russians' plates. As proof against any tampering, we had released the speech hours before to both the Western and the Soviet press. It was obvious that the Soviet press would suppress the speech. If we did not ourselves hand a Russian translation of it to the Politburo members, the Soviet political elite would learn practically nothing of its content.

The leadership apparatus of the Soviet Union generally learns what the West has to say only at second hand, either from official papers or from the press. Its members can read only Russian papers, which at the time were selective to the point of transforming truths into untruths. The newspapers attributed motives and purposes to Western political figures that were cut to the measure of the image Soviet ideology had created of the West. Finally, Moscow newspaper reports and commentaries were meant to propagate and legitimate Soviet policies.

Could the men assembled in the Palace of the Czars—with the exception of Gromyko and Andropov, then head of the secret service— possibly know what the West was thinking about their actions? Could they know what I thought? It seemed necessary to place our opinion before them in black and white—even at the risk not only of their being surprised at the content but also of their reacting with outrage at such high-handedness. Of course preparing the speech in writing had the secondary purpose of demonstrating to some Western skeptics how and with what words the German chancellor had entered the lion's den.

Brezhnev's after-dinner speech was short and limited to generalities; it had a hortatory tone but was utterly factual. The second half of his address, dealing with the collaboration of the Soviet Union and Germany, was even rather cordial. My reply was more than twice as long, so that I was forced to speak rapidly. But I spoke softly and courteously; I was exceedingly polite not only in my tone of voice but also in my phrasing.

When it came to the two most controversial topics, however, I expressed myself loudly and clearly. I laid the blame for the crisis in Afghanistan at the Soviet door, and I insisted on the total withdrawal of Soviet troops. I also blamed the Soviet Union for the situation that had made the NATO TNF resolution of December 1979 necessary, and I appealed to my Soviet hosts to agree to beginning negotiations without any preconditions. Of course in closing I spoke of Germany's wish for peace, of the horrors of the last war, and of our willingness to collaborate with the Soviet Union. But I added, "Now it is important to prevent new and dangerous imbalances that could jeopardize what we have already achieved between us."

The expressions of the Russians who read along as I spoke soon indicated surprise, then irritation, and finally anger. Suslov, who was sitting next to me, at some point in the middle threw his translation demonstratively and noisily onto the table. I thought this would be the moment of my downfall, but I continued to speak in a soft voice, without batting an eyelash. When I looked across the table, I was relieved to note that Brezhnev was in no way disconcerted. He followed my text—with which he had been familiar for two hours—without looking up from the paper.

When I finished, Brezhnev rose to his feet and applauded. Suslov, Kosygin, and all the others followed his example. The Politburo had felt my respect for the world power that is the Soviet Union; though these men were annoyed, they were not offended. Because they had understood perfectly the seriousness of my desire for peace and collaboration, they were ready to accept my candor.

Probably it had been many years since the Soviet leadership had heard such undisguised reproaches from abroad. Some members of the leadership had become nervous, as shown by the little groups of gesticulating men talking to each other after the dinner. Some of the Russian guests seemed to feel that they had been taken unawares; they might have been thinking that the whole thing was unheard-of—I didn't know.

Hardly had I finished than Brezhnev crossed to my side of the table to tell me that we would have to talk further. I therefore retired rather quickly. Apparently Brezhnev needed time and opportunity to digest the effect of my words. I had the impression that I had set something in motion, but I did not yet know what it was.

Late that night or the following morning I heard that our hosts were annoyed. The general secretary, I was told, had spoken as a statesman, while the chancellor had merely made a lot of noise. The Soviet journalists tried to use this line to make their German colleagues nervous. The German delegation waited rather tensely for the Soviet reply, which was to be made in the morning session. At the Soviets' request the meeting was postponed by an hour to eleven o'clock—a sign that on the Soviet side matters were not going according to plan.

In the meantime we followed the schedule that had already been determined in Bonn and drove to the memorial to the Soviet soldiers at the wall of the Kremlin and to the Lyubino cemetery, where the German soldiers were buried. Although it was merely a "working visit," I placed two wreaths there to demonstrate that we Germans did not want to forget Hitler's war, that we would not allow the horrors of the past to be repeated.

The Soviets had not established special cemeteries for their twenty million war dead, nor is it easy to find individual soldiers' graves anywhere in the country. Instead there are innumerable war memorials; it is here the dead are remembered, and it is here memorial services are held. That is why the Soviet leadership found it very difficult at first to honor the German desire for common gravesites for the German war dead and to allow the Federal Republic to take care of these military cemeteries. The former enemy was to be permitted something denied their own dead? We must gratefully acknowledge that in the course of the years the Soviets little by little enabled us to care for and visit German military cemeteries.

That morning, July 1, 1980, the Lyubino cemetery showed every sign of hurried preparation. The grass that had been cut the day before had not yet been raked; it was still lying at the sides of the path. Once again my thoughts went back forty years—the faces and names of childhood friends who had fallen in the war rose in my memory.

The following day the *Münchner Merkur* reported, "The ghosts of the war formed a guard of honor at the graves of Lyubino." That could indeed be said. The war ghosts were also present at the Kremlin wall—as they had been present the previous day at our talks—and they would be present again today.

When Brezhnev opened the session, it very quickly became clear that the Soviet leaders had been consulting with each other. Brezhnev read from handwritten notes, he improvised now and then, and twice Gromyko helped out with specific wording. The gist of the statement was that the Soviet leadership was prepared, without conditions, without any delay, without waiting for the ratification of SALT II and before SALT III was begun, to negotiate bilaterally with the United States on limiting nuclear intermediate-range missiles, including the forward-based systems.

Thus the Russians had recanted their rejection of the treaty and the NATO TNF resolution. Would this be the breakthrough? I concealed my feeling of gratification. Instead I posed questions and asked for clarification. "You mention, for example, only the American FBS. You make no mention of the French, British, and Chinese intermediate-range missiles. Does this mean that these do not affect the situation?"

Gromyko replied, "We are dealing with the American FBS. The British, French, and Chinese weapons are not included because the intermediate-range missiles [which the NATO resolution was about] are American missiles. SALT III is another matter; in it we will deal with all the components. But here we have a narrower framework in mind."

I meticulously repeated what had been said and added, "Of course that includes the SS-20s, SS-4s, SS-5s, and Backfire bombers."

After a brief consultation with Brezhnev, Gromyko answered drily, "They say the more one has, the more one wants." The fact that he neither contradicted nor tried to set limits on this point made it clear that no element of the Soviet position was a mere psychological gesture.

I replied, "I shall pass on your suggestion to President Carter. Herr Genscher will fly to Washington tomorrow. . . . The sooner such negotiations are started, the happier we Germans will be. . . . We feel threatened by the Soviets' rapid deployment of intermediate-range missiles. Though we do not believe that you intend to use them in war, we fear them as a means of political pressure. By the way, I do not like using the term 'intermediate-range weapons,' since they are strategic weapons that pose a strategic threat to my country. . . ."

Now, in the summer of 1980, the negotiations proposed in the NATO solution might finally have begun. Six months had been lost to Soviet refusals. And now, as the result of the American presidential election, another six months had been thrown away. When Ronald Reagan was elected in November 1980, he had to be granted the usual six months to establish his administration. In reality, however, almost all of 1981 passed before the negotiations on intermediate-range weapons began; under the new acronym INF (for Intermediate-range Nuclear Forces), the talks opened on November 30 in Geneva. Two years had passed since the TNF resolution, almost three years since the Guadeloupe conference, and four years since my lecture at London's International Institute of Strategic Studies, where for the first time I had publicly called for such negotiations.

The Western European governments had wanted such negotiations since December 1979, since it was their countries that were being threatened strategically and existentially by the intermediate-range nuclear weapons; but conducting the negotiations was the business of the two superpowers. In November 1983 Moscow and Washington allowed the INF negotiations to end fruitlessly. Under Reagan, the White House had been unable to work up sufficient interest in the subject, and the Kremlin believed that by this time it had achieved adequate arms superiority in these new Eurostrategic weapons. Since Guadeloupe there had been changes of government in Paris, Bonn, and London; the basic shared strategic ideas of the Western European states had in the meantime made way for a lack of common purpose, and Europe's loss of influence in relation to the United States after 1981 eventually produced an even more precarious loss of influence in relation to Moscow.

This loss of influence, which would become a reality within a few short years, was not in any way in evidence in Moscow in July 1980. Quite the contrary; our visit had a happy ending. The Russians wanted to be respected as one of two equal world powers, and we had not denied them. They had hoped to teach their small German neighbor, of whom they were secretly also afraid, how to be afraid on their terms—and they had not succeeded. Instead we had told them, "Those who care about peace in the world must stop forcing their own political, social, and economic ideas on others." The Russians wanted peace and coexistence, and they wanted cooperation with their small German neighbor. As usual, the Germans advocated the same objectives, but they did not want them on Russian terms. The Russians understood and accepted this position.

The echo of the July meeting in Moscow was as loud abroad as it was at home. No one had expected the Soviet Union to be accommodating in the matter of Afghanistan; after all, Bonn had only minor interests in western Asia. But the fact that the door could once again be opened to arms limitation talks was considered a great coup. After Genscher brought him the news, Jimmy Carter spoke publicly on July 3 of "appreciation and admiration" for the German chancellor—quite a change from the suspicion publicly voiced by him and Brzezinski earlier. The following day there was a debate in the Bundestag during which Helmut Kohl, the leader of the opposition, was silent, while Strauss, then a candidate for the chancellorship, gave a not very convincing speech criticizing the Moscow meeting. This session finally confirmed that the visit was seen as an unconditional triumph by our government as well as abroad.

One more Moscow entr'acte remains to be recorded. Though it is not pertinent to the outcome of our meeting, it allows some interesting insights into the Soviet mind. On July 1, 1980, in accordance with my request, I was granted a two-hour talk with Marshal Dmitri F. Ustinov, who was accompanied by Marshal Nikolai V. Ogarkov and three or four other generals and an admiral. I was joined by Genscher, my friend Klaus Bölling (at the time state secretary and speaker of the federal government), and Hans-Georg Wieck, our ambassador to Moscow, who had first served me superbly ten years earlier in the ministry of defense at the Hardthöhe.

Ustinov, who was seventy years old, had in fact been a civilian armaments manager. Ogarkov, who was around sixty, had been in the military all of his career. When he was only thirty-three, Ustinov, a former metalworker, had been named people's commissar for armaments under Stalin; he had successfully carried out his job for the length of the war and had kept it until 1957—fifteen years altogether. After that date he had risen further in the hierarchy; a member of the Politburo, he had served as minister of defense since 1976. Without him the unprecedented buildup of the navy, space, and missile forces is unthinkable. He, like Brezhnev, owed the rank of marshal to the desire of the party to express its political primacy over the military. That evening, when I made a remark to Brezhnev about my talk with the two marshals, he replied, "Yes—but Ustinov is not military, he is our man."

Ustinov opened the talk with the remark that my book *A Grand Strategy for the West* had been translated into Russian and he had read large parts of it. Some of its ideas were obviously sensible and understandable; but others were open to debate. As our talk proceeded, I tried to make him see that though the Bundeswehr was well armed and fit for action, because of its equipment and its limited mobility it was in no position to advance into territory beyond its borders. The purpose of our army was to defend in a small radius on our own soil. It was important to me that he and his experts be persuaded of this fact. I had already explained the situation to Brezhnev six years earlier, but it had been my impression that the general secretary's skepticism had not been allayed.

Ustinov did not hesitate. "You know, Leonid Brezhnev is well informed on military matters. He is familiar with the subject. That is why he is perfectly able to judge whatever you told him. . . . As far as manpower, technology, and organization are concerned, we believe that your army is one of the best. Discipline and technology are held in high regard in your country, and you, Chancellor, have contributed to this attitude. . . . But you are a little too modest in what you claim about the German army and its limited radius of action." Then he went on to give special praise to the Bundeswehr's Leopard tank. But inevitably he came back to the German military radius of action. In 1941, he pointed out, Hitler had not had a perfect organization of reinforcements either, but Germany had had no trouble conjuring up plenty out of thin air. Besides, German industry was highly efficient; should the need arise, great numbers of tanks could be built in no time at all.

The talk finally turned to Carter's and Brezhnev's meeting in Vienna the previous year, at which time Ustinov and Ogarkov had met with Harold Brown, at that time United States secretary of defense, and General David Jones, then head of the Joint Chiefs of Staff. Ustinov complained that no progress had been made since MBFR, although the Soviet Union had offered to reduce its troops by 30,000 men if the United States would reduce its troop strength by 12,000. This led to a lengthy dispute between Ustinov and Genscher on the reciprocal proposals of the last twelve months. Ustinov was well informed on the details. Finally Ogarkov said, "If we go on this way, we'll need another twenty years! Why don't you accept our proposal of freezing the current situation?"

I answered that this was not an acceptable solution without agreement on an upper limit identical for both sides.

So in the end the arrangement remained the same: Let us declare the existing state of comparative strength to be the state of balance and perpetuate it by an accord. Our discussion on the Eurostrategic intermediate-range missiles ran a similar course and also resulted in no new ideas. The two marshals claimed that the SS-20 program was merely a modernization. They rejected my detailed references to the multiplication of the threat with the claim that the number of launchers and the sum of all nuclear service charges (that is, the sum of explosive values) were unchanged. Ogarkov added that if the American FBS were included, NATO had double the number of warheads held by the Soviet Union.

I responded quite firmly. "Marshal, you have almost three times as many warheads on intermediate-range missiles as you did in 1970. You can hit three times as many cities with them, you can reach my hometown of Hamburg even from the other side of the Urals with your SS-20s, a feat that was impossible with your old missiles. All your weapons do not threaten the United States—they threaten Germany!"

At this point, for the only time, Ustinov went beyond the line set by the Politburo to make the concise reply: "That is correct."

After discussing Soviet naval armaments, I spoke of the comparatively small role of the West German navy. It would, I assured my audience, remain small in future; we had no plans to enlarge it. Ustinov objected that originally we had built submarines of only 350 tons, but now, ostensibly under pressure from the United States, we had a fleet of 1,800-ton submarines. He pointed out that we had gradually raised the upper limit of other classes of ships as well and were building 6,000-ton warships. Furthermore, it was technically possible to build warships of any size in Kiel, Bremen, and Hamburg.

I replied that since the days of Hitler no large warships had been built in any of these three German ports. Jokingly I added that I promised to send him a picture postcard in the event, but I doubted it would happen in my lifetime.

Ustinov liked black humor; he said that considering his age, he probably wouldn't be there to receive such a postcard. Nevertheless, Moscow would have to include the potential of the German shipyards in its calculations.

Both marshals struck me as highly intelligent. In addition, they were well informed; they never needed sources for any details. In our talk, which was carried on in a relaxed and collegial tone, they appeared confident but not overbearing. My spontaneous impression was that these were men of a caliber in no way inferior to that of their Western colleagues. As far as the discussion was concerned, they always (with the one exception noted) hewed to the line set by their leadership, neither moderating nor going beyond it. Ogarkov was, as it were, the operational reserve, while Ustinov played the leading part. I sensed that both of them took the Bundeswehr very seriously, even though it was comparatively small. They demonstrated their thorough knowledge of the German fighting forces and clearly showed their concern.

I had no reason to question Ustinov's wish for peace. Nevertheless

I was just as certain that he—and perhaps even more Ogarkov—considered the Soviet Union's material and quantitative superiority to be the best assurance of peace. The fact that such an enormous superiority would have to be disturbing to the Germans had apparently not played a large role in their thinking so far. However, when I listed some of the German cities they could destroy with their SS-20 missiles, they did seem to have a certain measure of understanding for me and my line of reasoning.

According to Western calculations, for years these two men, as heads of the entire Soviet military machine, spent 12–14 percent of the Soviet gross national product on their fighting forces. This was an enormous percentage compared to the less than 7 percent of the American GNP and the less than 4 percent average of the GNP of the Western European nations. This quantitatively large slice of the Soviet economic pie was also qualitatively superior. The army had been given not a vertical cut but a horizontal section—that is, the top layer, particularly rich in calories. The meager bottom crust had been left to Kosygin and Tikhonov to feed the civilian sector.

I don't know to what degree the two marshals sought support for the invasion of Afghanistan or whether they understood how much the Afghan adventure was harming their reputation in the world and especially in the United States. Whatever the case, they were integrally involved in increasing the missile buildup, and obviously they lacked any political instinct for the reaction of the people and nations threatened by it.

Calling them militarists would be an oversimplification. They were merely callous in pursuing Soviet security interests and seemed genuinely surprised that the world reacted by speaking of a Soviet expansionist drive. Like Brezhnev himself, they seemed honestly concerned with preserving peace; but they did not understand that they were the ones who were jeopardizing peace, without intending to. They were typical Russians.

The Gerontocratic Rapids

I SAW Brezhnev only once more after this meeting, during a working visit in Bonn in late November 1981. It was my seventh personal encounter with him. Our first had been at the dinner on the Venusberg during Willy Brandt's chancellorship; then there had been my two visits to Moscow and Brezhnev's return visit in 1978, as well as the meeting in Helsinki and the one in Belgrade, where we had had a talk when we were both attending Tito's funeral.

The old man's ideas had not changed very much; but now he was really ill and frail. He clung to his self-imposed task of consolidating the Soviet sphere of influence, which had been considerably enlarged in his time, through agreements with the West and through détente. One of his colleagues told me that Brezhnev did not want to leave too many unsolved problems for his successor. But that is exactly what happened—in particular the great economic and international problems of his country, which he had been unable to solve, were passed on to his successor.

In the course of our meetings he had personally come to trust my candor, even though he was totally unwilling to accept my security policy. Now he was troubled by his inability to understand Ronald Reagan's intentions and actions. In November 1981 he obviously hoped that I would supply him with a key to understanding the new American president. In the meantime he had become totally dependent on Gromyko when it came to the reasoning and subject matter of all discussions.

Since the INF talks between Paul Nitze and Yuli Kvitsinsky were scheduled to begin in Geneva in a few days, Eurostrategic weapons once more played a leading role in our talk. Brezhnev did not bring up anything of special significance—with possibly one minor exception. At the time some Soviet officials still hoped to be able to undermine Western Europe's determination to rearm and were doing everything they could to increase Western nervousness. I therefore said at one point in our conversation, "General Secretary, you must please understand clearly that if the impending negotiations fail, I would risk the survival of my government to bring about armament by the West, and every conceivable West German government will agree to the stationing of new American weapons unless, by the end of 1983, a breakthrough in the mutual limitation of intermediate-range missiles occurs. . . . In the West, however, we have gained the impression that the Soviet leadership puts more stock in the peace movement than in its own negotiations." Brezhnev and Gromyko fully understood that I was speaking deliberately and with conviction. Besides, they had heard similar sentiments in their talks with the heads of the West German political parties.

Then both listed a number of complaints about Reagan—and more especially about Caspar Weinberger. When it came to Reagan, they simply did not understand him; they probably just took him to be a cynic. In Weinberger they probably saw an actual warmonger. I made it clear to them that Reagan, on his side, could not understand the Soviet stance. In the eyes of Washington, Brezhnev's proposal of a moratorium could only mean that the indisputable superiority in Europe the Soviets had achieved was to be perpetuated. Finally I said, "I once told Ronald Reagan that Leonid Brezhnev doesn't really want war. Today I want to tell you: Ronald Reagan also wants peace. He said to me, 'I want to negotiate with the Russians, to go on negotiating, and to negotiate some more, until they understand my position.' Reagan will need time. Even a successful governor of the state of California comes to the presidency with about as much international experience as your first secretary in Kazakhstan. At his age, however, he will be the best judge of what he is capable of. Then—like his predecessors Nixon, Ford, and Carter—he will, I'm sure, want to meet with the leader of the Soviet Union. After all, you got along best with Nixon; you'll see that Reagan will take his bearings from Nixon."

This last meeting, too, received favorable notices from both the world press and our own media. To my surprise it was also approved by the Japanese press and even by the papers in Israel, where during Menachem Begin's time not many good things were written about me. Bonn, it was said, had first of all persuaded Reagan to make the public offer of a mutual zero option and had then convinced Brezhnev to make a counterproposal. In spite of a tiny remnant of mistrust here and there, the world understood that we had firmly interpreted the Western position on arms reduction to the Soviet leader and that Brezhnev had accepted. These were, the newspapers commented, good enough opening positions with which to begin negotiations in Geneva.

I believed these judgments to be on the mark. But I knew better than the newspapers that at the time the Reagan administration was not actually pursuing a clear course of compromise. Meanwhile sections of my own party were waiting with much too much impatience, emotionally heightened, for a breakthrough; they were inclined to be intolerant both of delays and of tactical caution. Some went so far as to silently accept permanent Soviet superiority by denouncing balance as always synonymous with competition for superiority in arms. The leadership of the Social Democratic Party, through Willy Brandt, allowed itself to appear to tolerate such tendencies; that this appearance was not deceptive was proven in 1983, when the leadership and a majority of the national party convention emphatically and euphorically rejected the second half of the TNF resolution on the stationing of Eurostrategic intermediate-range nuclear missiles. Herbert Wehner and I, Defense Minister Hans Apel, other friends in the federal government, the parliamentary group, and the party found it increasingly difficult in 1982 to swear the Bundestag majority to using common sense in foreign policy. At the same time Moscow had come to believe seriously that with the help of the peace movement it would be possible to sneak past the TNF resolution and to prevent the stationing of Western intermediate-range nuclear forces.

In its thirteenth year the SPD-FDP coalition was beginning to crumble. Foreign Minister Genscher, who was clearly playing an active role in this process, had begun in the summer of 1981 to speak publicly of the necessity of a "change." By the beginning of the following summer our partners in Washington and Moscow understood that the success of my parliamentary vote of confidence in the spring of 1982 could not prevent the collapse of my government much longer.

After my resignation in October 1982 the West German government gradually lost its international influence, in spite of Genscher's efforts on behalf of international and collective strategic continuity. The two world powers, tacitly agreeing that there was no need to arrive at an understanding at the Geneva INF negotiations, were no longer obliged to pay attention to Bonn. Chancellor Kohl found the confusing game of two-track diplomacy toward the Soviet Union—transparent on both tracks—too complicated; he therefore soon gave it up and reconciled himself to the supposed inevitability of American deployment of weapons on Western European and therefore German soil. The Reagan administration was delighted with his position. But after a short time it turned out that Washington's respect for Bonn and its desire for serious consultation with the convenient new German government was gradually decreasing.

To be fair, the temporary change from Brezhnev to Andropov in November 1982, then the shift from Andropov to Chernenko and finally, in March 1985, to Gorbachev did not exactly invite active diplomacy on the part of the West. Probably even if the West had acted jointly on the basis of a shared overall strategy, it would have had great difficulty arriving at a viable outcome of negotiations with the Soviet Union, because the internal insecurity of the political class in Moscow was palpable. Only when Gorbachev was firmly in the saddle did the summit meeting between the American president and the Soviet general secretary that I had long advocated come about—in Geneva in late November 1985. The Europeans and West Germans, however, retained only the role of friendly, applauding audience. They forwent introducing their own interests, just as they did a year later, when Gorbachev and Reagan met a second time, in Reykjavik, to discuss the fate of the world.

In the seventy years of its existence the Soviet Union has had four great, historically significant national leaders: Lenin, Stalin, Khrushchev, and Brezhnev. Gorbachev is likely to be the fifth. His four predecessors were despots of the Russian type once embodied by the Moscow grand dukes and czars, even though Stalin was originally a Georgian— but then Catherine the Great was not a Russian either, but a German princess. It seems reasonable to me to count on such "Russian" continuity at the head of the Soviet Union for the foreseeable future as well—no matter whether and to what extent Mikhail Gorbachev is successful in the reforms and changes he is initiating.

Gorbachev quickly rid himself of several old Politburo members who had not—unlike Suslov, Kosygin, Ustinov, and Arvid Pelshe—already died along with Brezhnev, Andropov, and Chernenko; this gesture rejuvenated the top echelon, and it may be that the new men will prove to be more flexible and less conservative than their predecessors. Many

Soviet citizens are hopeful. In Germany's interests, and in the interests of Germans in both West and East, I sincerely wish that their hopes are fulfilled.

But to the extent that in the West we share these hopes, we should be cautious: Though the greater vitality of younger men as opposed to their intellectually rigid and risk-fearing predecessors may lead to greater mobility in matters of foreign policy and security, it may also lead to a greater willingness to take risks. It seems to me inadvisable to base our own policies on the theory that Russian-Soviet expansionism will cease. In any case we will have to keep alive the possibility that one day Brezhnev's strategy will be revived, though perhaps by other means.

Therefore, if we are to be prepared, a study of the Brezhnev era is advisable. Unlike Lenin, Brezhnev did not enrapture his people as a prophet. He was not widely hated as Stalin was. Nor is it likely that he will be turned into a figure of fun, like Khrushchev with his changeable, choleric temperament. Sooner or later observers outside the Soviet Union may well come to see him as the archetype of a Soviet leader; such a view would, to be sure, be at considerable variance with Gorbachev's ideas.

New administrations often present their people with an extremely negative opening balance sheet, assigning the blame for it to their predecessors. Carter and Reagan took this position, as did Kohl—and so did Gorbachev, blaming Brezhnev. The more darkly the predecessor and the era associated with his name are depicted, the easier it is to promise new beginnings for new initiatives—and to be believed. Later, viewed from a greater distance, the breaks often seem far less significant. In any event, they tend to affect domestic policies far more than the foreign policies of the nation in question. But frequently the change on the domestic scene is simply more strongly marked in the consciousness of the period. The supposedly new reality of the national, social, and economic processes is often largely an illusion—though at times such an illusion can be very useful. Deng Xiaoping certainly did start far-reaching renewal in China—leaving the memory of Mao Zedong pretty much intact, by the way; in citing the negative balance of his inheritance, he limited himself almost exclusively to the Gang of Four and their crimes and errors (which he was justified in attacking). Whether Mikhail Gorbachev will be able to bring about a categorically similar change in the Soviet Union cannot yet be determined.

Today conversations with Soviet Russians—old acquaintances, for example—Gorbachev's speeches, and party and government statements make it clear that Andropov and Chernenko are not among those held responsible for the paralysis Gorbachev has diagnosed. As far as Andropov is concerned, such an attitude makes sense, since he tried to advance the generational change in the Soviet leadership strata; for example, he promoted Gorbachev when the latter was still quite young. It seems to me probable that if Andropov had lived and remained in office, he would have tackled many of the reforms Gorbachev is now pursuing. For these reasons alone Gorbachev is not interested in diminishing his memory. The West will probably long remember the downing of a Korean jetliner in the late summer of 1983 and Moscow's subsequent helplessness, which occurred during Andropov's time in office. Otherwise he left no significant marks on foreign policy; his tenure was too short.

The same holds true for Chernenko. Domestically his tenure from February 1984 to March 1985 was probably no more than a brief, posthumous extension of the Brezhnev era. Brezhnev himself had picked him out as his successor, presumably because he considered him congenial. There is good reason why Chernenko is no longer mentioned in Moscow.

But there is abundant mention of Brezhnev, who headed the Politburo and the Soviet Union for almost two decades. As far as I can see, the criticism to date has addressed the first half of his era less than the second. At present it is focused mainly on domestic events, very little on foreign affairs. Brezhnev's and Gromyko's arms control diplomacy is undergoing significant changes, but the Brezhnev doctrine, limiting sovereignty of nations in the Socialist camp, was used to justify the invasion of Czechoslovakia; forced arms buildups; political, military, and economic extension into the Middle East, into East, Southeast, and West Africa, into Afghanistan, and into Nicaragua—all these are, for the time being, outside the bounds of criticism.

Of course attitudes toward President Andrei Gromyko may be playing a part. Under Brezhnev Gromyko was the executor of foreign policy for many years, though he did not become a full member of the Politburo until 1973. On March 11, 1985, he proposed Gorbachev's name to the Politburo for election to the office of general secretary. Even today he seems to be playing an important role in the Politburo, at least in matters concerning foreign affairs. Alexander Yakovlev, Eduard A. Shevardnadze, and Anatoli Dobrynin are on a lower rung when it comes to foreign policy.

I paid a private visit to Gromyko in February 1987, when I returned to Moscow for the first time in almost seven years. I had accepted an invitation by my friend Kurt Körber to a German-Soviet discussion at the Bergedorfer Gesprächskreis that he had established. Both of us were happy about the reunion. Gromyko seemed relaxed, unruffled, cheerful; at moments he was even witty. Of course we talked about old times. Gromyko recalled our first meeting eighteen years earlier in the Spiridov Palace, with Alex Möller and Egon Bahr. We also talked about current problems of foreign policy and arms reduction, about German-Soviet relations, and about Gorbachev's proposed economic reforms. But Brezhnev's name did not come up.

A final word on Brezhnev: When I heard that he had died on November 10, 1982, I was genuinely saddened. I had had a long shared history with this sometimes harsh, sometimes sentimental Russian leader. His desire for peace was sincere. But I had to take his desire to expand Soviet power just as seriously. Brezhnev's ideological-philosophical basis was narrow, but he had a unique and sure instinct for his nation's interests. The Soviet Union's military superiority and his desire for peace did not, in his mind, contradict each other. Whether he always saw through the military maps and statistics and the resulting necessity to build up the Soviet Union's armaments, which his military branch presented to him, I have come to doubt; especially in his last years this may or may not have been the case.

In 1983 Bruno Kreisky remarked to me that there was a tragic element in the fact that for a number of years Brezhnev had not understood the international process. Now that he had been succeeded by Andropov, who was capable and highly intelligent, the man at the helm of the United States had little to offer that was substantive. I could not raise strenuous objections to this harsh judgment; I merely pointed to events in connection with the shooting down of the Korean passenger plane and added my doubts as to whether Andropov, rather than the military, was really fully in control of the executive.

In domestic affairs Kreisky's characterization of the final years of the Brezhnev era was unquestionably accurate. The aged and sickly general secretary had been unwilling to tolerate innovation and struggle. He had made his peace with the clumsiness of the bureaucracy; he wanted peace and quiet. He believed he had secured his nation's external peace, and he was reluctant to disturb the domestic peace through changes. The people around Gorbachev are probably right in seeing the second half of Brezhnev's time in office as a period of domestic and economic stagnation.

Will
Gorbachev Make
Basic Reforms?

I F REAGAN'S countrymen liked to call their president a great communicator, the term applies in equal measure to Gorbachev. He speaks persuasively; his speeches, tailored for television, are highly effective—not only with the Soviet public but just as much in Eastern Europe, where hopes for him are high, and especially in Western Europe—in the West altogether. He does not recite carefully crafted tactical or bureaucratic pronouncements; instead, he presents his arguments in a way that is both powerful and likable; the listener can follow his thinking and therefore finds it logical.

The West felt Khrushchev to be arrogant, at times even boorish; Brezhnev seemed boring; but Gorbachev is interesting. At present, when public opinion—the public's likes and antipathies—are largely molded by television, this skill is extremely valuable. Without it, and without television, it is unlikely that either John F. Kennedy or Charles de Gaulle would have been able to achieve such profound effects far beyond the borders of their own nations. Of course the talent required to deliver a good television speech is not enough in the long run; it must be combined with basic abilities and traits: the power of analysis and judgment, the courage not only to express both of these but also to develop ideas based on them and to draw practical conclusions, leadership qualities, a realistic, accurate eye for what is possible in a given situation, and finally, steadfastness and perseverance in pursuit of set objectives. And all these must be surrounded by an aura of ethical and moral responsibility to one's own people and the world.

Gorbachev will have to be in power longer before we can judge whether and to what extent that great television communicator possesses these basic skills. His analytical faculties and courage are beyond question. Whether they are combined with sufficient domestic and particularly economic imagination, as well as the acuity and perseverance to "drill through thick boards" (Max Weber), remains to be seen.

But his initial effectiveness has been breathtaking. Soviet functionaries I have known for years speak of "new thinking" when they mention "reform" (*perestroika*) and "openness" (*glasnost*), even "democratization"; there is a sense that they feel inwardly involved. The newspapers now print critical articles; sometimes they are even critical of the army. All of a sudden *Pravda* has become interesting, the *Literaturnaya Gazeta* even more so. Television is carrying controversial discussions and commentaries. Andrei Sakharov and other exiles have been allowed to return to Moscow, and some dissidents (among them a number of Jews) have been granted the emigration permits they have long been seeking. The extent to which the curtain has lifted is still small when compared to the freedom of expression that prevails in the Western democracies. But this new beginning fills many Soviet citizens with hope for more. The intellectuals and artists have so far been the greatest beneficiaries of the changes, and their hopes are the highest—as is true of Soviet émigrés living in the West, who are devoted to their country with all their heart and soul.

Others, however, are skeptical or even pessimistic: They remember earlier disappointments. The actions of the leadership after the serious accident at the Chernobyl nuclear reactor on April 26, 1986, raised some questions. The authorities initially withheld some facts and glossed over others, and for a long time the large numbers of dead and evacuees were kept secret altogether. This attitude made it clear that even Gorbachev finds it easier to ask for openness than to practice it. In the same way, in the same year, the extent of the uprisings in Kazakhstan was kept secret.

For a long time now the birthrates in Kazakhstan, Turkmenistan, Uzbekistan, and Kirghizia—republics with considerable or increasing Islamic influence—have been much higher than in Russia proper, and for a long time they have been a source of concern for Moscow, as are the nationalistic demands for greater autonomy in those republics. It is difficult to believe that openness and democratization will benefit the USSR's non-Slavic populations to the same extent as they will the Slavs—that is, the Russians, Ukrainians, and White Russians, who altogether make up little more than half the total population (a fact particularly noticeable in the Red Army). Gorbachev has publicly opposed the nationalism that is gaining ground in Central Asia, Georgia, and Armenia, as well as in the Baltic states; *Pravda* has trivialized it as "local patriotism." The more openness and democratization are introduced, the more crushing the Soviet Union's problems of nationalities could grow; unless they are resolved or controlled, I consider a reversal of the newly introduced freedom of expression very likely.

My impression is that this danger is even greater in the area of economic reform. Expectations have been aroused whose satisfaction in the foreseeable future seems improbable to me. To this day, in fact, nothing has changed for people at work, in the stores, and on the street—except that alcohol in every form has become a scarce commodity. People roam through the streets and stores, carrying shopping bags and plastic bags—just in case they stumble on something useful for sale; the lines outside the shoe stores, for example, seem to me no shorter in 1987 than they were in 1980.

The thirteenth Five-Year Plan, beginning in January 1991, will noticeably improve the supply of consumer goods—at least, that is what the people have been told. The precondition is that in 1989 the general elements of this plan will be decided, with the details settled in 1990. But at present—in 1987—conversations with Soviet economists provide only inadequate ideas about how to meet the promises made to consumers. Discussions in the economic sector of the Soviet Union and among economic officials, as well as the discussions of both groups with political functionaries, involve controversy—which in itself is a good symptom, not a bad one. But to date no clear conclusions have been drawn. The chief difficulty is that so far analytical criticism has undervalued the problem so much that it cannot arrive at logical plans leading to decisive actions. When the mental construct is lacking, a society oriented to a system of regulations and their (often careless) execution cannot count on economic success.

The task facing Gorbachev is greater than the one Lenin set himself in 1921, when he established the New Economic Policy (NEP). He cannot take advantage of experience gained in a market economy, and he cannot appeal to the Soviet citizen's own material interests. Though the latter is conceivable—and in fact in isolated cases some thought has been given to effective income and wage differentials based on production—it would be at odds with all past custom and even current ideology. That is why Gorbachev has not gone much beyond calling for greater discipline at work and restricting the supply of alcohol.

For the moment the discussion of reforms is centering on a small area of the domestic economy—reorganizing the nationalized industries (the "socialist industrial plants") and restructuring the Moscow ministries and planning boards; over twenty ministries alone cover the various branches of the economy. Furthermore, there is talk of allowing a small segment of agricultural production to engage in a free market, with prices freely set; this would apply to what the collective farmers raise on their "own" land and to the "excess production" of the collectives. At the same time more rigorous state quality control of industry is being introduced in place of the previous internal controls; it is probably that the new quality controls are the chief cause of the decline in industrial production noted since the end of 1986. All these innovations go back to Andropov, who for his part was inspired by Kosygin, by Professor Yevsei G. Liberman, and by the Novosibirsk economists' paper of 1982. But so far that is almost all.

The "reconstruction" of the economy is supposed to be completed by the end of 1990. If the present, very fragmentary sketches are all there is, a categorical increase in the Soviet Union's economic production beginning in 1991 is presumably an illusion.

Even the present modest suggestions find very considerable resistance the moment they are implemented. The proposed law concerning the socialist industrial plants proposes giving the industries freedom of decision in a number of areas (though not in investments); but what is lacking are "cadres"—that is, leaders who are capable enough and brave enough to make such decisions. The risk of making a decision that will subsequently turn out to be inadequate or wrong is not balanced either by sufficient training or by commensurate incentives. Political functionaries want to see the mechanisms for sanctions tightened, business functionaries fear the loss of their permanent positions. Of course the latter is equally true for the government bureaus and functionaries that deal with the distribution of whatever goods have been produced. What is evident on the lower and middle levels as universal inertia also occurs on the top rung, in the form of substantial ideological resistance. This resistance is directed against the mobilization of individual material interests, as opposed to the general "social interest." It insists that in the interests of the stability of the social and national order it is essential to maintain the traditional administrative centralization. Only a small number of all the people involved in industrial activities are committed to the reforms; they are among the cultural and technical intelligentsia. What is absent is a positive mass movement, which does not exist even within the party. Gorbachev has been able to obtain a resolution from the Central Committee to replace a number of people who seemed unsuitable to him; but it is quite obvious that even this initiative gave him enormous difficulty. As yet he is far from working in an atmosphere open to reform.

This may be the main reason the overall organizational plan of the attempted economic reforms has not yet been submitted. But I am inclined to believe that no one in Gorbachev's immediate circle has yet worked out a general concept. It seems that it is considered enough for the moment to take some initiatives in the right direction and to trust to the future for pragmatic progress.

In a conversation with Andrei Gromyko in March 1987 I said I was following with interest the establishment of greater intellectual freedom and the admission of criticism in the Soviet Union. But if in three or four years there is disappointment that the economic expectations raised today have not been realized, such newly liberated criticism would be directed at the inadequate economic leadership as well. "I'm afraid that under those circumstances the Soviet leaders will once again restrict the freedom to criticize." I asked Gromyko when he believed the mass of consumers would start to see economic improvement.

Gromyko replied, "We are optimists. In the past we have not made full use of socialism's potential. The ideal would be to bring out its total value. Today we want to tell people the truth. That requires a restructuring of public opinion and economic leadership. Of course as a result people are going to make greater demands. We make every effort to satisfy them. But because expectations will continue to rise, there will be those who are still not satisfied even in five or ten years. We are convinced that our policy will be successful in the future."

In his general ideas Gromyko did not deviate from Gorbachev's basic line. Of course detailed economic disquisitions can hardly be expected from a foreign minister. Nevertheless I took his broad (and, for Gromyko, unusually optimistic) answer as a sign of the fact that even in March 1987 the leadership circles of party and state had not yet arrived at any far-reaching general plan for restructuring the Soviet economy.

The discussions I had with Soviet experts during that same visit only confirmed this impression. For example, a person with whom I had often talked during a twenty-year period—Valentin Falin, the former ambassador to Berlin—used the phrase "socialist market"; but the meaning of this concept was never clear. When I spoke to an economics professor, she told me the intended restructuring of the economy was not at all Soviet-specific; the same ideas were being used in many developing nations. She pointed to the spread of modern communication technology, to the "technological revolution" in general, to the transition from manufacturing to service economies. Like Falin, she surprised me by speaking in detail about the dependence of the Soviet Union's economic development on the course of the international economy. Economic security through self-sufficiency is no longer thinkable, she said. Economic want in one nation inevitably leads to setbacks in others, thanks to international interdependence; she illustrated this point with various examples. Previously no one in the Soviet Union had ever referred to Soviet vulnerability on the international front, though in fact it was obvious. Her statement indirectly reflected the new and accurate recognition that the outcome of the intended economic restructuring depends entirely on the course of international economic processes.

Until now Soviet exports have centered on oil and natural gas (their share of all Soviet exports to the German Federal Republic has been about 80 percent in the last few years). The enormous up-and-down shift in the international prices of these two energy sources since 1973, as well as the strong fluctuations of the American dollar, in which these prices are set and which serve as the currency of energy contracts, has seriously affected the continuity of the Soviet economy because the country's foreign-currency balance fluctuates accordingly. Now the Soviets are talking about expanding their exports of manufactured goods, about joint ventures to be established with foreign enterprises for this purpose, about free trade, and about their hope of joining IMF and GATT; complaints are heard about embargoes and the lists of the Coordinating Committee for East-West Trade Policy. There is even talk to the effect that in future Soviet heavy industry itself will be allowed to dispose of 30 percent of the foreign currency earned by exports.

Of course it is entirely possible that greater attention on the part of the Soviet Union to the international economy and greater participation in its division of labor can have positive effects on Moscow's future foreign policy. In the meantime, however, the concerns of the Soviet Union are still largely focused on the domestic economy. Only if the country succeeds in selling a greater quantity of the industrial goods demanded on the world market and receives hard currency in exchange will its domestic economy be able to profit from an expansion in foreign trade. But the road to that point is a long one.

It is in the interests of all the Soviet Union's neighbors—and of the entire world—that Gorbachev's economic reforms succeed. In all probability failure would throw Moscow's sphere of action back to the field of international power politics. It would be an illusion, however, for us in Germany to expect that the expansion of Soviet trade will provide more than an occasional stimulus for our own industrial activities; the point of departure, which is often completely overestimated both at home and abroad (especially in the United States), is much too small. The share of German exports to the Soviet Union is a mere 2 percent of our total exports—meaning that it amounts to less than half the amount of our exports to our tiny neighbors such as Austria and Switzerland. Nevertheless, the Federal Republic of Germany has, for a long time, been the Soviet Union's principal trading partner in the West and thus the principal source of foreign currency for the Soviet Union. It is in West Germany's political interest to maintain this privileged position; we can assume that it will continue to provide opportunities to use Moscow's interest in expanding Soviet-German economic relations to promote German national interests.

In view of the Soviet Union's very slight export efforts to date on the one hand and Moscow's minimal tendency to take on international commercial indebtedness on the other, a rapid increase in Soviet imports is not something we should count on. Aside from a few technological key products, we cannot expect sudden incentives for the restructuring and increased growth of the Soviet economy. What must happen is that modernization and growth arise first of all in the domestic economy. Redistribution of resources would most quickly lead to success. At the very least, the hierarchy of the four principal sectors— military spending, investment, consumer goods, and industrial production—must be altered to the detriment of military spending. The security complex of the Soviet leadership and its obsession with the military, which originated in Stalin's time and has held sway for more than forty years, are the principal reasons why Soviet economic growth is still so slow. I tend to believe that this circumstance in large part motivates Gorbachev's welcome change of course in Soviet policies on disarmament and arms limitation. Given the strong position of the Russian military, such a motive has not yet been articulated. But I can easily imagine that the Soviet generals are considerably disconcerted by the proposals Gorbachev has made, beginning in Reykjavik in late 1986.

Both Gorbachev and Reagan committed a serious error in Reykjavik, and after the conclusion of their deliberations they jointly capped these with a third mistake. Gorbachev's mistake was wanting to surprise the

Western superpower and its leader with an all-inclusive disarmament proposal. Realistically he could not expect to bring about a disarmament agreement with Reagan that would cover all bases then and there; at best he could hope to reap a tactical, rabble-rousing advantage in world opinion by making what appeared to be a persuasive proposal, which Reagan nevertheless rejected (because of his own plan to remove the American nation from the risk of war by the use of the Strategic Defense Initiative, or SDI).

Reagan's mistake was that he agreed to discuss Gorbachev's comprehensive packet of proposals then and there, without preparing himself sufficiently. The American president should have obtained a comprehensive idea of the proposals and their advantages and disadvantages by asking a series of questions, he should have agreed to study them carefully, and he should have offered to meet a second time in eight or ten weeks. Instead he allowed the impression to be created that a constructive disarmament proposal on the part of the Soviet Union had failed for no better reason than his obsession with SDI.

The mistake shared by both statesmen was that they parted without setting the date for another meeting, even without issuing a joint press release. Instead they announced—though separately, nevertheless agreeing in substance—that their deliberations had failed.

Subsequently both sides understood very quickly that their own countries, their allies and clients, and the world in general would not be willing to accept the simultaneous announcements of failure as a sufficient effort. As dissatisfaction and sometimes vehement criticism spread, both governments quickly rushed to wipe out the negative impression by promising to try again. Both governments realized that promises were no longer enough and that an actual agreement had become an urgent necessity.

It was presumably domestic considerations, however, that chiefly motivated both heads of state to resume serious discussions on arms limitation. I have no doubt that Gorbachev carefully studied the examples of economic reform under the halfway comparable conditions that were available to him—Lenin's NEP, Deng Xiaoping's economic reforms, and the economic policy incrementally developed over longer periods of time under János Kádár's leadership of Hungary. He needs a success in arms reduction especially for economic reasons.

Gorbachev's opposition to Reagan's SDI plans is also largely based on economics. Technically the Soviet Union is quite able to develop and manufacture equivalent military equipment, from tanks through fighter planes to nuclear submarines, military satellites, and antimissile systems;

as a rule Western military advantages are limited to only a few years. Nevertheless, it always costs the Soviet Union considerably more to achieve the same results. Gorbachev had no reason to fear that when it came to SDI he would not be able to hold his own in military technology with the United States. What he did have to fear was that a race in this field would take a still greater share of the Soviet gross national product.

On Moscow's Red Square with my wife, Loki, and daughter, Susanne, during
a private trip to the Soviet Union in the summer of 1966.

Soviet Foreign Minister Andrei Gromyko welcomes members of
the West German SPD delegation to Moscow, August 21, 1969.

State visit to the Soviet Union in October 1974: *top,* signing the mutual final
statement; *bottom,* Loki and I speak with Mrs. Brezhnev, Premier Kosygin's
daughter, and Mrs. Gromyko.

My first meeting with East Germany's Erich Honecker occurred at
the 1975 Helsinki Conference, a forum that marked the high
point of East-West détente.

A positive relationship with French president Valéry Giscard
d'Estaing contributed to a hitherto seldom-seen spirit of
harmony and cooperation in the Western alliance during the 1970s.

COURTESY HELMUT SCHMIDT

Leonid Brezhnev in Langenhorn: *top*, on the flight from Bonn to Hamburg; *bottom*, Brezhnev seated under the collected works of Marx and Engels.

COURTESY HELMUT SCHMIDT

"For the first time he seemed to me a little helpless": Gromyko's last attempt to dissuade the West German government from adhering to the TNF resolution in November 1979.

Moscow, July 1980: from left to right, Foreign Minister Hans-Dietrich Genscher, State Secretary Klaus Bölling, Kosygin, Gromyko, myself; at far right, West German ambassador Hans-Georg Wieck.

Bonn, October 1981: My last meeting with Leonid Brezhnev.

Richard Nixon's competence in the sphere of foreign relations
captured my immediate admiration.

November 11, 1969: Meeting of the NATO Nuclear Planning
Group in Warrenton, Virginia.

Old friends: I counted Arthur Burns (*above*) and former High Commissioner to Germany John McCloy (*below*) among those Americans whose advice and opinions carried weight.

Due to his preeminence in advocating aid for developing nations, Robert McNamara is for me characteristic of American social idealism.

BUNDESBILDSTELLE

First meeting with Gerald Ford, Washington,
D.C., December 1974.

As a guest at the White House, 1976: from left to right, President
Ford, myself, Vice President Nelson Rockefeller, Secretary of State
Henry Kissinger, and Foreign Minister Genscher.

COURTESY HELMUT SCHMIDT

To the present day a great deal of mutual trust has characterized my
friendship with Henry Kissinger.

Washington, D.C., July 1977: Differences in opinion over U.S. policy
toward the Soviet Union were already apparent during my first meeting
with Jimmy Carter, here with Foreign Minister Genscher and
Secretary of State Cyrus Vance.

President and Mrs. Carter, Loki Schmidt, and myself at a state dinner.

Guadeloupe, January 1979: The initial conception of what was to become the TNF resolution. To several observers it was incredible that a West German chancellor took part in a meeting next to the heads of government of the Western nuclear powers. From left to right, Giscard d'Estaing, myself, Prime Minister James Callaghan of Great Britain, and Jimmy Carter.

Carter's reaction toward the Soviet invasion of Afghanistan led to new tensions between Washington and Bonn. The president was especially influenced in his policy by National Security Adviser Zbigniew Brzezinski (here between Carter and West German ambassador Berndt von Staden in Washington, March 1980).

In the autumn of 1980 the SPD-FDP coalition won the West German
parliamentary elections, and I became chancellor for a third term.
The government's economic policies and the TNF resolution stood at the
center of my accession speech.

An in-flight, preconference briefing.

Venice, June 1980: Participants in the sixth world economic summit. From left to right, Prime Minister Suzuki, Prime Minister Trudeau, myself, President Giscard d'Estaing, Prime Minister Cossiga, President Carter, Prime Minister Thatcher.

Bonn, May 1981: My first official meeting with Ronald Reagan. I initially trusted in Reagan's intentions to bring about arms-control talks with Moscow. I was to see, however, that the president's assurances could not always be relied on.

Alexander Haig (*above*) unfortunately did not act with the same circumspection as Reagan's secretary of state that he had earlier exhibited as NATO commander in chief. More difficult, however, was my rapport with Secretary of Defense Caspar Weinberger (*below*).

Beijing, October 1975: Reviewing the honor guard at the airport with Deng Xiaoping.

A visit to the "Forbidden City."

A historical figure: Despite his ailing health, Chairman Mao Zedong's charisma and vivacity were unmistakable. In a conversation spanning several hours he repeatedly returned to one point: the inevitability of conflict between China and the Soviet Union.

By the end of the 1970s Hua Guofeng was deemed to be the most powerful man in China. He was to be deposed in 1981.

Beijing, September 1984: Nine years after my initial trip I visited China again, this time as a private citizen. My reunion with Deng was especially cordial.

Tokyo, October 1978: State visit to Japan; *above*, with Prime Minister Takeo Fukuda; *below*, being received by Emperor Hirohito.

Arms Reduction
by Treaty:
A Historical
Opportunity

F OR GORBACHEV, intermediate-range missiles could be an opening to the process of arms reduction. This approach also had a strong strategic attraction; in the meantime American intermediate-range missiles had been deployed in Western Europe, and their nuclear warheads could put objectives on Soviet soil out of commission.

After the expectation—fostered during the Brezhnev era—that the SS-20 missiles could be used to force Western Europe's political hand and to arouse fear and psychosis turned out to be false, it was in the Soviet Union's strategic interest to remove the Western counterthreats. For this reason today's Soviet leadership even seems prepared to give up its intermediate-range missiles pointed at Western Europe.

Should all intermediate-range missiles really be withdrawn from Europe by both sides, it would be a great, even if somewhat late, personal triumph for me. For the proposal of the reciprocal zero option, first formulated in 1979, is mine. Brezhnev rejected it in 1980 and 1981. Reagan accepted it in 1981. Without a Western arms buildup the Soviet Union would not have been willing to give up its intermediate-range missiles.

But now there is opposition to the zero option from within the West. To be sure, there is little basis in fact for the concern, cited by several

European and American politicians and generals, that withdrawal of the
intermediate-range missiles would leave Western Europe exposed to the
danger of a conventional attack. Some of the Western generals who
think in strategic terms—such as American General Bernard Rogers,
who was still commander in chief of NATO fighting forces in Europe—
and some of the Western politicians of a military cast of mind—for
example, Manfred Wörner—raised the argument that should the Soviet
Union launch a conventional attack, complete withdrawal of intermediate-range missiles would rob the West of the chance to use defensive
nuclear weapons in a first strike. To support this argument, they
pointed to the Soviet Union's numerical superiority in the area of
conventional forces in Europe.

The argument cannot stand up to closer scrutiny. For one, the alleged numerical conventional superiority of the Soviet Union has held
steady for the last forty years; actually it was much greater before the
Bundeswehr was established. Soviet numerical superiority was no less in
the 1970s, when the Soviet Union started deploying SS-20s, and in
1979, when NATO resolved to deploy theater nuclear weapons beginning in 1983. What motivated the Western statesmen who participated
in the resolution was achieving a balance not with the established forces
of the Soviet Union but rather with their new SS-20s.

For another, the extent of today's Soviet conventional superiority is
often exaggerated, especially by the United States. Even when I was still
serving as minister of defense, I was never really worried by the larger
number of Soviet conventional troops because I was always convinced—
and still am—of the Bundeswehr's combat effectiveness in the case of
attack from the East and because the German Federal Republic—as well
as France and all other Continental allies—has not followed the American example of abolishing the draft. Because we have maintained compulsory military service, we can quickly mobilize fully trained reserves;
these do not have to be transported across the Channel or the Atlantic.
The Western European fighting forces have a high deterrent value—a
fact I confirmed in my discussion with Ustinov and Ogarkov as well as
on other occasions. The deterrent would be considerably strengthened
if the French, German, and Benelux fighting forces were finally to be
integrated. In any case, the armed forces at hand are quite sufficient to
discourage any rational Kremlin leadership from seriously considering
attacking Western Europe by conventional means.

The nightmare of the West's hopeless conventional inferiority will
stop being justified when German troops have been fully put in position. But the strategy of "flexible response," suggested in 1962 and

resolved by the alliance in 1967 as a response to this nightmare, is fully suited to crippling the defensive combat effectiveness of the Bundeswehr. In reality, since 1967 military plans and maneuvers have provided for no real flexibility. Rather, the NATO leadership has invariably worked with the idea of rapid escalation; it assumed and in its maneuvers rehearsed the early use of nuclear weapons by the West. When I became minister of defense in 1969, I realized that if actual hostilities ensued, this strategy could lead to the loss of millions of human lives in both Germanies within a very few days.

I considered it completely unrealistic to believe that if we needed to defend ourselves, our soldiers would go on fighting once a nuclear weapon had been exploded on German soil. I thought it was equally absurd of NATO to believe that in such a situation our soldiers would continue to offer resistance, fighting more fanatically and suicidally than the Japanese, who capitulated as soon as the two atom bombs fell on Hiroshima and Nagasaki in 1945, even though not a single American soldier had yet set foot on the Japanese home islands. As commanding officer, I was therefore fully determined to give no assistance whatever to Western escalation of nuclear warfare in the (unlikely) case of a Soviet conventional attack. Nevertheless I thought it prudent not to say so; it was, after all, conceivable that some uncertainty about possible Western reaction might well have a deterrent effect on the Soviet Union.

It is time to replace the strategy of "flexible response" with a new plan, perhaps the deployment of sufficient conventional forces using integrated German, French, and Benelux troops under the joint command of the French. Such a plan is also very much in France's enlightened interest; Paris should try to imagine clearly the situation France would find itself in if the Bundeswehr had to give up defensive warfare because Germany had been destroyed by nuclear weapons!

For the West the only function of nuclear weapons must be to deter the East from considering a first strike from its side. This statement is true not only for Eurostrategic intermediate-range missiles of whatever operational range but also for long-range missiles (the so-called "strategic" missiles). It also holds true for so-called tactical nuclear weapons.

I spoke of this conviction as early as 1961 in my book *Verteidigung oder Vergeltung,* where I wrote,

> The thesis of the inevitability of nuclear defense is deadly nonsense. . . . Defense using limited nuclear weapons as threat is persuasive over a period of time only in [the case of] aggressions intended to use the same weaponry. Exclusively to deter *such* ag-

gressions NATO needs . . . *tactical* nuclear weapons in Europe.
. . . Actual defense against nonnuclear (conventional) attack in
Europe with tactical nuclear weapons would . . . most probably be
synonymous with large-scale destruction of Europe, at least . . . of
Germany.

It is in the interests of both the West and the Soviets to reduce their
mutual military potential by treaty. With regard to their nuclear weapons, the United States and the Soviet Union have been obligated to this
course for twenty years through the Nuclear Nonproliferation Treaty.
So far neither of them has lived up to this obligation—quite the contrary. A mutual zero solution in the area of intermediate-range nuclear
missiles would represent the first step since the end of the Second World
War toward actual disarmament arranged by treaty. Should this step
come about, I would know myself to have been justified in participating
in the NATO TNF resolution and in originating the idea of the zero
solution. Should it be destroyed by Western counterarguments, those
people might turn out to be right who at the time rejected the TNF
resolution.

As this book goes to press, the outcome of the Soviet-American
negotiations and the differences of opinion within the West concerning
the zero solution are still unresolved. Both West Germans and East
Germans will be deeply perplexed and concerned if the agreement being
striven for comes to nought. Both of us know that agreements require
partners. Both of us want to be partners in peace. Both of us want to
have the superpowers in the West and in the East as partners in peace
and not as firebrands.

Neighbors

A T THE MOMENT the danger of war in Europe is not very great, but it is not zero. The mutual arms buildups have hardly reduced the danger. There is no patented formula to guarantee the "eternal peace" Immanuel Kant presented to us as a desirable utopia. I will gladly concede that my ultimate objective of approximate parity of conventional—as well as nuclear—troops and weapons on land and sea and in the air is not enough to guarantee peace; Hitler was numerically inferior when he attacked almost every neighboring country in Europe. But the danger of being overpowered on the political or military level by a powerful neighbor is less if parity exists.

Parity must be paired with the willingness to talk together, to listen to each other, and to arrive at agreements. The Soviet Union, at least under its current head, Mikhail Gorbachev, is not a belligerent nation. But the generations of Russian expansionism will not allow us to see today's Soviet Union as a benefactor of humanity. It continues to be a huge, dangerously powerful neighbor. But it is not our "enemy"; it is for this reason that at the time I held the NATO high command I forbade the use of the term "enemy image."

The responses Gorbachev has aroused so far in Eastern Europe, in Western Europe, and in the United States are highly interesting because of their conflicting nature. Gorbachev has won over the great majority of the citizens in the Soviet Union's client states in Eastern Europe by allowing the hope that his reform process will lead to a loosening and easing of conditions in their own nations as well. Some Czechs see Gorbachev as a kind of new Dubček two decades after the "Prague Spring." For the same reason the current ruling circles around Lubomir Štrougal and Vasil Bilak fear that the general secretary's reforms will go too far. While various minds in East Berlin agree with this assessment, the view is not shared in Budapest and Warsaw: János Kádár and Wojciech Jaruzelski favor Gorbachev's reforms, trusting that they will lead to greater scope for their own reform policies and a reduction of Moscow's control of their governments. It is conceivable that Gorbachev will be willing to allow the heads of state or party leaders in Eastern Europe some additional decision-making powers. He might even grant some additional rapprochement between Eastern and Western Europe; after all, he himself likes to speak of the "European home," a term in which he includes the Soviet Union.

However, the political heads of the Eastern European nations will have to think twice. For one, even Gorbachev—no matter how much he seems to be about to rein in the overall expansionist strategy of his nation—will never permit nations in the Warsaw Pact to resign from the military alliance and the joint strategy imposed on them by Moscow. Anyone foolhardy enough to try such a maneuver would probably pay a high price. The fact that until now Ceauşescu has been allowed to get away with his willful domestic and international escapades is not proof to the contrary; for one thing, it is fully assumed that he will be replaced within the foreseeable future; for another, he can hardly damage the Soviet Union outside of Romania—and if need be, Soviet troops are nearby. This latter consideration holds equally true for the Warsaw Pact nations that border on Western democracies—Hungary, Czechoslovakia, and the German Democratic Republic, where sizable numbers of Soviet troops are stationed. For this reason, and not only for domestic considerations, the leaders of the German Democratic Republic in particular will approach further overtures in favor of unifying the divided German nation with the utmost caution. Although economically they are the most successful, Honecker and the leadership of the East German party will respond with particular care to every signal from Moscow.

The second and at present the more important reason for caution among Eastern European Communist leaders lies in the uncertainty about Gorbachev's economic success. Whatever the outcome, it will be several more years before he can achieve it. He is without a doubt by far the most intelligent, most energetic, and most modern leader the Soviet Union has had for years; but if he should fail because his reforms do not succeed or because they make excessive demands on his party functionaries, the probable result will not be a return to the phlegmatic callousness of the Brezhnev era but more likely a deep relapse into tyranny by the secret police, into a centrally administered command economy, and internationally into dictatorship over the client states of the Warsaw Pact. For a long time to come there would be no thought of human rights, much less of "democratization."

If some well-to-do person lives next door to a very poor and oppressed but sometimes inconsiderate family, who look on him with suspicion or even envy, he has a personal interest in wishing these neighbors progress and improvement in their living conditions; he may even decide to help out in this regard. Such is the situation of Germans in the Federal Republic; we have a high living standard, as opposed to our neighbor, the Soviet Union, whose tanks and fighter planes are stationed only minutes from our soil. It is therefore only natural that most Germans hope that Gorbachev's reforms will be successful. They suspect the new man will be just as unable to overturn the historically evolved forms of the state and society as Peter the Great was three hundred years ago, but in their own interest they wish him as much success as was granted that first great Russian reformer.

All the nations of Western Europe will arrive at this insight. The clever Chinese must surely feel the same, since they, like the Germans, live next door to the Soviet Union. Many Americans find it harder to make up their minds. Some, quite simply, are reluctant to give up their ideological image of the enemy. Others, like Henry Kissinger, point out that a Soviet Union that is successful in its reforms and economically improved will be a more significant power factor in the world than before. This prognosis may well be accurate; nevertheless, the general wisdom that a satisfied neighbor is more pleasant than a hungry one remains true. Whether or not the Soviet Union will subsequently return to an overall expansionist strategy cannot be predicted. That is why caution on the part of the West remains advisable: maintaining deterrent parity as the basis of Western security and on this foundation building a many-sided collaboration with the Soviet Union with a view to its economic, technical, scientific and, simply, civilizing inclusion in the international scheme.

When I spoke with Gromyko in March 1987, he said, "We are convinced of the future success of our policy; but it requires a peaceful domestic and foreign policy."

I offered him my best wishes. "Your success is in everyone's best interest: the interest of both the peoples of the Soviet Union and its neighbors in Europe."

"That is well said," Gromyko commented. "All of us live in the same European home, and we will always take your hand. You yourself can make a great contribution, since you continue to exert great authority all through Europe."

I found this a very charming remark and replied, "The hand of George Shultz is among the hands you must take."

Gromyko responded, "I have met Shultz frequently, and I agree with you. Sometimes our discussions have been heated . . . but Shultz is a man you can talk to. He does not do all the talking; he knows how to listen. He plays his part well."

Then Gromyko asked my opinion of the current situation of German-Soviet relations; he was referring to a derogatory remark Chancellor Kohl had made about Gorbachev. "Time has left that interview behind," I replied. "What is important is that an American-Soviet INF treaty is achieved this summer; if there is too little time and as a result the ratification debate in the United States stretches into the election year of 1988, there is little hope of ratification. The new president would not be in office until January 1989; presumably he would begin new negotiations, so that any outcome open to ratification would not be available until 1990 or 1991." Would Gorbachev be able to wait that long?

The sooner a treaty was signed, the better, Gromyko answered. But if the Americans had neither the desire nor the will, the Soviet Union was prepared to wait.

It was my impression, I told him, that both Shultz and Reagan had the necessary will. "Chancellor Kohl as well, by the way. The fact that you are now proposing a zero solution is quite in keeping with the erstwhile West German government. Of course, the situation has changed in the meantime because you have stationed your short-range INF in the German Democratic Republic and Czechoslovakia; the decision of whether an INF agreement can come about is based on a satisfactory inclusion of the short-range INF in the treaty."

"We are aware," Gromyko countered, "of the fact that you originated the proposal of the mutual zero solution; we are prepared to treat the SR-INF in the same context. Your statements concerning the Soviet proposals have a solid basis. When you were chancellor, we already knew there could be no real world peace as long as there are nuclear weapons. But in the past we concentrated too much on the European region; now we realize that a global solution is necessary. . . . I don't know whether the dinosaurs were vegetarians or beasts of prey. But I do know that in retrospect the nuclear dinosaurs will look horrible! There are too many analyses, too much haggling, too much risky business. Homo sapiens must pinch himself to become aware of the risk."

I had not spoken to Andrei Gromyko for six years. He seemed candid and relaxed. I thought, For Heaven's sake, let's take these two men, Gorbachev and Gromyko, at their word! On the flight back to Germany, thinking about my talks in Moscow, I remembered an event from my youth that had made a lasting impression on me. When I was fifteen and sixteen, I borrowed the great Russian nineteenth-century romance writers and novelists, one after the other, from the public library near the Landwehr railroad station. I read these works with the rapturous absorption of the adolescent. Different impressions of Russian culture were later added to these early encounters, and all my life I have known that the writers, painters, and musicians of Russia were a part of Europe's cultural continuum; even during the war against the Soviet Union I never abandoned this belief. And now, in 1987, even the Communist leaders of Russia are finally discovering their membership in the "common European home." I must admit I was moved. I had to pull myself together so that emotion and sympathy would not seduce me into an illusion.

We Germans must never forget Hitler and his war, all the atrocities committed by Germans. I know that we are in no way morally entitled to feel that they are balanced out by Stalin's outrages. But I also know that even in Bismarck's day czarist Russia was a dangerous and powerful neighbor—and the Soviet Union is still more powerful. It is by no means an international charitable institution. But we must not think of it as the enemy! We must see it as our neighbor and strive for good neighborly relations with it.

II

The United States:
The Difficulty of Being a World Power

I N the nearly forty years since its founding, the Federal Republic of
Germany has had six heads of government. Each had a different
style and different ideas about domestic and foreign policies. But
none of them forgot for a moment that in the last analysis the security
of our state depends on the United States' strategy and its commitment
to assisting its European allies.

Yalta and Potsdam were the inevitable consequences of the American
decision in 1944 to establish the second front against Hitler on French
and Italian soil rather than follow Churchill's suggestion that the invasion center on the Balkans. No German chancellor is politically entitled
retrospectively to criticize the Yalta resolution; but German policy must
always be based on the political and military situation of the divided
Europe and divided Germany that were created in 1945.

In the years just after the war the Germans were not at all certain
whether and for how long the division would remain. But they knew
one thing: Without the United States and its advocacy of their freedom,
the Western occupation zones from which the Federal Republic
emerged in 1949 would have been at the mercy of the Soviet Union.
Without the great help of the Marshall Plan, Germany's stupendous
economic reconstruction would never have been possible. Without the

airlift, Berlin would have been lost. Without NATO, democratic
Europe could not have been kept in existence.

It is true that from 1949 on, Konrad Adenauer had some serious
disputes with Washington, and Ludwig Erhard, Kurt Kiesinger, and
Willy Brandt after him were involved in similar confrontations—for
example, over the so-called Radford plan for a peripheral defense of
Europe from Spain and Gibraltar; over the MLF, the NATO plan for
a multilateral nuclear Polaris naval force; over "compensatory" payments for United States expenses for American troops in Germany; over
the 1969 Geneva treaty on banning nuclear arms; and over the German
Ostpolitik. But even on such occasions no West German chancellor ever
lost sight of the existential significance of the alliance with the United
States. And none who sought compromises with the Soviet Union to
secure the peace ever forgot the categorical difference in the relation-
ships of the Federal Republic with the two superpowers.

We are linked with the Americans by shared values concerning freedom and the role of the individual, the open society and the democratic
form of government. We are separated from the Soviet Union, on the
other hand, by their dehumanization of people; their ideology, which
is forced on their people with doctrinaire zeal; and the totalitarian
system. The basic rights guaranteed by our constitution and the values
they express do not have their origin in Russia; the ideas of our state
are rooted in the West. They were first embodied in national practice
in London, in Philadelphia, and in Paris.

I held these convictions when I first became a member of a national
government in 1969, and I have not changed my opinions. Thirteen
years later, when I was preparing for my resignation, on the eve of my
fall I called together the ambassadors accredited in Bonn. My address
was brief. Directing my remarks to the United States, I said, "We will
not forget: The intellectual heritage of the individual's right to liberty
comes to us . . . from Franklin, from Jefferson, from Washington. And
we also know what we owe to George Marshall and millionfold American generosity since the war. . . . Millions of Germans have read not
only *Uncle Tom's Cabin* but also Thornton Wilder and Ernest Hemingway. Jazz has become part of the culture of all of Europe. All this is a
single, interconnected culture! . . . It remains our mission to see to it
that subsequent generations on both sides of the Atlantic will maintain
our mutual friendship."

The following morning—October 1, 1982—I addressed the Bundestag for the last time as chancellor: "The North Atlantic alliance reflects
the mutual interests of Europe and North America. . . . Only together
can all of them preserve their security and their liberty, their peace. At

the same time NATO is one of the most important links in German-American friendship. . . . We are united by fundamental values, no matter how different we are from each other. In such a friendship mutual criticism is both necessary and helpful; anyone who suppresses criticism of a friend cannot remain a good friend in the long run. Anyone who does not express his own interests to his friend can lose respect and friendship by this omission. Precisely because I have been a critical partner of four American presidents and administrations, I affirm once more at this moment my belief in German-American friendship."

It was important to me that the two speeches assure both our Western friends and allies and our Eastern neighbors of the steadfastness of German foreign and security policies, which would not change in future. Many listeners may have found this a risky move, and their reports to their governments back home may have included question marks concerning the future. I, however, felt fairly sure of my prognosis based on my analysis of the German position. And I had stressed one point for years: Without constancy, without accountability on the part of our nation, its security and its interests would be in jeopardy.

Kohl's government actually made efforts toward constancy, though not prudently enough; Franz Josef Strauss' inclusion in this constancy also signaled a new personal domestic policy for him. Kohl, Genscher, and Strauss are only in part responsible for the fact that in 1984 Moscow tried to propagate a different interpretation of the situation. There was no "change" in the foreign and security policies of the German Federal Republic in 1982 and 1983, and there has not been one since, even though at times the public exhibition of mutual pats on the back by Kohl and Reagan may have looked like it.

The situation in the United States, however, proceeded quite differently. The changes in the presidency—from Johnson to Nixon in 1969, from Ford to Carter in 1977, and from Carter to Reagan in 1981—brought about major changes in America's foreign and security policies; in the two latter presidencies the interests of Europe and Germany were seriously affected. Even in his earliest international actions Jimmy Carter jeopardized one of the most important preconditions of the policy of negotiating with the Soviet Union he had set his sights on. Without intending to, or even realizing what he was doing, he undermined Soviet confidence in the continuity of the United States' strategic objectives and intentions. I will never forget Carter, in May 1977, asking me in a private discussion, "Helmut, couldn't the two of us remove the Berlin Wall?"

Astonished, I asked in my turn, "How? By what method?"

Carter replied, "I thought you might know of a way."

Of course neither I nor anyone else in the West knew of a way.

This incident taught me how little my counterpart understood of the situation in divided Europe and how ignorant he was of the power of the Soviet Union and its interests.

When Carter's successor, Ronald Reagan, spoke publicly of the Soviet Union as "the evil empire" and freely expressed his aversion to that nation, when Washington seemed to pursue the objective of military "superiority" over the Soviet Union, this repeated naïveté upset me no less; this time it had gone to the other extreme.

Carter frankly explained to his European allies, as well as to the Soviet Union, that the SALT policy of his predecessors, Nixon and Ford, had not gone far enough, although in fact they had based their position on a realistic policy for limiting strategic arms—a policy which we, the European governments, had championed and which we had publicly supported with our full authority. Now everything was to be renegotiated and new positions adopted.

Four years later, after we had loyally backed Carter's new SALT policy, his successor, Ronald Reagan, explained to us that Carter's SALT policy, too, had been a mistake; in fact, the entire idea of détente was nothing but an illusion. These were by no means the only off-on switches to which the European allies and the politicians in the Kremlin were exposed. For even during both presidents' terms in office there were crucial tacking maneuvers in foreign policy, all having considerable bearing on Germany's interests. Bonn was compelled to react to all these changes—as were Paris, London, and the rest of the NATO membership. This response required both a readiness to compromise and our own perseverance. These events are what I wish to report on.

In all the phases, even the many about-faces, I always admired the vitality of the American nation, and I could never entirely suppress a pinch of envy. This vitality is borne on waves of optimism and moral idealism. In part it may be rooted in the influx from Europe, the centuries during which the ocean brought people whose drive for freedom was especially strong and who were prepared, confident of their own strength, to build up a viable existence from nothing.

The spaciousness of the territory extending to the Pacific allowed for enormous expansion; the seizure of land at the expense of the original Indian inhabitants and their large-scale extermination happened with naive matter-of-factness. At the same time the spaciousness of their own country was and remains one of the reasons for Americans' international restraint, which, aside from a few imperialist adventures and the interlude of the First World War, lasted until the Second World War. This basic tendency to isolation, according to the motto "Let the world leave us alone, and we will not interfere in its quarrels," and the Monroe Doctrine continue to play an important role in United States policy and will do so in future. Connected with isolationism is a considerable lack of knowledge of the world; what the American people know about the geography, history, and politics of other peoples and nations outside the "Western hemisphere"—more precisely, outside the *North* American continent—is comparatively little. For centuries the historical image of most Europeans was strongly Eurocentric in focus and continues to be so; but that at least encompasses a large number of peoples and nations. But the world image of most Americans—and of most American politicians—does not go far beyond the borders of their own country. This is the reason for the American naïveté in assessing and dealing with other nations and their interests that we have often enough observed.

As a member of the West German government and as chancellor I never doubted the almost complete harmony that basically prevails between the United States and ourselves; nevertheless, I was compelled to endure a great many differences of opinion in important areas. Many conflicts could be nipped in the bud; others could be easily resolved.

Essentially there are three categories of differences of opinion between Europe and the United States:

1. Short-term discontinuities in United States foreign policy, such as Carter's embargo on nuclear fuel to the German Federal Republic; the affair of the neutron weapons; the prologue to the boycott of the Olympics; the treatment of Poland after 1981; the so-called pipeline embargo by Reagan in the summer of 1982.

2. Disputes concerning the crisis of the United States' overall strategy toward the Soviet Union; concerning the United States' ignoring the Soviet Union's strategic intermediate-range missiles pointed at Western Europe and the German Federal Republic; and in principle concerning the United States' abandonment of the policy of détente after 1976 and of SALT after 1980.

3. Differences of opinion about managing the chain of international economic crises; for example, the first dollar crisis of 1969–1973, which triggered a crisis in the world currency system established at Bretton Woods; the structural worldwide economic crisis as a result of the explosion in oil prices of 1973–1974 and again—even more grave—in 1979–1980; the second dollar crisis of 1977–1979; and, as the result

of the record United States budget deficits and their far-reaching financing from abroad, the third dollar crisis, beginning in 1985.

Only a small number of the differences of opinion mentioned in the first category were bilateral—that is, concerned only West Germany and the United States; the differences of opinion in the second category concerned the United States and its European allies as a whole and were thus multilateral; this was even more true of the controversies in the third category. Many disputes could have been avoided or resolved with only minimal frictional loss if the political class in the United States knew even approximately as much about Russian-Soviet history, Europe, and the international economy as the political leaders of the European nations know about America and the Soviet Union.

Europeans must constantly test and supplement their knowledge of the United States. By the end of the war, what I knew about America was not very much. During the next twenty years I had to increase my store of knowledge, and for that purpose I visited the United States frequently. I made many American friends during my trips, and I shall always be grateful for their generous hospitality—in the intellectual realm as well.

First Impressions
of America

I N SCHOOL I learned practically nothing about America apart from the Monroe Doctrine, the part the United States played in the First World War, Woodrow Wilson's Fourteen Points, and Black Friday on the New York Stock Exchange in 1929. Matters stood not much better for American literature: Outside school I had read *Moby Dick* and, of course, as a child, *Uncle Tom's Cabin, Tom Sawyer, Huckleberry Finn,* and some Mark Twain short stories; in addition, a couple of books by Jack London and Edgar Allan Poe's horror stories; the deepest impression was left by Thornton Wilder's *The Bridge of San Luis Rey.*

But those of us who grew up in Germany at the time had no idea of the American Revolution, of the Declaration of Independence, of the Declaration of Human Rights, of Thomas Jefferson, Benjamin Franklin, or George Washington. Of course we knew nothing about American democracy or Alexis de Tocqueville, nothing about the emancipation of the slaves under Abraham Lincoln, and we had heard almost as little about the splendid American literature of the twentieth century.

Franklin Delano Roosevelt was presented to us as a "plutocrat," which was intended to mean an exponent of government by wealth. This debasement of American capitalism, suspiciously close to cheap-

ened Marxism, fell on fertile soil in me: my Aunt Marianne, my
mother's sister, had nothing good to report from her own experience.
Because of the Depression, she had returned to Hamburg from the
United States shortly before the outbreak of the Second World War.
A singer whose career had never taken off, she had spent the previous
fifteen years giving piano lessons in Minnesota. Things had not gone
well for her; though she spoke appreciatively of her American friends
and of our relatives in Duluth, who had taken her in and helped her
time and again, she also brought back negative impressions. In a word,
at the time war broke out, my knowledge of America was minimal, and
my ideas of its economic and social conditions had a negative cast.

It was only the anti-American propaganda during the war that made
me suspect that the United States must have its good points as well—
otherwise, why would Goebbels go to such trouble to debase it in our
eyes? Even at the beginning of Hitler's campaign against Russia in
June 1941 I knew that we were done for. I recalled Napoleon's march
on Moscow, his monumental retreat; I was persuaded that Russia's
vastness was invincible. At the time I got into a quarrel with one of
my uncles, who was deeply outraged when I declared in the summer
of 1941 that after the war all Germans would be living in holes in the
ground or, at best, in barracks. In December 1941, when Hitler's
hubris provoked America to declare war on Germany, I recalled the
crucial role the United States had played in 1918. I was appalled and
felt confirmed in my prognosis of German postwar conditions. At the
time German troops had penetrated deep into Russia, were almost at
the gates of Moscow; and yet we were already fighting for survival and
to avoid capture. Those of us who were soldiers therefore pushed
aside any thoughts we might have had about the larger meaning of
events.

It was only three winters later, after the collapse of the Ardennes
offensive at the Battle of the Bulge, that I met Americans for the first
time. More precisely, I met their artillery fire, their Thunderbolts and
Lightnings, but I did not see a single American soldier. They invariably
waited to attack until we were worn down by the massive artillery fire
and by the oppressive American command of the air—the American air
force had what amounted to a monopoly from dawn to dusk—and until
we had beaten a retreat. I thought there was no sense in fighting the
Americans and British, and I said to my commander that we should
allow the Amis to get as far as possible into Germany and to concentrate
instead on beating back the Russian armies. He was outraged at my
suggestion and rejected it, but he did not report me. Perhaps, like

many German soldiers at the time, he too believed that an American-Russian conflict would soon break out in Central Europe, but he did not say so.

I had imagined the end of the war and its consequences as much more terrible than they actually turned out to be. It is true that the winter of 1946–1947 was desolate; people starved and froze in the ruins of the cities, which had been swelled by the influx of millions of refugees from the East. But in September 1946 James Byrnes, the American secretary of state, spoke in Stuttgart, and his words allowed the Germans to get a perspective on the future once again. Barely two years later the United States withstood Stalin's blockade of Berlin. We saw the political and military risk the American government was willing to assume, and we admired the pilots of Operation Breadbasket. This was the time when the Germans' hopes and faith turned to the Americans.

My eyes had been opened even earlier to the truth of the United States. During my university years in bombed-out Hamburg, from late 1945 to the summer of 1949, I spent little time on my studies. We veterans found it a little difficult to take university life and the faculty altogether seriously—though there were brilliant exceptions, professors we revered. A considerable part of my time was given to earning a living, another part to my political education. In late 1945 I had begun working with the SPD, and soon afterward I joined it formally. The rest of the time I had left was given over to general education. Now at last, thanks to Ernst Rowohlt's edition of books on rotary presses and in newspaper format, my generation had a chance to read modern literature from other nations. Finally I read Walt Whitman, Theodore Dreiser, Sinclair Lewis, Upton Sinclair, William Faulkner, Thomas Wolfe, F. Scott Fitzgerald, William Saroyan, Ernest Hemingway, John Steinbeck, and all the others. I was carried away by the richness and power of this literature.

Whenever we could afford it, we went to the Kammerspiele, a small, cold theater in Hartungstrasse. Ida Ehre, who ran the company, produced contemporary plays from abroad, using the most primitive means but engaging outstanding actors (herself included). I shall never forget a production of Wilder's *The Skin of Our Teeth* with Hilde Krahl in the role of the maid.

In that starvation winter of 1946 we all lived on 896 calories per day. But now and then Aunt Marianne received a CARE package from our relatives in Duluth, and she shared her coffee with the whole Hamburg family; America was clearly a land of miracles—and there could be no doubt that the Americans were a generous nation, from George Marshall and the Marshall Plan right down to Uncle August in Duluth, Minnesota.

The time between the end of the war and the foundation of the Federal Republic was one of turbulent transition, a time that in spite of hunger and widespread misery meant a marvelous intellectual liberation and development for many of us. Two events late in this period enriched my understanding of the United States. One was the currency reform of June 1948, which the then economic director of the British-American zone, Ludwig Erhard, combined with the abolition of most ration cards and food coupons. These were great economic feats. For the first time in my life I lived in a functioning market economy, something I had merely heard about at university and had understood only abstractly, without being able really to imagine it. Until now there had been only the black market for us: One American cigarette had cost 6 marks; to get a basket of potatoes and one loaf of bread, my wife had to knit sweaters night after night.

A year later I wrote my thesis on the currency reforms in Japan in 1946 and in Germany in 1948. I understood that the currency reform in Japan had been attempted much too soon, when the supply of goods was totally inadequate, and that therefore it could not help but fail. But I also realized that German currency reform, two years later, owed its success to the Marshall Plan. One of the figures behind the German reform, the young American Edward A. Tenenbaum, was unfairly ignored in Germany. He was the intellectual link between the American military government and the German experts. Lieutenant Tenenbaum from New York was the son of Jewish emigrants from Poland. He deserves a monument in German economic history.

The other event was my friendship with an American who had been a German Jew from Hamburg, Eduard Heimann of the New School for Social Research in New York. Lectures by this outstanding university professor, and especially discussions with him into the small hours of the morning, opened my eyes and broadened my view. I began to understand, for example, why Marxism must lead to an ethical abyss; before he emigrated, Heimann had been a religious socialist, a member of the circle around Paul Tillich; so I heard about Catholic social theory for the first time. Heimann also persuaded me to read the writings of the American Revolution. With all his love for his new home, he was just as much influenced by his European education, and his intellectual roots reached deep into the historical and cultural earth of Germany as well as the intellectual soil of the French, Spanish, and Italians. It was probably inevitable that "freedom and order" became his credo: Free-

dom he had found firmly established in the United States, while the
insight about the necessity of order was probably something he had
brought with him from Europe. Eduard Heimann was the first great
American I encountered at close range.

Shortly thereafter I took my first trip to the United States. Since then
there have been almost a hundred more; except for Idaho and the two
Dakotas, I have visited every state and learned an enormous amount in
the process. If America is measured superficially, by French or German
standards, much will remain incomprehensible, other things will seem
disconcerting, and still others will even arouse dislike. On the other
hand, the American who takes his Southern mentality or his pioneer
nature as the standard by which to measure Europe but who does not
know much of its two-thousand-year history or its linguistic and cultural
variety must also find many things incomprehensible. Since Americans
and Europeans, however, are dependent on each other and will continue to be so, both sides should make strenuous efforts to get to know
each other better. Jet planes, telecommunication satellites, and television offer the technical means for us to approach each other and learn
from each other. However, since German television, for example, has
for years shown us our American friends first in the guise of soldiers in
Vietnam and then overwhelmingly as decadent capitalist clans in Dallas
and Denver, and since American television for the most part has presented Germans as Hitler's soldiers or even as henchmen of the SS, and
shortly thereafter as militant pacifists, mutual understanding has been
made increasingly difficult.

I combined a business errand with my first visit to America in 1950.
For several weeks I was to represent the port of Hamburg at an international fair at the navy pier in Chicago. Although except for my time in
Chicago I spent only two days each in New York and Duluth, I saw a
great deal on that trip. I was instantly fascinated; my liking for America
began right there.

The port of Hamburg had been destroyed. What my two bosses—the
then Hamburg economic senator Karl Schiller and the director of the
port, Ernst Plate—and I took to the exhibit were merely plans and
models for its reconstruction. We were soliciting confidence in Hamburg's future. In truth we had nothing to offer yet. And yet interested
American visitors came to our exhibition booth: "Very interesting. But
there's one thing I want to know: How are the Russians behaving in
your Hamburg? Did they actually agree to your coming here?" The
questioners did not realize that Hamburg was in the western part of the
divided country; how could people in the American Midwest know? At

the time the citizens of Hamburg didn't know whether Seattle was in the United States or in Canada.

When my two bosses left after the official opening, I moved to a cheaper little hotel, and in this way I quickly met a number of people informally. I read American newspapers and magazines and listened to the radio. In the evenings I strolled through the Loop and gawked at America. One trait impressed me even then, and to this day—thirty-five years later—I always put it in first place when the American people are under discussion: its enormous vitality.

A great dynamism and an inclination to optimism—though this goes with a tendency to simplify circumstances and problems at times beyond the limits of what is admissible—allow that typical American stance of "Don't worry, we'll manage." This fundamental attitude eventually leads to success.

In 1950 Senator Joseph McCarthy was much in the news; a majority of the simple people seemed to have been enraptured by his exalted Communist hunting. Though it bothered me because the man seemed too me like a megalomaniacal pocket edition of Marat and his accusations reminded me of the Nazis, the fanatical mischief wrought by McCarthy, which was damaging to many of his fellow citizens, could not shake my love for America.

The most personal experience of my first visit to America was the generous friendship of my relatives in Duluth, which I enjoyed for a long weekend. When I arrived at the train station, I was welcomed by a large number of roughly contemporary cousins (all of them second cousins) and their spouses. The women claimed to be the city's maids of honor and kissed me one by one. My uncles' and aunts' welcomes were not quite so effusive but cordial nevertheless. A quarter of a century later, when I was chancellor, my wife and I spent a day in Duluth. There was a ceremonial reception, and the entire clan met once again in the large home of my cousin Philipp Hanft—most of us a little gray at the temples by now.

In 1950 the real reason for my visit was to bring thanks for the CARE packages on behalf of my Aunt Marianne and the Hamburg family. I was asked many questions about Germany, but there was not a word of accusation about Nazi crimes or the war that had cost so many American lives. Uncle August took me to the factory he ran, a small, simple iron foundry. The plant, with about fifteen or twenty employees, seemed to support the whole family. What was fascinating to me was that the parking lot held exactly the same number of cars as there were workers—everybody had his own car! We would not have dared to dream of such a thing in Germany; in fact the motorization of the masses did not achieve a similar extent until the 1970s.

They must have read my astonishment on my face. In any case the following day my uncle made me a tempting offer: "Stay here. We'll find you a job in the foundry. We even have an empty house for you. All you have to do is ask Loki and Susanne to follow." There it was again, the heart-warming American spontaneity and a generosity so great as to bowl you over. We could not make up our mind to leave Germany, although at the time we kept a fairly miserable home with four families in a four-room apartment. But we maintained the friendship with my relatives, with whom I share merely a great-grandfather, and with their children.

More American friendships accrued during the 1950s, especially after I was elected to the Bundestag in 1953. At that time I first came to know Henry Kissinger, who was working on strategy as a young associate professor at Harvard; later our acquaintance turned into a firm friendship. In those years I also met Robert Bowie, who later, under Kennedy, headed the planning staff in the State Department; I also met Herman Kahn, Donald Brennan, William Kaufmann, Hans Bethe, Edward Teller, Robert Osgood, and Roger Hilsman. I came to understand the role played by Albert Einstein, and I grasped the tragedy of J. Robert Oppenheimer. In particular I learned about the role of Congress, which differs so thoroughly from that of both the Bundestag and the British House of Commons.

During my travels through the United States I saw for myself the calm, relaxed authority that emanated from President Dwight David Eisenhower. He had ended the Korean conflict and brought the American troops home. In June 1953 he had not intervened in the uprising in East Germany, and he had held back during the disturbances in Hungary as well. He respected the Soviet zone of influence in Europe that existed de facto though it was not specified by treaty. He did not, however, allow Moscow to take precedence over the United States. I trusted him and his balanced foreign policy.

At that time the Democratic Senator Mike Mansfield (whom I met again twenty-five years later, when he was the American ambassador to Tokyo) wanted to bring home the American troops stationed in Europe. Wilhelm Mellies, deputy head of the SPD under Erich Ollenhauer until 1958, and I were among the many who tried in vain in the 1950s to persuade Mansfield that withdrawal would be an error in strategy. I thought Mansfield's idea, which had become an obsession with him, was dangerous because it would of necessity lead to a huge superiority of Soviet troops in Europe. This was the time when the necessity of strategic parity began to take hold of my thinking.

We also visited Senator James W. Fulbright, who was considered the outstanding thinker on foreign affairs in Washington. Fulbright did not share his colleague's opinion; he felt the lack of his administration's global strategy for peace.

It was at that time, too, that we learned that the American Senate is not so concerned that Republicans support the Republican administration (as was and is taken for granted in Europe for any ruling party) but that the Senate as a whole, transcending party, sees itself first and foremost as the deliberate control and balance to the president and his administration. The clever interplay of the two floor leaders (Lyndon Johnson for the Democrats and William Knowland for the Republicans) would have been seen in Bonn as a betrayal of the party—though it has to be admitted that in general, defeats in parliamentary votes would bring far more serious consequences to European government than a similar defeat for an American president.

During one of my early visits to the United States I called on Walter Lippmann, at that time the dean of political journalists, whose widely syndicated column I admired. To this day I feel great admiration for the top people in American journalism—Marvin Kalb, Joe Kraft, Flora Lewis, and James Reston have always been excellent seismographs to me. Most American newspapers are terribly provincial in their reportage, which rarely goes beyond local events; they can hardly hold their own with European local papers. But some of the columnists syndicated throughout the country are among the best in the world, as are some of the newspapers, such as the *Christian Science Monitor,* the front page of the *Wall Street Journal, The New York Times,* and the Washington *Post,* as well as such weekly newsmagazines as *Time* and, though less reliably, *Newsweek.*

To me the American *International Herald Tribune,* published in Paris and distributed in various European locations, is the best daily newspaper in the world because it combines three advantages: balanced international reportage in concise articles, an excellent overview of the United States, and a variety of rich, high-level commentary that draws on many American sources. In the age of television, which satiates the public with a wealth of channels and programs, the influence of newspapers on American opinion is comparatively slight, but the press influences the political and economic elite.

As representative, minister, and chancellor I have always freely exposed myself to the influence of newspapers. I have spent up to an hour and a half a day reading newspaper reports and commentary, and not merely the summaries prepared by the press office. The idea that I am hostile to the press, which is raised occasionally, is based on an error. It is true that I have always detested giving five-minute interviews on the stairs, as it were, in the elevator, or on the edges of a meeting, and I have often enough felt that interviews in which I was asked incompetent questions were an affront. I have always known that the term "journalist" is a collective noun which, like the generalized "politician," encompasses people with widely varying qualifications; in both worlds the range goes all the way from quasi-criminal to statesman. But I always gladly rearranged my schedule to make room for an interview with Kurt Becker or Hans Reiser, with Katharine Graham, Anatole Grunwald, or James ("Scotty") Reston.

The few great American political television interviewers are outstanding. Often they are superbly informed and exceptionally discerning. They put intelligent questions, compelling the person they are interviewing to put his thinking on show. They do not, following a preconceived opinion, drive him into a corner or into irrelevancies. Of course there was the additional factor that an interview with Barbara Walters or Walter Cronkite not only was intellectual fun in itself but also furnished an excellent vehicle to bring German politics to the citizens of the United States, both intellectually and emotionally.

Whenever I was in Washington, I always called on George Meany, the president of the powerful labor organization, the AFL-CIO, and later on his successor, Lane Kirkland. It seemed to me just as important to know the opinions of the heads of the unions as to hold discussions with outstanding industrialists and bankers. In the early years I owed a great deal to David Rockefeller in particular. Of course during my visits to the companies and large factories of the country I spoke with as many people as possible. From Detroit to Seattle, from Cleveland to Houston, from South Carolina to California I collected my impressions. Almost everywhere I was generously given information. But the country's achievements were also spectacular! In the mid-1950s American industry was still far superior to German production.

Visiting Hollywood's film industry, Wilhelm Mellies and I spent an afternoon watching Grace Kelly, who was making her last film. Many years later I saw her again, together with Raymond Barre and his wife, when she was the Princess of Monaco; we danced an old-fashioned waltz. Her death in an automobile accident soon thereafter touched me deeply.

From Hollywood our travels took us to the Boeing plant in Seattle, where we were shown the first civilian 707, which had just been developed from a military long-range tanker plane. It would soon set out on its triumphant flight throughout the world. When I was chancellor, I always flew 707s when I traveled abroad.

Thirty years later I paid another visit to Boeing; I felt highly gratified that Lufthansa was spoken of in the most laudatory terms; the German airline had become highly regarded throughout the world. In the early 1950s I had been charged by the Hamburg provincial government to help the company during its early days. Today my old friend Heinz Ruhnau is the chairman of its board.

Kennedy's Star

I HAD a close-up view of some stretches of the presidential election campaign of 1960. The German Social Democrats profited from Kennedy's campaign tactics and tried to apply some of them to Willy Brandt's Bundestag campaigns in 1961, 1965, and 1969—often successfully. Our real fascination with Kennedy, however, did not begin until after his narrow victory over Nixon; it set in with Kennedy's inaugural speech. Its content, language, and style enraptured the Germans as well as his own countrymen.

Kennedy's image and his radiance, the achievements as well as the failure of his short era will undergo many supplements, deductions, perhaps even revisions in the American historical records and in international historical discussion. I too have ambivalent memories of the Bay of Pigs disaster, the dangerous and careless meeting with Khrushchev in Vienna in 1961 that preceded the building of the Berlin Wall, and the United States' becoming enmeshed in the Vietnam War, which France had already lost. But I am disgusted by the observation, heard frequently in the United States in more recent years, sometimes uttered cynically, at other times hypocritically, to the effect that in view of the disaster of the Vietnam War, Kennedy had been murdered just in time. I was a witness to the weakness in leadership at the time the Wall was erected; I will never forget August 13, 1961, when ten thousand and more Berliners gathered on the square outside the Schöneberger town hall to express their outrage and their fear, but also their hope of Kennedy's intervention. The then mayor, Willy Brandt, at that time the outstanding leader of the Berliners, had obviously not received satisfactory agreements from Washington. I heard his speech on the radio: He reassured his Berliners at the same time that he restrained them from rash and dangerous action. This approach was characteristic and represented a rhetorical master performance. It was not until a few days later that Kennedy sent his vice president, Lyndon Johnson, to the deeply shaken old German capital. In short, in 1961 I had my doubts whether Kennedy, who clearly lacked foreign-policy experience, would have enough judgment and decisiveness to master international crises.

These doubts were erased in October 1962 by his incomparable operations to resolve the Cuban missile crisis. At the time I was minister for domestic affairs in Hamburg—that is, quite far removed from national politics, and even more so from international affairs. Nevertheless, the threat of armed conflict between the two nuclear superpowers, the dangers of a new world war, were very clear to me. At the weekly conferences with Councilor Hans Birckholtz and the department heads of the ministry for domestic affairs, we spent more time discussing the international crisis—though we were in no way responsible for solving it—than on Hamburg's community matters.

We admired the American president; almost daily we debated among ourselves the options at his disposal for whatever the next step was—but Kennedy and his team invented something that did not even exist historically or under international law: a partial naval blockade of the island nation, which was minimized by being called a quarantine, without a shot being fired. I was deeply impressed by Washington's ability to undo the knot Khrushchev had tied with his unbridled adventurism without making the latter look like the big loser—Kennedy went to a great deal of trouble to allow the Soviet leader to save face.

The Cuban missile crisis and the way it was resolved deeply influenced later developments in the relationship between the two nuclear world powers as well as the relations between the United States and its European allies—especially de Gaulle's France. It is true that this influence was not always or entirely in a positive direction. In 1962, however, Kennedy's achievement was most evident. The president fulfilled many Germans' hopes of a political leader: an idealist with a grand vision and a little ingredient of romance while at the same time a man with practical, proven successes. According to a widespread public illusion, an ideal statesman is someone who can develop a stirring vision of the future; but at the same time he is held responsible for turning this vision into reality. He is supposed to be likable—perhaps even radiating a bit of erotic attraction—and a great speaker; but he is also expected to be infallible in making his calculations. At the same time that the public wants him to be a "realist," he is supposed to be truthful and clear. These traits and skills, never yet found combined in one person, the Germans found only partially in Schumacher, Adenauer, and Erhard. But now it seemed that a young American president fulfilled all these desiderata at once.

Under this impression many Germans were prepared to entrust themselves to American leadership without reservations. We would also have been prepared to make sacrifices for German-American friendship if Kennedy had asked us to. His Philadelphia speech of July 4, 1962, seemed to demonstrate a new reality to us: This American president understood Europe, he was offering Europeans an equal partnership with his own nation. I experienced this impression only once more in later years—with Gerald Ford.

We loved Kennedy, and because of him we loved the United States. When he was killed, the dismay and grief in Germany were no less than in his own country. Along with our grief came the first breath of the fear of the political future that has visited the Germans frequently since, sometimes softer, other times more strongly.

On the evening of November 22, 1963, I was giving a speech at a conference of the Social Democratic party in Hamburg. As I was speaking, someone handed me a note telling of Kennedy's assassination. I interrupted my prepared text to read the message out loud. It was impossible to go on speaking or listening. I said, "This death shocks all of us. It changes the world. Let us quietly go home." The people acted as if they had been clubbed: dazed, uncomprehending, and grieving. They rose and silently left the hall. A star had gone out. We had never felt so close to the American nation as we did that night.

Johnson Causes Erhard's Downfall

T HE Johnson years robbed many pro-Americans of their illusions—a change of attitude increasingly clear in retrospect. It is true that it took several years for this sobering effect to transfer to Europe and to Germany. The first cooling-off was followed by the resistance to the Vietnam commitment and ended in the despair at the meaningless sacrifice of America's youth in the rice paddies of Southeast Asia.

After Kennedy's death emptiness set in. In our view President Johnson lagged far behind the expectations his predecessor had aroused. In spite of his propagation of the Great Society and the unquestionably substantial sociopolitical steps by which American society seemed to imitate the European welfare state in the 1960s, there was a clear lack of generosity—at least in relations with Europe.

Under Johnson the mid-1960s saw two confrontations with the American administration. The first was in connection with the project, originated by Kennedy, of a multinational fleet of carriers for nuclear missiles (the so-called Multilateral Force, or MLF). At the time I suspected that the Americans had a twofold motive in promoting this plan. The first was the belief that realization of a two-pillar theory might be substantially advanced by European participation both in nuclear-strategic deterrence and in disposition over these nuclear weapons. The other was the intention to counter France's retreat from NATO, which was increasingly imminent after the Cuban missile crisis. That event had made it unmistakably clear to all Europeans that peace in Europe was wholly dependent on purely American decisions. At the moment the crisis was coming to a dramatic head, de Gaulle unequivocally linked France's fate with that of the United States. As far as I could tell, he was acting as a model ally, never asking for details.

During my time in the European Parliament in Strasbourg, however, I had come to know some of de Gaulle's French followers and their views on America. Therefore I imagined in the early 1960s that de Gaulle would try—not least because of the experience of the Cuban crisis—to free France from its total strategic dependence on the United States. I worried about the consequences of such an effort on the part of the Gaullists, since they could drive a deep wedge into the alliance. A similar way of thinking, taking its direction from de Gaulle, developed in Germany as well, especially in the Bavarian Christian Socialist Union. The representatives of the CSU, headed by Strauss, were considered secondary Gaullists in Bonn, while the rest of us were counted among the so-called Atlanticists. After de Gaulle pulled France brusquely from the joint integrated military organization of NATO in 1966, German secondary Gaullism began to die down.

The MLF project entailed almost insoluble difficulties and therefore endless discussions, both in the United States and in Europe. England made its own, modifying proposal (Allied Nuclear Force, or ANF). Were the occupation troops to be multinationally mixed? Who would decide about who was to be detailed? Would the participating European governments be allowed veto power over decisions by the American high command? And if these questions were answered in the affirmative, would the MLF be able to function? Would it be a persuasive deterrent force to Moscow?

Within the ranks of German Social Democrats this discussion also took up a fair amount of time. Max Brauer, the mayor of Hamburg, whom I respected highly and who was without a doubt a close friend of the United States (where he had lived during the Hitler period), was the leading exponent of the opposition. Because of my anti-Gaullist sentiments, I was an advocate. But what was much more important was that Fritz Erler, at that time the leading expert on foreign affairs in the Social Democratic Party, finally came out in favor of affirmation.

The 1964 federal party congress followed Fritz Erler, handing Brauer a bitter defeat at the end of his political life. But a few months later, in December 1964, Johnson dropped the project overnight without proposing an alternative. Those of us who had put our prestige on the line to back a plan of strategic importance to the United States felt we had been duped and had lost respect at home. That was when I understood for the first time that it is domestically risky to commit oneself to a policy advocated by the ruling power if that power cannot be relied on to stick to its guns.

The second confrontation occurred in the summer of 1966. The German-American agreements on balance of currency in favor of the United States were about to terminate. The question was whether to renew or extend them; to come right down to it, it was a matter of relieving the American balance of payments, which had been skewed by, among other things, the expenses for troops stationed in Germany. The United States also funded such outlays for its troops and other military installations in France, England, Italy, Belgium, and so on, but these nations were not being asked for "currency offsets." For this reason I considered this demand, levied exclusively against Germany, as a disguised collection of occupation expenses, which were certainly no longer current. Given the friendliest possible interpretation, it was a contribution exacted from the German partner alone.

Chancellor Erhard was setting out on a visit to President Johnson in late September 1966. His departure was preceded by a debate in the Bundestag that also discussed a broad American press campaign that had unfolded in the United States in the vanguard of the state visit, to pressure Erhardt to make concessions. The American government was unwilling to agree to the nuclear "right of codetermination" requested by the Bonn government. Instead Bonn was being asked to make larger payments, termed partly currency balance and partly recompense for American weapons and equipment, which the United States had pressed on the Bonn government in large amounts.

In this debate I proposed that on the occasion of the visit we withdraw the demand for nuclear "codetermination" raised by Erhard's government but refuse to enter on new obligations in connection with the balance of currency agreements of July 1964 to the same amount. The West German government found this suggestion worthless.

Erhard's visit to Johnson ended in a humiliation for the chancellor. In a Bundestag debate a few days after his return I asked that he lay on the table the extent of the obligations he had confirmed or newly agreed to. Since Erhard had apparently overdrawn the account of German capacity, he could not accede to the request.

Erhard was too soft to reject Johnson's unreasonable demands. The result of the negotiations conducted at Johnson's ranch in Texas was not acceptable and was seen as an additional symptom of his inadequacy. Only a few weeks later his own party dropped him, and for the first time since 1930 the Social Democrats came to participate in the government.

I do not believe Johnson and his advisers had deliberately intended to contribute to Erhard's downfall; presumably they had not given a thought to his situation at home; if they had, they would have been more accommodating and would have helped him to achieve a success that he could show off to the German public and the Bundestag or that at least could have helped him save face. Thus in 1966 the American lack of international experience and the egotistical inconsiderateness of an American president helped to bring down a chancellor and start a change of coalition in Bonn.

There was no need to mourn the Erhard-Mende government; it was ripe for replacement. Viewed historically, the Social Democrats' participation in the government had long been overdue. Nevertheless, the event left a bitter aftertaste. I thought of it more than ten years later, when Presidents Carter and Reagan repeatedly took action over the heads of their European allies or did not honor official agreements; just like Johnson, unaware of the domestic consequences for their allies or ignoring them, they made difficulties for me several times while I was chancellor.

Much as Johnson played an essential part in Erhard's fall and the collapse of the coalition of the CDU-CSU and the Free Democratic Party in 1966, fifteen years later Reagan, though unwittingly, had a part in shattering the social-liberal coalition of the Social Democratic Party and the FDP. This happened because he pursued his Soviet policy and his economic policy without regard to the interests of Europe and most especially Germany, thus disconcerting many members of my party. Of course in both instances domestic and economic factors also played an important part, especially the FDP's main raison d'être, which is to change coalition partners with some regularity.

I did not get to know Johnson, his cabinet members, and his advisers more closely, with the exception of McGeorge Bundy and Robert McNamara. Bundy impressed me as highly educated and at the same time energetic and resolute; it was easy to have confidence in him. I continued to see him occasionally in later years; the Vietnam experience had turned him into a strategic thinker, and every conversation with him was fruitful.

The same was true of McNamara. I often visited him during the

1960s, when I made frequent trips to the United States as a Hamburg senator and as chairman of the SDP parliamentary group. This was both during his term as secretary of defense and later, when he headed the World Bank. He always insisted on thinking through all possible strategies, and he exercised the utmost intellectual stringency. As secretary of defense he drew the consequences of the approaching stalemate between Washington and Moscow as early as 1962 and freed the United States from the nuclear strategy of massive retaliation that had been official policy until then.

Even more than his share in the responsibility for the Vietnam War, the Cuban missile crisis has since shaped McNamara's thinking and given him a strong ethical orientation beyond his strategic and economic competence. Once, late in the 1960s, we were talking about Vietnam and Nixon's and Kissinger's efforts to end the war; I asked him why the preceding administration had not made the same attempts. His answer took me by surprise: "Bobby could have done it." But Robert Kennedy had fallen out with Johnson a long time before and left his administration, and in 1968 he too had been assassinated. After John F. Kennedy's death McNamara thought very highly of the equally charismatic younger brother. On the other hand, he held it against Johnson that he had not made any serious effort to end the Vietnam War; this was also the reason he had resigned as secretary of defense in late 1967.

McNamara saw his work at the head of the World Bank as more than a complex multinational chore; it was a moral mission, and he brought all his skills to it. McNamara was the first politician who understood the primary significance of developing agriculture in the developing countries and who explained to them that they were able to feed themselves. He was especially convincing because of his unconditional personal support of the people of the underdeveloped nations. Therefore McNamara, who had not been raised to be a member of the Democratic Party, became for me a symbol of that social idealism that had always marked large segments of the Democratic Party on the East Coast since Roosevelt's New Deal.

It is easy for a German Social Democrat to reject the traditional conservatism of the Southern Democrats but otherwise to feel drawn to the Democratic Party and the labor movement. I felt the same way until, as chancellor, I had to face foreign statesmen and negotiate with them. Then I began to understand: Though affinities on the basis of party membership can be useful at times in foreign affairs, what really matters are the judgment and discernment of one's counterpart in any encounter, his ability to get any given policy enacted at home, his reliability and his consistency. Measured against these, it is fairly unimportant whether someone is a Republican or a Democrat.

Since 1969 I have worked with four American presidents and their administrations—most happily with Gerald Ford, who is a Republican, distinctly less comfortably with Jimmy Carter, the Democrat, and with Reagan, who once again is a Republican.

Nixon: The Strategy of Balance

WHENEVER the talk in Europe is of Richard Nixon, the Watergate scandal automatically comes to mind; Nixon's name makes us feel uneasy. I have sensed this reaction frequently whenever I called him, with conviction, a high-ranking international strategist.

Nixon must have been well prepared for his international role when he was elected president in late 1968 after campaigning against Hubert Humphrey. I met him for the first time a year later. In November 1969 my American counterpart in the defense department, Melvin Laird, invited the members of the NATO Nuclear Planning Group to a conference at Airlie House, a farm in Virginia. The second day the president entertained us at breakfast in the White House. Italy's Manlio Brosio, at that time NATO secretary general, introduced us to the president, we ate our cereal and scrambled eggs, and then Nixon spoke for about ten minutes on the world situation. What he said was neither profound nor new, and certainly it was not original—his remarks were little more than exalted small talk, meant as a polite gesture to us. When Nixon finished, Brosio rose and told him quite bluntly that what he had said was really not sufficient—we had hoped for a little more substance.

Nixon was a little startled. Then he reflected for a moment and launched into a second speech, lasting about three quarters of an hour, completely off the cuff (I was sitting next to him and could see that he was not speaking from notes). The most important man in the Western alliance conjured up in front of our eyes an improvised but nonetheless persuasive picture of the world. He analyzed conditions in Vietnam, the role of the People's Republic of China and its growing significance, the situation of the Soviet Union and the necessity of cooperation with it, especially in order to arrive at a limitation of strategic arms (later called SALT). Nixon spoke about the Middle East and its problems. In particular, he went into detail on the overall strategy of NATO. In effect he did not deviate from the two important plans NATO had adopted in December 1967: on the one hand the Harmel Report and its two-step strategy of combining military security with political détente and on the other the military strategy of flexible response.

I was certainly not the only one to feel instant respect for Nixon's competence. Back in Bonn, I went to see Willy Brandt. He was getting ready for his first visit to Washington as chancellor, and I advised him to take his preparations very seriously so as to be able to represent our German interests and intentions in the general context of Western strategy when he was speaking with Nixon. The American president, I told him, knew his business; in any case he understood a great deal more about strategy in dealing with the Soviets than Johnson, who had disappointed Brandt so badly in Berlin.

Looking back from the perspective of the 1980s, I still cannot understand Nixon's behavior in the Watergate affair and the scandal of the tapes, but I empathize with the reaction of the American public and the Congress all the more. On the other hand, Nixon's foreign policy and defense ideas can stand comparison with those of his predecessors and successors very well. There is more: Nixon's opening to China; the retreat of the United States from Vietnam, which he struggled for and finally achieved—though not without circuitous means and delays; his strategy of balance with the Soviet Union, outstandingly marked by the ABM treaty and SALT I; his understanding of the interests of his European allies; his judgment and capacity to act in international affairs—all of which clearly distinguish Nixon from Johnson, Carter, and Reagan.

Of course his advisers and cabinet officers played a part in his foreign policy practices, Henry Kissinger above all. But it is doing Nixon an injustice to think it permissible to interpret him as the executive instrument, as it were, of Kissinger's ideas. In the case of the opening to China, reversing a policy that had been chiseled in stone with unusual obstinacy for twenty years, it is obvious that Nixon planned it before placing Kissinger—who was brought to him by Nelson Rockefeller—on his staff.

In 1986, twelve years after Nixon's resignation, he and I had a personal exchange of views. We met at his office, located in a New York high-rise and decorated with many historical photographs. The outward occasion was a television interview; Nixon loyally supported President Reagan's position even while he managed to stress his own differing opinion. He seemed more self-assured than I had expected him to be, grandly ignoring the past. His overview of the current world situation was stupendous; he had mastered the important details—an aspect that was even more glaringly evident in private conversation than in front of the rolling cameras. I was impressed and felt confirmed in my judgment that the Western world had lost a significant strategist in Richard M. Nixon—through his own fault.

During the early years of the Nixon administration my immediate counterpart in Washington was Melvin Laird. Right from the start we had a cordial relationship, which continues to this day. At that time Laird was, of course, preoccupied mainly by the Vietnam War. It was his job to promote the "Vietnamization" of the war, an objective Nixon adopted in early 1970, so that American troops could gradually be withdrawn from Vietnam. Because he had served in Congress a long time, Laird was an experienced politician. He suffered from resistance to the war, which was rapidly growing among the youth of America, and he wanted to free his country from this burden.

I followed the step-by-step American troop withdrawals with inner empathy, almost in a state of suspense. But the announcement in the fall of 1972 that universal compulsory military service was being abolished worried me. Laird explained that, given the troop withdrawals, the United States no longer needed so many soldiers, and there were no other projects in which he could use them. It seemed to me, however, that the compelling motive was to calm public opinion in the United States. I feared that in Germany—and in my own party—voices might be heard to demand that we should follow the example of our principal ally, place the Bundeswehr on a voluntary basis, and also abolish the draft. There were already ideas about a short "militia" term.

I was annoyed by all this for two reasons. One centered on memories of the Weimar attempt at democracy, which had failed in part because the Versailles Treaty had forbidden universal compulsory military service and the Reichswehr could therefore not be anchored in the new democracy but developed into a "state within the state." Therefore I saw conscription as a factor that helped to insure the fundamental democratic nature of our armed forces. I have not changed this conviction from the mid-1950s to the present day.

For another, abolishing the draft in the German Federal Republic—which would probably have been joined by other European members of NATO—would have sharply increased the Soviet Union's numerical troop superiority in Europe. As far as land forces were concerned, after all, the Bundeswehr had become the backbone of the joint defense of Central Europe.

We succeeded in keeping the discussion that was beginning in our country in check. Melvin Laird appreciated our efforts. He always showed understanding for the political problems of his European colleagues, a trait that distinguished him clearly from his sometimes rather overbearing successor in the office of secretary of defense, James Schlesinger, who was not at all troubled at inspecting an honor guard of the Bonn watch battalion with his hands in his pockets. My friend Georg Leber, my successor on the Hardthöhe, was very troubled indeed!

Laird also understood at once why I was compelled to oppose the planned deployment of ADM (Atomic Demolition Munitions, rather misleadingly called "atomic mines" in German newspaper jargon) along the line of demarcation. When I became minister of defense in 1969, this plan was already included in a project managed by a military NATO committee. I objected vigorously: Since the other side could not be prevented from moving barbed-wire fences and spring-gun installations, it was all the more important that our side not deploy nuclear weapons on the border. An additional point was that positioning these weapons along the border would, in the case of overt hostilities, have turned any attempt at conventional defense into a fiction and therefore irrelevant. With someone less confident than Laird my opposition might have occasioned a crisis in the relations between Washington and Bonn; some newspapers on both sides would have questioned my loyalty to the alliance. Thanks to Laird's understanding, the plan could be tabled without this move's being made public. Laird knew what you could ask of one's allies and what would be going too far.

Instead we jointly started the so-called European Defense Improvement Program (EDIP) in December 1970. Besides its military purpose, which is primary, the program had the secondary, political purpose of making it clear to Moscow that despite the Vietnam War, which at the time was being intensely watched by the whole world, the defense of Europe would not be neglected.

In reality, however, a sense of neglect did arise in the capitals of

Western Europe in the early 1970s. This feeling was connected not only with the Vietnam War and Nixon's and Kissinger's intense concentration on ending it but also with the SALT negotiations. These bilateral verbal encounters between Washington and Moscow, which largely excluded the European allies, found their resolution in May 1972 in the SALT agreement on limiting the number of strategic missiles and the ABM treaty on limiting antimissile weapons. Furthermore, this sense of insecurity was connected with the catastrophic developments in the international currency system together with the American attitude of "benign neglect" on this subject, announced on August 15, 1971, by Secretary of the Treasury John B. Connally.

In April 1973, five months before he was named secretary of state, Henry Kissinger proclaimed the "year of Europe." In Europe this declamatory act—which, by the way, had no practical consequences—aroused only disbelieving astonishment, mixed with mockery.

In the meantime, however, the uneasiness and finally the shock of Watergate had reached Europe. People both in the United States and in Europe first began to withdraw some of their confidence in Nixon when his troops marched into Kampuchea in 1970. Beginning in 1969, the mistrust aroused in Europe by the overtly exclusive SALT negotiations was understandable; but we felt that there was no justification for the Nixon administration's initial mistrust and obstruction of Willy Brandt's *Ostpolitik,* especially the August 1970 treaty with Moscow.

Washington's skepticism was almost entirely washed away in September 1971, with the Four Power Agreement (which paved the way for the friendship agreement with the German Democratic Republic of late 1972). Both SALT and *Ostpolitik* followed the guidelines laid down in the Harmel resolution of 1967 for an overall strategy by the Western alliance toward the Soviet Union—an alliance Nixon endorsed at the time he took office. But one thorn remained: Nixon had no personal ties of friendship to any of his European colleagues—possibly with the sole exception of de Gaulle; Nixon never made any secret of his admiration for the president of France. For most Europeans, Nixon remained a mysterious figure for his entire term in office.

During the Nixon years I kept in close touch with Henry Kissinger, who was Nixon's security adviser until the middle of 1973 and served as secretary of state until the end of 1976. My reason was not only that we had known each other for a long time; close exchanges were absolutely essential if we were to recognize and understand what changes in American policy were setting in or were already in place. Nixon's complicated nature, imbued with suspicion of his own administration, had led, as we saw even in Bonn, to a situation where Secretary of State William Rogers and his most important officials in the State Department not only had less influence but also a much narrower perspective over foreign and security policies than was the case in the corresponding ministries in Paris, London, and Bonn. Of course we paid calls on our counterparts in the State Department and the Pentagon, but the crucial information and ideas could be obtained only from Kissinger in the White House.

The First
Dollar Crisis

I N July 1972 I moved from the defense ministry to the finance ministry (for six months I was also in charge of the economic ministry as a so-called double minister). At that time I was about to set out on a routine trip to Canada and the United States. It turned into an occasion to say good-bye to the men who had been my colleagues, Donald McDonald and Mel Laird, and to pay introductory visits to my new counterparts in charge of finance, the liberal John Turner in Ottawa and George Shultz in Washington. I had not met either of them before, but I was to develop a lifelong friendship with both, as I had done with Kissinger and Laird.

The same was true for Arthur Burns, the white-haired president of the Federal Reserve Bank. Nine years later, in 1981, Arthur was named American ambassador to Bonn; he was an ambassador whom I not only respected but for whom I felt a great liking, even though he was often enough compelled to advance opinions of his government that were opposed to mine. By the standards of the diplomatic service Burns was by no means an ideal ambassador—his freely given opinions made him much too independent for that. But because his thinking embodied the American virtues, he was a great ambassador for his nation. He contributed a great deal to mutual understanding; Reagan could not have sent Bonn anyone more suitable.

Arthur was a wise man, with shrewd economic discernment, encompassing political and life experience, incorruptible moral integrity—and all this was combined with a very modest private life style. In August 1983 Loki and I spent two or three days with Helen and Arthur Burns—and their Yorkshire terrier Hansi, who was terribly spoiled by Helen—in their summer home in Vermont; the ambassador had installed a primitive art studio and a workshop in the barn of the tiny old wooden farmhouse. There was a second workroom for writing in a hut in the woods, without water or light, and of course without a telephone. There we philosophized about everything under the sun, about the United States and Germany, about Christianity and Judaism—as we had so often done in Bonn, when we sat and talked until the small hours of the morning.

In July 1972 these encounters were still far in the future. All I knew was that my friend Karl Klasen, who at the time was president of the Deutsche Bundesbank, thought very highly of Burns, who was his counterpart in the American Federal Reserve. It was the time of the first great dollar crisis, which brought the two men in touch almost weekly, sometimes daily. The worldwide system of pegged exchange rates, which had been created in 1944–1945 at Bretton Woods, was in bad shape because the dollar was steadily falling in value on the international markets. This situation had not been foreseen either in the textbooks or in the tenets of the central banks and the International Monetary Fund.

As I soon learned, there was no one among those in charge on either side of the Atlantic who had either a solution or the authority necessary to impose a solution. The summer of 1972 was relatively calm with respect to monetary policy—in retrospect it was the calm before the storm. In Washington, in July 1972, I restricted myself to asking questions of my new American partners, Shultz and Burns. Of course I knew the German view of the problems from the lectures by my cabinet colleagues Alex Möller and Karl Schiller, who had headed the Finance Ministry before me, and from the discussions about the proper role of the German mark in this chaos and our tactics in regard to monetary policy; we carried on these discussions often while Brandt headed the cabinet. In my conversations with Shultz and Burns I could therefore let myself throw in an occasional observation along with my questions. I was and still am in principle a supporter of pegged exchange rates because they best serve the international division of labor—that is, free international trade—and therefore all participating national economies. I cited the appropriate arguments. I will never forget Arthur's response: "Your talk makes a lot of sense, young man." Young man? I was fifty-three years old—but I felt flattered.

What were the reasons for the crisis? The Bretton Woods system was pegged to the dollar, which was the yardstick for all other currencies. The dollar was identified with the price of gold; an ounce of gold was worth $35.00. Every foreign central bank could buy gold from the United States at that price; conversely, the United States could buy dollars or any other currency it might happen to need and pay for it in gold. Under this system 4,000 German marks, for example, were the same as one dollar (parity) in the fall of 1969, or, to put it another way, 140,000 marks had the same value as an ounce of gold.

Now if a country needed dollars—for example, to pay a deficit in its trade balance—it could borrow the dollars to start with; but in the end it had to pay these to the United States Federal Reserve System in gold. If, on the other hand, a country had a trade *surplus,* a credit balance accumulated in its central bank in the currencies of its partner states or in gold; both together formed the so-called currency reserves.

Long before a central bank gives away its own currency or gold, the importers of goods and services must pay their bills. For this purpose they buy the foreign currencies in which they have to pay in the currency market—at that time mostly dollars—using the currency of their own country. In this way the dollar or the other required currencies become scarcer and more expensive—that is, their own exchange rate worsens. On the other hand, their exchange rate improves when the exporters exchange their earnings in foreign currency into their own currency on the currency market. This process leads to an increased demand for their own currency and to an increased supply of the foreign currency. That is why persistent export surpluses lead to a rise in the rate of exchange, while export deficits lead to a decline in the rate of exchange of one's own currency.

The Bretton Woods system provided for this contingency: It allowed for a rise or decline in the rate of exchange up to a percentage of the dollar parity of each currency. Once the upper or lower limit was reached, the central bank in question was required to intervene; that is, no later than the moment when the lower limit has been reached, it must sell as much of its foreign currency reserves as necessary and at the same time remove its own currency from the market so it does not fall below the limit.

In practice the "foreign currencies" involved were almost exclusively United States dollars. The dollar was not only the parity standard for all participating currencies but also the crucial intervention and reserve currency. Furthermore, in international trade it was the overwhelmingly employed "transaction currency"—that is, most international exchanges were billed and paid for in dollars.

When a deficit country had exhausted its possibilities for credit, or when it feared for the remaining stock of its currency reserves, it could request a devaluation of its own parity by the International Monetary Fund; the dollar parity of its own currency was thus lowered. This freed the particular country from the burden of intervention at the same time that it led to an artificial price reduction for its exports and a rise in prices of its imports; thus the hope existed for a better adjustment of the balance of payments and preservation of the new parity.

Neither devaluation nor appreciation is popular in the affected country. The rise in import prices leads to domestic price increases and thus to inflation; the rise of export prices, on the other hand, arouses fears in industry and labor about foreign markets and unemployment. Not only did the Bretton Woods system take into account this lack of popularity, which could cost the government in question prestige among the voters, but the International Monetary Fund also issued suggestions on how to avoid the situation: It advised nations suspected of having to devalue to reduce their budget deficits and their money supply. In other words, nations with a weakness in balance of payments were urged to curb their homemade inflation.

But this was precisely what the United States had not done; the Vietnam War had made huge demands on the budget, and the deficit had been financed by the American capital market with the aid of a generous money supply. Prices therefore rose in the United States, the dollar lost some of its buying power, trade deficits became chronic, and the dollar touched on the lower limit, where intervention was mandatory.

Beginning in 1968, Bonn was extremely disturbed by these developments. The Deutsche Bundesbank, under pressure from the United States, was the first to give up gold as the form in which the United States met its obligations, accepting instead interest-bearing United States Treasury notes. At the end of 1969 we revalued the German mark against the dollar for the first time. In August 1971 Nixon abolished the convertibility of gold against the rest of the world. The same year the mark was formally revalued against the dollar for the second time.

None of these maneuvers led to any lasting resolution. But the constant interventions in the German mark led to unwelcome high money supplies in Germany, so that inflationary processes began to set in.

The drama had many acts, and I do not intend to describe them here. Among the indirect consequences were the resignation of two German finance ministers, my friend Alex Möller in May 1971 and his successor Karl Schiller (who was serving in a dual capacity as finance minister and economic minister) in early July 1972. Now I was the finance minister who was facing the problem. I understood that at bottom Shultz's and Burns's thinking was similar to that of Karl Klasen and myself. The four of us were committed market economists and passionate supporters of free international trade. At the same time we were convinced that for both purposes a pegged currency exchange, though not essential, was the best precondition.

Both the men I was dealing with, however, also knew that Nixon would not be changing his economic policies and had no desire to do so; after all, it was an election year. Though Washington's academic circles were humming with monetary policy suggestions of every possible kind, it was hardly worth the trouble to spend much time discussing them. Nixon was more likely to attempt to confuse his own people about controlling the inflationary policy (which Johnson had set in motion) by government loan and price controls (a move he implemented on August 15, 1972, against Shultz's advice) than to attack the evil at its root. Benign neglect would continue to prevail.

In July 1972 I flew back to Bonn knowing only too clearly that we too were facing national elections in the fall. Until then there was little we could do about the massive rush of speculative dollars from the whole world on the German mark, which, it was suspected, would be devalued again, other than to use government control of foreign currencies to expand the money market supply with marks and consequently defend ourselves against a worsening of our inflation rates as best we could. At the time the dollar stood at 3.22 German marks.

In the course of 1972, and during the early months of 1973, international activity aimed at preventing the worst grew to a nearly hectic pace. The United States continued to refuse to make the dollar scarce by selling gold or foreign currencies and thus supporting its exchange rate. The French finance minister, Valéry Giscard d'Estaing, and I were in close touch, as I was with Shultz and his highly skilled deputy, Paul Volcker. Finally we founded a private club that soon proved its efficiency; we called it the Library Group. It consisted of Shultz; Giscard; the British finance minister, Anthony Barber; our Japanese counterpart, Takeo Fukuda; and myself. For a long time it remained a secret from the public, even from the committees of the International Monetary Fund; it took its name, which was known only to us, from the place where we happened to arrange the first meeting: the library of the White House.

Except when the five of us met, Paul Volcker was the most important go-between (my secretary of state, Karl-Otto Pöhl, had a lot of traveling to do, too). Volcker had been given the use of a military plane without windows, which Pöhl and I called the Flying Submarine. This was when I learned to appreciate Volcker's firm convictions and his always reliable factual knowledge, as well as his prudence and discretion. We understood each other, although for a long time he had to defend a fundamental position espoused by his government that we could not endorse, and although I had trouble understanding his speech (for a long time I thought he was a Southerner, which was quite wrong: he came from New Jersey).

Later Volcker went to work for the American central banking system. After serving as president of the Federal Reserve Bank in New York, he became chairman of the Federal Reserve Board in Washington; this made him a counterpart of Pöhl, who was the president of the Deutsche Bundesbank. Even earlier, however, I had admired Volcker as a beacon in the turbulent economic policies because of his inflexibility, especially during the second and third dollar crises. Later on, during the crisis of budget policies in the Reagan administration, he became in effect the United States' economic statesman.

In the early 1970s the political leadership of the United States had allowed Shultz's predecessor, John Connally, to commit the country to widespread neglect of the dangers connected with the progressive devaluation of the dollar. The government could not make up its mind either to correct the inflationary budget and monetary policy or to intervene in the currency markets, as it could have done on the basis of its immense gold reserves. The United States could also have borrowed foreign currencies. But the other important currencies (especially those of Europe and Japan), in consideration of the prices of their own exports, could not be appreciated every few months at will. And neither Paris nor Bonn, neither London nor Tokyo was prepared to inflate its own economy through steady massive dollar purchases—that is, by intervening with its own currency to support dollar parity. In March 1973 the members of the Library Group therefore had no choice but to agree to freeing the exchange rates, or "floating" them. Immediately the dollar sank to 2.83 German marks. By the early summer of 1973 it fell to 2.58 marks.

In Bonn these changes were celebrated as a major gain in prestige, and I had to ward off the well-meant congratulations of laymen. In fact Valéry Giscard d'Estaing and I were deeply worried about the further consequences of the float. We realized that, with the end of the system of pegged currency rates, we were about to enter into a completely new climate, a new era. For a long time we had fought delaying actions. We

also tried to hold together at least the most important European currencies, subsequently creating for that purpose the European Monetary
System (EMS). But six months later came the first oil price explosion,
whose catastrophic effects on the international economy—in which the
dollar glut had originally been involved—none of us had foreseen.

As early as the 1960s my friend Alex Möller, Willy Brandt's first
finance minister, had taught me an important doctrine: Monetary policy *is* foreign policy. Foreign policy considerations also compelled the
European allies to support the currency of their most important member for as long as such a decision could be justified on economic
grounds. But the leading power was no longer willing to accept those
restrictions on its own freedom of action concerning monetary and
budget decisions, though these restrictions are and should be essential
to regulated, dependable currency parity. The United States surrendered the leadership of monetary policy, and thus in practice some of
its de facto leadership of the West. In all this George Shultz acted as
a loyal servant of his president's policies. It may be that he temporarily
flirted with the thesis, at that time widely supported in the United
States, that the international price of a currency is best adjusted by the
market—that is, supply and demand in the daily currency market.

During the crisis there were, of course, confrontations with the
United States, most especially between Shultz and Giscard. Finally all
the participating finance ministers were conscious that they were risking
not only the reliability of their governments' monetary policy but also
their prestige. To my astonishment, in 1973 I saw myself in the position
of having to resort to strong words to mediate a heated argument
between Giscard and Shultz.

Among the few amenities in the career of a finance minister are the
yearly meetings of the World Bank and International Monetary Fund,
which alternate between Washington and one of the other member
states. In September 1973 the Library Group met in Nairobi, the capital
of Kenya, on the occasion of one of these meetings. To me, the untouched countryside of East Africa is among the most beautiful in all
the world; it stretches from ocean beaches through savannahs and
woods to snow-capped mountaintops. Several nature parks offer the
European enchanting panoramas and thousands of wild birds and mam-
mals. Karl Klasen, his colleague Heinrich Irmler, Loki, my daughter
Susanne, and I seized the opportunity to fly to the Ngorongoro Crater
and the Serengeti. It was an exciting adventure: lions, leopards, buffalo,
rhinoceros, elephants, gnus, and many varieties of antelope. While we
were picnicking in the wild, a kite stole the sandwich out of Klasen's
hand.

On the flight back our tiny single-motor propeller plane flew into a hailstorm. The stones clattered on the cabin roof and the wings, and we could not see a thing; the lightning bolts merely lit up the towers of clouds into which we were occasionally thrown. Of course there was neither radar nor radio beacons, but we could hear a loud *beep, beep* coming from the instrument panel at one-second intervals. When we asked what the sound meant, the pilot informed us, "We're losing altitude." He had completely lost direction; the East African mountains were close by, and we were all afraid that we would crash into a mountainside. We could hear the pilot's radio conversations with the tower in Nairobi; the tower spoke to him soothingly and gave advice. When we finally returned unharmed to the light of day and were approaching Nairobi, the tower commented, "Very, very fine." We thought so, too, and after landing we expressed our gratitude and joy for the rescue with whiskey and planter's punches. A few years later we heard that our pilot had crashed.

The Nairobi session brought together almost all the international friends in the same hotel—and, in the evenings, in the same bar. The confusions of monetary policy were behind us, and the oil price shocks had not yet appeared on the horizon. We were cheerful and enjoying the happy mood. It was the most pleasant international conference I ever attended. Of course our final act was to spend a night in the Tree Tops Lodge and observe the elephants from on high. After the lively days in Nairobi the sight of these pachyderms reminded me of the first European summit I had attended.

In the end we had all learned that we could rely on our colleagues' word, transcending all differences of opinion. This knowledge also led to personal friendships: Giscard and myself, Giscard and Shultz, Shultz and myself—as well as with Fukuda, who would later be prime minister of Japan, and Anthony Barber, the British chancellor of the Exchequer, who unfortunately soon left the international scene and entered private industry as a banker in London.

During this time George P. Shultz became my closest friend in the United States. In the exchange of views between us, which has now lasted some fifteen years, I am sure I often said more than was absolutely necessary; but Shultz said rather less. He was an excellent listener but cited trenchant reasons for finding flaws in what the other had said. We had become finance ministers at roughly the same time, and both of us already had a good deal of experience in government. Shultz had served as secretary of labor and head of the Office of Management and Budget (OMB) in the White House. Before that time he had been an adviser to the Eisenhower, Kennedy, and Johnson administrations. His past

included a brilliant academic career in economics; nevertheless, jettison-
ing the Bretton Woods system confronted him with an entirely new
economic challenge—as it did all of us. Like myself, George is a committed believer in a market economy and free trade, and he opposes inflationary economic policies; this attitude unites us.

Intellectually and politically he is incorruptible. It is true that his
loyalty to Nixon was greater than his excellent judgment. Even a decade
later, as Reagan's secretary of state, his loyalty to the president would
prove to be his guiding principle. When Nixon imposed price and wage
controls against Shultz's advice, Shultz telephoned me to let me know
about this decision in advance of the public announcement: "Helmut,
I don't have to tell you that this is happening against my belief and
against my advice." When, however, in March 1974 Shultz understood
the extent of his president's misconduct in connection with Watergate,
he drew his conclusions and announced his resignation, which was
accepted in May. Almost at the same time Giscard and I also left our
finance ministries. As early as a year later, when we were preparing for
the first so-called international economic summit at Rambouillet, the
three of us met again, Shultz acting as President Ford's private emissary.
Then seven years passed until, after a successful period as head of
Bechtel, the world's largest engineering firm, he returned to American
government service in June 1982, this time as secretary of state.

A few days after his nomination the London *Economist* tried to put
itself into my place as chancellor. An article composed in the form of
a letter read in part:

> After four years of mounting horror at American inconsistency
> under President Carter, you have gone through 18 months of
> mounting irritation with President Reagan. . . . Now, . . . one of
> your oldest friends from finance-minister days has taken over as
> secretary of state in Washington. George Shultz is not yet a foreign
> affairs expert—but he is well travelled, widely connected at the top,
> humorous, shrewd: not such a compromiser as everyone thinks,
> rather determined. . . . George Shultz rarely promised but always
> delivered. You hope he can do it again. . . . If George is there,
> maybe it's worth starting over again.

In fact, I felt more or less like this in the summer of 1982. As it was,
we already had an appointment for a private visit at his home in Palo
Alto in late July 1982; when I arrived there, George had already been
installed as secretary of state, and the Senate had confirmed him unani-

mously. We spent several wonderful days together; Obie Shultz (the nickname is probably a variant on her maiden name, O'Brien) is a considerate hostess. We talked about everything under the sun. In the evenings we were generally joined by friends or other guests; Henry Kissinger and Harry Lee Kuan Yew, the prime minister of Singapore, also came to stay for one or two nights. In short, it was a restful meeting of old friends. Every night Shultz and I used to sit and relax in his hot tub in the garden. He asked a lot of questions, which I answered the same way as had always been our custom: candidly, without regard to tactical considerations and prestige. I gave him only one piece of advice: "George, don't forget one thing: Your president cannot afford to name three secretaries of state in one term. You are therefore in a very strong position should there be a difference of opinion on some important problem." My friend merely smiled—and we gazed at the stars in the clear summer sky of the Bay area.

In July 1982 the oil price explosion of 1973–1974 was already almost a decade in the past, but the effects of the oil price explosion of 1979–1980 could still be felt everywhere. When we shifted to an international system of floating exchange rates in March 1973, we had not foreseen these explosions. But in the spring of 1973 we had in any case agreed that developments in the area of monetary and currency policy would have a considerable effect on both international trade policies and the world's energy supply and that therefore they must be considered questions of international politics. In 1973 Shultz and I agreed to raise these questions at future international conferences "under the aspect of their paramount significance for foreign policy." In March 1973 Shultz proposed expressing himself publicly to the effect that general floating of exchange rates was merely a temporary, passing arrangement; the participants were assuming an eventual return to pegged parities. However, the construction of a new international currency system based on pegged but flexible parities presupposed the foreign currency markets' settling into new parity levels beforehand. We also reached an agreement concerning our further way of proceeding: During 1973 and 1974 we intended the development of the new international monetary order to be within the scope of the International Monetary Fund and its member bodies.

But in reality, as a result of the Yom Kippur War, the Arabic leadership of the OPEC cartel, which had not been very successful until then, drastically reduced the amounts of oil it offered for sale in order to force the West to change its policies in the Middle East. Subsequently oil prices rose steeply, increasing fourfold within the few months from September 1973 to April 1974.

Now the fly in the ointment of floating exchange rates quickly became evident. For one thing, the governments were freed from the responsibility of having the exchange rates of their currencies correspond to some officially determined parity; many governments exploited this freedom to allow more strongly inflationary monetary and budgetary policies in general.

The tendency to inflation spread because ever larger numbers of governments were prepared to accept large budgetary deficits and because each of the central banks took care that the budgetary deficits could be financed by an expansion of monetary policy. Some governments, such as the British, even expressly advocated this point of view because, as they noted, the higher price of oil decreased the buying power of the national economies, making it necessary to increase the money supply in compensation.

The balances of payments of the oil-importing nations began to show high deficits, which were soon paired with rapidly growing surpluses among most of the OPEC nations. Since these surpluses were immediately invested in interest-bearing notes issued by Western commercial banks, the banks found themselves recycling petrodollars, as the phenomenon came to be called. That is, through credits the banks financed the balance-of-payment deficits of the oil-importing nations. In this way the growth of international credit volume was accelerated; both governmental and private international debt grew at a rapid pace.

Since the international oil trade was traditionally invoiced and paid in United States dollars, the international dollar credit volume in particular was expanded. To simplify the process, new financing practices were invented; the so-called Eurodollar market—a phrase that only a few years earlier would have met with total incomprehension—developed into a flourishing trade; in many places outside the United States newly licensed banks sprang up like mushrooms, and they raked in a pretty profit with cheap dollar credits.

The American Federal Reserve, which was responsible for the dollar, was powerless in the face of these events. Furthermore, it did not even fully understand the dangers connected with them. Nor did it recognize the dangers inherent in the fact that American private banks were providing *long*-term credit financing to the oil-importing nations whose balances of payments were weak; the banks seemed to be taking in sufficient amounts from Arabic depositors. But these deposits were *short*-term! The situation was basically similar for the commercial banks doing international business in England, Germany, and the other affected nations. Every three months 8 to 10 billion American dollars in short-term notes flowed from Arabic sources to Europe, and these monies were immediately converted into international long-term loans. These were the causes of the international "debt crisis" of the developing nations in the 1980s.

At the time I had not anticipated the debt crisis in this way; two other matters worried me. First, I was concerned with the solvency and ability to make payments of those banks that were dealing in currencies other than their own and thus were neither subject to supervision nor, in case of emergency, entitled to support by their own national central banks. I thought a banking crisis was not out of the question—not, as it turned out, mistakenly. Second, I was afraid that none of the oil-importing nations could in the end avoid a crisis in the balance of payments and as a consequence a deflationary crisis with massive effects on employment.

I drastically expressed these worries in a public address in Rhineland-Palatinate: We were entering on demanding times, I said, and would have to be prepared for severe restrictions. Alluding to Churchill's famous wartime speech, I spoke of sweat and tears. This reference offended Chancellor Brandt, who insisted that the economic boom must not be attacked. I acquiesced, but on November 5, 1973, I wrote a concerned private letter to Secretary of State Henry Kissinger. In it I suggested that a private conference of diplomats, oil specialists, and currency experts in the important industrial nations be held in order to develop a joint policy for the Western governments. It was essential, I wrote, to exchange views and experiences in order to arrive at mutual cooperation and a common policy toward the OPEC nations.

At first my suggestion did not fall on fertile soil with Kissinger because in November 1973 friction between Washington and Bonn had developed. These tensions were fed by the media. Without Germany's knowledge, the United States government had put together ocean transports bound for Israel from its military arsenals in Bremerhaven, thus turning the Federal Republic into a source of military reinforcements in the Yom Kippur War. Willy Brandt was fully justified in taking offense. It was not until February 1974 that the Washington energy conference grew out of my suggestion. Henry Kissinger discussed it in detail in his memoirs.

French President Georges Pompidou did not send his finance minister, Giscard, as I had hoped, but instead dispatched his foreign secretary, Michel Jobert, and heated controversies arose between him and

Kissinger, who was our host. Brandt had sent both Walter Scheel, his foreign minister, and myself; as chairman of the council of the European Community, Scheel was to speak for that body, while I was supposed to represent German interests. I did so, standing with Kissinger against Jobert, who was quite bellicose and took France's role in the world far more seriously than the ominous economic problems we were there to discuss and which he did not understand.

The conference had no immediate results. The structural crisis of the international economy thus began without the most important governments' agreeing on a diagnosis, much less on treatment.

My Friendship with Gerald Ford

T HE Washington energy conference, which was overshadowed by American-French differences, was my last act of teamwork with the Nixon administration. After that I saw Nixon only one more time while he was president, at a NATO meeting in Brussels in late June 1974. I had just become chancellor, and questions of foreign policy were in the foreground. That is why we touched only briefly on the problems that had not been solved at the Washington energy conference. Nixon complimented me on the role I had played at the conference, though his remark was not really appropriate. He seemed to me both tense and unsure of himself; he resigned six months later.

I had not previously had close contact with former Vice President Gerald Ford, who now assumed the presidency. It had been a surprise when Nixon proposed Ford for the vice presidency in October 1973, after Spiro Agnew, who had been elected in 1968 along with Nixon, had resigned because of tax irregularities. Ford had named Nelson Rockefeller to the vice presidency, so that now the two leaders of the United States had come into office in ways that were unusual though fully in conformity with the Constitution.

The indictment and legal proceedings against former President Nixon were still ahead; the world speculated whether Nixon would be found guilty. In order to avoid further shock and internal division of the nation after Vietnam and Watergate, Ford pardoned his predecessor after a few weeks. This, too, was in accordance with the Constitution, but once again was highly unusual—and almost beyond the comprehension of Europeans, since European constitutions do not recognize such a procedure (that is, a pardon *before* the legal verdict). When I learned of Gerald Ford's decision, I said to my colleagues, "Ford is one hell of a brave man."

Since Nixon was now out of the picture, some of the media pounced on Ford. In the two and a half years of his term he was treated pretty unfairly by the media in his country and especially by American television. This predominantly negative attitude was initially transmitted to Europe. But during the great Conference on Security and Cooperation in Europe in Helsinki in late July 1975 and during the first economic summit in Rambouillet in November 1975, European statesmen learned to appreciate Gerald Ford as a reliable partner in foreign affairs; they also trusted him on a personal and human level—despite unavoidable conflicts of interest and differences of opinion.

The Soviet leadership under Leonid Brezhnev, who probably did not fully understand the domestic significance of the Watergate affair, was reassured by the fact that Henry Kissinger was once again nominated as secretary of state; under Ford there seemed to be no danger of any fundamental change in the United States' international aims and methods. Even before Helsinki, the meeting between Ford and Brezhnev in Vladivostok in December 1974 probably swept away any doubts that might have remained.

I myself met and spent time with Ford eight times in extended conversations or negotiations during his brief period in office. Our first meeting, in Washington in the late autumn of 1974, was basically devoted to becoming acquainted. Beginning in May 1975, we met three times at short intervals—first in late May in Brussels on the occasion of a large NATO meeting, eight weeks later in Bonn during Ford's visit to the Federal Republic, and again a few days later in Helsinki.

During his visit to Bonn at the latest I developed a great personal confidence in the new president. That feeling has never been disappointed; nor did Gerald Ford ever take me by surprise, perhaps by making unilateral decisions, arrived at without consultation. On the contrary, he continued Nixon's foreign policy in almost every respect; during his presidency the United States—from Bonn's point of view—became an increasingly reliable and dependable partner and NATO leader.

So NATO's dual "grand strategy," as it had been formulated jointly in late 1967, remained in force: both joint security *against* the Soviet Union through joint defense capability and cooperation *with* the Soviet Union, especially in the area of arms limitation by treaty through SALT and MBFR. Of course Europe understood that, beyond these decisions, the United States had to respect its own interests along with overall Western interests in those regions that transcended the geographically definable territory of NATO; this situation was not a new reality.

In 1975 one of our trivial differences of opinion was the question of the attitude to take toward Portugal and Spain. On May 29, 1975, a discussion took place in Brussels between Ford and Kissinger on one side and myself on the other. The following dialogue ensued:

SCHMIDT: Could you possibly be somewhat more reserved in your address to the NATO Council in regard to Spain than your draft provides?

FORD: Do you want me to leave Spain out altogether?

SCHMIDT: No, but perhaps the whole passage referring to Spain could be reformulated somewhat. To us in Europe the whole Spanish problem looks a little different than it does to the United States, for whom Spain is primarily a strategic factor. The Franco era is obviously coming to an end [Francisco Franco died on November 24, 1975]. It is still not clear who will take the helm. We should be encouraging those we hope will govern after Franco. That means we must deal not only with those who are in power now.

FORD: We are now negotiating a treaty for a military base, and we assign a high priority to it. Should these negotiations fail, the alliance would suffer appreciable disadvantages. So we have to walk a tightrope.

SCHMIDT: Yes, certainly. But so that you can be sure of your bases and your special strategic ties with Spain beyond today, you should talk about it with tomorrow's rulers as well. What is also at stake is the United States' standing in Europe. No one should be able to say of the United States that it was supporting the wrong regime.

KISSINGER: We in America apply the same theories to Spain that you Europeans apply to Portugal: We are unwilling to support any movements that cannot be controlled. . . . The latest development in Portugal shifted the weight in favor of the communist-leaning officers.

SCHMIDT: It's too early to form a final judgment about the outcome of that business. Portugal is going through an economic decline, it is facing a desperate situation in that area. Even Mario Soares, whom I believe to be a courageous man, is unlikely to be able to deal with it [in 1974, after his return to Portugal, Soares first became foreign minister; he ruled the country from July 1976 to 1978]. Though the communists are well organized, when it comes to finances they are entirely dependent on Soviet aid. I do not believe the Soviet Union is prepared to supply economic help to Portugal in the grand style for long.

KISSINGER: The public confrontations between the communists and the socialists have one advantage, at least—the idea of a popular front can't arise.

FORD: What can the United States now contribute that would be useful to what happens next?

SCHMIDT: Prevent the Soviet Union's open intervention in Portugal. To be sure, so far Moscow has been rather cautious; it prefers to send Romania or East Germany to do its dirty work.

KISSINGER: That's right. But even a Romanian or Yugoslav sort of communism would have dangerous effects on NATO.

FORD: How would the Europeans react if the Azores seceded from Portugal and declared their independence?

SCHMIDT: The Eastern European propaganda machines would present it as the result of American interference. Western Europe, however, would accept a separation of the Azores if the situation in Lisbon becomes untenable. But today that is not the case. Therefore at present a declaration of independence on the part of the Azores would not be justified in the eyes of Western Europe.

I was expressing the opinion of most of my European colleagues. We thought the chances were particularly good for a shift to democracy in Spain—and we supported *all* democratic parties and labor unions to the best of our ability. Prime Minister Adolfo Suárez, the opposition leader (later prime minister) Felipe González, and especially King Juan Carlos played their parts to perfection. Today little is left of Francoism; in the meantime Spain has joined both NATO and the European Community.

The situation was somewhat different in Portugal, because that country had been a member of NATO from the outset. But since the end of António Salazar's dictatorship and most recently under Marcello Caetano, the Portuguese revolution had drifted far into communism domestically. Some of the military personnel who appeared for Portugal in the governing bodies of the alliance and of NATO expressed astoundingly naive views, some of them vulgarizations of Marxism. This was true as well and especially for Vasco Dos Santos Gonçalves, the head of government, and Costa Gomes, the head of state. I could therefore easily understand why Ford and Kissinger were turning a cold shoulder to the Lisbon regime. But even in the case of Portugal we still hoped for a turn to democracy, even though we could not overlook the East bloc attempts to underpin the communist element in the government, which was strong to begin with. Portugal too has since become a member of the European Community, after the dilettantish, semicommunist regime was abolished in 1976 by President Mario Soares. Granted, changes in Portugal's domestic policies have not so far made as firm an impression as Spain's.

In both cases Bonn gambled on positive changes and tried to contribute to that end, while Washington was skeptical. But influenced by Europe, Ford and Kissinger in fact chose not to draw the consequences that seemed to them obvious. Until then, events on the Iberian peninsula had confirmed the European assessment of the situation. For similar reasons it later seemed to me correct to oppose the forces in Europe that seemed to want to escort Turkey out of NATO when Turkey returned to a military regime. I was just as determined when I countered the American wish to force Andreas Papandreou's Greece out of NATO in view of measures he took that appeared destructive and provocative.

Of course the problems of the Iberian peninsula were not the most important topics of discussion between the Ford administration and the West German government. I focus on them here only because—with one exception, to which I will return—there was no serious difference of opinion between Washington and Bonn. Much more important in our consultations were questions related to SALT I and MBFR, and then of course the 1975 Helsinki Accord; the structural crisis in the world economy, especially oil and energy questions; the currency problem; and the Middle East and China—and finally, the purely bilateral topic of the German military payments to the United States, which I wanted to end once and for all.

As far as MBFR was concerned, Ford wanted to see rapid progress that he could show off at home. He hoped that before the actual presidential election campaign began, he would be able to withdraw some of the American troops from Europe in the train of a reduction agreement; he would be able to present this withdrawal as a success to the Congress in Washington. He had the impression that both the Soviets and the West were playing too many tactical and arithmetical tricks during the negotiations.

Ford wanted to move the matter forward, and this wish coincided with my views. As early as the late 1950s and then again ten years later as defense minister, I had advocated the establishment of a troop balance in Europe; I had expended a considerable sum of spoken and written words on this effort—without results. I therefore found Ford's attitude all the more gratifying. But the two of us did not have enough influence to propel the sluggish and pedantic MBFR negotiations in Vienna forward.

Nor did our opinions on SALT II differ. In November 1974 Ford and Kissinger had met with Brezhnev and Gromyko in Vladivostok. Obviously they had come very close to complete agreement on SALT II. Two obstacles remained, however. One had to do with internal American politics—the upcoming election in 1976, since what could have been achieved would presumably be attacked by both sides: both by certain Democrats, who would have found the agreement not far-reaching enough and by the right-wing Republicans, headed by California Governor Ronald Reagan, who would have denounced the agreement as harmful to the United States—these were the same people who, for ideological reasons, were suspicious of Kissinger's policy of balance and therefore were condemning it. Ford therefore wanted to wait to conclude SALT II until after the presidential primaries in the summer, and possibly until after the presidential election in November. So he took his time.

On the other hand, he also needed time to overcome the other obstacles: the Backfire bomber, on which the Soviets had just begun production, and the intermediate-range SS-20 missiles. In a private conversation in May 1975 Ford and I spoke very candidly about these new difficulties.

I could certainly understand why Ford was concerned with these domestic considerations, and his calculations did not annoy me. I counted on the probability of his reelection, and I never doubted that during his second term he would bring about the SALT II agreement, which was very important to Germany. As far as the Backfire bomber and, even more, the SS-20 missiles were concerned, Germany, of course, had an urgent interest in including them in the bilateral balance at which SALT II aimed. Since the Cuban missile crisis, the superiority of Soviet nuclear intermediate-range missiles in Europe had seemed to me to pose a danger, and while I was defense minister I had discussed the subject repeatedly with Melvin Laird. I was therefore glad that Gerald Ford not only understood this concern but also shared it. He specifically promised that the SS-20s and Backfires would be included in SALT II. At the time we did not put our understanding on the record. Given our personal confidential relationship, there seemed no necessity to write it down—and besides, we were not at all eager to rouse any sleeping dogs.

In May 1975 the Helsinki Conference on Security and Cooperation in Europe had not been entirely planned. In fact, it occurred in late July. There were no differences worth mentioning between Washington and Bonn concerning the contents of what was to become the Final Act and the section that dealt with the declaration of principle concerning the preservation of human rights in Europe, as well as the other political questions to be discussed in Helsinki.

President Ford's two-day state visit to Bonn at the end of July 1975— that is, just before the Helsinki Conference—therefore turned into a brilliant success for both sides. Ford's statements on Berlin and the overall defense of Europe, which he made in a small Hessian town before troops of both nations, allowed no doubt whatever of America's constancy. What we said jointly about Helsinki and the CSCE Final Act proved to everyone that in Germany the opposition of the CDU-CSU was totally isolated when it rejected the Helsinki Final Act as inadequate. But even leaving this aspect aside, we made great strides forward.

Like almost every eminent guest of state, Ford stayed at Gymnich Castle near the federal capital. The official talks were held in the Schaumburg Palace in Bonn, which had served as Konrad Adenauer's residence while he was chancellor (the move to the new chancellery had not taken place until three years later). On the wall of my office was a good and impressively lifelike portrait of August Bebel, painted in the last year of his life, that had been a gift to me from Alfred Nau. A conversation about the great Social Democratic leader, the history of the German labor movement, and the growth of the German Social Democratic party revealed, to my surprise, that the United States secretary of state was extremely knowledgeable; the American president, for his part, had a detailed idea of Bebel's great opponent, Bismarck. In the case of Kissinger, who was among the intellectual elite of the East Coast, and who in addition had been born in Germany, a knowledge of German history might have been assumed. But it seemed to me unusual in someone like Jerry Ford. I did not find a comparable familiarity with the history of my country in either of his successors.

Over dinner the conversation turned to German expressionist painting, and particularly to Emil Nolde. Hitler had ostracized almost all expressionists, had removed their paintings from the museums, and had had them destroyed or dumped them at auctions abroad. Several expressionists had not been allowed to exhibit, while others were forbidden to paint altogether. Influenced by the art classes in the Lichtwark school in Hamburg, I had been a fan of German expressionism since I was a boy, and my enthusiasm had grown over the years. In 1937, when I was eighteen, the exhibition "Degenerate Art" organized by Hitler convinced me completely of the degeneracy of National Socialism. As chancellor I used every opportunity to help the expressionists to find their well-deserved breakthrough into the awareness of both Germans and foreigners; compared to the French *fauves,* they still played only a subordinate role in the world. That was also the reason I had furnished the new chancellery with expressionist works of art, which always caused comments from foreign visitors.

This was true of Ford and Kissinger as well. We talked about Nolde's undervaluation in the American art market. Kissinger suggested a group exhibit in the United States to give the American public its first thorough overview of German expressionism. Such an exhibition was in fact mounted at the Guggenheim Museum in 1981; by now, as the guest book shows, many Americans have also made the pilgrimage to the Nolde Foundation in Seebüll, a few kilometers south of the German-Danish border.

President Walter Scheel invited Ford and Kissinger for a boat trip on the Rhine, together with prominent European guests and a large contingent of American journalists. It was a beautiful summer night. Thousands of people crowded the landing stages, and the wine queen of Linz offered the Fords a goblet of good wine. Later there was the dark outline of the Siebengebirge, hundreds of lights on the Rhine, talk about all sorts of things, including Adenauer ("Over there, in the dark, is Rhöndorf; that's where he had his house. That is why Bonn was made the capital"). Betty Ford had just undergone an operation for cancer and still felt weak; she really needed rest. But out in public she played her part magnificently, and everywhere people applauded her with all their hearts.

Our guests seemed happy: Everything taken together resembled the image of Germany the German immigrants had brought with them to America in the late nineteenth century. It was a picture of Germany our guests had preserved—in spite of Hitler and Auschwitz. Of course the Hofbräuhaus, the Nibelungs, sauerkraut, and "old Heidelberg" would have fit the picture just as easily. And a year later, on the occasion of the Bicentennial of the United States, when I invited Jerry Ford to a reception on board our training ship *Gorch Fock,* the sailing vessel dressed overall with flying pennants also fit the romantic image of Germany held by many Americans.

Nevertheless, neither Ford nor Kissinger was so naive as to think that the obvious liking of their German hosts or the tipsy Rhine journey was a full characterization of the German Federal Republic, its problems, its fears, and its hopes. Both were realists: the president as a result of the experiences of a long political career as a congressman, during which he had had to campaign to get reelected every two years—when he had had to take other people's concerns seriously. And the American secretary of state, only yesterday a Harvard professor, who knew more about modern German history than many German participants on the midnight cruise.

Both realized that the permanent division of the German nation must present a grave problem to all Germans; they knew that the division had caused not only visible wounds but also internal ones. And they recognized our hopes for healing. In these matters Ford was neither callous—he did not say, "You Germans will just have to accept the situation"—nor did he arouse illusionary expectations. After this trip *Time* magazine wrote, "No country in Europe is more pleased with Ford than West Germany. Chancellor Helmut Schmidt . . . found Ford well briefed, informed, serious. . . . What [the West Germans] treasure more than anything, however, is the sense of stability and calm they perceive in the Ford administration." This assessment was correct on every count.

Only a few days after Ford's visit to Germany we met again in Helsinki. Two things stood out during the days in Finland: the matter-of-factness with which the United States appeared as a European power and was accepted as such, and Gerald Ford's reserve and natural dignity. Even more important was the relative ease with which Gerald Ford, Valéry Giscard d'Estaing, Harold Wilson, and I arrived at arrangements for an international economic conference of the heads of government of the major industrial democracies. The idea had originally come up in a conversation between Giscard and myself. We had been thinking about a kind of continuation of the old Library Group on a higher level. But at first Washington had hesitated; its relationship with Paris had been marked by caution, at times even traces of mistrust, since the de Gaulle era. In Bonn, Ford and I worked out a joint concept, and in the meantime a good personal relationship between Ford and Giscard had also developed. On a bright summer afternoon, sitting around a garden table in Helsinki, therefore, we made plans for the first summit; so as to keep it from falling into the hands of the bureaucrats, we agreed to have all preparations made by people we would personally charge with the task. We also quickly agreed on the necessity of Japan's participation; I especially welcomed this move because it would keep Germany from being the only vanquished nation at the table. By the time Gerald Ford left Europe in early August 1975, he had made many friends among those who were governing the old continent. He had reason to be pleased with them, and they with him.

A few months later, the first of the so-called international economic summits, which was held in Rambouillet—by this time Italy had been invited as well—proved that Ford was discerning about both the economic situation of his own country and the international economy. He could boast of some success in fighting inflation, but he was not willing to exaggerate his achievements in this direction in view of the danger of growing unemployment. Paris and Washington deferred to each other on monetary policy, though without concrete results. Nevertheless, this accommodation removed an important obstacle to the reform of the IMF statutes and the impending North-South dialogue.

Despite the clear reservations of Japanese Prime Minister Takeo Miki, we parted in the awareness that the economic crisis, which had by now overtaken all nations, must not seduce us into a trade and monetary war of all against all, as had happened during the crisis of the early 1930s. Everyone had understood the strategic importance of sensible economic measures that took the international situation into consideration, and everyone was assured that all other participants had the same view. Our foreign and finance ministers had helped to bring about this atmosphere of trust, no one had given the media at home any sensational releases for domestic consumption, and all had once more witnessed a self-assured and relaxed American leadership. In my view all this counted for much more than the lack of specific agreements, which I had not expected in any case. On the contrary, from the outset we had lowered our expectations as much as possible.

Nine months later—the interval was a little too short—there was a second meeting of this sort in Puerto Rico, which Jerry Ford had called. For the first time Canada was included, and Pierre Trudeau turned out to be a productive participant. This second meeting, which turned the summits into a tradition, was also a success, in the sense that all participants agreed that the structural crisis of the international economy could be overcome only by joint action.

During the following meetings the intimate nature soon became lost. Nevertheless these summits always have a great political value: They allow for a relatively informal exchange of views on acute problems, and they stimulate an understanding of other nations' positions, especially among heads of governments and nations who are new to their office. They thus make possible a realistic assessment of the other leaders' future actions, and most important, they strengthen trust among the participants. "Nations have interests," it is said—which is true. But these interests are interpreted and pursued by the leaders, and different personalities at the head of the same state will act in very different ways. That is why it is useful for us to get to know each other well. And that is why the often-reprinted catchphrase to the effect that an international conference is useful only when it is certain from the outset that "something will come of it" is false.

The three great summit conferences of 1975—in May in Brussels, within the context of NATO; in July and August in connection with the Helsinki Conference; and in November in Rambouillet—in my opinion showed the West at a high point of unity. There was no doubt about the joint "grand strategy," there were no mutual suspicions and bitterness, and there was confidence in a moderately imposed American leadership that forebore playing out its role in public.

All this was not altogether lost after the change in the presidency in Washington, but it did crumble. When Valéry Giscard d'Estaing, Jim Callaghan, and I now meet occasionally in Vail in the Colorado mountains at Jerry Ford's invitation, and we sit of an evening over a glass of whiskey, the conversation may move away from current problems and turn nostalgically back to the mid-1970s. One or another of us, feeling somewhat melancholy—and at the same time a little arrogant—might say, "Of course in those days the world was better governed than it is now." And the rest of us take it as it is meant: with a grain of salt. Then one of us says, "Cheers" and raises his glass, and we drink a toast.

The end of the Nixon-Ford-Kissinger era was, as we can clearly see today, the end of the successful phase of the West's overall strategy that had been formulated ten years earlier, in December 1967, by Pierre Harmel in his report "The Future Tasks of the Alliance." But in 1975 and 1976 we could not have known.

As I wrote earlier, there was an important German-American problem Ford and I had to solve. It had long been my opinion that the constantly renewed medium-term agreement on German financial contributions for American troops in Germany must stop. As mentioned above, only Germany had to make these payments, though American troops stationed in other European countries also burdened the American budget and, since they were largely paid in the particular national currencies, the American balance of payments as well. The more I understood the economic context, the less acceptable it seemed to me that the Germans were the only ones who had to pay and that therefore the impression of a moral obligation had arisen. After all, the American troops were on German soil in the interests of other European nations as well—and primarily in the American interest, besides. Neither Paris nor Brussels, The Hague, or Ottawa made similar demands, although they too had stationed troop contingents on German soil.

I was always an opponent of any kind of special treatment of Germany within the Western alliance, and special treatment by the United States alone was especially out of the question. Nor was it acceptable to let the idea of an American-German master-vassal relationship arise even subconsciously on either side of the Atlantic. That was the principal reason—not so much the financial considerations—I wanted to end the German payments, which ran to billions of marks and which we had been making for decades. The reasons the United States was insisting on special payments by Germany were also less matters of the budget and the balance of payments and more psychological and political. I understood as much. The fact that this problem had hammered the last nail into the coffin of Ludwig Erhard's chancellorship a decade earlier was for me an eloquent admonition to proceed carefully.

Gerald Ford's good common sense, as well as his cabinet's certainty that Germany was a reliable ally—plus our own conviction that remaining allied with the United States was in our own best interest—made the negotiations easier. When in July 1976 we had an exchange of letters that finally brought the matter to a head, we, as well as our foreign ministers, had discussed the problem several times without arousing public attention. The crucial sentences in my letter to Ford of July 29, 1976, had been agreed upon by the two of us ahead of time. They read:

> . . . Therefore, I wish to note our agreement that the traditional balance of payments offset has lost its relevance. However, military procurement by the Armed Forces of the Federal Republic in the United States, which has formed the basic element of past such agreements, can be expected to continue as in the past. . . . The Government of the Federal Republic of Germany welcomes the intention of the United States administration to transfer a combat brigade to North Germany. It attaches special importance to this step to strengthen the defense capability of the alliance, and is prepared in this exceptional case to make a single payment of up to 171.2 million Deutsche Marks toward the cost of the military accommodation of the brigade. However, the Federal Government deems it important to state that this special, single contribution does not establish any obligation on the part of the Federal Republic of Germany to pay stationing costs which, under the Status of

the Forces Agreement and the supplementary agreement thereto, are the responsibility of the stationing power.

The stationing of an additional American brigade in Schwanewede near Bremen thus furnished the occasion for a one-time final payment; since it was small, it did not affect the economy, and it allowed the Americans to save face. The plan to shift this brigade from the United States to northern Germany was primarily attributable to the two defense ministers, Georg Leber and James Schlesinger. Clearly in this case Schlesinger did not enjoy Ford's approval from the outset, and the president must have felt somewhat pressured. In fact, I repeatedly thought I sensed that Ford was displeased with Schlesinger; in November 1975 he replaced him with Donald Rumsfeld.

Ford and his advisers—Henry Kissinger, Donald Rumsfeld, and Brent Scowcroft (who had succeeded Kissinger as national security adviser in November 1975, allowing the latter to concentrate entirely on the State Department)—had proved to be open-minded partners in ending the currency offset. Precisely because they did not boast of America's leadership role, it was easy for us to acknowledge the extensive leadership the United States in fact exerted. Concerning all essential questions of world politics—whether China or the Middle East, the overall Western strategy toward the Soviet Union or the position each of us should take in the international economic structural crisis—we either agreed in the first place or at least were able to work out a sufficient consensus. This was true of the relationship of Washington and the governments of the European partner states in general; it was especially true of German-American relations.

One difference of opinion occurred in November 1975 because of New York City's financial crisis. This American metropolis, a center of private financial trading and the world's stock markets, is also a conglomerate of industry, trade, business, and services and a cultural center of American civilization—and it is frequently on the edge of being ungovernable. Extreme wealth and widespread poverty, even flagrant misery, live cheek by jowl in the city. Whenever I looked at New York's problems, the concerns of European mayors seemed to me comparatively slight.

I admired all the men, from Fiorello La Guardia to Edward Koch, who managed to administer such a city halfway decently and successfully. By comparison, the administration of Hamburg, my hometown, is a piece of cake. The economic crisis that manifested itself in increasing unemployment beginning in 1974 brought considerable financial difficulties to almost all the great cities of the world; everywhere expenditures for social welfare grew rapidly, while tax revenues did not. But New York City found itself in an unusually severe budget crisis.

I could only speculate how far New York had previously lived beyond its means. But in the summer and autumn of 1975 rumors made the rounds concerning its supposedly imminent inability to pay its bills, and I was disquieted by the open controversy about the necessity of financial aid from the federal government, which was allegedly refused. New York's financial collapse could easily become a model for other cities that found themselves deep in debt—and not only American cities. A collapse of the interest rate of municipal bond issues could spill over onto Europe and other parts of the world, especially as it would originate in one of the world's financial centers; after all, almost every metropolis everywhere had been living beyond its means.

The city, its political representatives, the governor of the state of New York, and the Democratic opposition in Congress put the Republican president under pressure, especially because New York State was also affected. Ford too feared a precedent, though with different implications—that is, a number of other cities might come forward to raise claims of their own if New York were to be given federal help. He therefore made it a condition that the city, ignoring the countless pressure groups, must first of all impose budget cuts and thus create the conditions for permanent financial recovery. This suggestion corresponded in principle to my own way of thinking. Nevertheless, I was convinced that the city must not be allowed to fall into a situation where it was unable to pay its bills.

In early October 1975, on my way to Washington, I was asked at a press conference in New York what I thought. I made the mistake of responding to the questions. The New York media interpreted my answers as critical of the president's position. Two days later, when I met with Gerald Ford, my conscience troubled me; whatever I had said on the subject, I should not have allowed myself to be drawn into a public discussion of my host country's domestic problems in the first place. With a short reply the president courteously passed over the matter but carefully listened to my view of the matter. A few days later he arrived at an agreement with New York City.

When Ford won the primary contests over Ronald Reagan by a hairsbreadth, I was glad; I did not know Reagan, and I valued Ford highly. In November 1976, when he lost the election to Jimmy Carter, who to me was another unknown quantity, I was concerned. Ford and I had worked very closely together, as had our foreign ministers,

Genscher and Kissinger. Our collaboration had gone far beyond the area of the alliance and the overall strategy toward Moscow. We held the same views on the future role of the People's Republic of China, on the important role of Anwar Sadat and on the Middle East in general, on the role of OPEC, on the situation of the developing nations and the possibilities of providing them with the help they needed, on the economic crisis—and we had helped each other in all these areas. I was deeply grateful to the departing president of the world power that was the United States. In a long letter of farewell of November 23, 1976, I wrote:

> Among all other things you restored the integrity of the presidency and the White House and thereby trust and confidence of hundreds of millions of people—Americans and foreigners—to the United States. . . . I feel that no other German chancellor ever felt so free, on such friendly terms and so reliably rooted in a sense of friendship with an American president as I have felt with you during your presidency. . . . When I myself and the coalition parties supporting my Government in the Federal Republic of Germany won the federal elections in October by the skin of our teeth, we probably just had that bit more luck than you. Quite certainly, one of the causes for our success in the elections was that German voters were conscious of the excellent relations existing between the United States and my country, for which you deserve much of the credit.
>
> I am sure I have not always been an easy partner for you—but how could it have been otherwise when every head of government has to represent and protect what he believes to be the interests of his own country. This indeed makes mutual confidence all the more precious. . . .

Of course, my wife and I also thanked Betty Ford, whom we had come to value greatly. In my letter to the president I expressly mentioned the great help given us by Henry Kissinger and Ford's secretary of the Treasury, William Simon. In closing I stressed the role played by our superb personal relationship.

Gerald Ford thanked me warmly for my letter, and we promised each other that we would continue to cultivate our personal friendship. In fact, to my great satisfaction and enrichment, this close friendship has continued to this day.

My farewell letter to Kissinger and his reply were of a similar nature. When Kissinger handed his office over to his successor, Cyrus Vance, we had known each other for almost two decades. I had first met Henry Kissinger in the mid-1950s, when he had won international recognition with an intelligent book about nuclear warfare. I had not been at all in agreement with the thesis of the book, but I owed many interesting ideas to it. In 1960, when in a book of my own I set out to develop alternative ideas by summarizing the British and American literature on military strategy, which was as yet almost unknown in the Federal Republic of Germany, and comparing them to the position dictated by West German interests, Kissinger helped me in various ways. The same was true in later years, when he had long since become security adviser and later secretary of state. I believe that now and then I was of some help to him as well.

Conceptually as well as operationally Kissinger always saw the overall strategy of his nation as a unified whole. His basic moral values were typically American, but he was much too rational to use America's power as a policeman for moral uplift, as many Americans tend to do when it comes to international policies. Kissinger was a strategist of the West-East balance—advocating neither the striving for superiority that was later so noisily propagated by the right wing of the Republican Party under Reagan nor yielding to the Soviet expansionist drive or Soviet armament ambition, as he was sometimes accused of doing. While he was chancellor, Willy Brandt had had occasional problems with Kissinger, who in the early stages mistrusted the motives behind the German *Ostpolitik*. I, too, had my differences of opinion with him now and then, but far more often I agreed with him. At that time, most of all, there was an extraordinary degree of mutual trust. To this day, more than a decade later, nothing has changed.

Jimmy Carter:
Idealistic
and Fickle

I N January 1977 President James Earl Carter took his place on the world stage. A former governor of Georgia, he came bereft of any experience in international affairs. His qualifications consisted instead of a great store of goodwill, a considerable intelligence, and an unmistakable personal sense of mission. This last trait was probably also responsible for his victory over Ford. It is likely that the election would have had a different outcome if America had already overcome the disappointment, humiliation, and shock of the Vietnam War and the Watergate scandal. Many Americans hoped Carter would lead the country to a new beginning.

As always, Europeans were markedly more skeptical. The European governments had no need of a new beginning in Washington; instead, they had high hopes for a confirmation of America's overall strategy and its consistency in pursuing it. These hopes were soon dashed. From the moment he assumed office, Carter left no doubt of his intention of making a considerable change in the United States' attitude toward the Soviet Union. The strategy of the Nixon-Ford-Kissinger era would not be continued. After a relatively short time it also became evident that Carter was not at all consistent in pursuing his new line. Resistance from other governments, his own scruples, and his critical intelligence repeatedly led to revisions of the insights and intentions he had so recently articulated.

In retrospect the most frightening aspect seems to me the fact that he largely changed his assessment of the Soviet Union in fewer than four years. In his last year in office, after the Soviet invasion of Afghanistan, he declared publicly that he now correctly understood the true nature of the Soviet Union. This statement expressed public admission of his basically false estimate of Moscow during the earlier years of his administration.

From my European view of the situation, Carter's first response to Soviet policies in 1977 contained serious flaws. The accusation he publicly leveled over and over, that Soviet citizens were deprived of all human rights, could not, of course, alter their lives in any way, but it would inevitably embitter the Soviet leadership. The failure of Carter's human rights campaign could have been foreseen, as well as his disappointment that it failed. He lacked any knowledge of Russian history, tradition, and mentality. He did not know that civil rights in the sense established by the English, American, and French revolutions did not exist for Russians and had never existed. Nor did he realize how sensitive the reaction of the Soviet leadership to his campaign would be; the Soviets saw it as a hostile attempt to undermine their dominance.

Of course an American moralist and idealist can envisage worldwide pressure on the Soviet leadership, exerted with all the political and economic tools at America's disposal. He can also harbor illusions about the success of such a campaign. He can even achieve quite far-reaching agreement in the West and in parts of the East. But he must be aware that the Kremlin has hegemony over a number of other states and over countless millions of people and that it can tighten the ideological, police, and military screws when that seems advisable.

Therefore Bonn was not the only capital that feared a worsening of the situation for people living in Eastern Europe, especially the hundreds of thousands of Germans who had been waiting for exit papers for a long time. Other governments in the Council of Europe were equally worried about the danger to détente implicit in Carter's human rights policy. Europeans had seen from the outset that the human rights section of the Helsinki Accord could be realized only after favorable political and economic developments in Eastern Europe, and even then only very slowly and in small steps. We hoped there might be gradually increasing freedom of action for the governments in Warsaw, Budapest, Prague, and East Berlin; we feared a relapse into the brutal manipulations of the Brezhnev days. Our memories of Budapest in 1956, of

Prague in 1968, of Dubček and the powerlessness of the West in such situations were only too vivid.

In the spring of 1977, when Jimmy Carter was ready to resume the SALT negotiations, which had been interrupted during the election year, he first sent his secretary of state, Cyrus Vance, to call on the most important European allies. Vance knew Europe and the rest of the world well; he had previously undertaken operational missions in the international area. Many European politicians, myself among them, had come to value Vance long before he held office. He was knowledgeable, sensitive to others' interests, an important member of the Council on Foreign Relations in New York, experienced in international dealings, reliable—and a gentleman through and through.

Quite clearly Vance had been given an impossible job: He was to persuade the Kremlin to go far beyond the joint declaration of intent for SALT II that had been aimed at by Ford and Brezhnev a good two years before, in Vladivostok. The two heads of state had wanted to replace the SALT I interim agreement on nuclear strategic offensive weapons, which would expire in the fall of 1977, with a medium-term treaty; Carter wanted the same thing. But Carter was striving for considerably larger reductions in the arsenals of both sides than had been envisaged in Vladivostok.

I was greatly worried that this proposal would make Brezhnev's position much more difficult. He was not only the man in the Kremlin most important to SALT, he had also been the one who had brought about the Soviet willingness to compromise in Vladivostok; Carter was forced to rely on his will and influence. In my estimation it was important not to compromise Brezhnev in the eyes of the other Politburo members. Someone who continually compromised the Soviet leaders by waging a human rights campaign could hardly hope to persuade them to go beyond the old agreements for arms limitation to actual disarmament.

I told Vance that the Soviets would be dismayed. Carter's ways of thinking, which could not help but remain mysterious to them, would lead them to suspect intentions they could not decipher, and as a consequence they would reject the proposals. Secretly Vance seemed to agree with me, but his president had given him explicit instructions to strive for deep cuts in both weapons arsenals. To this purpose he was to submit to the Kremlin a new, comprehensive draft.

In fact when Vance visited Moscow, the Kremlin reacted as expected: Brezhnev and Gromyko insisted on the agreements hammered out in Vladivostok and made no counterproposals to Carter's idealistic plans. The American president thus suffered a defeat, particularly since he had deliberately allowed his proposals to be made public even before the Moscow meeting, stressing the necessity of diminishing the large stockpiles of long-range missiles. But that was precisely the weapons category in which the Soviets had superiority; how were they to give it up without gaining an advantage in another area?

The failure of Carter's suggestion for deep cuts placed him in a double dilemma. For one, he was now compelled to work out a new concept. For another, he had handed the opponents of SALT a yardstick against which a short time later, in 1979, they could measure the SALT II agreement, which was clearly weaker—and thus they could simply reject it.

In that same year, 1977, Carter gave the American opponents of SALT a further argument: He canceled the planned B-1 long-range bomber program in favor of modernizing the existing B-52s. No matter how well founded his decision to go against the plans of the Nixon-Ford administration may have been, it gained Carter the reputation—which he could never again shake—of being too "soft" on the Soviet Union. His SALT negotiating position was actually weakened by his abandonment of the B-1, since the Soviets had already accepted its introduction. In addition, no provisions had been made for the resumption of SALT negotiations. Not even a date had been set.

Given this muddled situation, in the course of 1977 the Europeans had plenty of time to become better informed about the ideas on SALT II that were then being considered in Washington and to analyze them. In the course of this analysis it became clear to me that, in contrast to Ford, Carter had given no thought to including the Eurostrategic SS-20 intermediate-range missiles and the Backfire bomber—which the Soviets had for some time been deploying in relatively high numbers every month—in the limitation of strategic weapons he had in mind. His plan involved limiting only the cruise missiles that were carried on long-range airplanes; Washington did not consider that the Soviet cruise missiles that were directed exclusively at European targets might well be a threat.

At first I was very reserved in expressing my worries about this negotiating concept. I could not immediately figure out whether what was behind this neglect of Soviet intermediate-range nuclear missiles, which were aimed almost exclusively at Western Europe and therefore chiefly at targets in the German Federal Republic, was primarily the fear that otherwise some of the American nuclear weapons stationed in Europe would be included in the negotiations or whether it was a matter of being considerate of the French and British intermediate-range missiles.

Some Europeans suspected that the refusal to include the intermediate-range missiles directed at European targets in the negotiations concealed Washington's intention merely to reduce the strategic threat to American territory without being bothered by any European security interests. I thought that a mixture of all three motives was probable. The increasingly brusque rejection of my arguments, however, reinforced my impression that the third motive was in fact the crucial one.

During 1977 I personally expressed my concerns to the president and repeatedly to his national security adviser, Zbigniew Brzezinski. When I visited Carter in Washington in mid-July 1977, I had previously held conversations with Tito, Kádár, and Gierek; I was therefore able to communicate to him the great value even the Communist leaders of Eastern Europe placed on Brezhnev's acceptance of détente and the depth of their awareness that by no means every member of the Politburo in the Kremlin shared this acceptance. I advised Carter to give Leonid Brezhnev an advantage over his colleagues by providing him with exclusive information. When, for example, Carter had decided to assume the domestic and international risk of discontinuing the B-1 bomber, he could have informed Brezhnev ahead of time.

Carter objected that so far the Russians had not understood his policies. He asked me whether I thought it possible that the reports Anatoli Dobrynin, the Soviet ambassador in Washington, sent back to Moscow were not accurate. I pointed out that Dobrynin's reports would certainly have to go through the Moscow foreign ministry, where they would be evaluated, before they reached Brezhnev's desk—if they even got as far as his desk. It was therefore advisable, I continued, for the American president and the Soviet general secretary to cultivate a personal contact. Carter seemed to want to take up this suggestion; but to the end of his term in office there was no lasting personal relationship between Carter and Brezhnev. The situation vacillated from suspicion (1977) through brotherly kisses (Vienna in 1979) to bitter reproaches (a year later).

My other suggestion, which I first advanced with diplomatic caution, that Eurostrategic intermediate-range missiles be included among the weapons negotiated in SALT was much more important to me than Carter's and Brezhnev's personal relations; but my ideas in this area fell on deaf ears when it came to Carter and his advisers. The roughly six thousand nuclear warheads, mounted on weapons of the most varied sort, which the United States controlled on West German soil alone were declared in Washington quite benignly to be "theater nuclear weapons"; in the same way, the Soviet nuclear missiles designated for use on European soil were seen the same way. The range of these weapons was not great enough for either side to reach the territory or even the capital of the other world power (with a few insignificant exceptions on the southwestern edges of the Soviet Union, which could be reached from the eastern Mediterranean). In essence, the only people threatened by the missiles were those living in countries allied with the world powers; and so the world powers did not take the problem very seriously.

Even the language that had come into use was absurd: The possibility of becoming the victim of nuclear destruction was designated a "strategic" quality; the possibility that people in the European nations might be destroyed was assigned merely a "tactical" quality. In addition, and quite unnecessarily, it seemed almost blasphemous to Europeans to hear talk of "theater weapons," meaning theater of war. Seventy-five million Germans were said to be living at the center of the imagined "theater of war," and it was easy to imagine that in case of armed conflict the "theater" would essentially remain limited to the two German states. For psychological and semantic reasons alone I therefore generally spoke of "Eurostrategic" weapons threatening my people.

I explained to Carter and Brzezinski over and over that we could not accept a situation that placed such a high value on the nuclear threat to and vulnerability of the United States that it must be urgently limited and at the least brought into balance (though I shared that opinion) while at the same time the equally obvious nuclear threat to and vulnerability of Germany was being neglected. I could not accept a view that took this latter danger to be so unimportant that no effort need be made at either quantitative limitation or approximate balance. Every time we talked, I expressed my increasing concern. I mentioned it to both the Americans and the Soviets, using the same wording and the same arguments. Later I gained the depressing impression that Leonid Brezhnev was able to understand my worry better than was Jimmy Carter.

I saw Carter as well as Vance several times in 1977. During this time it was obvious that Brzezinski's influence over the president was growing. The national security adviser was given increasing liberty for his international operations, and it became increasingly clear that the people in the White House frequently passed over Cyrus Vance, whom we all respected, and the State Department. As a result of his growing influence, Brzezinski called on me twice in 1977; he presented himself unabashedly as the self-assured agent of a world power. He probably thought of himself as a practitioner of realpolitik, but he was a hawk as far as Soviet policy was concerned.

The president, for his part, was a moralist. Carter and Brzezinski both overestimated the ability of the White House to shape the world merely by taking stands. This attitude became especially clear a year later, when the United States mounted a huge propaganda campaign to keep Mohammed Reza Shah Pahlevi in power without any thought to the cost—that Khomeini's successor regime would remain an archenemy of the United States for the foreseeable future.

Carter's idea of the superiority of his moral position and his overestimation of the ease with which international politics could be manipulated, combined with Brzezinski's inclination, as the representative of a world power, quite simply to ignore the interests of America's German allies—there had been nothing like it in German-American relations since the days of Lyndon Johnson's dealings with Ludwig Erhard.

Differences of opinion surfaced even in the first six months of the Carter administration. Only a few days after taking office in January 1977 Carter, speaking through his vice president, Walter ("Fritz") Mondale, urged us to entertain an expansive monetary and financial policy. This suggestion, which met with no response, recommended a concentrated Keynesian policy of deficit spending, to apply to the whole Western world. Pointing out that worldwide inflation would be the inevitable result, we rejected the proposal. We also withstood Carter's attempt, by withholding shipments of nuclear fuel to us, to force us to break our contract with Brazil by refusing to make technology for the civilian use of nuclear energy available to that country. According to the Nuclear Nonproliferation Treaty, we were thoroughly entitled to such shipments.

On the Double Track of the TNF Resolution

I N the summer of 1977 disagreements as to the proper response to Soviet SS-20s armament were added to our other differences of opinion. In September I took a great deal of time to make Brzezinski understand the strategic position of both my country and the divided German people. The political threat to the Federal Republic of Germany by the Soviet Union's rapidly growing SS-20 armada played the principal role.

My effort had only slight results. Brzezinski felt that none of these matters was for Bonn to worry about, that they concerned only the United States. Should the Soviet Union ever threaten the Federal Republic with SS-20s, the United States, using its strategic nuclear weapons, would be in a position to counter the threat.

At the outset Carter agreed with his security adviser; like Brzezinski, he lacked any understanding of my concern; nevertheless he remained cordial and courteous. Fifteen months later, however, there was a quite different outcome—not, of course, before a number of serious additional disagreements and only after I had voiced my concerns in a speech to the International Institute for Strategic Studies (IISS).

This address, which I held in London on October 28, 1977, was later sometimes called the hour of birth of the so-called TNF resolution, the instrument used by the North Atlantic alliance in response to the deployment of SS-20s in late 1979. In fact—my text leaves no doubt—I did not pursue the goal of responding to Soviet preliminary arming with Western rearming; rather, I demanded that both Eurostrategic nuclear weapons and conventional fighting forces in Europe be included in the arms limitation the two superpowers were striving to achieve in SALT II. Going further, I requested that the subject of so-called enhanced radiation weapons (ERW) introduced by Carter be investigated from the standpoint of the effect these new nuclear weapons would have on arms limitation efforts.

For the rest, my speech mainly addressed current economic problems. In this context I raised a number of topics on which Bonn and Washington also had different views—for example, energy policy and approaches to East-West trade. I made an effort to speak in a courteous tone of voice, and I avoided any pointed remarks; I deliberately ended with two complementary quotes from recent statements by Carter and Brezhnev. Nevertheless the international audience realized—at least during the subsequent conversation at dinner—that the German chancellor was emphasizing matters that were clearly at odds with what was favored by the new American president.

Washington was first surprised, then angry, and finally perplexed. Subsequently, in 1978, the White House revised its thinking concerning Soviet Eurostrategic weapons. The United States administration understood that in fact it was imperative not to neglect what we called the gray zone (an expression that referred to the strategic area covered neither in the MBFR talks, which had been going on for years in Vienna, nor in the current SALT negotiations).

In late 1978 Carter suggested a four-power meeting for January 1979, to take place on American soil; in fact it took place on the French Antilles island of Guadeloupe. The agenda covered questions of international and security policy. The fact that the head of the West German government was taking his place beside the heads of government of Great Britain, France, and the United States, a visible fourth in the NATO leadership group, caused raised eyebrows among some observers.

We met in the shade of palm fronds on the Guadeloupe beach. Brilliant sunlight and a mild ocean breeze put us in a pleasant mood. During the discussion Carter brought up the problem of the gray zone. It was clear that this question troubled me in particular, he began; in order to remove this bone of contention, he was proposing that American intermediate-range missiles be deployed in Europe to oppose the

Soviet SS-20s. Such a move would reestablish parity. Carter asked my opinion, but I preferred to remain quiet for the time being. Since I had not been prepared for this suggestion, I merely pointed out that the two other heads of government represented nuclear powers and that I preferred to wait and learn their position. And that is the procedure we followed.

I could not make out whether or not Jim Callaghan had expected the topic. In any case, he said that in the end such a step would probably be necessary, but that it should be taken only if Soviet-American arms limitation negotiations on the gray zone were to lead to a negative outcome. Callaghan urged that such negotiations be undertaken soon.

Valéry Giscard d'Estaing seconded this suggestion, though with one significant qualification: Because the Soviets, with their ongoing deployment of SS-20s, already had a great advantage, such negotiations could drag on indefinitely, until they ended in failure; the Soviets, after all, held the better cards. Therefore the United States would have to set a time limit on the negotiations before they ever started. If, after the agreed-upon time had run out, no resolution had been achieved, the American intermediate-range missiles would be deployed. What was crucial was that the Soviets understand this determination from the outset.

I was the last to speak. I agreed with Giscard. It was clear to me that such a step would not meet with undivided approval in Europe and in my own party. But I had long been convinced of the necessity of parity, especially in the gray zone. For a long time I had wanted the West and the East to negotiate the matter. It was obvious that such negotiations could hardly be successful without a Western pawn. But since the Western pawn consisted of no more than a declaration of intent possibly to station their own intermediate-range missiles four years later, it was to be expected that the Soviets in the meantime would mobilize their propaganda machine against such plans and that these efforts would be concentrated on Germany. That is why I stressed the fact that the Federal Republic of Germany must not be the only country to make its land available for stationing the American intermediate-range missiles; the territory of other European NATO states must also be open to deployment if action were actually to be taken. In view of de Gaulle's doctrine, still in effect under Giscard, concerning France's nuclear autonomy, it was clear to me that France would not participate under any circumstances.

Carter accepted the solution thus worked out by his three principal European allies. This agreement was the genesis of what later came to be called the TNF resolution, which was formalized by the NATO council of ministers ten months later, in December 1979, and which was to give rise to fierce altercations, primarily in Belgium, Holland, and West Germany. In 1980 it was also the object of fierce altercations with Carter—but I will touch on that later. In Guadeloupe, however, the sun was still shining. The future role of China, the situation in Iran, the position of the Soviet Union, and the problems in the Middle East occupied the foreground of our further discussion.

The Guadeloupe meeting was harmonious and pleasant for the four wives as well—and for Carter's young daughter, Amy, who was along this time as always. The "ladies' programs" customary at all state visits or conferences arranged by protocol are often boring if not torturous for the wives. Many people who watch television reports believe it must be a great pleasure for the politicians' wives to represent their country in a quasi-official capacity. In reality the opposite is more often the case—just as the wives and families of leading politicians must always make enormous sacrifices in private life. But on Guadeloupe the situation was different: There was a splendid evening party on an old Creole estate belonging to friends of Giscard's. We learned how to open coconuts with a machete and were in a cheerful frame of mind. My wife has a particularly happy memory of spending half a day steering a large trimaran that had just crossed the Atlantic.

Carter continued Nixon's China policy. Gerald Ford had sent future Vice President George Bush to Beijing as his personal representative. Carter raised the American presence in China to a full-scale embassy and initiated regular diplomatic relations. In the eyes of the European governments such behavior was logical and sensible. The Federal Republic of Germany had taken the same step even earlier; we had been counting for a long time on China's impending role as a world power, though it was hard to calculate how much time would have to pass before that day. However, we carefully avoided exploiting the Kremlin's fears and playing Beijing off against Moscow. We never forgot that the Soviet troops stationed farthest into the West were only an hour east of West German borders, and Soviet planes only minutes away. By contrast, China was far distant. It would take decades for its fighting forces to be even approximately equal to Soviet military might. Most of all, in spite of the theory of the inevitability of a third world war, advocated during Mao Zedong's lifetime, Beijing had no occasion to intervene in West-East tensions other than occasionally and peripherally; when such an occasion did arise, the Chinese leadership usually made do with psychological propagandistic commentary.

From the entirely different geographic perspective of the United States, at first glance the situation might seem very different as well. When Beijing wanted to buy American as well as European weapons, Brzezinski thought for a time that this would be an opportunity to create additional tension between China and the Soviet Union and to link it to American foreign policy. We Europeans united in advising Carter against this approach; he followed this advice. He was already finding it hard enough being understood by the Kremlin.

Partial Success

in the

Middle East

THE definitive normalization of American-Chinese relations aside, Carter's principal successes in foreign affairs were the Panama Canal treaties and his contribution to the partial success of Egyptian President Anwar Sadat's magnificent peace mission. Sadat had traveled to Jerusalem in November 1977. At Carter's initiative, the Camp David process involving Sadat and Israeli Prime Minister Menachem Begin culminated in March 1979. As host, he mediated the discussions and finally brought about the peace treaty. This initiative, as well as his personal travel diplomacy in Cairo and Jerusalem, represented an enormous risk for Carter as far as the response at home was concerned, especially as by this time the revolution in Iran had given rise to sharp criticism of his policies concerning Teheran. The partial success attained by the peace accords will always have to be judged as Carter's achievement.

Bonn played only a secondary role in this process. It consisted of conversations held on the edges, as it were, with the Saudi king and with Crown Prince Fahd—who, as prime minister, was a person of some importance—and of many contacts with Sadat, who was seeking an exchange of opinions with me anyway. Aside from the return of the Sinai Peninsula, which was of crucial importance to him, Sadat was unable to achieve his goal—autonomy for the Palestinians in the West Bank and the Gaza Strip. Nevertheless he accepted as the price of his endeavor a precarious isolation for Egypt from the other Arab states. Cairo clearly understood the danger not only to the country but also to Sadat personally. Since in his generosity Sadat was taking such risks upon himself, the United States apparently did not believe that it was necessary to take any special measures to keep this risk to a minimum.

For us in Bonn there was no reason to intervene, though I was concerned enough to note that because the peace accords held no solution for the Israeli-occupied territories in the West Bank and the Gaza Strip, they might isolate Egypt within the Arab League and therefore make it increasingly dependent on the United States. I was also very aware that the process could not help but show the United States as the unconditional ally of Israel and therefore alienate especially the Saudi leadership.

Until this time Riyadh had kept very quiet; at the outset the Saudis had tolerated Sadat's initiative, though without formally approving it. King Khalid's hopes rested on a "solution" to the problem of Jerusalem: that is, internationalization of the area containing the holy sites, with the flag of the Prophet flying over the Dome of the Rock, the site from which Mohammed had ascended to heaven, the Israeli flag flying at the Wailing Wall, and a comparable symbol to mark the Christian memorials. Jerusalem would be the holy place of the three great religions of the world. Although the pricing policies of OPEC, which had turned international economics upside down, would have been impossible without Saudi leadership, Washington had dealt cautiously with Riyadh until this time. The Saudis were all the more disappointed by Camp David, which disavowed their vision of a peaceful solution.

The European heads of state met in Venice on June 12 and 13 and agreed on a declaration on the Mideast. We based our statement on United Nations Resolutions 242 and 338 as well as our own positions since 1977. We stated that we intended to consult with the various parties and to take action according to the outcome of these conversations. The members of the European Community felt obligated to do no less in view of the traditional ties between and common interests of Europe and the Mideast. Carter expressed indifference to these proposals. Israel's influence on the American media and thus on American domestic policy apparently seemed to him to be too strong and a balanced Mideast policy therefore was too risky. The European proposals therefore went unanswered.

But just then a chain of cataclysmic events fundamentally changed the overall situation in the Middle East. In January 1979 a revolutionary uprising of the masses had toppled the Shah's regime, which in its last period had been truly megalomaniacal. A phase of chaos and crisis lasting several years was followed by the establishment of the fanatically anti-American (and anti-Western) Khomeini regime.

In December 1979 the Soviet Union had invaded Afghanistan and after two years of Soviet intervention had blatantly installed a communist satellite regime.

In November 1980 Iraq invaded the border regions of Iran. Contrary to all Baghdad's expectations, this adventure would lead to a long and bitter war.

American authority in the entire Mideast region diminished rapidly after November 1979, when the Iranis occupied the American embassy in Teheran and took fifty-two American citizens hostage. This action was first tolerated by Khomeini and subsequently overtly supported. The amateur preparations and weak execution of a failed military liberation action dealt the final blow to Carter's reputation.

It was possible to argue about whether the use of military force was justified in this instance. Vance had apparently voiced concern on the question of international law as well as other considerations—but in any case, he resigned before the operation was actually carried out.

However, all previous political attempts to influence Teheran had remained fruitless, and thus almost everyone was prepared to grant Washington the right to defend the life and liberty of its citizens in Iran. Obviously there was no one left in the chaos that was Iran who had the authority to guarantee the safety of foreign nationals.

Furthermore, two spectacular actions of a few years earlier were roughly comparable: In 1977 terrorists had hijacked an airplane transporting almost a hundred Germans and had diverted it to Mogadishu, Somalia, where they held the passengers captive, threatening them with death; the passengers were rescued by force. There was also the forcible rescue of the hijacked Israelis in Entebbe, Uganda. In both cases the rescue operations were carried out far from the home nation and by the use of armed forces secretly flown to the scene. The operation in Mogadishu had been risky because it had to be improvised within a very few hours. Nevertheless, it had been much easier to carry out than the Entebbe operation, because the president of Somalia, Mohammed Said Barrah, had given his approval.

The effort to free the American hostages in Teheran was an even more difficult operation than Entebbe. But there was plenty of time to prepare. It was all the more important to plan carefully and provide adequate matériel and personnel strength, especially as the rescue mission had to travel several hundred miles from its landing site to Teheran and back. The overly hasty scrubbing of the operation when it had hardly begun, the obvious nervousness of the people carrying it out, the confusion at the operation site—all these caused me and other heads of government to feel some doubt as to the effectiveness of the Americans' conventional forces deployed in Europe. Of course none of the European governments let these feelings be known. Reagan's bombastic landing operation on the little Antilles island of Grenada in 1983 did nothing to allay these doubts.

The Soviet air defense's outrageous shooting down of a Korean passenger plane that had deviated from its course strengthened my doubts as to the solidity of the American operations capability. Of course the Soviet reaction was scandalous; the West came to know all about the separate steps that led to the final action through the recorded radio contacts. United States radar reconnaissance over the North Pacific, especially around Kamchatka and Sakhalin, should have realized that a deadly drama was unfolding. But the Korean passenger plane was not warned, and the Soviet command center was not informed that a tragic misunderstanding was beginning to unfold. I still have the feeling that in the American armed forces regulations play too large a role and that training the junior officers to make independent decisions is neglected. There are many signs that the desire for independence among the lower ranks and commands is even discouraged. In any case, even tactical fighting decisions are made far too high up, "far from the line." In the Second World War, too, it seems that tactically clever military leaders such as George Patton and Omar Bradley were the exceptions that proved the rule.

Of course when there is an acute threat that nuclear weapons will be involved, leadership must come from the state's political leaders. It is probable, however, that the military leadership system of the United States is too closely tailored to this eventuality. Even aside from that circumstance, the accumulation of more than 30,000 soldiers and officials in the Pentagon is evidence of the top-heaviness of the military apparatus. The Carter administration was in no way responsible for this situation; it took over a clumsy existing system; granted, it made no attempt to reform it.

The failure of Carter's rescue mission in Teheran was the climax of an inappropriate American policy toward Iran. In the 1950s the Shah, with help from the United States intelligence service, had survived a putsch attempt by the popular premier, Mohammed Mossadegh; since that time the American construct of the Central Treaty Organization (CENTO) Pact, with Iran as its anchor, had essentially supported the Shah. That was the beginning of the American predilection for the man on the Peacock Throne. The fondness remained long after the CENTO Pact had stopped having any significance and long after Reza Pahlevi had lost all contact with reality.

The Shah ruled the country primarily with the help of his secret police, with the help of the military, and finally—after the first oil price explosion, which he had helped instigate—with the help of overwhelming financial power. This seduced him into an effort at industrialization so precipitous that neither the traditional social structure nor the infrastructure (ports, streets, electricity supply, and municipal services) could keep pace with it. Excessive demands were thoughtlessly made on the land and its citizens. All opposition was brutally suppressed. The upper ten thousand, on the other hand, lived in the lap of luxury. Corruption and self-enrichment reached an extent I had never seen in any other country.

As early as 1975 a short visit to Teheran had persuaded me that this regime could not last long. The only one who opened her mouth at the court of the Shah without being asked by the king of kings was the intelligent and brave Farah Dibah. I have seen such courtly submission only one other time in my life—at the "court" of Nicolae Ceauşescu, whose family clan exploited his country in the name of Marxism and just about deified the head of state.

Quite a few German businessmen, as well as businessmen from other European nations and the United States, made pilgrimages to Teheran in those days; everybody wanted a piece of the prosperity. Western executives peddled their wares, and all admonitions to exercise caution fell on deaf ears. In 1977 the various opposition groups began to demonstrate; the government responded with bloody measures to suppress them, and the chain of mutual escalation came to a climax in 1978.

In January 1979 the Shah left the country. It was not until the last few weeks before his flight that Washington understood how serious the situation was. But now the United States was being made to pay for neglecting to contact any of the opposition groups, especially the Shiite Muslim forces which in the end established a government. Their rule, which was no less dictatorial than the toppled reign of the Shah had been, was under the spiritual leadership of Khomeini, who banished and defamed the Shah. From one moment to the next, the United States had to redefine its entire Mideast strategy and secure new bases of support. At the outset many of the crucial forces were against Washington; after the Soviet invasion of Afghanistan, however, the fear of the Soviet Union felt in almost the entire region had turned in favor of the United States.

Because of its great distance from the dramatic changes in the Middle East, the Federal Republic of Germany probably found it easier to recognize the objective problems than Washington, which was more directly involved. Through its appearance of overt partisanship for Israel and against the Palestinians, the United States had increasingly alienated the Islamic world, in the end even the conservative and pro-Western states in the region. Furthermore, the abrupt abandonment of the Shah after so many protestations of friendship shocked both Saudi Arabia and Egypt, in spite of all the criticism these nations had leveled at the monarch. When Washington was unwilling even to grant Reza Pahlevi exile, Sadat came to the aid of the man who was by this time terminally ill and brought him to Egypt. When Carter added insult to injury by making public accusations of Pakistan's Zia ul-Haq, he largely gambled away his position in the region.

Carter's reaction to the Soviet occupation of Afghanistan was equally badly thought out. He launched a partial trade embargo (especially affecting wheat) and announced a boycott of the summer Olympics to be held in Moscow in the summer of 1980; Brzezinski made polemical speeches on the necessity of "punishing" the Soviet Union. But their means were not adequate, nor did the allied nations agree on such action; in recompense Brzezinski had his picture taken for release in the international press showing him standing at the Afghan border holding a submachine gun. Carter cut back on United States diplomatic relations with Moscow and gave up working for the ratification of SALT II.

There was little chance of ratification by the United States Senate in any case. By ending the process, Carter now tried to make a foreign affairs virtue of a domestic necessity. The primary campaign for the presidential election of November 1980 was in full swing, and Ronald Reagan, a Republican candidate for president, criticized the SALT II agreement in the sharpest terms. All through the country strong anti-Soviet sentiment grew. Carter tried to adjust to this trend, but neither his authority nor his power were sufficient to control it, to preserve a perspective, and to hold on to the decision-making power over the political process regarding the Soviet Union.

Nevertheless, the Carter administration managed in a relatively short time to redefine a number of strategic points for a future American policy on the Persian Gulf. The relationship with Pakistan was smoothed out; Washington and Islamabad needed each other by this time. Agreements on bases were made with Oman, Somalia, and Kenya. Since the overall American strategy would not allow direct military support of Israel—while on the other hand relations with Saudi Arabia, which had been disappointing in many regards, had cooled—Egypt willy-nilly became an anchor of the American position. But this situation put an additional burden on Sadat's domestic situation and placed him in even greater jeopardy as far as foreign relations were concerned; the seeds of discontent grew when in late 1980 the first maneuvers of the newly created Rapid Deployment Forces (RDF) were held on Egyptian soil.

But all these efforts also had another side: Both the "left-wing," self-styled "progressive" Arab governments and the traditionalist-conservative regimes of the region gained the impression that the United States was striving to achieve a position of hegemony in the Mideast. This idea caused them to fear that *both* superpowers would intervene directly in the Iran-Iraq war, and since the Soviet forces seemed far away, anti-American sentiment prevailed. The official statement by Reagan's secretary of state, Alexander Haig, on March 18, 1981, concerning the "strategic understanding" between the United States and Israel only accelerated this trend.

Just as unnecessary was Reagan's military engagement in the minefield of Lebanon in 1983, which had such an unfortunate outcome and which was hopeless from the outset. No one in Europe understood exactly how this military action was supposed to clarify the confused conditions there.

Paris and London have a greater knowledge and understanding of the Middle East than Washington has, and also a great deal more experience. This experience with the political and religious powers of the region go back for generations along both the Seine and the Thames. Madrid has even older—though more limited—insights into the Arab mentality. Nevertheless—or rather, precisely for this reason—no European government and certainly not the European Community had the idea that the West might offer or put into practice a "solution" to "the problem of the Middle East." Europe knew that the last time there had been a long period of peace in the region, or at least a large part of it, was under the Ottoman Empire. But today such an empire is impractical both in fact and ethically. The Ottoman and Habsburg empires collapsed with the First World War; any idea of establishing similar control over the Mideast or the Balkans must remain a fantasy. This truth was brought home to both Washington and Moscow.

The Americans are more optimistic in this respect. They do not understand that young Palestinians' acts of sabotage against a foreign military occupation that has lasted for twenty years cannot simply be condemned wholesale as "international terrorism." The fight against such acts will remain unsuccessful as long as the causes of the bitterness are not removed or substantially relieved. The Americans do not understand Moslem extremists' readiness, deeply rooted in Arab tradition and religious mentality, to sacrifice themselves; this readiness is most strongly marked among the Shiites in Iran but also exists in Lebanon, where it visibly shocks the world almost every day. The Americans do not see that the situation in Lebanon by itself raises a dozen problems that cannot be addressed in isolation. The region from Cyprus to Kurdistan and from the Blue Nile to the Khyber Pass holds out another several dozen difficult, unsolved, and sometimes insoluble problems.

The Americans grandly ignore the internal dynamics of the region and its ethnic, religious, and economic problems, focusing instead on the imperiled right to exist of the State of Israel, on the provision of a sufficient oil supply for the Western world, and on checking further Russian penetration into the region.

These were the principal concerns during the Carter years, and the Europeans, including the Germans, shared them. They will continue to be the troubling factors in future. The European governments intervened hardly at all in the Middle East policies of Kissinger, Carter, and Reagan—if for no other reason than that they do not possess the military and economic means necessary for such intervention. However, at times we looked upon Washington's unstable and in part one-sided policy with a good deal of concern. We Europeans have helped where and how we could: At Carter's request, my government, for example, made great national and international efforts to provide economic stability for Turkey, and Egypt became one of the foremost recipients of German development aid. France helped in Chad and Lebanon, as did Great Britain and Italy. Europeans are conscious that at best the West can defuse an explosive situation here or there or tone down a war in the region and that it must time and again prevent any development potentially threatening to the world by shifting its influence appropriately.

We Europeans also know that Soviet influence in the region can no longer be removed altogether; if it is pushed back in Egypt or Somalia, it bobs up again in Ethiopia, in South Yemen, in Libya, Syria, and Afghanistan. Though in the European view the West is thus compelled to try to check the Soviet Union, a certain restraint is also required. But the consequences of a large-scale war or an explosion in the region are incalculable for the Kremlin as well—and the Kremlin fears terrorism no less than the White House does.

The governments of the European nations allied with the United States therefore agreed substantially with Washington concerning the West's principal interests. But because Europeans understood the Middle East better, their reactions to the United States' often unstable policies, which generally aroused great hopes, were restrained. The Europeans knew they could pursue their vital interests only in concert with the Americans, who for their part should have known they needed the support of the Europeans. Thus the preconditions for a shared overall strategy on the Mideast were in no way different from those for a shared overall strategy toward the Soviet Union.

Carter's Foreign Policy Collapses

B Y the beginning of 1980, I realized Jimmy Carter was profoundly worried about his chances of reelection that November. His foreign policy was increasingly being shaped by short-term considerations of the effect it would have at home. This was not only true for his moves on Iran; it was even more valid for his attitude toward the Soviet Union. In his relations with the United States' allies, and especially in his dealings with West Germany, he began to show a lack of regard and consideration. Therefore to be seen standing shoulder to shoulder with Jimmy Carter became a domestic risk for many European governments—as it certainly did for me. I too had to face elections in the fall of 1980, and Giscard's presidential elections were coming up in the spring of 1981. After the crisis in Afghanistan broke out, Carter managed to quarrel with both of us about conditions his own administration had brought about through sheer carelessness.

Only two weeks after the Soviet occupation of Afghanistan, Carter began to doubt Giscard's reliability in case of a far-reaching confrontation with the Soviets—completely unfairly, as I knew and as I explained to the American president in a long telephone call on January 11, 1980. On that occasion I stressed how essential it was not to break off communication with the Soviet Union during such times of crisis. Carter replied that the Soviet Union had to be shown that it would be punished for its deeds, and that was why it was important for all of us to declare ourselves in unmistakable terms. The word "all" for him included all the allies, from Begin to Giscard and myself.

Carter was to deliver his State of the Union message on January 28, 1980. In view of the most "dangerous threat to world peace" since the Second World War he affirmed the United States' determination to remain the strongest nation; the Soviet Union would have to pay a "heavy" price for its aggression. After these strong words he announced some very limited American steps: a ban on Soviet fishing in American coastal waters, limitation on the export of certain agricultural products and high-technology equipment, and finally, should the Soviets continue to occupy Afghanistan, a United States boycott of the Olympic Games in Moscow. On this last point he begged me the very next day, in one of his many short, personal letters, to support him; it was, he wrote, "the most significant and effective action we can take to convince the Soviet leaders of the seriousness of their invasion. . . ."

Carter had not discussed the joint Western reaction he was outlining with his allies ahead of time. Though we had only minor objections to the individual steps, we saw clearly that there was no logical and self-contained overall strategy for managing the crisis. Therefore Prime Minister Francesco Cossiga of Italy, supported by Bonn, asked for a comprehensive consultation (for which he proposed the circle of the seven participants in the international economic summit). Carter was willing, "even if the French do not agree" (!). A telephone conversation once more revealed Carter's animus toward Giscard. Of course I defended the French president, and I once more urged a joint decision. Not only was it important, I said, to deliberate the next step and the one after that; we would also need to know what measures we might have to take down the line.

The five-member consultation (without Japan and Canada) was conducted by foreign ministers in the last week of February at Gymnich Castle—too late, since on February 11 Carter had already sent a personal letter to all participating nations announcing a dozen elements of the punitive action he was carrying out against the Soviet Union. But the letter made no mention of how the Soviet leadership might be brought to the point of declaring its mission in Afghanistan at an end and retreating without losing face. Washington's attempt to force Brezhnev to retreat with a dozen pinpricks was hardly persuasive; after studying this long letter, I had to ask myself whether Carter was sincere in his efforts to achieve a Soviet retreat from Afghanistan.

Though the situation was quite different in many ways from that at the time of the 1962 Cuban missile crisis, the latter did offer two lessons that could be applied to the Afghanistan crisis: The United States had to be prepared to use its power to overcome the crisis, and to do so in a manner that the Kremlin could not mistake. And it had to be sure to avoid publicly humiliating the Soviet Union; instead, it had to offer Moscow the opportunity to arrange the situation without a major loss of prestige.

On February 20 I urged Cyrus Vance to proceed along these lines. Fortunately Vance had not formed his view of the situation exclusively from the media reports. Furthermore, he was a good listener. I asked him what the United States planned to do if the Soviets refused to leave Afghanistan, as seemed likely, and what was planned in the not improbable case of incidents in Iran or the Gulf region, which would make the situation even more volatile. After all, I pointed out, the United States was very weak in conventional weaponry in that part of the Middle East. I warned against supplying arms to the People's Republic of China in a demonstrative way that might leave the Soviet leadership with the feeling of renewed encirclement, even though that was not the intention.

Vance replied that the United States' political and economic relations with China had been cultivated only superficially, but that the Soviets now understood that the time when the United States treated the two Communist great powers the same way was over. He believed that the "energetic reaction" on the part of Washington to the Soviet occupation of Afghanistan would lead to a Soviet retreat and the restoration of the status quo ante—that is, a neutral Afghanistan. In any case, the United States intended to keep its channels to the Kremlin open. Nor did it intend to put SALT I and SALT II in jeopardy. It was possible that SALT II would again be proposed for ratification in 1980, arms limitation talks would be continued, and all in all the "basic framework of East-West relations" was to be "kept alive."

In that case, I pointed out, Brzezinski and his submachine gun in the Pakistani refugee camp had sent the wrong signal. If the Soviets were to decide that a new round in the arms race was about to begin, they might decide to make use of the relative superiority they enjoyed at present, since they could not win an arms race. However, we Germans had reservations about any new arms race, and we certainly did not want to be drawn into one as America's only ally. The same was true for our position on trade actions against Moscow; we had commercial treaties with Moscow that we were unwilling to break. I protested against the repeated American criticism of our defensive efforts and pointed out our mobilization strength. I went on to say we could not forget that sixteen million Germans were living in East Germany under Soviet domination and two million Germans in West Berlin; anyone who talked about punishing the Soviet Union had to understand that it would be quite simple for the Soviets to punish the Germans in return. "We want to, and we will, be on board the American ship. But the engines should not be fired up to full strength before knowing where the journey is to lead. . . . We do not wish to make sacrifices for their own sake."

Speaking of the new trade sacrifices expected of us, Vance said that the sanctions directed at Iran "were correct; the threat worked." But I knew that it had not worked and that trade sanctions against the Soviet Union would have no more effect than pinpricks.

Vance answered my question about Washington's assessment of further developments in the Mideast by saying that the United States was aware of the necessity "of solving the Palestinian question." I, on the other hand, did not credit the United States with either the determination or the ability to bring about an agreement on the Golan Heights, the West Bank, and the Gaza Strip. But I did not say so.

American doubts as to the French president were also voiced on this occasion. I replied that the United States was our most important ally but France was our closest one. Washington should not try to play off Paris and Bonn against each other. We would do everything to avoid such manipulation. On the other hand, I shared Giscard's opinion that the Soviet Union must not be allowed to drive a wedge between Europe and the United States. But without timely information *before* action was taken, it was difficult for Bonn and impossible for Paris to act in concert with the United States.

As for the necessity of a better understanding within the alliance, Vance agreed with me. It was clear that he cared about closer contacts. Our conversation also revealed the discord between the State Department and the White House. For example, Vance said he never used the expression "punishment." He also let me know that as far as the boycott of the Olympics was concerned, the allies had been inadequately informed of the president's intention and that members of the administration, who in his view should have known better, had been responsible for this oversight.

Vance was both candid and understanding. Talks with him were always fruitful. In this case they prepared me well for my next visit to Washington, which took place two weeks later.

In the main my talks with Carter on March 5, 1980, touched on the same topics I had previously discussed with Vance; both sides expressed the same opinions. Only a few more points need to be noted. Carter once again voiced his doubts of Giscard's reliability; furthermore, he remarked, French defense policy assigned a higher priority to nuclear and intervention forces than to conventional ones. Since February 5 he had felt that for domestic reasons France was embarking on a neutralist position; he was "deeply concerned" by this turn of events. I realized that Carter still had not understood either the soul of France or the mind of the French president. I explained to Carter the domestic two-front confrontation Giscard was facing in his reelection campaign. I had no doubt, I said, that France could be counted on in any serious situation. That was exactly what Giscard meant when he declared publicly that France had never yet hesitated to meet its contractual obligations. No other leading politician in France was as close to the United States as Giscard.

I did not feel that I had persuaded Carter. The American president seemed to be in a position where he could accept only black-and-white descriptions. An example was his obstinate insistence that Europe must participate in the Olympic boycott. He lacked any awareness of the difficult position in which his unilateral announcement of the boycott had placed Giscard, other European leaders, and myself. Three times before Carter made his public statement, rumors had caused me to inquire of Washington whether there was any such intention; as late as four days before Carter made his announcement, I had put the question to Warren Christopher, his assistant secretary of state, who happened to be in Bonn. Trusting the negative answer I received each time, I had let the German athletic associations know that there would be no boycott of the Olympics. It was, then, a total surprise when Carter announced the boycott after all and, without consideration of the domestic humiliation he was causing his allies, demanded that they cooperate with his decision immediately.

I told the president that in the end we would be standing on the right side, but that given the unfortunate prologue, I needed time. Some European governments, especially Margaret Thatcher's, were quick to declare their participation in the boycott. But when the Olympic summer games opened in Moscow, almost all the NATO member states were present.

On March 5, in the course of our discussions on the Olympics, I asked the president what he intended to do once the Olympic games were behind us, the boycott was in place, but the Soviet troops were still in Afghanistan. To persuade the Soviets to retreat, it was necessary to use both pressures and incentives simultaneously. Brzezinski had mentioned a trinity made up of Western unity, Islamic unity, and Afghani resistance, but I knew Islamic unity could not be had without solving the Palestinian question.

Carter replied with disarming candor that he did not believe the Soviets would leave Afghanistan. So I began to understand that what he was after was domestic prestige. For the sake of his prestige, Giscard and I were supposed to give up ours—and for the sake of a hopeless operation, the German chancellor was also supposed to sacrifice the vital interests of his fellow Germans east of the Federal Republic's borders. I determined to make no more concessions, and I rejected both the limitations on trade with the Soviets and the idea of alternative Western summer games.

On the topic of the Palestinians, Carter said he expected that by perhaps May he would have to step in again. Such an action might involve unpleasant confrontations with Israel, since the United States was closer to the Egyptian position than to the Israeli one. A few months later, however, the world realized that Menachem Begin had had his way entirely, no matter how unpleasant his dealings with Carter may have been. Beginning in the summer of 1980, Begin staked everything he had on Carter's defeat.

Before we turned to the social part of my visit, I informed the president that I intended to visit Brezhnev; however, no date had yet been set. Carter made no comment. Later, however, he vehemently opposed my visit to Moscow; I made the trip nevertheless.

At the end of our discussions Carter and I issued a joint communiqué. Though differences of opinion could be glimpsed between the lines, they were not clarified but concealed as much as possible. I left Washington with the depressing awareness that the leader of the Western alliance was not sure of his own course, that he was changing tack from day to day, and that therefore there was no relying on the consistency of his course. I made great efforts, however, during several public appearances and with the media to allow no doubt as to the fundamental German loyalty to the alliance. But I also made no secret of our close alliance with France.

The reports and comments of both the American and the German media on March 6 and 7 were quite uniform. In the East the reaction was less certain: TASS spoke of German subjugation, while Radio Moscow and the Polish media claimed that Schmidt had resisted American pressure. I found my own assessment expressed in the *Financial Times* of London, namely that the value of my trip to Washington consisted in having increased the United States' understanding of the fact that the allies had differing interests and relations with the Russians and that this led to reactions of differing emphasis. The Danish *Politiken* hit the nail on the head: "Regardless of what has been said, it has been difficult and at times impossible for the Western allies to receive clarification on what has been decided in Washington . . . and how far the requested support by Bonn and others was supposed to go. . . . If President Jimmy Carter expected to persuade Chancellor Helmut Schmidt of his ability to maintain a carefully considered foreign policy, it can be said that he had nothing but bad luck."

Franz Josef Strauss, who would be on the hustings against me in the fall of 1980 as the candidate of the CDU-CSU for the chancellorship, basically shared my view; he too wished adherence to our treaty obligations to Moscow, an absence of overreaction, and a period of reflection before participating in the Olympic boycott. Strauss visited Carter a few days after I did. If he had deviated notably from my line in Washington, I am sure Brzezinski would have told the media about it. But—perhaps disappointing some—Strauss exhibited statesmanlike behavior and preserved our common interests.

Eight weeks later, on May 7, I met with British Prime Minister Margaret Thatcher in London. It was with satisfaction that I heard her express views on American foreign policy similar to ours: that Washington lacked a perspective on the connections among the Afghanistan crisis, the Iran crisis, and the conflict in the Mideast. As far as the last point was concerned, the pro-Israeli position in Washington was sure to grow stronger until the November elections. Should the nine member states of the European Community introduce a resolution in the United Nations Security Council concerning the Mideast conflict, the Americans would probably veto it. Carter's policy was being decided to a frightening degree by campaign considerations. This estimation was confirmed in the approaches to the sixth international economic summit, which took place in Venice on June 22 and 23.

On April 16 I announced to Carter by telephone the impending decision by the West German government to recommend to the national Olympic committee that Germany stay away from the Olympic Games. The following day the decision was communicated to the German sports associations, and the formal cabinet decision followed on April 23. I had, as Carter knew, declared as early as January to the Bundestag, and had reiterated this declaration in Washington, that it was up to Moscow to create the conditions that would make participation possible; but this had not occurred. I was counting on the German sports associations to comply with the recommendation. We had, I assured them, come to our decision with a heavy heart.

At the same time I had called Carter's attention to an idea, which I had expressed in several public speeches, that seemed to me appropriate in the context of the TNF resolution to allow the Soviets to save face while agreeing to the arms limitation negotiations desired by the West. The proposal boiled down to an interim agreement between Washington and Moscow, in the form of two unilateral public declarations, not to deploy any intermediate-range missiles until the end of 1983. Such a moratorium would not put the West at a disadvantage, since three more years were required to produce the Pershing 2, while without an interim agreement the Soviets could expand their great lead by the end of 1983. An interim agreement would limit the Soviet advantage to the position that could be attained in any case, while allowing the impression of a balanced agreement under which the actual limitation negotiations specified in the TNF resolution could begin. I hoped, I said, that this proposal would be of interest to the American disarmament specialists.

Carter replied that, given the "shaky situation in Italy and Holland," it was important to avoid the appearance of tampering with the TNF resolution. He advocated sending my suggestion along with an explanation to the other NATO partners and making it clear that it did not represent any deviation from the TNF resolution of December 12, 1979. I agreed, and that is what was done. For the rest, I told Carter, I would be extremely annoyed should anyone try to jeopardize the December decision. Carter thanked me, and we agreed to publicize the substance of our long telephone conversation. I also used the idea of a moratorium in a public address in Düsseldorf—much to the displeasure of Foreign Minister Genscher.

In May there were several critical statements by members of the American government about an alleged lack of loyalty on the part of the Europeans toward the United States. Most particularly, there was anger in the White House about Giscard's meeting with Brezhnev in Warsaw in May. At the end of May *Business Week* carried an article, inspired by Washington, which attacked Giscard and me equally. It made the senseless claim that I was losing my (alleged) ability, thanks to my friendship with Giscard, to prevent France's secession from the alliance (!); furthermore, my proposal of an interim agreement had abrogated the TNF resolution. My impending trip to Moscow was called a "heaven-sent" propaganda opportunity for the Soviets; I was said to be on the way to neutralizing Germany. I could not take such nonsense seriously—but

Jimmy Carter did, and presumably the inspiration for this and similar concoctions came from his staff.

In any case, I received an astonishing letter from Carter, dated June 12, which Washington immediately leaked to the press. In the first sentence the president referred to "conflicting press reports." Some of them "incorrectly have claimed that you have proposed an East-West freeze on TNF deployments, and others imply that you called on the Soviets to cease further TNF deployments for a fixed period of time. In view of your upcoming trip to Moscow, I thought it would be appropriate if I took the immediate opportunity to state once more our views on this matter." Carter explained that the United States would not agree to any proposal that provided any freeze, moratorium, or renunciation of further deployment of new or additional intermediate-range missiles, not even for a limited time. He knew, the American president went on, that I continued to support the TNF resolution emphatically. He himself supported an immediate and unconditional start to exploring limits on intermediate-range missiles; he would urge the Soviets to halt the deployment of their SS-20s; but he would not accept a freeze until 1983, even if this were binding on the Soviet Union alone; the United States would continue its swift deployment of intermediate-range missiles. In view of the fact that the texts of my speeches had been officially transmitted to the White House, the letter seemed odd, since it was based entirely on news reports. The real source of Carter's anger was my impending meeting with Brezhnev.

The release of the letter to the Washington press was pure spite. To all appearances someone was eager to vent his spleen—someone who had never been able to decide whether the Germans or the Russians were the archenemy of the Polish people, from whom he was descended. For me the crucial point of the letter was the one-sided emphasis it placed on the deployment of Western intermediate-range missiles; by contrast the letter lacked all mention of the arms limitation negotiations with the Soviet Union decided on by the alliance, of which, under the TNF resolution, there were still three and a half years left. Until this time the Soviets had refused such negotiations; now it seemed to my colleagues and myself that at heart Brzezinski was happy with the situation and that Carter cared only about showing the American public that he was being firm in dealing with Moscow but that he really had no interest in the success of my mission to Moscow.

Four days later I answered Carter's letter tersely and without addressing the substance in detail. I suggested we talk in Venice, and this talk took place five days later, on June 21. Before our encounter an interview with Henry Kissinger appeared in the *Stuttgarter Nachrichten,* in which he said about me, "I have great confidence in Schmidt as a man and as a political leader." I admit that reading this made me all the happier because at the same time Dr. Kohl and Dr. Zimmermann, the leaders of the opposition, were unconditionally taking Carter's side in the Bundestag.

For the American president the atmosphere of the impending meeting of the seven grew worse because in the meantime he had called the June 13 Mideast resolution of the nine heads of government of the European Community—which had coincidentally been concluded in Venice—a "blow against Camp David." On the other hand, Cyrus Vance, once again a private citizen, speaking at Harvard warned his fellow citizens against the belief that they and only they could direct the world in its course. He added, "We Americans cannot allow ourselves to become prisoners of our emotions."

The city of Venice showed off its full splendor under gleaming skies. All international conferences are held on the island of San Giorgio Maggiore. The former Benedictine monastery, which is more like a palazzo, has been renovated into a conference center. Even the motorboat approaching diagonally through the Grand Canal offers a breathtaking view of the monastery chapel; on the ride back the main island, with the Doges' Palace and the campanile of San Marco, as well as the facades of the palazzi along the shore, dominate the view. It would take a heart of stone not to be overwhelmed anew each time at the beauty of this wonder of the world. This time, too, as I was on my way to my discussion with Jimmy Carter, my spirits soared.

I felt wonderful politically as well. I knew that the other European leaders, Giscard foremost among them, would support me. But most especially I had understood that for domestic reasons Carter was at present much more dependent on my good behavior than I was on his. For his prestige at home and in the world had suffered; mine had not. I was not interested in challenging Carter; rather, I wanted to settle our dispute. I wanted to have free rein for my trip to Moscow, and I wanted to be sure for the rest of 1980 that the White House would not continue to hamper me unfairly. I wanted to maintain the logic and reliability of my line. What was most important to me was insisting on American-Soviet negotiations to limit the Eurostrategic intermediate-range missiles. With this idea in mind I set out one beautiful afternoon, accompanied by Foreign Minister Genscher and my foreign policy adviser, Ambassador Berndt von Staden, to visit the American president, who was accompanied by his new secretary of state, Edmund Muskie, and Brzezinski, his national security adviser.

Presumably none of those present had any idea that after the humiliation of June 12 I had planned to assume an uncharacteristic hardness. The discussion began with the topic of Afghanistan; Carter put a number of questions and asked me about the briefing Giscard had given me about his recent meeting with Brezhnev in Warsaw (of course Giscard had informed the American president directly). In the course of this conversation about the West's position vis-à-vis the Soviet Union I reverted to Carter's June 12 letter and vehemently and in great detail rejected the claims he had made: "This letter has unfortunately become an important focus of the Bundestag election campaign. It is a fact that the very day it was sent it was also released in Washington to the press. This procedure seems to me close to an insult . . ."

CARTER: I cannot agree to that.

SCHMIDT: To date there has never been a decision to which we Germans have pledged ourselves that we have reneged on. Nor is there any reason for you to assume that in future we will not keep our pledges and—

CARTER: No, we're not assuming anything of the sort!

SCHMIDT: In your letter you made reference to misleading press reports, although you already had the actual text of my speech in your possession. Neither Secretary of Defense Brown, who called on me recently, nor your Ambassador Stoessel questioned this speech; nor was our ambassador in Washington asked about it. I could easily understand if there should be some doubt about a speech at some time or another, but then it is possible to ask. That didn't happen. The indiscreet release of your unjustified letter attracted a lot of attention. By comparison, I have been very reserved. If I were to proceed with equal indiscretion, I am sure that would have serious repercussions in your country.

May I remind you that in March I informed you that I would work against German participation in the Olympics. I kept my word, and at great political cost at home I managed to get your recommendation accepted; but as a result I am just about isolated in Western Europe.

In the same way, I stand practically alone in Western Europe with respect to the INF program because I am sticking to our agreement. Perhaps I may also remind you in this context about the history of the cruise missile addendum to SALT II and the history of the INF resolution of Guadeloupe and Brussels. When I first called your attention to this problem, I was given to understand that I should keep silent because it was a matter that concerned the United States, not Germany. I did not go public until later, in the fall of 1977; that was what brought you to the Guadeloupe decision and finally all of us to the NATO resolution. I'm politically married to this resolution, I won't abandon it, and I will not change my mind.

At this point I also reminded Carter about the affair of the enhanced radiation, or neutron, weapons (ERW). In this case, too, I noted, I had not changed my mind, and he could have counted on my steadfastness. Instead he had changed his own opinion, on which I had relied. "We always kept our word; last December I even risked my political survival at the Social Democratic Party congress for the INF resolution. If, after all that, anyone thinks that I am not true to my word, I do feel insulted."

CARTER: I have no such suspicion.

SCHMIDT: It is a regrettable fact that your letter affected the German-American alliance. . . . Perhaps I may remind you that you urged me to reflate the German economy by one percent of our gross national product. At the time I pointed out that such a move might lead to a deficit in the German balance of payments, and that in fact is what occurred. But since I had given you my word, I kept it. It cannot serve any useful purpose to insult an ally who keeps his promises.

I am speaking very frankly here, and in a foreign language to boot. Perhaps it would sound less harsh in my own language. But in neither language does it make sense to mince words. . . . We do not need warnings of that sort. I hope that together we can prevent this letter's becoming a wedge between Americans and Germans. Such a wedge, by the way, would help neither of us win reelection.

For decades I have participated in discussions between the United States and my country; for example, concerning the Radford plan; for example, concerning the MLF, which President Johnson later abandoned; for example, concerning McNamara's new military strategy, which turned out to be correct. I lived through all these disputes; I know they're normal. But since the alliance made its resolutions concerning INF, there has not been a disagreement between us in the matter. At the time we agreed on two points: These weapons were to be stationed on European soil, and the preparations were to begin at once, so that deployment could begin by the end of 1983. At the same time we agreed that you would negotiate with the Soviet Union on mutual INF limitation. So we were agreed that the number of the weapons to be stationed in the West would depend on the outcome of negotiations. In the ideal case, then, a zero solution, in which there is no deployment at all, is conceivable. We were agreed on all this. I will stick to it.

Now it has become clear that you *cannot* deploy before the fall of 1983. Consequently I suggested that in view of this fact both sides refrain from deploying additional INF for the next three years. In actuality it would be only the Soviet Union that would have to halt its deployment process—that is, the Soviets would be asked for a unilateral halt, since they are deploying steadily all the time, while three and a half years will pass before the West can deploy any weapons. I am disappointed that Washington could not understand this. For my part, I never used such words as "moratorium" or "freeze."

But today I too am beginning to doubt whether the United States is sincere in wanting to negotiate with the Soviets! Perhaps you are afraid that while negotiations are ongoing, the Congress will not approve the funds for development and production. But it would not be the first time you have produced without, in the end, deploying. The B-1 bomber is an example—

CARTER: No one in my administration believes that Germany will not go ahead with carrying out the resolution. But when you gave your speech in April, you caused an international stir that had its roots in Germany. At the time you telephoned me to discuss what we should do; consequently messages were sent to Holland and Belgium, among others. But then you said you were sticking to your statement. That made Belgium, for example, extremely uneasy, and it caused problems in Italy as well. I do not believe that was how your statement was meant; but I think that it was not well considered. After the difficulties in Belgium and Italy, I wrote to you in order to clarify the American position. We are opposed to a moratorium and a freeze because that would freeze the imbalance. It would, in effect, amount to sanctioning the current extent of Soviet deployment of SS-20s. The United States will never agree to a production stoppage. . . . I believe that it is not your intention to delay the deployment [of Pershing 2s] in Germany, the beginning of which is planned for August 1983. But we differ on the question of whether you should have made your statement, which led to confusion in Holland, Belgium, and Italy. I do not doubt your intentions, but I regret your statement and I regret that, because of it, we are having these confrontations. Besides, the American position isn't determined by concerns about the defense budget or funding for arms production. In fact, Congress wants to spend more money for defense than my budget draft calls for.

·   ·   ·

Then Carter returned to the topic of Afghanistan, his various embargo measures against the Soviet Union, and American nonparticipation in the Olympics: "Some of our allies supported us more, others less, in this. We two don't have any argument on the subject, but I don't agree with your way of proceeding."

If we agreed on the subject, I threw in, then I really could not understand his letter.

"I wrote the letter on the basis of misleading press reports," Carter admitted. "But what matters to me is to make it clear that the United States is not prepared to promise that they won't be deployed. Because, as I said, that would be tantamount to sanctioning the Soviet deployment, and how would we be positioned if after the three years the Soviets were to propose that negotiations should continue? It would place us in a difficult situation—"

"But then why," I asked, "did you agree to the cruise missile paragraph of SALT II?"

Carter justified his action. That paragraph, he said, was only one element of a larger package; alone and of itself, it would not have been to the United States' advantage.

"You will remember," I persisted, "that I advised against that paragraph. I foresaw the INF danger when the United States dismantled its intermediate-range missiles in Italy and Turkey after the Cuban missile crisis. In 1969 I expressed my views in a book about the questions of military parity.

"In this context I want to point out one thing: Germany is a small country; sixty million people live in an area no larger than your state of Oregon. And there are more than five thousand American nuclear warheads in that area; naturally, to the Soviets they are five thousand targets. I am prepared, if necessary, to station another hundred weapons in this thickly settled area. You with your huge territory are much better off."

The conversation then turned to financial aid and debt conversion in favor of Turkey as well as debt conversion in favor of Pakistan. Carter mentioned the enormous costs to the United States of its military presence in the Indian Ocean and the Far East. Now, he said, bases in the Mideast were under negotiation.

I called his attention to the fact that the Mideast governments were also entitled to some assurance that they would not be victimized by revolts; for this reason we Europeans had come to an understanding with Secretary of State Vance that the nine European Community nations would take an initiative to expand the security-related United

Nations Resolution 242. But now President Carter had announced on television that he would veto such a resolution in the Security Council. "The situation was similar," I continued, "a few months ago in regard to the Olympics. Both Mr. Brzezinski and Mr. Christopher told us a few days before my executive declaration that the United States was not planning to decide against participating in the Olympic Games. Accordingly, I did not mention the problem in my speech. But the following Sunday I let it be known that you had, after all, decided in favor of nonparticipation."

At this point Brzezinski jumped in. "In speaking to Senator Biden, you were critical of American policy in general and figures in the American government in particular!"

"If necessary," I retorted, "I can fight with the best of them."

Brzezinski flashed, "And we know how to fight back."

Carter put an end to this exchange. "I never criticized you. I think now we'll understand each other better."

I stressed once more that it would be beneficial if the Soviet Union were to declare that it did not intend to deploy any further SS-20s. Carter repeated that he could not share this view, since verification was possible only for emplacement construction. I countered that Soviet agreement would, of course, have to be verifiable. At this point Secretary of State Muskie also joined the conversation. He noted that if there were a moratorium, the Soviets would demand that it would have to apply to production. But in that case a moratorium would disadvantage the West more than the Soviet Union.

I said, "The Soviet INF are not directed at the United States but at Europe, the Middle East, and China. Should none of these affected parties have the right to say to the Soviets, 'Stop additional deployment of SS-20s'? At this point I must repeat my question: Is the United States serious in its intention to negotiate?"

In response Carter explained that the Americans had offered to negotiate with the Soviet Union. But abrogation of the TNF resolution was out of the question, he said. I emphasized that we too would reject any such move. It was my impression, I said, that it might be possible to persuade the Soviets to withdraw their demand for abrogation of the NATO resolution as a precondition for the resumption of negotiations. We would have to make it easier for the Soviets to back off from their own preconditions. To my question as to whether the Soviet Union would negotiate SALT III before SALT II was ratified, Carter replied that I should try to find out the answer while I was in Moscow. I explained my intentions and closed with a preliminary draft:

This is what we will confirm:

1. There is no chance that the Soviets can drive a wedge between us Germans and our allies.

2. The Soviets must understand that the Federal Republic of Germany is irrevocably committed to the principle of military parity in Europe and the world as the precondition for cooperation with the Soviet Union. By the way, I prefer the term "cooperation" to the concept of détente.

3. The Soviets must understand that this is why we continue to stand behind the alliance's INF resolution; and

4. they must understand that we are just as determined as anyone else to refuse to accept the invasion of Afghanistan.

5. Furthermore, they must understand that with the same determination with which we stand behind NATO and the European Community, we back the Helsinki Final Act, which was signed by thirty-four nations, and our treaties with the Soviet Union, Poland, and the German Democratic Republic. These treaties include economic cooperation with the Soviet Union within the framework of both COMECON and the OECD consensus.

I closed by promising that at the end of my talks in Moscow both sides would understand that it had been necessary to talk with each other and to listen to each other: That, after all, was the art of diplomacy. "The Soviets are asking us for a declaration on matters of fact, but their draft is not acceptable to us. As a precaution, we are preparing a press release that will be limited to a description of the visit [to Moscow]."

The conversation then turned to the credit aid for Poland, which both Carter and I wanted; Poland was undergoing its first balance-of-payments crisis. Finally we came back to Afghanistan and the Palestinian question.

In the end I summed up the crucial points of our talk. It was my impression, I said, that we were of one mind on the essentials. "Don't you want to tell that to the press? You could also add that you have convinced yourself that Germany will not abandon the INF resolution. And why not say something positive about Genscher's and my trip to Moscow?"

Carter nodded and summed up the Afghanistan situation. The Russians would have to clear out of the country altogether; recognition of the Karmal regime was out of the question.

My discussion with Jimmy Carter was much more important to me than the matters under review by the economic summit meeting, which began the following day. At the beginning of the session devoted to questions of international policy Francesco Cossiga asked me to summarize the current situation. I gave a survey covering conditions from the conflict in the Middle East through the occupation of Afghanistan and the situation in Iran to the crisis in East-West relations. Of course I also alluded to our own intentions in Moscow. My summary met with general approval. Even Jimmy Carter, whom I had spared and had not criticized at all, could not hold back.

The following day Brzezinski took upon himself the task, which was surely not a pleasant one, of giving the press a background briefing in order to make sure that the normal climate was preserved. He specifically invited the *Frankfurter Allgemeine Zeitung,* which normally tended to back the CDU-CSU; on June 25 the paper carried a six-column story on the briefing. Brzezinski presented the political declaration of the seven heads of government on Afghanistan in such a way that it seemed to include everything Carter had said since January (which was not the truth; for example, the word "punishment" did not occur). In answer to the question of whether it would have been possible to avoid the discords of recent weeks by an earlier agreement at the highest level, he spoke with a candor that pretty much exposed his own government: Such an effort had been impossible if only because there was no agreement on the top level of the United States administration; it was only now that consensus had been achieved among president, secretary of state, and national security adviser. Asked about the disagreements with me, Brzezinski replied that the president's letter had been based on "mistaken press reports." But that was all settled now: "Everything is clear with Chancellor Schmidt." This sentence served as the newspaper's headline.

Otherwise the international press responses were mixed. *La Repubblica* wrote, "Carter has not persuaded Europe." The *Corriere della Sera* added that Carter had had to undergo much soul-searching to arrive at the belief that the channels to the East had best be kept open; that was why he was now welcoming my visit to Moscow. *The New York Times* took a similar view: "President Carter was challenged to explain why he was so suspicious. . . . Mr. Carter finally agreed in public that maybe these meetings could be useful, despite his original doubts." *Le Figaro* hit the nail on the head: "A modest balance . . . but, to be fair, everything went off more smoothly than expected." The Soviet and Eastern European media published only propaganda positions. As a whole, the economic questions took second place to the international problems in all the assessments. The response was overwhelmingly positive measured against the very minimal expectations.

My own summing-up was ambivalent. On the positive side I counted the following: the entente with Valéry Giscard d'Estaing had held up once more, the Europeans appeared united, Carter and Brzezinski had moderated their position. We now had a clear basis for the talks with Brezhnev and Gromyko, which would take place in a few days. The negative side of the ledger listed the fact that it seemed never to have occurred to the American president to pursue the second part of the TNF resolution actively and actually to begin negotiations to limit the Eurostrategic SS-20 missiles that had already been produced by the Soviets and that were rapidly multiplying. Carter quite obviously thought of nothing but showing himself firm in his relations with the Soviets because of his reelection campaign. But this firmness was merely a pretense—with which he fooled himself as well. Because in fact he was not prepared actually to put pressure on the Soviet Union when it came to Afghanistan.

At the time one of my colleagues said, "Considering Eurostrategic nuclear weapons, we wanted to restore parity through disarmament; the United States, on the other hand, was aiming at the same objective through rearmament." It seemed to me that consequently the American position hardened. But I believed that a lot of time remained to exert some influence before the end of 1983. When at the time Rudolf Augstein wrote despairingly in *Der Spiegel*, "We do what the Americans tell us to; East Germany does as the Soviets order them to. But at least *we* are still allowed to grumble," I did not share his resignation for a moment. I knew that in American election campaigns foreign policy always had to be the whipping boy for domestic propaganda and mutual recriminations, to a much greater degree than happens in Europe. But the American campaign would come to an end in early November.

When, on July 3, 1980, just returned from Moscow, I read Jimmy Carter's paeans of praise about my negotiations in the Kremlin, my first reaction was relief: he could hardly change his mind again before the election in November.

I saw Carter only once more during his presidency, in the White House on November 10, after Ronald Reagan had won the election. I made use of the opportunity to meet the president-elect in Washington as well. My farewell visit with Carter went off pleasantly. His Southern hospitality and his personal friendliness set the mood.

Domestic Reasons for the United States' Lack of International Continuity

WHEN President Carter took office, he made it clear to America's allies, who had loyally cooperated with the Ford administration, that much of what they had supported in international affairs had unfortunately been a mistake; he would begin an entirely new policy in many areas and expected our cooperation. When President Reagan followed him into office four years later, this drama was repeated in reverse. According to traditional European concepts, the international policy of the Nixon-Ford-Kissinger era might have been called a centrist policy; Carter initiated a 90-degree turn to the left, and Reagan continued with a 180-degree turn to the right.

Both changes had multiple causes, but they were rooted almost entirely in American domestic affairs, in their structures and structural changes, in the partisan power struggle, in the attitudes and trends among the citizenry and the political class. Of course the mind sets and prejudices of the two new presidents, both of whom arrived in Washington with little experience in foreign affairs, played an important role. Both brought with them to the White House their own people (among them very few women), who had stood by them during their time as governor and subsequently during their years of running for office. These aides and advisers always had a great deal of experience in domestic and party politics, but most of them had no knowledge whatsoever of foreign affairs. This was as true, for example, of Hamilton Jordan and Jody Powell on Carter's staff as it was of Edwin Meese and "Judge" William Clark during the Reagan period.

Earlier presidents had also brought their personal confidants to the White House and entrusted them with highly influential positions. But until the first half of the 1970s two groups with international experience had always represented a sufficient counterweight in the arena of international politics. One was a large number of outstanding career diplomats and career officials in high positions, who provided continuity; the other was a large reservoir of discerning private persons, who were committed to foreign affairs and who had already served earlier administrations.

This reservoir, earlier frequently called the "establishment," had both its forum and its center in the Council on Foreign Relations in New York. Its members were lawyers, bankers, some industrialists, and academics. The council published (and still publishes) the excellent periodical *Foreign Affairs*, under the editorship first of Hamilton Fish Armstrong and later under William Bundy; the quarterly contributes substantially to the function of the council as a forum. The Council on Foreign Relations successfully drew carefully chosen young people into its discussions and prepared them at first for modest tasks; in the course of their careers they often took on top-level missions in the State Department, the Pentagon, the White House, or other centers of international policy—from trade agreements to disarmament.

For the most part these were men who felt the praiseworthy urge to devote some years of their lives to public service and who were financially in a position to afford this sacrifice. In the meantime they pursued their professions, kept themselves current on all developments, and were almost always prepared to serve whatever government or president was in power, even in honorary positions—be it as private adviser or as a member of such commissions as American administrations establish from time to time. After the Second World War, John McCloy was for a long time the chairman of this group and, as it were, its prototype; later David Rockefeller and Cyrus Vance played a significant role in the council.

This establishment produced a great number of outstanding people who served their country—and the world—in sometimes invaluable ways. The majority were Republicans, but many Democrats were also in the group; what was crucial was that they had to be "left" Republicans or "right" Democrats, but in any case men of the center who thought responsibly on the international level. It was precisely for this reason that they could preserve the continuity of United States foreign policy through changing administrations—at least until the domestic split during the Vietnam War.

A German politician who came to New York and was invited to meet with the council felt this to be a great honor; furthermore, he found it a good opportunity quickly and fairly effortlessly to take his bearings concerning the American government's position on the situation in the Mideast, its relations with the Soviet Union or Berlin, what its intentions were or what its intentions were likely to be in the near future.

Of course within this establishment various currents, even controversies, were evident. But here the visitor was dealing with people who really knew the countries and problems they talked about; they had sufficient money, time, and opportunity for travel; they spoke or understood at least one foreign language. They were at home in the world, and it was profitable to talk with them. Robert Roosa, George Ball, and later Peter Peterson and Felix Rohatyn are council members I hold in fond memory.

The foreign policy elite, which had very silent but effective ways of seeing to its own succession, was thus largely a matter of the East Coast. Of course some of the top people from Harvard and MIT in Cambridge were among them, as were some from the Ivy League universities of Yale, Princeton, and Columbia. From the 1960s I recall with pleasure Professors Robert Bowie, William Kaufman, Klaus Knorr, Marshall Shulman, Henry Kissinger, Zbigniew Brzezinski, and many others. Of course this clublike, loose mesh of people also included some outstanding business leaders who were both talented and unassuming but had no direct social ties; among them were the successive heads of the AFL-CIO, George Meany and Lane Kirkland.

Any European in the 1950s and 1960s who needed information on the United States' current thinking on foreign affairs needed only a few days and a couple of conversations with members of this group. It was not necessary to travel to the United States every year if now and again he would attend some of the private international conferences; I gratefully recall the yearly so-called Bilderberg Conferences that Prince Bernhard of the Netherlands organized and ran, and the yearly meetings of the London Institute for Strategic Studies under the leadership of Alistair Buchan. Some of the United States senators active in foreign affairs—such as Jacob Javits, Charles Mathias, Henry ("Scoop") Jackson, and Charles ("Chuck") Percy—always participated in these two- to three-day international conferences. Conversations with Dean Acheson, George Kennan, and Paul Nitze, which might occur during such meetings, were a treasure trove of information and enlightenment.

If, in addition, the European was able to talk with the governor of New York, Nelson Rockefeller, or with one of the senators in Washington who were most knowledgeable about domestic affairs, he could without much effort order his impressions of the United States' foreign policy outlines within the framework of the nation's internal tensions. In this way America became quite transparent to the eyes of European politicians. We were not surprised whenever, a few years later, one or another of the men we had had such good conversations with reappeared as a cabinet member or deputy secretary or head of a department; in such cases we could safely assume that the man's views were the same ones he had espoused in our earlier talks. America was consistent. There was no occasion to fear a general change of direction by 90 or even 180 degrees when a new administration took office.

This consistency and reliability in United States foreign policy visibly diminished during the Vietnam War. The war and the questions about the meaning of the sacrifices it demanded, as well as the prospects of political success, polarized the American political class. Many lost some of their composure (as well as their good manners); others were plagued by serious doubts about the international role their country was supposed to be playing, an attitude due in part to the opposition of their own sons and daughters. In the course of the 1960s the characteristic significance of the old East Coast establishment to foreign and security policies passed its peak.

The Carter administration, and the Reagan administration even more, replaced the dominant foreign policy influence of the East Coast, which primarily looked across the Atlantic to Europe, with influences from the South and the West Coast of the vast country. People there were more likely to look to Mexico, to the Caribbean, and westward across the Pacific. At the same time, as the 1970s went on, there was a shift in the fulcrum of economic dynamics, in United States economic growth, as well as a noticeable population transfer to Florida, Texas, California, and other states, away from the East Coast and the Midwest, which for many generations had been the home of industrial growth. The newly flourishing regions were more vital but also more naive when it came to foreign affairs; a certain amount of contempt for both Washington and the old establishment could not be ignored.

New slogans and new guiding principles emerged. Jimmy Carter was influenced by the concept of a global economic triangle of the United States, Europe, and Japan, an idea that originated with the so-called

Trilateral Commission under David Rockefeller; in the late 1970s the concept of the Pacific Rim was added.

In the view of many Californians, the world's economic growth had found its new dynamic center in that region. There was a hope that the commercial capacities of Japan, Korea, Taiwan, Hong Kong, and Singapore could be expanded under American technological and preferably entrepreneurial leadership and thus made at least an additional cornerstone of global foreign policy and strategy. By comparison the role of Europe moved to the background of this concept.

Certainly these ideas are also affected by illusions about the peoples of Asia and their interests. The average American's knowledge about the Japanese—their history, culture, and mentality—is even less than their knowledge about Europe. This is even more true of China and its five-thousand-year history and culture; but it is equally true, for example, of the Islamic nation of Indonesia, with its more than 160 million inhabitants and more than 13,000 islands.

America knows very little of the internal Asian conflicts—for example, the resentment felt toward the Japanese by the Chinese, Koreans, and Filipinos because of Japanese imperialism from 1930 to 1945 or the subconscious fear that Chinese communism might exert control once more. The typical American has little idea of the envy the Southeast Asian masses feel for the economic success and affluence of the Chinese living in Malaysia, Thailand, Indonesia, and the Philippines.

While the members of the old East Coast establishment not only shared a language with England but also were fairly fluent in French, German, and Italian, hardly any American politician speaks Chinese or Japanese or Indochinese. Understanding of Asian peoples is underdeveloped. America will have to find out that given the great differences in cultural traditions and social structures, it will be possible to guide the Southeast and East Asian nations in the direction of American interests and objectives in only very limited ways.

But such experiences are still in the future. In the meantime Japan's enormous economic boom, as well as economic upswings in the newly industrialized nations of East and Southeast Asia and China's economic reform under Deng Xiaoping, are all bewitching developments. The new line of vision of many Americans toward the coasts beyond the Pacific is a fact. Europeans would do well to make their arrangements accordingly, because they must retain their influence on the United States' global thinking and acting. That is why since 1976 I have repeatedly suggested to the ministers of the German federal cabinet and my staff that whenever they went to the United States, they visit not only

Washington and New York but travel to the west and the south of the country as well. I myself—even while I was chancellor and in spite of all time constraints—have followed my own advice.

In July 1979, during one of these visits to California, George Shultz invited me to be his guest in Bohemian Grove during the traditional yearly summer encampment. This weekend gave me one of the most astounding experiences I ever had in the United States. Later I went to Bohemian Grove a second time, and my impressions intensified.

The landscape in which the encampment (the term used) takes place is uncommonly beautiful. The valley, a few meters wide and several kilometers long, is protected along both slopes and on the valley floor by venerable sequoias, some of them a thousand years old. Though the sky can be glimpsed through the loosely grouped treetops, the horizon is concealed. It was very quiet, with a total absence of traffic noise; the only sound was an occasional blare of music from somewhere or other. Some paths crossed the valley, as did a brook, which carried water from a small lake to the Russian River at the foot of the valley. (The name of the river recalled the time when Alaska was part of Russia, and Russian hunters and settlers pushed their way south as far as central California.) Earlier visits to California had introduced me to the sequoia groves in the Muir Woods north of the Golden Gate Bridge; they had always fascinated me. By comparison Bohemian Grove is a tiny area; but the beauty of nature alone is worth the long car trip.

Even more interesting is the cameraderie among the men (women are barred) who meet in Bohemian Grove, which got its name from the exclusive Bohemian Club in San Francisco, where there is a long waiting list for membership. The encampment in the grove is not a large common camp; the two thousand or so men who spend the weekend together live in five or six dozen small camps, almost entirely concealed by trees and bushes, scattered along the hillside. Some of the camps consist of log cabins, others of wooden huts, still others are made up of tents; there are electric light and running water. The meals are simple and substantial but well prepared. Almost all the men wore colorful shirts and trousers, some of them in glaring plaids, such as Americans wear when they return to Mother Nature. The members of the encampment visited each other for music (some played great Dixieland, others classical quartets), for sociability, or for chats. The atmosphere was relaxed and cheerful.

In July 1979 there were also two or three joint functions on the lakeshore and in small outdoor theaters built into the wooded hillside. The "lakeside speech," held by the water, usually deals with politics or economics and is delivered by one of the prominent members or one of the guests (I, too, was once granted this honor), who is introduced by another participant in the encampment. The listeners sit in the grass, facing the lake; many of them are great experts in the field under discussion and they are in no way uncritical. But the entire event proceeds casually, with a touch of boyish romanticism and the dash characteristic of television Westerns.

Some of the camps produced short lectures followed by a discussion. I recall one afternoon in a neighboring camp attended by three of the then "presidential hopefuls"—George Bush, Alexander Haig, and Ronald Reagan. I can't remember whether they had already announced their intention to run; whatever the case, during the foreign policy discussion, which was led by the prime minister of Singapore, Harry Lee Kuan Yew, Henry Kissinger, and myself, they were cautiously reserved.

This weekend allowed me an illustrative glimpse of America's elite. The politicians who were present were, for the most part, guests of one or another of the club members. But these members were artists (I met Isaac Stern there), writers (such as Herman Wouk), physicians, attorneys, bankers such as Peter Peterson, and industrialists like David Packard—whom I had met ten years before, when he had been deputy secretary of defense under Melvin Laird and who was one of the owners of the worldwide firm of Hewlett-Packard—and Steve Bechtel Senior and Junior, who headed another worldwide firm with my host, George Shultz. It is true that some of the participants came from the East, the Midwest, and the South; but altogether I cannot imagine a greater contrast to the somewhat cool and stylish New England atmosphere in the Council on Foreign Relations or the River Club in New York. In Bohemian Grove we were in our shirtsleeves, we were direct, relaxed, carefree—and yet not shallow. This was without a doubt also an establishment, but of a very different kind. The difference was much greater than that between, say, Bavaria and the northern German seaports.

Gerald Ford took a different route to bring leading figures from the various sectors of the American society closer to each other. He hosts an annual weekend in a hotel in Vail, Colorado, in the heart of the Rocky Mountains. Under the aegis of the conservative American Enterprise Institute, about two dozen chief executive officers and independent owners of major corporations and banks gather. They are joined by about the same number of foreign colleagues as well as foreign statesmen, members of the cabinet, outstanding economists, senators, and congressmen, as well as experts from various American think tanks. Though the group works hard in workshops and in plenary meetings, sociability is not forgotten. These meetings bring together not only the west, south, and east of the United States, but also the various political groups within American society. Such events are not only useful but, in view of the increasing fragmentation of the political class, also necessary if a broad political and foreign affairs consensus is to be restored in the United States.

The decline of the old East Coast establishment and its significant replacement by the South and the West were not the only developments that contributed to the dissolution of the unified political class. Another was the formation of a class of professional intellectual politicians who never run for office but offer their services to the elected politicians and the candidates—at times even force them on them—as expert advisers and executive officers. They are supported by various institutions, where they work whenever they are not in government service.

Such think tanks have existed in the United States for some time; for Europeans the Rand Corporation, for example, brings to mind the field of military analysis; at a very early stage it produced such lucid minds as Albert Wohlstätter, whose essay "The Delicate Balance of Terror" in *Foreign Affairs,* published in the 1960s, was one of the first to arouse a consciousness of the sensitive nature of the balance of nuclear strategic deterrence. In the course of the last two decades many more or less comparable institutions have been added to the earliest ones. In contrast to the old ones, the new institutes are specifically partisan. The American Enterprise Institute tends to be Republican, while the Brookings Institution has an overwhelmingly liberal and Democratic orientation, as has the Carnegie Endowment for International Peace. Opposed to these, at least since the Carter period, are the conservative Georgetown Center for Strategy and International Studies as well as those foundations that are adjusted to the Republican right wing and are rapidly gaining ground in both financial donations and significance: the Hoover Institute in Stanford, California, and the Heritage Foundation in Washington.

During the four Carter years the Committee on the Present Danger, which stood fairly far to the right, was an enormously productive pool of those who were concerned about Carter's overall strategy. Eugene Rostow and Paul Nitze were the driving forces; both had come from the old establishment, and both assumed important posts in the Reagan administration in the area of disarmament policy. During the 1940s Nitze, along with Dean Acheson and George Kennan, had been one of the American thinkers who had taken a farsighted, responsible position on overall strategy; together they had conceived the Marshall Plan.

Service to the interests of their own country took precedence over their party affiliation.

I had known Nitze since the 1950s. To this day I have great faith in his discernment and personal integrity. When Reagan named him to head the delegation that was to negotiate in Geneva with the Soviets on the limitation of Eurostrategic intermediate-range missiles, I was reassured. I could not foresee that the young Richard Perle would grow into an uncommonly talented opponent to him (and to Rostow, who was head of the disarmament agency). Perle impeded and undermined the progress of the negotiations with tactical cleverness and intellectual brilliance.

This assistant secretary came from a different school of new career politicians. Perle was not a member of one of the large think tanks; he had been one of the crucial figures on the staff of the conservative Senator Henry ("Scoop") Jackson. Today senators' personal staffs may consist of up to a hundred people, all of whom are paid by the state. Many of the younger, coming professional politicians, who are waiting for their chance, are drawn to these jobs. The atmosphere on these staffs is one of both professional competence and intellectual rivalry, as well as strong partisan polarization. These staffs also serve as springboards for jobs in the federal government; in many cases the young men's political ambitions mislead them into underestimating the experience and discernment required of lifelong professional soldiers and career diplomats. With the help of their mentors in the Senate and the House of Representatives, such people frequently swell the ranks of those in subordinate positions. But once they have succeeded in obtaining one of the coveted positions in the executive, they pull others from their group whom they believe to be congenial up with them.

The continuing displacement of career officials from almost all the leading positions is one of the most important reasons for the lamentable lack of consistency in American foreign policy; the increasingly broad adaptation of the leadership personnel to public opinion, which is principally formed by television, is just as pernicious. Nowadays, when a new president takes office, he names hundreds of new assistant secretaries and ambassadors. The number of people who leave their positions and missions is in the thousands, and almost all posts are filled with party members or sympathizers of the new president or his party. Of course the secretaries are also replaced, and the departing president takes almost all his documents with him. By the time the new president has completed the process of familiarizing himself with the position, almost a whole year has passed.

In contrast, when a new chancellor comes to power in the Federal Republic of Germany, the ambassadors are as a rule not replaced, and there are changes among only a few deputy ministers; filling positions with persons outside the career bureaucracy is the rare exception. When I was a minister and chancellor, my personal advisers were also career officials. Even more important was the fact that during my eight and a half years as chancellor I had four foreign and security policy advisers one after another, and all of them were outstanding career diplomats (three of them subsequently became ministers in other governments— that is, they attained the top level of the career bureaucracy). Though the law allows deputy ministers and generals to be retired at any time, this step is seldom taken in Bonn for political reasons. When there is a change of government, the change of personnel is concentrated on the ministers and the civil service and parliamentary state secretaries. In Great Britain the practice is similar but even more restrictive.

The advantages are obvious: Whenever a new prime minister or chancellor assumes office, he finds first-rate experts in place; they are familiar with the history and all aspects of the complicated problems the new man is eager to solve. He must come to terms with their ideas; but once he has made a decision, he can rely on his officials to carry it out loyally. In this way a significant consistency of foreign policy is preserved not only in London and Bonn but also in most European capitals even through changes of government. This continuity leaves the other governments with the important sense of reliability and trustworthiness. This component of personal continuity is generally supplemented by the prime minister's, chancellor's, or president's own considerable instinct for foreign affairs. Almost all of them have been prepared by their political careers to assume national responsibility; thanks to years of dealing with the foreign and security policies of their nation, they know that only in very few cases can an abrupt change of course be successful. Neither Georges Pompidou nor Valéry Giscard d'Estaing replaced Charles de Gaulle's overall or nuclear strategy with a different concept. Edward Heath did not retract the decision of his predecessor, Harold Wilson, to stop maintaining fighting forces east of Suez. When Wilson once again followed Heath, he did not push the United Kingdom to withdraw from the European Community. Helmut Kohl made every effort to continue his predecessor's *Ostpolitik*—despite the sharp criticism he had previously leveled at this policy when he was a member of the opposition.

Washington, on the other hand, is characterized by each new person's rich imagination. Almost every president announces his own foreign policy or overall "doctrine." This discontinuity cannot help but evoke insecurity, caution, even suspicion among the United States' allies as well as its opponents. The changes in the personnel pool from which persons active in the White House, the State Department, the Pentagon, the disarmament agency, and the diplomatic corps are drawn are endless. Since 1976 the presidents' lack of experience in international affairs has aggravated the situation. In Washington the career diplomat has little standing; therefore, as well as because of the fairly low salary, many first-rate people leave foreign service relatively early; many are frightened away from adopting that career in the first place. Instead, the campaign contributions of private citizens play a considerable role in their being named to ambassadorships. And yet the United States still has excellent career diplomats (I gratefully recall, for example, Walter Stoessel as ambassador to Bonn) and has produced outstanding outsiders as ambassadors (such as Arthur Burns, who later was ambassador to Bonn).

On close observation it becomes obvious that only the fighting forces, as a self-contained apparatus, remain relatively unaffected by the regular personal-political torrents. The army can promote its best people in relative peace and quiet through multiple assignments and place them in influential positions at a fairly early age. Because of such procedures, these men have often acquired a sagacity on overall strategy far beyond the military aspects, which has benefited the Europeans through the figures of good commanders in chief (the position of SACEUR—Supreme Allied Commander Europe—traditionally goes to an American). Thus, while serving as SACEUR, Generals Lyman L. Lemnitzer, Andrew J. Goodpaster, and Bernard Rogers often showed greater understanding of the interests and necessities of their European allies than did the Pentagon. As SACEUR during the late 1950s and early 1960s Air Force General Lauris Norstad was both an effective ambassador for Europe in Washington and a superb ambassador for the United States in Europe. During the second half of the 1970s Alexander Haig played an equally outstanding role as SACEUR. Subsequently, as Reagan's secretary of state, he acted with less prudence than he had shown earlier in Brussels and still earlier during the 1974 presidential crisis in Washington.

The outstanding American military role is, however, impaired by the deep-seated rivalry among army, navy, and air force (plus the marine corps). When defense expenditures increased enormously under Reagan and his secretary of defense, Caspar Weinberger, based on the idea that Carter had neglected them, I gained the impression that the way the additional budgetary sums had been assigned to the various services was based not on strategic considerations but rather on a crude proportional quota. For similar proportional reasons the Eurostrategic Pershing 2 had to be a weapon of the army rather than the air force. A general who thought in terms of overall strategy, such as David Jones or Maxwell Taylor, could put his analytic skills to use only after becoming chairman of the Joint Chiefs of Staff or supreme commander in Europe, only after being appointed to the White House, perhaps only after retiring from active service.

Occasionally, when talking with American friends, I would complain about the lack of consistency in their country's foreign policies; the conversation then inevitably turned to the fact that excessive demands were made on every president and that each reacted differently. By European standards the American president holds both of the most important national offices: He is both head of state, with an almost imperial status, and head of government. Simply from the point of view of protocol, the former office consumes a great amount of time; the president can hardly find the time customary in European nations to receive visits from foreign heads of state. Such heads of state as the royal rulers of England, Spain, Holland, Belgium, Norway, Sweden, and Denmark or the presidents of France, the Federal Republic of Germany, Italy, and Austria are also charged with the unwritten but enormously important task of ideologically integrating all parts of society and visibly carrying on the tradition of the country's and their society's basic values. Most recently Spain's King Juan Carlos, Italian President Sandro Pertini, and German President Richard von Weizsäcker have fulfilled this mission admirably and to everyone's satisfaction. For the American president, on the other hand, this function is made much more difficult by the fact—inherent in the system—of controversy with the majorities in the Senate and the House of Representatives, especially as for all practical purposes he also exerts the function of head of his party. What comes to his aid is the amiable tradition of the American people to "rally behind the president" and his crisis management whenever an international problem grows acute. This support was felt, for example, by President Carter in the case of Camp David and again when the Americans were taken hostage in Teheran. Reagan could count on it for his bombing attack on Tripoli.

The actual function of the president, to be the head of government (called the "administration" or "executive branch"), also suffers from having too many expectations placed on it. There are very few of the weekly cabinet meetings, so common in Europe, devoted to joint discussion and joint decision making; frequently a cabinet meeting in Washington has no other purpose than to allow television to applaud. In the majority of cases the freedom of action of an American secretary is clearly less than that of a Western European minister. With a very few exceptions, the president hardly ever sees his cabinet for a report; his personal staff keeps him informed on their opinions and activities. His staff gives instructions to the cabinet members, a practice that leads to blurred borders of cabinet responsibility and seduces the White House staff members into openly judging whether a cabinet member is a good "team player"—that is, whether he dutifully allows White House staff members to guide him.

The crucial staff members, predominantly trained during campaigns, first of all establish domestic or public relations norms; when William Clark became Reagan's security adviser, he had only the vaguest notions of his country's foreign and security policies. Neither in July–August 1982 in the case of the "walk in the woods" and its rejection by Reagan, nor in 1983 in the case of the announcement of SDI and the claim that this system would make all nuclear weapons obsolete, was he able to assure a prior thorough examination of the complex materials—because he had not even recognized the problems. In both cases the White House never understood that the interests of the allies were affected as well.

Even if the president does not feel drawn to a deeper foreign policy analysis, theoretically the vice president might still intervene. But despite presidents' frequent announcements of their firm intentions to make full operative use of their vice presidents, despite Americans' memory of the three events when vice presidents Truman, Johnson, and Ford were abruptly placed in the presidency, the vice president is invariably pushed aside by the White House staff. When Nelson Rockefeller was the vice president, he sarcastically explained to me that his responsibility was limited to representing the United States at earthquakes and funerals.

It is also conceivable, again theoretically, that the White House chief of staff, at least, would insure an all-encompassing global view. McGeorge Bundy, for example, as chief of staff in Kennedy's White House, performed this service. But precisely in the critical times after 1976 and after 1980, when such a role would have been most desirable, the chiefs of staff have lacked this qualification. Neither James Baker nor Donald Regan saw to it that President Reagan made his own clear-cut decisions to put an end to the perpetual quarrels between Secretary of State Shultz, who thought in international and qualitative terms, and

Secretary of Defense Weinberger, whose points of reference were military and quantitative.

The United States' European allies learned long ago not to take the statements on foreign policy enunciated in the presidential candidates' election platforms too seriously. But they have also had to learn that they could rarely know ahead of time what the elected president would actually do. They can never be sure that their talks with the secretary of state, the secretary of defense, the national security adviser, trade delegates, or the president's personal emissaries really do provide them with full disclosure of America's policies. They are uncertain how long a decision will remain in effect. They note with concern the growing populism of current American foreign policies and the increasing influence of senators, representatives, and their staffs. The allied governments feel that today Washington is considerably less reliable than during the period from Eisenhower to Ford, and thus they act more cautiously. They fear the next change of course; no one knows when it will happen and where it will lead.

Changing
Global Strategies

S INCE the end of the Second World War there have been four phases—or three changes—in overall United States strategy vis-à-vis the Soviet Union, and with it Europe. Two of these course changes were caused by external events and international developments; they were well founded and viable. The third change abandoned all previous strategy without replacing it, in the fourth phase, with a newly defined or definable overall strategy. At least, no such strategy is discernible to this day.

Of course in all four phases of American overall strategy some important components remained. No American leader would ever have let his country be overtaken by the Soviet Union in matters of military and power policy. Washington has always been aware of the necessity of setting limits and containing the Soviet-Russian expansionist drive. And there has never been any change in the determination to drive the Soviet Union out of territories where it has illegitimately established itself. The changing leadership of the United States has at all times been aware that these objectives require a number of allies, especially in Europe. The tendency to isolationism, which has been influential in American history and is still latent, has never been allowed to prevail. Not without interruptions but still fairly consistently, all four phases of American global strategy have aimed at at least a partial, limited cooperation with the Soviet Union. These elements of consistency, however, have been stressed to different degrees in the four phases, and less constant components have been added in each phase. Furthermore, the individual elements have also been subordinated to new overall concepts that have been embellished with new slogans or catchphrases and then presented to the country itself, to the allies, to the Soviet opponents, and to the rest of the world with an impressive amount of rhetoric.

If we ignore the catchphrases, we may characterize the four phases as follows: first, the short phase of the fruitless attempt to work together with the Soviet Union; second, the longer era of the Cold War, the arms race, and the vain attempt at a "rollback"; third, the time of accepted balance between the two superpowers through mutual assured nuclear destruction; and fourth, the phase of renewed Cold War and arms race.

The first American global strategy was conceived even before the Second World War ended. It grew out of the collaboration of the wartime anti-Hitler alliance. In Teheran and Yalta, and later in Potsdam, there was a concerted attempt to order the postwar world; in San Francisco the United Nations was founded as a joint effort. The attitude toward the Soviet Union that grew out of this cooperation gave rise to the Baruch Plan and the Marshall Plan. Neither of these was entirely altruistic; both represented offers to the Soviet Union—and to all the European states that had suffered the consequences of the war—to establish peaceful conditions and to concentrate on economic recovery.

However, Joseph Stalin rejected the United States' offer to abolish nuclear weapons and pushed ahead with the development of Soviet nuclear armaments so as to close the gap with American arms. He also rejected American economic aid. The other Eastern European states also refused to participate in the Marshall Plan. Supported by the presence of Soviet troops, Moscow concentrated on consolidating the Communist regimes in Eastern Europe. It was consistent with the Soviets' global strategy for them to demobilize far fewer of their troops than the United States did. Moscow was, in fact, intent on maintaining a sizable military force.

Stalin's attempt to establish a satellite government in Greece in 1947, and especially his Berlin blockade of June 1948, led to the first definitive fundamental change and thus to the second phase of American foreign policy. Truman responded with the airlift for West Berlin and most importantly by establishing NATO. At the same time the process of unifying the three Berlin zones occupied by the Western powers was initiated. Stalin responded by practically eliminating all non-Communist parties in Eastern Europe and establishing the Communist-dominated German Democratic Republic. A few years later both German states were integrated into the alliances of the opposing world powers; in this way they were turned into the frontline bastions of the world powers in Europe. Even before the 1940s ended, the Cold War was in full swing.

This epoch was characterized by the arms race between East and West and by the battle for spheres of influence in other parts of the world. The attempt to turn Korea into a Far Eastern outpost of the Communist system of alliances caused the Korean conflict in 1950 and was the background of John Foster Dulles' efforts to encircle and push back the Soviet Union through worldwide American alliances. Not without some justification, Washington at the time saw the Soviet Union and the People's Republic of China as a power grouping with a joint strategic objective (the break between Beijing and Moscow did not occur until the late 1950s). The logical solution was the development of a confrontational strategy toward the Soviet Union—that is, a global anti-Soviet overall strategy on the part of the United States.

The causes of this fundamental change in overall American strategy were to be found in Soviet conduct, which did not change, even after Stalin's death in 1953, under either Georgi Malenkov or Nikita Khrushchev. The suppression by force of the freedom movements in East Germany in 1953 and in Budapest in October 1956 outraged the American sense of justice (as it did almost all the rest of the world) and offended America's basic humanistic values. But at the same time this brutal use of power revealed the real impossibility of intervening successfully in favor of the oppressed without risking a major war. On land the United States forces were unquestionably inferior, and their superiority at sea and in the air had not been enough to win in Korea. Superiority in the area of nuclear weapons remained the last refuge in case of an impending defeat on European soil.

This situation brought about the American military strategy of deterring the Soviets with threats of massive retaliation with nuclear weapons—an approach soon adopted by NATO. The West threatened Moscow with nuclear destruction if the Soviets attacked. Some Americans—such as the chairman of the Joint Chiefs of Staff in 1956, Admiral Arthur W. Radford—went so far as to more or less give up the idea of conventional land-based troops as more than "tripwires" for the nuclear destruction of the enemy. Others—such as General Maxwell Taylor, who in 1957 had just retired as army chief of staff—instead posed the question: What happens if we can't or won't use nuclear weapons? Taylor logically called for adequate conventional forces.

In fact during the second half of the 1950s the United States' nuclear superiority gradually came to an end. During the Suez crisis of 1956 Khrushchev threatened the French and British with his country's limited number of rockets with nuclear warheads; Washington urgently advised Paris and London to terminate the Suez operation. The Berlin crisis lasting from 1959 until the Wall was built through Berlin in August 1961 justified Taylor's question. It is true that during the October 1962 Cuban missile crisis Khrushchev backed off when faced with the danger of a nuclear confrontation with the United States. But at the same time the Kennedy administration understood that a qualitative nuclear balance was rapidly approaching: whichever country used nuclear arms against the other first would die anyway—even if the second to do so.

This insight into the developing second-strike capability of the Soviet Union forced the transition not only to a new military concept but beyond it to a new overall strategy by the United States and the West. From now on it was important that both world powers understand that their mutual capacity to destroy each other must lead to voluntary—and ideally even to contractual—mutual limitation of their overall strategic objectives and actions. From this insight the third phase of the American-Western overall strategy toward the Soviet Union developed step by step. Roughly, if inadequately, it is defined by the term détente. Though major tensions remained and the arms race continued, for the first time there were attempts to agree on arms limitation, which were successful by the end of the 1960s.

At first the United States found it difficult to explain to its European allies why the apparently comfortable strategy of massive nuclear retaliation should be given up and replaced by a strategy of "flexible response." It took McNamara five years to persuade his European colleagues in the defense ministries in 1967 that in future not every circumstance should call for the use of the big nuclear stick. That same year NATO came to the same conclusion in the Harmel resolution: security against the threat from the Soviets both through its own defense efforts and through mutual arms limitation. In other words, there was a willingness to collaborate with Moscow that had not been seen since 1948. Of course this policy had been made easier by the break between Beijing and Moscow, which had attained international significance in the early 1960s.

In this third phase of the overall strategy as well, neither the United

States nor the other world powers were prepared to accept Soviet expansion or to grant the Soviets military superiority. Nevertheless Washington, London, and Bonn arrived at a number of treaties with Moscow that stabilized the balance. Paris had a part at least in the Four Power Agreement on Berlin. This process was not seriously endangered either by the Western outrage at the violent shattering of the Prague Spring in 1968 or by the sad result of American intervention in Vietnam. The Soviet Union, too, did not make the Vietnam War, which lasted well into the 1970s, a pretext for rejecting negotiations and treaties; it, too, understood that its own security interests demanded a limited cooperation with the West.

This third phase was the most fruitful and peaceful period so far in the coexistence of the two world powers. SALT I and the ABM treaty were breakthroughs that would have seemed impossible as recently as ten years before. The same was true of the complex of treaties that grew out of the German *Ostpolitik*. The absolute high point was the 1975 Helsinki Conference on Security and Cooperation in Europe (CSCE). But the Helsinki Conference also demonstrated the growth in freedom of action the European states had won in the meantime. After all, the basic principles of both the Harmel doctrine and the CSCE had been developed by Europeans, who were beginning to pursue their own interests. Of course the sphere of action of the Eastern European states was relatively small, but it was greater than ever before or since. Almost without exception, the governments in both parts of Europe had their own interest in maintaining and further developing this period of partial cooperation and the overall strategic concept on which it was founded.

Nevertheless this policy burst apart in the course of the later 1970s; even before Ronald Reagan came to office, it seemed to have come to an end. This was in part due to the Soviet Union's disturbing behavior, but also in part to the shifting mood and changing objectives of the United States. As for the Soviet Union, it seemed that a serious misunderstanding had occurred in the Kremlin. There had been agreements with the West, and especially with the United States, on a variety of issues. The Nuclear Nonproliferation Treaty (NPT), the Four Power Agreement on Berlin, the ABM treaty, and SALT I had been concluded, and finally the Helsinki Final Act had been signed. Now the Politburo believed that the Soviet Union could seize political and military advantages in those areas not covered by the treaties.

Moscow did not appear to have foreseen that Washington and the West together would not accept the recent expansion of Soviet power positions without retaliatory measures. The Soviet Union therefore engaged in heavily building up its deep-sea fleet, building up its Euro-strategic SS-20 missiles, supporting Vietnam in its conquest of Kampu-chea, invading Afghanistan, and expanding Soviet military power in Arab, African, and Central American nations. The Soviets seemed to act on the assumption that they had acquired carte blanche for any opera-tion at all that was not specifically interdicted by bilateral treaties. Furthermore, the Kremlin created the impression that the ABM treaty had been violated by erecting a huge radar center in Krasnodar, which seemed tailored to the whole country's antimissile defenses (instead of merely serving a single target region, as the ABM treaty permitted).

All this caused a deep-seated disillusionment and bitterness in the United States. President Carter, his administration, and his followers were disappointed as well. Apparently there had actually been a strong belief that détente in Europe and the arrangement between Moscow and Washington furnished some sort of unwritten guarantee of good behavior on the part of the Soviets. American conservatives blamed Carter and his idealism. The reactionary right went considerably fur-ther; this group had long ago made "détente" a dirty word; even under the most favorable circumstances it would not have ratified SALT II. Now these critics did not hesitate to claim, with as much bitterness as smugness, that they had always said this would happen. Carter, they pointed out, had led the United States into a position of weakness.

It was true that Carter had not acted on any overall strategy of his own. In the area of arms limitation he had set himself higher goals than his predecessors in the Nixon-Ford-Kissinger era, but he had achieved less than they had. He had weakened the internal cohesion of the alliance without meaning to and without even noticing the result. In his last year in office he underwent a turnaround change by adapting completely to the strongly heightened domestic pressure; he an-nounced a policy of "strength" vis-à-vis the Soviets. In January 1981, when he handed the office over to Ronald Reagan, the United States no longer had a concrete plan concerning the Soviet Union.

But except for a hefty increase in the defense budget, the new crew did not bring a draft for a new strategy into office. Nor, in the years since then, has it developed any overall strategy that is self-contained and logical.

Since 1980 the race for unlimited arms buildups has been dominating the picture. Reagan's March 1983 announcement that all nuclear threats to the United States were being invalidated by the still un-developed Strategic Defense Initiative (SDI) system was groundless, if only from the technical point of view. Politically it was equivalent to a cancellation of the ABM treaty; only the date was left open. Moscow was faced with the necessity either of developing similar defensive systems or of improving and increasing the number, weight, and warheads of Soviet offensive missiles in order to run under the SDI shield or to "saturate" it—that is, to overpower it by force of numbers.

In the fall of 1984, during his second election campaign, Reagan offered to make the SDI system available to the Soviet Union after it was fully developed; presumably only a very few people took the offer seriously, and the president himself soon seemed to understand that this proposal, aimed at the television public, was absurd because the Soviets could never take it for granted that Reagan's successors would keep the promise.

Television Democracy Reagan Style

TELEVISION tempts politicians to tell the broadest stratum of the people what they are supposed to want to hear, as determined by public opinion polls or by guesswork. These statements are couched in the simplest, most vivid, most posterlike formulas.

Ronald Reagan is a master of this device. As a populist he is far more successful than Carter was—and Carter as a populist put Ford and Nixon to shame. In Mikhail Gorbachev the Soviet Union for the first time has a leader who deals with television in a similarly virtuoso way; he is quite capable of impressing both the Soviet and Western television public. Reagan, on the other hand, addressed himself almost entirely to the American electorate, overlooking the fact that overly simple ideas and overly plain language are far less successful in Europe than in the United States.

Reagan's renunciation of ostentation and fake stateliness served him well in the United States. In his personal behavior, too, he is artless, friendly, modest, and tolerant. His language is uncomplicated. In short, in conversation Ronald Reagan is pleasant if not especially stimulating. I gained this impression as early as the autumn of 1978, when Reagan—who was getting ready to run for president—visited me in the chancellery.

Reagan and I agreed on two important points at that time. The first dealt with the necessity of fighting inflation, which at the time was running about 9 percent in the United States but barely above 2 percent in West Germany. The American situation was not only the result of the first oil price explosion of 1973–1974 but also the heritage of the inflationary financing of the Vietnam War. The second point concerned Carter's treatment of the Eurostrategic intermediate-range missiles in SALT II. Reagan criticized Carter because the latter had not been considerate enough of the Europeans' security interests and had seen the SALT II negotiations with the Soviets as exclusively a bilateral matter. Of course he was not telling me anything I did not know only too well.

It is true that in 1978 we did not see eye to eye where SALT II was concerned. Reagan rejected SALT II in the form it took at the time, while I was hoping for negotiations to proceed to the point where an agreement could be concluded, and I thought that whatever SALT II failed to cover could later be taken care of by SALT III; I believed that a failure to conclude a SALT II treaty would document to all the world the inability of the two superpowers to fulfill their obligations to reduce their nuclear weapon potential as stated in the Nuclear Nonproliferation Treaty. Such a state of affairs would enhance global insecurity. More than two years later, after Reagan had taken office, it became clear that he was actually honoring Carter's SALT II agreement for these same reasons, even though the agreement had not been ratified.

Before he assumed office, Reagan and I met two more times, the second on the occasion of my farewell visit to Carter in November 1980. Reagan had been elected but had not yet taken office. For the time being he was living in the small Jackson House a few steps and only one block from Blair House, the official guest residence, where I was staying. Our conversation—as well as my subsequent talks with his advisers William Casey, Arthur Burns, Alan Greenspan, Richard Allen, and Caspar Weinberger, as well as the new majority leader, Senator Howard Baker—again turned on economic questions. The new crew, which was still in the process of being brought together, was hoping for a combination of lower taxes, a lower rate of inflation, and a higher defense budget. To me this idea seemed fairly optimistic (a few months later Weinberger, the new secretary of defense, told me that his defense budget would be increased by 16 percent in real dollars the following year and 6–7 percent the year after that!).

But I kept my criticism to myself and centered my talk with the president-elect on the necessity of arms limitation. I was convinced that the Politburo's sense of reality was such that it would not let Reagan's hard anti-Soviet campaign rhetoric frighten them into abandoning negotiations with the new president. I was less certain that Reagan was willing to negotiate. However, he dispelled Foreign Minister Genscher's and my fears with the impulsive matter-of-factness, which clearly grew out of his political instincts, with which he spoke about the impending arms limitation negotiations. He would, he said, be conducting them with vigor and great tenacity and purposefulness. "We will negotiate and negotiate and negotiate," he said at one point. Genscher and I were reassured and satisfied as we flew back to Bonn.

And when barely six months later, at the end of May 1981, I paid my first state visit to the president, I found no reason to doubt his determination to conduct arms control negotiations with Moscow. I thought it particularly noteworthy that in a joint communiqué dated May 22, Reagan had committed himself to "execute both elements of the NATO resolution of December 1979 [the TNF resolution] and to give them equal weight." Even more reassuring was the fact that Secretary of State Alexander Haig had already initiated preliminary talks on the impending negotiations on limitation of intermediate-range missiles and that President Reagan assured me that the actual negotiations would get under way before the end of 1981.

These assurances were very important to me for both international and domestic reasons. I felt justified in trusting Reagan's willingness to negotiate, not only with regard to Brezhnev but also as far as the doubts within my own party were concerned. I considered it normal that Reagan's brand-new officials would take about a year from the time he took office to start on concrete negotiations. After all, four years earlier I had been angered at the rashness with which an insufficiently prepared president had tried to commit the Soviet Union to a completely new course without considering his predecessors' negotiations; and of course it had not worked for long.

Although in the autumn of 1980 I had just been elected to a third term after a decisive election victory of the social-liberal coalition, that coalition was quite brittle. Opposition to the TNF resolution developed in both parties. At the same time the economic crises caused by the second oil price shock in 1979–1980 gave rise to repeated disagreements as to the appropriate economic policy for the West German federal government and the Deutsche Bundesbank. The leaders of the large unions and even Heinz Oskar Vetter and Aloys Pfeiffer, the heads of the Deutsche Gewerkschaftsbund (trade unions congress), who until that time had been among my most reliable supporters, grew nervous in the face of increasing unemployment. They knew as well as I that our national resources could not defend us against the effects of worldwide exorbitant oil prices and high interest rates. Though Germany still had the lowest interest rates as well as the lowest unemployment rate in the European Community, the labor leaders were being pressured by their membership and officials.

Even worse was the growing tendency of some spokesmen of the left wing of the Social Democrats, including the circle around the chairman, Willy Brandt, to voice the suspicion that the United States and the Soviet Union were to be measured by a double standard and that the example of the TNF resolution was presenting the Federal Republic of Germany as merely a bridgehead of American interests in Europe. The left wing of the SPD would have preferred to see the TNF resolution simply canceled, without replacing it with another treaty. Some of the speeches presented the Soviet Union as almost less dangerous than the United States under Reagan. The new far left in West German politics, the Green Party, followed its ecological-anarchist-pacifist principles even further. And some of the leftists within my own party opportunistically began to try to go the Greens one better.

It was clear to me that the strategic security interests of Germany and Western Europe called for carrying out *both* elements of the two-track TNF resolution in preference to preserving my own government. It was therefore for intraparty reasons that in May 1981, a few days before a trip to Washington, I made my conviction public both to a North Rhine–Westphalian and a Bavarian delegate conference. The press reaction to both speeches was dramatic. The right-wing German media said my speeches were a "shrill accompaniment" to my trip and wrote about my having my "back to the wall." The more liberal and left-wing papers responded sharply: "Can the United States still count on Germany?" and "If the administration makes it through the autumn . . . ."

Washington, however, was backing the German chancellor, especially as a few days previously François Mitterrand had taken Valéry Giscard d'Estaing's place and Washington had only very vague and—because of his intended coalition with the French communists—quite mistaken, negative ideas of his policies. The *Washington Post* and *The New York Times* had demanded that the United States "meet Schmidt halfway" and had decided that "Schmidt Needs Friends." On May 21 Joseph Kraft wrote, "America's best friend in the world today is probably the visiting chancellor of West Germany, Helmut Schmidt. . . . The internal troubles burdening Schmidt arise in large measure from his willingness to stand up as a friend of the United States in its struggle against the Soviet Union." And the previous day James Reston had claimed, "He is Washington's strongest ally in Europe . . . he is welcome here for several reasons."

Reagan and Haig had presumably arrived at similar conclusions. Whatever the case, the visit was a success for both sides, though not where the important question of international economic controls was concerned. Our long conversations explored all the areas of international politics without uncovering any disagreements worth mentioning. Reagan accepted my invitation to Bonn (his visit took place the following year, in June 1982), and my visit became the occasion for Reagan to announce the appointment of my old friend Arthur Burns as ambassador to Bonn. More important than these was the fact that Reagan and I understood each other personally. I am certain that an important element of this ease was his preparation by Alexander Haig, who knew Germany and myself very well from his days as SACEUR. I was not exaggerating when at the end of the visit I announced about the new president, "I like this man."

I liked more than his manly charm. What particularly impressed me was the way he had psychologically and physically overcome the consequences of the assassination attempt that had occurred less than two months before and that had left him severely and painfully wounded.

My understanding of why this man was so popular with his people was perhaps more instinctive than rational: He is relaxed; he speaks only after taking a brief moment for reflection; though he uses very simple images and words, the listener is not concerned that he might change his mind overnight. Reagan is proud, and proud of his country; he examines almost all problems as an American and *only* as an American. Nevertheless, he is able to listen to a European.

Reagan also listened with interest to my description of the new French president. I had encountered Mitterrand on various occasions before he took office. Reagan had not met him yet. I made an effort to explain to my American host why we could both assume that the change from Giscard to Mitterrand would not lead to a basic change in French foreign and security policy. I told Reagan I intended to stop off in Paris on my way back in order to inform the new French head of state immediately about our Washington talks. Reagan welcomed this plan and asked me to convey his respects to Mitterrand.

At the conclusion of our three discussions on May 21 and 22 I was relieved and believed that after four years of insecurity I was once again dealing with a consistent and therefore reliable American president. Reagan was fully determined to consult in depth with his allies and to avoid any surprises. The fact that later his administration followed this intention only in part—that, for example, we learned about Nitze and Kvitsinsky's "walk in the woods" of July 1982 and the formula for compromise on Eurostrategic weapons that had been discussed there only after the proposal had been rejected and only through leaks in the press—dashed my expectations. But in May 1981 I could not know any of that. The fact that Reagan abolished Carter's grain embargo against the Soviet Union for domestic reasons—that is, in line with agricultural policy—did not come as a surprise to me.

The positive international media response to our meeting was no surprise, either. A few days later my secretary of state, Kurt Becker, summarized his report on the German media response with the statement that the meeting had aroused friendly comments everywhere and that the personal relationship between the American president and the German chancellor was generally seen as a positive one. The American media shared that view. The newspapers in the Western European nations sang the same tune, but they added two angles: Regarding the American policy of high interest rates, Reagan had not accommodated Europe. And they stressed the confirmation of the close entente between France and Germany—correctly, as I thought then and think still.

My positive evaluation of Reagan was strengthened a few weeks later by the course of the seventh international economic summit in Montebello, outside Ottawa. Both Reagan and Mitterrand were attending one of these meetings for the first time. Both fitted well into the relaxed atmosphere that had become almost traditional by now. The clever, reflective, and outwardly almost always cheerful Canadian prime minister, Pierre Trudeau, was a clever host; he had called the meeting in a large log cabin–style hotel in an almost untouched landscape. None of us could help but feel well here—most especially Reagan. During one of the intermissions I drove him through the park in an electric golf cart. Other participants had similar kinds of fun, and there was a lot of laughter. I had known Trudeau for years, and to this day I have a liking for him. As chairman of the conference, he saw to it that the proceedings in Montebello ran a brisk but relaxed course.

As I remember, Reagan's contributions were remarkable only for their stress on aspects of the situation that concerned trade policy. He is a believer in free trade, and even later, in the years of the great trade deficits caused by his own budget deficits, he generally resisted the strong protectionist pressure which the Congress, many American trade unions, and large segments of American industry exerted on him. Reagan's fundamental free trade attitude admittedly went hand in hand with a strong tendency to trade sanctions, embargoes, and the like. These latter he saw as instruments of American and Western foreign policy, not as means of international economic and trade policy. It was almost inevitable that a year later, in June 1982, during the economic summit in Versailles at which Mitterrand presided, a vehement dispute would break out between Reagan and his socialist-Colbertian French counterpart on the issue of trade policy. Outside the area of trade policy, Reagan's economic knowledge and judgment were minimal.

In the course of our various meetings during 1981, and especially in January 1982, three of Ronald Reagan's characteristic traits became more and more noticeable. First was his ability and tendency to interpret complicated matters merely in a simplified version and, simplifying them even more, to draw political conclusions from them. Second was his unshakable belief in the superiority of those factors and skills that had made his country great in the course of two hundred years—capitalism and free enterprise, optimism and moral idealism, as well as the tendency to use brute strength and even to take the law into one's own hands where the administration of justice was absent. The third was his astonishing ability to speak to his people in the same way they talk to one another.

This last skill was particularly evident on television. Millions and millions of Americans could recognize themselves in Reagan. Johnson and Nixon had appeared to them as not quite transparent tacticians; Ford did not have enough time to create a personal image; Carter was eager to make conversions—he did not appear to the American television audience as a sovereign who rose above the mundane. Reagan, however, gave Americans the instinctive feeling that he was one of them, someone they could trust. American confidence in the person of the president was, typically, always greater than approval of his policies, whether it be his decision to curtail social expenditures in favor of defense spending, his attitude to Nicaragua, or his budget deficit policy.

I consider it possible that because of the foreseeable sinister consequences of his daredevil budget policy, Americans will sharply criticize Ronald Reagan soon after the end of his second term as the man responsible for oppressive domestic and foreign indebtedness (insofar as they look backward at all, which is not usually an American strong point). Nevertheless, it would be a mistake to forget that in the first six years of his presidency Reagan represented his people more firmly than any of his predecessors since Kennedy had. Americans felt that he represented their best interests.

This was true even of many of his fellow citizens whose thinking and assessments were very different. I was astonished to hear George Shultz speak of Reagan as a "leader" as early as 1979. I was even more surprised when Lauris Norstad, who had hardly favored Reagan's candidacy, told me in the autumn of 1981 that he considered Reagan the first truly political leader; America had lacked such a head for a long time. This fact also gave the West in general a great opportunity to see the world situation from a new vantage point. Five years later I was talking about the president with a sophisticated American friend. I was complaining about Reagan's simplistic assessments on the basis of his black-and-white images of the world. My friend replied, "You're quite right, but Reagan has the right political instincts."

This observation cannot be contradicted where Reagan's ability to rule and to lead through the medium of television was concerned. Even Kennedy was skillful at making use of television. But the United States now has almost as many television sets as it has inhabitants, and television is ubiquitous and almost omnipotent. Reagan understood in masterly fashion to make unusually effective use of his moments on the screen. Granted, this skill has its dangerous reverse side. For one, the effect on the public that was to be brought about by Reagan's art of presentation became a crucial question for his staff when considering whether a particular policy should be pursued or rejected; factual and substantive criteria became secondary. The decisive issue became not whether a policy was necessary but whether it would "go over" with the public. In addition, any politician who must announce something that will be undesirable or uncomfortable to the public or even a large segment of it, anyone who supports a position that provokes criticism or public debate needs not only eloquence but also time. But television allows very much less time than it takes to read a newspaper. As a result Ronald Reagan simply ignores all unpleasant truths.

Television journalists like to ask a single question—at most two or three—on a current event, and the answer to it is neatly introduced into the latest news or feature program that same day. If I asked how long my answer could be, I was given one of two replies; I was told either "A minute and thirty seconds" or, ironically, "Stick to the tried and true rule—long questions and short answers." In such a situation there were several possibilities: *Without* regard to a favorable television effect, one can make one's opinion clear in a few sentences; *with* regard to the television audience, one can utter some pleasantries without treating the actual subject with any clarity, or one can go still further and tell the public what it wants to hear. In such situations I have often cursed the so-called brief interview. The more one accommodates public opinion or expectation, the greater is the danger of losing direction and leadership.

Acting in front of the camera was Reagan's job for many years. But the movie actor or television announcer speaks words written by others—he does not learn to ad lib or improvise. Aside from a few live television duels with an opposing candidate, Reagan's television scripts are, as a rule, carefully prepared; the public is unaware of the fact that they are actually being read. In June 1982, when Reagan addressed the Bundestag during his official visit to Bonn, I was extremely impressed not only by the content and form of his speech but also by the ease with which he expressed himself, looking now to the left side, now to the right side of the hall, then to the center, effectively combining rhetoric and gesture. Only later did I learn that his carefully edited text had been projected onto the three panes of glass that screened him on three sides and which I had mistakenly supposed to be bullet-proof glass to protect him against a potential assassination attempt. In reality they were Tele-PrompTers. My late friend Nahum Goldman once said to me with biting wit, "Reagan? Nothing but an actor! But I have to admit, he's masterful at playing the part of a bad president!"

A bad president was not what Ronald Reagan was at the outset, certainly not to his fellow Americans. But just as surely he was and is an outstanding television actor. He is a genius at addressing and mobilizing Americans, their moods, their feelings, and their emotions. And together with all this—and this is true as well for his ghost writers and the larger part of his staff altogether—he has a fine instinct for the mood of his nation, both for current sentiment and for the ideals, idols, fantasies, legends, and rituals of America that lie on deeper levels.

Jimmy Carter and his staff had already found following the evening news and commentaries on television more important than daily perusal of *The New York Times,* the *Washington Post,* the *Los Angeles Times,* or the *Wall Street Journal;* only by watching the daily newscasts did Carter, Reagan, and their staffs gain an impression of what was current and what concerned their public at a given time. From these newscasts they arrived at their decisions of what was opportune and what inopportune—and from them grow many of the political statements and decisions of the following days.

The president has no need whatsoever to respond to an event that does not play on television. But once the television of the television-watching nation vividly presents an event—no matter how one-sided a segment of reality it is—the White House must take a position, in many cases the very same day, in time for the nightly news and feature shows, some of which are repeated the following morning. As a result political decisions are made in great haste and thus incorrectly. This is at times true even of decisions that are intended to present a positive show in order to distract attention from the previous day's ostensibly negative drama. Television theatrics frequently take the place of statecraft.

Out of such situations grew Carter's rashness in proclaiming the grain embargo and the boycott of the Olympic Games after the Soviet invasion of Afghanistan, as well as Reagan's declining a meeting of the American and Soviet secretaries of state after the Korean passenger plane was shot down and his embargo against Poland after Jaruzelski's imposition of martial law. The invasion of Grenada also served as a distraction from the humiliating picture of blown-up American barracks in Lebanon.

The effectiveness of television accelerates and provokes political decisions that should really be taken with greater care, such as Reagan's rash television announcement of SDI in the midst of a public budget conflict. Television also requires action even in cases where quiet diplomacy is much more likely to result in success; one example was Carter's miserably prepared mission to rescue the hostages in Teheran.

Europeans are often shocked when those in the White House "shoot from the hip." What they overlook is the fact that in Europe we are also marching along the road from parliamentary democracy to television democracy. In Europe, too, the speeches of the heads of government, their press conferences, and especially their television appearances are in increasingly questionable ways staged by scriptwriters, directors, lighting experts, and makeup artists. In Europe, too, the exigencies of television reporting have for a long time established agendas for the political leadership that differ from those customary in newspaper and radio democracies. It is true that the political reporting in our regional newspapers is still hugely superior to that in the American press, and the political sections of the European local press are certainly read. But even in Europe pictures make a greater impression than words, and that is even more true of the moving, colorful picture that appears to our sight along with the spoken word. The political victory march of the *Bild* tabloid in Germany or of the *Daily Mirror* and later the *Sun* in England, the intermittent dominance of the Parisian *France-Soir* on the newsstands, all this was merely an overture. In Europe, too, television's triumphal march is merely a matter of time, in spite of delaying tactics.

In the United States the triumph of television as an overwhelming instrument—and the source!—of the formation of political opinion has already taken place. Reagan was the first president who not only understood this but also made full use of it. His worldly wisdom was no greater than Carter's and his idealism—frequently far removed from reality—hardly less. Reagan's conservatism was good for his country after the Carter years; Reagan was considerably more consistent than his predecessor, and sometimes even obstinate. Though he was no more considerate of the interests of his allies in Europe, Japan, Canada, or Australia than Carter before him, the governments allied with the United States were relieved at his greater political consistency. However, they could not (and should not!) ignore his quality of being the television president. The man was effective because of his personal character, which he projected outward; because of his simplicity, his clear fundamental convictions, to which he clung; and because of his obvious sincerity. But most especially he was effective because of his ability to rally the American television audience behind him and to restore the nation's self-confidence. It remained to be seen whether he could overcome the great loss of faith in him that he suffered, because of his own naïveté and dishonesty, after the autumn of 1986 when the weapons deliveries to Iran and Nicaragua became known.

It was during a visit with Reagan in January 1982 that I first fully realized how much he himself was influenced by the images his countrymen saw every night on the television screen. The occasion was the declaration of martial law in Poland. My wife and I had the German habit of taking a short winter vacation at New Year's in a sunny southern clime—Mallorca, Ischia, or the Canaries. This time we had gone to the small golfing island of Sanibel in Florida. Reagan had heard we were there and had asked me to stop off in Washington on our way back. We arrived on January 4.

Two weeks before Christmas, Jaruzelski had declared martial law in Poland. Reagan himself had held a speech on November 18 that dealt in detail with matters of foreign and security policy. On November 25 I had had a long telephone conversation with Reagan in which I told him about Brezhnev's visit to Bonn, which had ended that day; I gave Reagan further details by the diplomatic route. From December 11 to December 23 I had met with Erich Honecker in the German Democratic Republic. So there was a lot to talk about. However, the events in Poland were the topic of greatest importance to the American president. This importance was due partly to the large percentage of American citizens who were of Polish extraction, but more especially to television, which, with its reports from Gdansk and Warsaw, aroused the whole American nation.

The entire American administration from the president down to

United Nations Ambassador Jeane Kirkpatrick, many senators, and many newspapers had exacerbated the emotionalism. Reagan had imposed a number of trade sanctions on the Soviet Union and an embargo against the People's Republic of Poland, and he was expecting his European allies to join in these actions. But he had not consulted these same allies beforehand and had informed them a mere six hours before he took action—just as, in his time, Carter had done. At the same time, however, his secretary of state had made it clear that Reagan had no thought of breaking off or at least interrupting the exchange of views with Moscow or the Geneva arms limitation negotiations. Nor did Reagan think to cut off the urgently needed American grain deliveries to the Soviet Union, since such an act would burden the American farmer; after all, he himself had resumed the grain sales in the spring of 1981. Reagan's trade-based reactions to the proclamation of martial law by Jaruzelski, who was seen and presented as Moscow's stooge, remained so limited in scope that they were merely of a pseudopolitical, symbolic nature. To the American television public, of course, Washington presented its measures as a step fraught with strategic significance; the president said publicly that the entire Western alliance must give Moscow a "distinct answer," and it was expected that the German chancellor would set an example for the other European allies.

At first I did not quite understand whether the excitement in Washington would eventually give way to cooler reflections and die down or whether escalation was imminent. After all, the American emotion was close to hysteria. Thus, for example, on January 4, 1982, the day I arrived in Washington, the *Wall Street Journal* announced that the time had come for me to take a stand. The article continued: "Mr. Schmidt's stance toward Moscow speaks of a demoralized leadership whose best vision of West Germany's future is as a Finlandized industrial vassal of a totalitarian empire." And another confused commentator warned, "No more Munichs!"

Because neither the politicians nor the editors of newspapers and television networks in the United States read European newspapers, they remained ignorant of my speech to the Bundestag on December 18 and the Bundestag resolution of the same date. Two weeks before my arrival in Washington, the Bundestag, acting with the federal government, had followed the debate with a unanimous statement directed at Jaruzelski's military regime in which it called for the "liberation of all prisoners" as well as the "restoration of the freedoms arrived at through a course of reform and renewal . . . [and] resumption of the dialogue with the patriotic forces of the Polish people willing to engage in reforms." The Bundestag had denounced the violation of the Helsinki Final Act by both the Polish military regime and the Soviet Union and had noted the Soviets' "open or covert threats of force against Polish independence from outside." In addition the Bundestag had suspended German economic aid to Poland for as long as "the measures of suppression of the current regime against the Polish people remain in force." But at the same time we had appealed to our own citizens to give individual moral and material aid to our neighboring people (which they did very generously). I myself addressed the Bundestag along the same lines; a week earlier, while still a guest in East German territory and speaking to the East German press, I had publicly taken a stand against outside interference in Poland's affairs.

The ten foreign ministers of the European Community, acting in sweeping agreement with the Bundestag's resolutions, had arrived at a joint resolution on January 4, 1982. Since the United States had by that time announced its economic measures against the Soviet Union, the ten further declared that they expected "close and positive" consultation with the United States. They specifically warned the Soviet Union against military intervention by the Warsaw Pact. The resolution of the ten was largely due to the steering influence of Foreign Minister Genscher.

Neither the American media nor the White House had taken any cognizance of these events. But some people in the White House had covertly informed the American media that Schmidt would be spoken to harshly and unequivocally on a number of issues, including the possibly serious consequences for the Western alliance that might result if the reaction of the Europeans continues to be as weak as it has been up to now. At the same time the media were fed the idea that the Americans might abort the pipeline agreement that was just then being negotiated between a European consortium and Moscow. The climax of these threats being spread by irresponsible men around Reagan was a suggestion that American banks might be persuaded to recall the loans they had granted to Poland, a move that would make large waves in Eastern European financial circles.

I decided to remain adamant on the matter. I found two aspects crucial that, it seemed, no one in the United States was prepared to state publicly. The whole world had witnessed the Soviet invasions of Budapest in 1956 and Prague in 1968, just as it had seen the invasions of Laos, Cambodia, and Afghanistan. These acts of violence against other nations by the Soviet Union or its Vietnamese allies had been met by worldwide outrage every time—as had the erection of the Berlin Wall in 1961. I had lived through all these events and had been shocked along with the rest of the world. But I also understood that on the one hand the United States had no effective power instrument to rescind these violations and that on the other it rightfully considered the threat of nuclear war too great to take the risk. In the case of Poland I understood clearly that any escalation on the part of the West could arouse the hopes of the freedom-loving Poles and tempt them to risk their lives and certainly their personal freedom while trusting in American or Western help—but that after some time Washington would arrive at the realization that the entire dramatic effort was in vain. The matter would be allowed to peter out, to be replaced by a new, more telegenic topic. I had no wish to participate in such an undignified scenario, which would ultimately hurt the Polish freedom movement and the Poles.

But I also had a specifically German motive, the inevitable result of German history during the Hitler era. No other nation, no other people had suffered more from German military occupation than Poland. The extermination camps in which millions of people were slaughtered had been situated on Polish soil, and most of the Jews who were killed were Polish Jews. After the war Stalin had forced the shift of Polish territory several hundred kilometers to the west and the displacement of many millions of Germans from their ancestral homes. As early as the 1920s the Weimar Republic, which had agreed with France on its western boundary in the 1925 Locarno treaty between Gustav Stresemann and Aristide Briand, had refused to bring about an "Eastern Locarno" as well, because it was unwilling to commit the nation to the German-Polish boundary, which had recently been created. Hitler, Himmler, and the so-called governor general of occupied Poland, Hans Frank, had taken the anti-Polish sentiment then prevalent in Germany (which, of course, had its reverse counterpart in Poland) and raised it to unimaginable horror.

In all the years after 1945 I was therefore deeply motivated by a wish for reconciliation between the Germans and the Poles; this will be my position in future as well, and I share it with many Germans. Reconciliation was a crucial motivation of Willy Brandt's—and later my—*Ostpolitik*. We had no doubt whatever that we must include in our calculations the fact of Communist rule, which had been established in the People's Republic of Poland under Soviet supervision. Any German intent on arriving at an understanding with Poland would have to conclude treaties with the government actually in Warsaw—whether the signatory was Wladyslaw Gomulka, Edward Gierek, Stanislaw

Kania, or Wojciech Jaruzelski. Any West German attempt to drive a
wedge between the Polish people and its government—to speak kindly
to the former while refusing to help the latter—was not only bound to
fail, it would also provide the Communist propagandists in Warsaw
with arguments against alleged "German revanchism." For years the
Polish leadership had turned the unwise speeches by a few functionaries
of refugee organizations—among them two CDU Bundestag representatives—against the Germans with great psychological success. Genscher
and I therefore would not even consider allowing Washington to maneuver the Federal Republic into a provocative role vis-à-vis Warsaw.

In addition, economic sanctions hit the little man in Poland more
acutely than they did the people at the head of the party. To help the
mass of the population in view of the acute scarcity of consumer goods
in Poland, we called on our citizens to send private food packages. The
Catholic and Protestant churches both provided very effective help in
this action by organizing mailings to clergymen and congregations
known to them by name. West German citizens sent millions of food
packages to Poland beginning at Christmas of 1981; by the summer of
1982 several tens of thousands of packages were still being sent off daily.
By this action we surely did not undermine the American trade embargo; but we did help countless Polish families. I was very proud of
the fact that so many Germans were not deterred by chauvinist propaganda from helping their Polish neighbors.

True, I found that the American media showed little understanding
for my position, which certainly was not influenced by any interests of
German business or our employment situation, as was flippantly im-
puted to me in the United States. But I had the satisfaction of meeting
with approval among many American friends with foreign policy experience. George Kennan stated publicly that he could hardly imagine that
the American sanctions would lead to a positive result. George Ball
called Reagan's sanctions "not majestic lions but toothless poodles,"
just as publicly adding the question, "When shall we learn that maintaining Western unity is more important than the ineffectual attempt to
intimidate Moscow?"

On January 5, 1982, the German ambassador to Washington, Peter
Hermes, had invited me and a number of old friends and their wives
to dine at the embassy. Of course the situation in Poland and the Soviet
Union's position were the principal topics of discussion. Though the
guests' opinions diverged, none considered for a moment that my government was simply saying what we thought the Soviet Union wanted
to hear.

John McCloy advised me that I should be firm in countering the anti-American and neutralist statements of some politicians, which had lately been heard in Germany; at the same time he reaffirmed his long and unshakable ties to Germany. Henry Kissinger went furthest in agreeing with the Reagan administration. He warned against underestimating American isolationism, which might join forces with American anticommunism in case of serious disappointment with Europe. He left open the question of whether economic measures against Poland would be effective, and he pretended that he lacked the expertise to answer the question. Gerald Ford replied that there were only two effective instruments of economic pressure: a grain embargo on the Soviet Union and a credit embargo on Poland. Both of these could be effective only if all the Western nations were truly united in participating, but the American administration itself was not even considering these measures. George Shultz agreed that these measures would, in fact, be effective only if the West took part in them as a unit, but such unity, he said, was a long way from reality. Lane Kirkland thought that compared with the public utterances, the measures taken by the Reagan administration were too weak. Senator Joseph Biden criticized the lack of sufficient consultation with the Europeans; the American sanctions had taken them by surprise, and, he claimed, the Senate had been misled when told that the Europeans had been consulted (which was probably true).

I myself could keep it brief that night. I pointed out that my speech to the Bundestag of December 18, the January 4, 1982, resolution of the European Community foreign ministers, and the joint statement President Reagan and I had released to the press shortly before this dinner had all said the same thing.

The detailed official communiqué was published the following day, January 6. With some satisfaction I pointed to our consistency and regretted the misleading reports in the American media. Consistency in foreign policy toward the Soviet Union was a precondition of the reliability of this policy; it was necessary, I said, if we wanted to be understood in Moscow. None of those present disagreed.

On the whole, that night I was conscious of a friendly affection. The fact that Betty Ford and Obie Shultz had come from the West and that Nancy Kissinger, the almost ninety-year-old John McCloy, and David Rockefeller from New York, as well as my old friends Melvin and Barbara Laird, Lane Kirkland and his wife, and Paul Nitze (at the time chief INF negotiator in Geneva) were there I understood to be gestures of great devotion. I was happy that not only my wife was included in these friendships but also my daughter Susanne, who for professional reasons was living in London and who therefore had shared in very little of the personal aspects of international politics in recent years. I do not think I am mistaken: The American participants in this party saw a friend in me.

During the day my wife had had a talk with American women during which politics inevitably came up. Loki reported on her various visits to Poland and her private conversations with Polish friends and acquaintances. The Poles, she said, were Poles ten times over, Catholic ten times over, and only then Communists once, at most. Loki found that such remarks evoked great astonishment. When she said that she had seen very different forms of Communism in various Eastern European nations, the reaction was the same. Clearly our American hostesses had only very sketchy ideas of the actually very differentiated situation behind the Iron Curtain.

The evening before, we had also entertained a few old friends: Secretary of State Alexander Haig; Paul Volcker, head of the Federal Reserve System; Ambassador Arthur Burns; and Senator Charles Mathias. Others in the party included Senator Robert Dole; the secretaries of Commerce and the Treasury, Malcolm Baldrige and Donald Regan; the President's adviser Edwin Meese; Congressman James Jones; Murray Weidenbaum from the Council of Economic Advisers; Lewis Preston from the Morgan Bank—the elite of the administration and the Republican Party, as it were. In this company, too, I regretted briefly but distinctly the fact that Washington had allowed the excitement of the media to mislead it about the German position. Otherwise they would have known that it was my belief that martial law had been declared in Warsaw only to anticipate Soviet pressure. They would also have known that a week *before* President Reagan's Christmas speech I had demanded that martial law be revoked, that the dialogue with Solidarity be resumed, and that all prisoners be released—as the president did subsequently. Economic sanctions—except for a grain embargo—would hardly affect the Soviet Union, since it imported a mere 2 percent of its gross national product from the West. I also pointed out that credit sanctions against Poland, such as the refusal to grant debt conversion for 1982, would cut two ways for two reasons. They would affect the little man in Poland, but they would also impact on the Western banking system, and therefore careful scrutiny of their possible consequences would be required. In general a joint analysis of all possible actions was urgently necessary; for even the United States—and myself as well—had no answer to the question of how the West should react to a possible further aggravation of the unfortunate situation in Poland. Furthermore, it was my impression that Jaruzelski was no puppet; he was first of all a Pole, secondly a military man, and only thirdly a Communist.

Secretary of State Alexander Haig was the member of the group who replied to my remarks. There could be no doubt, he noted, that Jaruzelski was not free to make his own decisions, that he was acting under pressure from Moscow; the Soviets had been demanding the imposition of martial law since September. Haig did not oppose humanitarian aid, provided "that it really reaches the Polish people; we cannot stand by and watch them starve to death." But the United States would be unwilling to grant credits to Poland as long as the government was oppressing the people. As far as consultation was concerned, he said that his deputy, Lawrence Eagleburger, had returned from talks in Europe with the impression that the Europeans were not prepared to participate in sanctions (which was correct). Therefore the president had guessed that he would receive a negative response in concrete consultations and had acted on his own.

This explanation seemed entirely plausible; I was therefore all the more puzzled by the American expectation that the European governments would join the unilaterally imposed sanctions retroactively. The most the United States could hope for on the question of sanctions was a self-imposed obligation on the part of the Europeans (and the United States' other allies, perhaps including Australia) not to undermine American trade actions against the Soviet Union through increased deliveries.

Haig said that the comments of the American mass media against Bonn's stance had surprised him, too. They had not been elicited by his department (which I believed) nor by the White House (which I did not believe). He confirmed that my December 18 speech had been almost identical to Reagan's later statements as far as the content went. Now it was important, he said, to create the impression that there was a "sense of action."

Besides attending these two evening parties, during those two and a half days in early January 1982 I visited the Foreign Affairs Committee of the Senate, had a long talk with Secretary of Defense Weinberger, and finally granted a long newspaper interview. Foreign Minister Genscher and secretaries of state Becker and von Staden were equally busy. We tried to do all we could to create a favorable climate for my talks with Reagan. The administration understood that its reproaches of us had been the outcome of their being taken in by the one-sided presentations of the American mass media, though it is also true that the media had without a doubt been infected by overeager members of the administration. In any case, the great speech bubbles soon collapsed soundlessly.

The following day the president initiated the topic of Poland with the remark that he was aware that the American media had dealt with me unfairly. He himself was in any case very happy with everything I said on the subject during my visit. After that beginning, it was not difficult to issue the joint communiqué. Some American commentators were satisfied with it but expressed their astonishment that the German chancellor had given in and "for the first time admitted that the Soviet Union shared the responsibility for the situation in Poland." Even now they were unwilling to recognize that a long time before, I had written a serious letter to Brezhnev on the matter—the only European head of government to have done so, by the way. Brzezinski (in private life for a year now) went so far as to state in *U.S. News and World Report* of January 11, "West German Chancellor Helmut Schmidt, while professing his commitment to Allied unity, is already acting like a neutral." But this was a rather grotesque exception. On the whole the American response was good.

The New York Times of January 7 raised an important point: The outcome, the newspaper noted, rested on the tacit understanding that negotiations with the Soviet Union would continue in spite of the Polish situation. This was in fact correct. However, the understanding was tacit only outwardly; in reality it had been explicitly elaborated between the two governments.

I was thoroughly satisfied with the overall outcome. The German media also commented positively on the results of the meeting—except for the Springer press and Franz Josef Strauss, who had accused us for days of "lack of dignity" and had used CSU connections to White House staffers to stir up anti-Bonn feelings. The strongest approval of Bonn's position was expressed in British, Italian, Dutch, and Scandinavian newspapers. These did not omit the appropriate references to agreement with the Vatican (which, as concerned Poland, the head of the Fulda Conference of Bishops, Cardinal Joseph Höffner, had not yet joined).

The French media tended to follow the somewhat sour reaction of François Mitterrand. At an internal session of the meeting of the ten European Community foreign ministers, Mitterrand's foreign minister had severely weakened his criticism of Poland's system of government as the true cause of the unfortunate situation, since he clearly had to respect the views of the Communist members of his government; suddenly the government in Warsaw could no longer be apostrophized as

a "Communist system." Outwardly, however, Paris acted especially outraged and particularly loyal to the alliance with the United States.
Nevertheless, even France did not participate in the American sanctions.

As early as five months later, during the eighth economic summit in
Versailles, a reversal set in: Reagan's insistence on introducing commercial measures as an instrument of foreign policy directed against the
Soviet Union led to a long, sharp public controversy between Reagan
and Mitterrand. Reagan attempted—once again unilaterally and without putting the plan to a vote—to undermine the European-Soviet oil
pipeline agreement through an embargo that would violate the sovereignty of the European nations by prohibiting partial deliveries by
American subsidiaries active in Europe. This move persuaded Mitterrand and the French press to adopt the position that Bonn had held all
the time.

I have described the controversy over the appropriate "answer" by the
West to the suppression of the Polish freedom movement at such length
because it illuminates the possible conflict between television democracy and political rationality. In this case rationality triumphed; all the
American measures were subsequently abandoned without much fuss,
though the situation in Poland did not substantially change. But such
conflicts can and will recur. Even in this case of conflict resolution
through smooth revision of the emotional standpoint, reason by no
means prevailed in the mind of the participants. Neither the majority
of the American media nor the administration admitted to themselves
the reality that the partition of Central Europe into two spheres of
influence (or into a Western sphere of influence and an Eastern power
bloc), which had been initiated at Yalta, could not be abolished by
television addresses, large gestures, and subsequent small actions.

Germany, as the instigator and loser of the Second World War, had
had no choice but to accept the partition, under which it had been
suffering for forty years; for the sake of peace, the Germans had also
made the boundaries forced on them the subject of nonaggression
pacts. In a different way, the Poles, too, suffer from the partition of
Europe, which made them subject to Soviet sovereignty; they have also
been forced to cede large tracts of their country to the Soviet Union.
At present it is impossible to foresee how the morally and historically
untenable situation of the division of Europe can be ameliorated. Every
attempt to use the will to freedom of the Poles, Hungarians, Czechs,
or Germans as a lever to force a restriction of Soviet-controlled territory
will run the risk of provoking violent intervention by Moscow; in the

end there are the threats of civil war and of international war. The idea of a "rollback" was shown to be unworkable in 1953 in East Germany, in 1956 in Hungary, and in 1968 in Czechoslovakia because—thank God!—it was not backed by any American contingency plan to run the risk of war with the Soviet Union. Nothing indicates that tomorrow the situation will be any different.

Most of the peoples of Europe have lived through worse war experiences than have the inhabitants of North America, who for generations have not been exposed to foreign troops on the soil of a destroyed homeland. That is why Europeans demand conciliation, understanding, balance, and guarantees that peace will be maintained by arms limitation regulated by treaty. But they are by no means prepared to let themselves be overwhelmed. Even the Poles would muster their national enthusiasm to defend their puny amount of self-determination against any Western attack. In the same way the citizens of the Federal Republic of Germany would defend their country against an attack from the East. But none of them—even the citizens of the German Democratic Republic—wish to be pushed or pulled by either of the two superpowers into a war or serious political conflicts with their neighbors. This attitude is not cowardice, nor does it represent "appeasement"; it has simply grown out of historical experience, political reason—and moral principles.

The consequences of this reasoning are bitter for the people of Europe, especially for those who long for freedom and democracy. Following their centuries-old tradition, the Soviet Russians have no great scruples about ignoring the longing for freedom of millions of people in their realm. The Americans cannot afford to minimize the will to peace of the people in both the eastern and western parts of Central Europe; such an attitude would deny their own outrage at the suppression of the people in the eastern sector. But the terrible, unendingly tragic dilemma of knowing oneself morally compelled to intervene but politically powerless to accomplish anything significant must be endured. It is very difficult to make this clear to a television audience expecting simple formulas and solutions.

In 1986 James Reston gave a lecture on the role of the mass media in American foreign policy. He said that the media were more than participants; unfortunately there was a danger they themselves and their activities would take the place of diplomacy and foreign policy. Of course this was not a role the media could actually fill. Television in particular was increasingly influencing the behavior of politicians and governments. Reston noted an "alliance" between government and media, but what was dangerous was the weight the politicians placed on their television appearances: They were mistaken "if they believed that in reality they are what they simply represent to the public." Conversely, Reston warned the media: "Because we in the media usually do not really know what the government is up to, the attempts to manipulate public opinion are limitless." The eye of the camera has made an enormous impression on public opinion and on the politicians. Reston's lecture ended with a reassurance that in the United States today, the press is better informed, less partisan, but more responsible than ever before. Though he was concerned about the influence of television on politics, he was reassured by the thought that of everything we had feared since the Second World War, hardly anything had actually occurred.

I understand Reston's irony. However, I myself am less doubtful of the influence of television on politics than of politicians' voluntary subjection to television drama.

The Temptation of
Économie Dominante

A LTHOUGH the awareness that common strategy and common action were a necessity was not lost on either side of the Atlantic during the days of Carter and Reagan, in practice this recognition was nevertheless increasingly neglected in Washington. The breach was to be filled only in part and only temporarily by the close collaboration between France and West Germany. The direction given within the European Community by the Giscard-Schmidt tandem in the second half of the 1970s radiated faintly to the entire West. But with three almost simultaneous personnel changes—from Carter to Reagan in the winter of 1981, from Giscard to Mitterrand in the spring of 1982, and from Schmidt to Kohl in the autumn of 1982—the constellation fell apart and has not been replaced to this day.

Reagan was also in no position to bring about a strong Western leadership. He was deceived by his popularity at home as well as public opinion in his country about the malaise felt in Europe—including in Germany—about the fact that a clear, shared overall Western strategy did not in fact exist. Its lack was evident primarily in two areas: first, vis-à-vis the Soviet Union, and second, regarding the viability of the world economy, which had been in jeopardy since 1973.

The economic disputes began within a very few weeks of Carter's inauguration in 1977. The new American president recommended an inflationary monetary and budget policy to us; further, he categorically demanded a reduction in our private-sector exports of nuclear reactors, hinting that if the Federal Republic of Germany refused to go along, there would be no further deliveries of enriched uranium for West Germany's own nuclear power plants. We rejected both demands. In the first instance we added the warning that the expansion of demand Carter had in mind for his own economy would merely lead to swifter inflation. In the second instance we explained our own economic interests in the area of employment and based our case on Article 4 of the Nuclear Nonproliferation Treaty, which granted the right to the peaceful use of nuclear energy. We further pointed out that we were carefully observing all international treaties relevant to this area. It took some time before Carter finally relented.

On the other hand, Carter's urging Germany and Japan to engage in generous "reflation" so as to bring the world economy back to a state of health remained a constant in his admonitions to us. At the economic summit held in Bonn in the summer of 1978, which I headed, we finally met him halfway, gaining in return the promise that intra-American oil prices would be released; that is, should gasoline and heating oil prices rise in the United States, the American demand for energy on the world markets would decrease correspondingly. Of course we later saw Carter do just the opposite; he used public financing to subsidize oil imports into the United States and thus drove up the Rotterdam spot prices for the whole world. The second OPEC oil price explosion was in the wind. We Germans, by the way, had set the pace with the right example, by passing on the entire increase in oil prices to the consumer. As a result we achieved a considerable reduction in oil consumption by industry and private consumers.

In the Federal Republic, after the summit meeting of 1978, the general expansion of demand proceeded along the lines of lowering taxes and investment programs which, adjusted each year, were to make up about 1 percent of our gross national product. In late November 1978 Carter told me that his tax cuts from the beginning of 1978 had also made up about 1 percent of the gross national product. He combined this information with the claim that now (that is, *after* the congressional elections in early November 1978) fighting inflation was his main problem; that was why he wanted to decrease the budget deficit for the fiscal year beginning on October 1, 1979, by half. I wished him good luck, because inflation in the United States was imperiling the stability of many nations. Ten days later I had a visit from the American

Republican presidential candidate, Ronald Reagan; he credited Carter's anti-inflation program to pressure from the Republican Party.

As early as late summer of 1979 it was obvious that the Carter administration was unable to get as firm a grip on the fundamental factors of its own economic development as continental Europe generally had. The downward trend of the dollar exchange rate was in full swing. Washington urgently suggested that the Deutsche Bundesbank intervene to a greater degree with German marks, so as to remove dollars from the market. But we could meet the request only to a limited degree because we took the risk of inflation in our own country seriously; every mark spent to support the dollar bloated the German money supply. To balance such inflation of the mark, it would have been necessary to institute high interest rates in Germany, which in turn would have depressed the state of the economy significantly and increased unemployment. I was willing to accept a cautious German cooperation, but at the same time I advised the United States to sell gold to support the dollar rate of exchange and higher interest there, where the real interest rate was almost zero.

At the end of September 1979 Finance Minister Hans Matthöfer and Deutsche Bundesbank President Otmar Emminger went with me to a meeting at Hamburg's Overseas Club with William Miller—the newly appointed United States Secretary of the Treasury, who had taken the place of Michael Blumenthal—his deputy, Anthony Solomon, and the chairman of the Federal Reserve Board, Paul Volcker. Volcker and Solomon are outstanding experts; that is why I secretly felt sorry for them when they could give no convincing answer to my matter-of-fact observation that in the final analysis foreign currency intervention would not be enough to restore the political confidence of the market participants in the economic development of the United States.

As always in such cases, I immediately informed Giscard, telling him, "The Americans are again asking us for monetary credits in marks, so as to support the dollar. I believe I'm going to have to give in a little. But the Americans will have to do something themselves in the way of higher interest rates and such. Washington will have to put its own house in order if it wants to ask us to help America."

Giscard shared my opinion and expressed it publicly. In fact, however, the Carter administration was in no position to put its own house back in order. On the contrary: inflation was increasing rapidly, as was unemployment. But the economic growth that was supposed to occur was minimal. The dollar, which had stood at 2.90 German marks at the beginning of the Carter administration, was worth only 1.71 marks in January 1980.

Nor was the Reagan administration able to place the United States budget and monetary policy on a sure footing. Admittedly, Reagan did manage a colossal upswing in the economic situation with the help of an economic policy which, though it was at first called "supply-side economics," in reality proved to be a policy of expanding national demand via rapidly increasing budget deficits of a magnitude not seen in the entire industrial world since the 1930s.

While Carter was unable to keep his budget promises, Reagan turned his, which went even further, into their glaring opposites by his manipulation of economic policy. Carter was punished for his mistakes while he was still in office; but it may well be that the American public will not realize Reagan's economic error until after he has finished his second term. Carter was simply not lucky.

Both the Carter and the Reagan administrations acted according to the comfortable rule that whenever the American public began to feel the unpleasant results of national economic policy, Japan and Germany (sometimes even the entire European Community) were to be made scapegoats. In Tokyo and Bonn we often heard the demand that we act as the "locomotive" of the international economy, although the wording varied from time to time; Japan was equally often exhorted to limit its exports to the United States through administrative intervention.

Whenever the United States enthusiastically launched a new economic experiment, its administration invited the world's other industrial nations to follow suit. This occurred in the early 1970s, when the system of pegged (but adjustable) exchange rates based on the Bretton Woods model was abandoned; it occurred again in the second half of the 1970s with the introduction of Carter's form of Keynesianism; and it occurred a third time at the beginning of the 1980s, with Reagan's form of Keynesianism, which became known as supply-side economics. In all these cases we were first invited to follow the allegedly good example of the United States. But in each case some time later we were even more urgently requested to participate actively in repairing the undesirable consequences and give up the drawing card. The locomotive theory has since grown into a monster of the Loch Ness type: It keeps coming up for air. The first optimistic call for a new beginning is invariably followed by a second call to change course, and the other nations are asked to help while their national economic interests are ignored. The third act then consists of dramatically aggravated conflicts of interest. These cannot be genuinely resolved in the fourth and final act but are more or less swept under the rug with mere declarations of intention.

Each time the American enthusiasm during the first act also grabbed a few German economists. In the case of abandoning the pegged exchange rates, a few professors of economics were happy to get on the same boat and tried with scientific theorems to fill the sails with wind. It was not until they realized, a few years later, that the absence of discipline in exchange rates and balance of payments left the leaders of many countries free to develop an inflationary budget and monetary policy that they moderated their stand. In the case of the deficit spending deliberately introduced by Carter, many of our business leaders and many minds on the political left applauded; they demanded that the West German government follow America's deficit example with grand investment and employment programs, to be financed by a drastic increase in the budget deficit. In the instance of Reagan's supply-side policy, it was especially German industry, the political right, and the FDP, as well as the Ministry of Economics and its head, Count Otto Lambsdorff, who insisted that we follow the American example of tax cuts. They did not realize until much later that basically "Reaganomics" was nothing more than a new version of the old inflationary deficit spending, though in a novel and more attractive form; while in 1981 they dreamed of tax cuts in Germany that would be equal to Reagan's, in early 1982 they began to demand a sociopolitically and domestically risky decrease in the relatively small German budget deficit.

In fact, since the beginning of the monetary and production crisis in the world economy, the Federal Republic of Germany had tried to steer a middle course. Together with Japan, Germany (like Holland and a few other countries) belongs to the nations most easily affected by the ups and downs of the chaotic disorder in the world economy. Both countries have practically no oil, while the United States and Great Britain are self-sufficient to a high degree and France disposes over extensive nuclear energy. However, not only are Japan and Germany dependent on energy imports and thus must bear their price fluctuations, but, because all raw materials are scarce within their borders, their overall economy is also integrated into the world economy to a high degree. Compared to the United States, the share of the Japanese gross national product that is exported is one and a half to two times as large, while in Germany the export share is three to four times that of the United States.

The governments in both Tokyo and Bonn understood that they must counter the two oil price shocks, which drastically reduced the buying power within our two economies. Our first step was an expansion of domestic demand and foreign trade indebtedness (Japan after 1973, Germany after 1979). These measures were intended to keep our economies viable and to set limits on the inevitable decrease in employment. But both governments were equally careful to follow these actions with budgetary consolidation. Japan was more successful than Germany in keeping up employment. Two reasons primarily accounted for this circumstance: First, the Japanese as a whole were much more easily satisfied. They voluntarily went without the urgently needed expansion of their inadequate social security and without improved housing, their labor unions were largely ineffective and the wage demands they made were very modest, and the successive governments of the Liberal Democratic Party (LDP) were neither compelled nor inclined to respect the unions. Second, the Japanese domestic economy was and is a market economy utterly controlled by the state; any comparisons with the United States, Great Britain, France, Italy, Canada, and Germany reveal that the Tokyo ministry for international trade and industry (MITI) is invested with very unusual rights of intervention, which are accepted by the enterprises. The Japanese government intervenes softly but most effectively.

Of course the Japanese governments and MITI have exaggerated the matter; during the 1980s, out of a mercantilistic mentality, they produced enormous surpluses in their balance of goods and services vis-à-vis the rest of the world. To do so, the Japanese gave up an increase in their standard of living, though it could have occurred, in favor of an increase in foreign debentures and investments abroad. During the 1980s Japan became the largest capital exporter in the world. The constantly repeated American accusations were therefore foreseeable, although the American government had little justification for them. Its need of capital imports was its own fault, and its contribution to the mismanagement of the trade and financial currents of the world was twice that of the Japanese in the opposite direction.

Under James Callaghan, Britain began by carefully following the line set by Carter; from 1979 on, under Margaret Thatcher, the line became harder and more focused on budget matters, congruent with a "monetaristically" grounded fiscal policy. Prime Minister Thatcher did not let herself be taken in by either Carter's or Reagan's enthusiasm; neither one version nor the other persuaded her to think for a moment of seeking the welfare of the British economy in deliberately triggered additional budget deficits. But since her economic policy was nevertheless not particularly successful, she was spared American interference.

To some extent Britain could therefore always afford to say what Washington wanted to hear without actually falling in with whatever course the White House was pursuing.

The reasons for the relatively slight success of London's economic policy lie in the aristocratic but quite undynamic mentality of British industrial management and in the philosophy of class struggle, carried over from the nineteenth century, which exists both in the labor movement and its supporters, including the Labour Party, and the industrial management, the upper classes, and the Conservative Party. The consequences were—and still are—comparatively minor industrial innovations and relatively small increases in productivity. However, London's banking and financial world, the so-called City, is an important exception to the general rule. Altogether we could neither learn much from the British example nor expect help from London in countering the Americans' expectations of us. It was always different when, for reasons of foreign policy, Washington demanded trade restrictions; then the traditional British belief in free trade ran parallel to Bonn's interests.

France's tradition had never supported free trade; since the days of Louis XIV the country had had a mercantile orientation. Nevertheless, Giscard and I usually pursued the same economic line, including our stance toward the United States. This wide-ranging economic agreement came to an end when Mitterrand assumed office. He combined three ideologies, evolved from different historical roots, into an overall concept; first, budgetary Keynesianism; second, socialism directed at nationalization and the welfare state; and, third, trade Colbertism. The consequence of Mitterrand's policy in the domestic economy was to accelerate inflation. Its result in the field of foreign trade led to a rapid decline of the franc's rate of exchange. Soon a correction in this economic policy became essential; it led to an increase in unemployment. Thus Mitterrand was all the more touchy about Reagan's attempts at trade patronage.

Consequently the economic summit held in Versailles in June 1982 witnessed a head-on confrontation between the two presidents. The so-called pipeline embargo (a misleading term, since it was merely a matter of supplying a few pumps) that Reagan imposed a few days after the summit aggravated the situation, until malevolent polemics were issued by all sides. Reagan's "crusade against trade with the East," as several European newspapers called it, surely made a good impression on the American television audience, since it was a concept easily understood by laymen. For the Soviet Union it meant no more than a policy of pinpricks, but the European allies saw this plan as an attempt to undermine their sovereignty and turn the United States into the economic commander of the Western world. The French media coined a term for the United States that became popular: *économie dominante*— the United States as dominating national economy. Similarly, an American political scientist spoke of an "imperious economy."

This concept was met with vehement protest not only in France; not a single government in the rest of the Western world, from Canberra and Tokyo through Ottawa to Europe, was prepared to accept the economic sovereignty of the United States. Though all of us found Reagan's vigorous presidency more reliable than the preceding Carter era, it was specifically in the economic arena that Reagan could gain neither credibility nor legitimacy.

Already a year before, in the summer of 1981, it had appeared that though Reagan could relatively easily enforce his major tax cuts, he would be unable to impose the budget cuts that would have to accompany the tax policy; in fact, he even increased defense expenditures to an outrageous degree. Every impartial observer could safely make the prognosis that state indebtedness would increase, balance-of-trade deficits would increase, and the dollar rate of exchange would fall (the latter two consequences set in only quite belatedly). The administration, however, denied any such inevitability. A certain Professor Arthur B. Laffer had turned out to be a splendid accomplice; with the help of a curve he had invented (the "Laffer curve"), he proved that there was no need to decrease expenditures because lower tax rates would allegedly lead to increased federal income. As late as January 1982 Secretary of the Treasury Donald Regan assured me that the national deficits on the order of $100 billion a year that I had foretold would absolutely not happen; in reality that same year the American deficit surpassed that sum, and in the following years it quickly rose to roughly $200 billion a year.

The budget deficits put an excessive strain on American savings and on the efficiency of the American financial markets and—as a result of the newly risen interest rates—stimulated tremendous capital imports. That is why today and for the foreseeable future the United States is by far the largest international debtor (even when we subtract all American foreign investments and claims). Reagan's initial economic success, which lasted quite a long time, and the rebirth of the typically American optimistic self-confidence he brought about first raised the dollar to heights it had last held in 1970. On February 26, 1985, the dollar stood at 3.47 German marks. But by the middle of 1987, as could have been foreseen, it had fallen back to 1.80 marks. The most important currency in the world has become a weathervane.

As far as I could see, a few men had warned against the administration's direction. Among them were the chairman of the Council of Economic Advisors, Martin Feldstein; Arthur Burns, who was one of the president's economic advisers as well as ambassador to Bonn; and especially Paul Volcker. Volcker was the only one whose arguments pointed not only to the foreseeable consequences for the United States but also to the consequences for the world economy. But their voices were drowned out, just like those of the European critics. Instead the administration and the Congress allowed themselves to be deceived by a paean of praise for the new economic policy. The chorus included the Nobel Prize–winner Milton Friedman and other professors as well as the cabinet members responsible for fiscal and budget policy, Secretary of the Treasury Regan and Budget Director David Stockman; senators and representatives did their best to spread the general euphoria. The mood lasted well into 1984; to my astonishment and that of many other critics, in the course of 1982 the recession was actually reversed and a major employment boom, which lasted several years, set in. Though, as expected, the federal debt grew and real interest rates rose, as did the deficits in the balance of goods and services in comparison to the rest of the world, the world was at first fully prepared to provide the United States with a high degree of savings, credits, and capital.

A series of factors worked in favor of the United States: increased capital flight from Central and South America and worldwide insecurity concerning the future of peace (the Israeli invasion of Lebanon, war between Iran and Iraq, American threats against Libya in 1981, the Falklands conflict between England and Argentina in 1982, and especially the increasing verbal Cold War between the United States and the Soviet Union). The increasing international insecurity made capital investment in the United States seem a safe haven. To this was added the relatively high real interest rates; after deducting for inflation, the United States rate for long-term loans stood at 5.7 percent, while in Germany it amounted to only 3.3 percent. The influx of foreign money that had to be exchanged for dollars for the purpose of investment in the United States led to a considerable demand for dollars and thus to a rise in the dollar exchange rate, and the hope of further exchange rate profits in turn attracted foreign savings. So for the time being it seemed the United States could easily finance its rapidly increasing deficits in the balance of goods and services.

But most especially the Keynesian employment multiplier grew, and unemployment decreased significantly. The traditional industries in the east and midwest of the United States were only slightly affected by this upswing. But the new technologies, which were located primarily in the south and west—as well as American workers' astonishing mobility and restraint on wage demands—contributed just as much to the persistent upswing as did the new self-confidence created by Reagan and the faith in the future of the American business community.

The European critics—myself among them—had expected a rise in American demand, but at the same time we had assumed that the American Federal Reserve System under Paul Volcker would pursue a relatively tight money policy. None of us had foreseen that foreign countries would correct the financial mishaps to such a degree. In the mid-1980s the American federal budget used up about one tenth of the world's total savings! In view of what seemed an exceedingly favorable American economic development, the warnings from Europe generally met with a lack of understanding in Washington.

Volcker's hard-money policy had markedly damped inflationary expectations, but President Reagan believed that the reduction in inflation was an effect of his supply-side policy. After a further reference to the United States' high interest rates, he said to me, "The Wall Street banks are to blame; they simply refuse to believe that we've conquered inflation." He was as unaware of the fact that the high American interest rates had led to an omission of the investments necessary for growth and employment in the rest of the world as he was of the danger that the quickly growing interest burden on those states that were heavily indebted to foreign countries—from Mexico and Brazil through Nigeria to Poland—might force major debtor nations to declare insolvency. The problem of interest and its effects on the world's economy were of no great interest to the Reagan administration until the end of 1984.

In 1981 and 1982 my concerns were largely shared by Burns, Volcker, and Kirkland, though Burns was always somewhat more optimistic. But the White House and the Department of the Treasury were not to be discouraged. Until early 1985 they were even indifferent to the rising dollar rate of exchange, which had the effects that American goods became drastically more expensive for the whole world to buy and American industry therefore had to let go of some of its foreign markets. This increase in the exchange rate, however, could not help but collapse within a foreseeable period of time because of the increasing trade deficit. The Treasury Department under Regan refused Volcker even the highly desirable paltry currency interventions that would have helped avoid short-term, erratic fluctuations in the rate of exchange and guarantee orderly market processes.

Only in 1985, after James Baker had taken over from Donald Regan, was there any awakening; but in the meantime the growth of the

American economy had markedly diminished. Now it was almost too late. Beginning in February 1985, the dollar retreated rapidly; in the spring of 1987 it reached almost the same low point it had suffered once before under Carter. There was no longer any hope of a quick cure for the American balance of payments. That was why the Loch Ness monster of the locomotive theory rose from the depths once more in 1985 and 1986. In the summer of 1986 Reagan personally requested all the United States' partners to make tax cuts. He himself and the Congress were just then engaged in a far-reaching restructuring of the American tax system, which admittedly incorporated the serious error that, as he explicitly declared, it would not let a single additional dollar flow to the deficit-ridden American federal coffers.

Reagan's demand was addressed primarily to Japan and Germany. Though the United States' own economic policy did not grant him any political legitimation for this step, it seemed that now, when the effortless increases in exports to the United States would come to an end, it was in the national interests of Japan and Germany (as well as Holland and other previous surplus nations) to provide for domestic economic growth by loosening both their budgets and their monetary policies. But the governments of both countries, shocked by the bad budgetary example set by the United States since 1981, had been gripped by an exaggerated savings ideology. Furthermore, they still lacked faith in the continuity of American economic policy; especially in the markets for textiles, agricultural products, steel, pipes, automobiles, telecommunications, and the like, they had learned the hard way about the egotistical will to power of the *économie dominante* and the United States contingency plan to violate the rules.

Since the Vietnam War and the abandonment of the international monetary system developed at Bretton Woods, the United States had lost its position as economic leader of the world. It was not in a position to utilize the yearly economic summit meeting (or the yearly IMF conventions) to win back the leadership because it could not develop a plan; thus the economic summit had only the very limited success of preventing the worst. But the European Community was equally unable to take a leadership position; in the course of its expansion from six to twelve members it had gradually lost the capacity to shape a joint economic will.

My attempts in 1981–1982 to give my American friends a sense of the international consequences of American economic activity, to persuade them to comprehend the destabilizing political dangers of European mass unemployment, and to offer them conceptual and cooperative economic leadership were fruitless. Viewed in hindsight and in connection with the collapse of the general strategy of the West after 1976, this negative outcome was just about inevitable. Henry Kissinger, who had long since returned to private life, was the only one of the statesmanlike thinkers in the United States who recognized the necessity of economic leadership of the Western world. Had George Shultz been named not secretary of state but United States "economic czar" in 1982, this efficient, rich, and powerful country might have been in a position to continue its great tradition of world economic leadership, which had begun with the ideas of IMF, the World Bank, the Marshall Plan, and the trade-political GATT "Kennedy round."

But Carter and Reagan acted without much concern for their economic partners, keeping an eye only on what they assumed to be America's economic interests. Their temporary economic successes blinded them to the fact that the huge aggregate of the American economy and the overriding dollar currency were having powerful effects on the world economy. They were conscious of their claim to supremacy, but they recognized the responsibility that followed from it only in their own short-term self-interest and only from case to case.

The United States has not yet understood that a purely national economic strategy is an anachronism in today's interdependent world economy. Just as in the areas of foreign policy and security strategy the United States cannot prevail in any corner of the world and certainly not against the Soviet Union without the cooperation of its partners, it must also cooperate with its partners for its own economic welfare.

Unfortunately at present the overall American strategy is being limited more and more to military armament and deployment. If Washington were to take its bearings from the fact that the seven participating states of the annual world economic summit taken together produce far more than half the total gross national product of the world, an overall strategy could be developed that would also include a joint economic policy for the common good and in order to ensure mutual trust between the industrial democracies, as well as for economic development help and in order to clean up squalid areas in the Third World that might otherwise fall under the grip of communist ideology and Soviet influence.

Helpful, Generous–
and Ruthless

S HORTLY before I left office, I read an essay by Warren Christopher in the Summer 1982 issue of *Foreign Affairs* concerning the team-work and the tensions in foreign policy between the Congress and the president. After four years as deputy secretary of state, Christopher had arrived at a conclusion with which I fully agreed: "We have not yet resolved the dilemma posed by our need to reconcile the imperative of democracy at home with the demands of leadership in the world." This statement applied not only to the relationship with Congress of the American president, who intends to play an international leadership role, but also to his relationship with the general media audience.

Indiscretions on the part of those who hold high office in the United States have become downright habitual. On the other hand, the American media exploit all available information, often unscrupulously. Both factors make it hard for the administration to analyze complicated situations in private, to define its own goals and possible lines of retreat in private, and finally to pursue its proposed objectives by means of confidential diplomacy. Bonn is surely a gossipy capital, but by compari-son the gossip in Washington sets a world record. This situation is all the more dangerous as by now the president has become extremely dependent on the national mood produced by the mass media.

A government's dependence on the mood of the media-consuming public is a characteristic of all democracies; it is a product of the sovereignty of the people envisaged by democratic constitutions. But emotional democratic politics should have some limits. Not least because of this reason our constitutions provide for representational democracy; otherwise one referendum after another would have to be held. I recall my embarrassment when, in the mid-1960s, the SPD opposition brought the Bundestag back from a summer recess because the tabloid *Bild* had managed to create a mass uproar over a relatively insignificant increase in postal rates by Erhard's government.

Another warning example was Carter's reaction to the inflated claim made by the media in the autumn of 1979 that the Soviet Union had installed an additional "fighting brigade" in Cuba. Although in fact Cuba had been receiving considerable military help from the Soviet Union for some time—as it continues to do to this day—the stationing of a new brigade was entirely out of the question. Of course, the American intelligence service and thus the president were fully informed about the situation. But the media's manipulation of public sentiment forced Jimmy Carter to engage in extravagant political action.

Conversely, self-confident presidents use television and its audience to make their policies plausible, acceptable and, if possible, popular. That is as true in the United States as it is in West Germany, and it applies by no means only to election campaigns, though in the Western industrial societies these have, to a large extent, turned into television races. Of course any statesman who can handle the television medium superbly can determine the issues and produce opinion. Ronald Reagan is a master of the art. But this method can lead to a reciprocal interaction between the television audience and the president that ends in a pernicious simplification of the actual problems. The greater Reagan's success on television, the more bluntly he adjusted his foreign and security policy strategy to its effect on the American public. His intervention in Libya in the autumn of 1981 and again in the spring of 1986 and his actions against Lebanon, Nicaragua, and Grenada are all clear examples of this process. But so are his refusal to take a firm stand on the bloody South African policy of apartheid and his silence when Israel invaded Lebanon. Reagan had no reservations about giving in to the American tendency—which was already strong—to see everything in black and white; he himself is marked to a great degree by thinking in terms of good guys and bad guys. This mind set found and still finds its strongest expression in his policy toward the Soviet Union.

When Reagan publicly called the Soviet Union the "evil empire," his words represented not only a superbly skilled populist but also his very personal view of the world. The American public's level of approval was great—but just as great were the worries of others that such language might be followed by corresponding action. Reagan and his previous officials Kirkpatrick, Regan, and Clark paid little attention—as Weinberger does to this day—to European concerns, not so much from disdain as from ignorance. What Reagan and his audience think is good for America must, they believe, also be good for Europe.

This view increasingly marked his attitude beginning with his second year in office; similarly, he became ever more open in his expectation that the SDI project, first formulated very vaguely, was in the joint interests of the Western alliance and that Washington's partners would therefore immediately and enthusiastically accept the plans for its realization. Washington completely overlooked the fact that before he announced the SDI project, the allies had not even been informed, much less consulted. Even afterward there was no retrospective mutual analysis and decision by the alliance about the idea of using outer space to wage war.

The procedure was similar when Reagan made the decision, while I was still in office, to reject an opportunity that arose during the July 1982 INF negotiations in Geneva to agree on limiting Eurostrategic intermediate-range nuclear missiles. And yet Washington was obligated to consult closely with its European allies in all phases of the Geneva talks; this had been one thing the Europeans had insisted on as a condition of the TNF agreement of December 1979. Especially the governments of Italy, Holland, Belgium, and Germany—the nations that had obligated themselves, if INF negotiations should fail, to station American Eurostrategic nuclear weapons (Pershing 2s) and cruise missiles within their borders beginning in December 1983—had the most burning interest in being consulted constantly. They could expect considerable domestic confrontation if the deployment went ahead, and if actual armament took place, they were likely to be faced with much more violent protests. At the crucial moment, these governments would therefore have to be in a position to explain to their parliaments and their public with conviction that the West had tried everything within reason to arrive at an agreement but that the intransigence of the Soviet Union had caused the failure. More important was their vital interest in the so-called zero solution—that is, the removal of the Soviet SS-20s and the sacrifice of their American counterparts, the Pershing 2s and cruise missiles.

This zero solution—in private Paul Nitze called it the zero-zero solution to stress its symmetry—had been thought up in Bonn; I had first proposed it publicly in December 1979 and repeated it several times. Reagan had adopted it publicly in 1981, for which I was grateful. The formula, which Nitze had developed during a walk in the woods with Yuli Kvitsinsky in Geneva, deviated from this optimum solution; but it would have made for a considerably diminished danger for Europe without the loss of parity. I myself would have accepted it at once if I had known about it. But once again, neither the West German government nor the other European governments affected were informed about this walk in the woods or even consulted. (I do not know if this is also true of England, a nuclear power that had also obligated itself to the stationing of cruise missiles should the talks fail.) Instead from America we heard outspoken criticism of the peace movements that were protesting the possibility that American Pershing 2s and cruise missiles would be stationed on their territories. These highly emotional demonstrations were taking place mainly in Germany, Holland, and England. Repeatedly we were asked whether we were still backing the TNF resolution, and Washington noted with concern that my own party was continuing its commitment only with the utmost reluctance.

On September 15, 1982, the increasingly undeniable ambivalence of Foreign Minister Genscher and the open disloyalty of Finance Minister Lambsdorff forced me to dismiss the FDP ministers, who had been confirmed in their desire for a change of coalition by the lessening of the Social Democrats' unity on issues of security policy. This act made the fall of the government, which occurred on October 1, inevitable. But it was not until weeks later that I, now an opposition Bundestag delegate, learned of the existence of the so-called Nitze formula, of the "walk in the woods," and of Washington's and Moscow's rejection of the plan.

It was obvious that an agreement was hardly possible any longer and that no agreement would be reached by the autumn of 1983. The contingency plan of stationing American INF in Europe would in all probability become a reality. In spite of this serious violation of the United States' obligation to consult with its allies, I, along with some deeply loyal Social Democratic friends, continued even after leaving the government to advocate deployment publicly because I considered maintaining the principle of parity to be of extreme importance. In the remote case that a mutual zero solution to the INF problem should still come about—as seems conceivable now, in the spring of 1987—we shall feel justified.

The American newspaper reports that retroactively enlightened

Washington's allies in the autumn of 1982 about the events in Geneva were based not on official press releases by the American government but on indiscretion. Possibly these leaks were intended to make the White House's rejection of the Nitze formula irrevocable. The entire episode was to be made to seem unimportant in American public opinion, and thus the Soviet rejection of the "walk in the woods" was also leaked. Later matters even went so far as to let the assumption arise that the United States had rejected the plan only after the Soviet rejection was an accomplished fact. The actual course of events, however, seems to have been quite different. The White House National Security Council had in reality dealt twice with the "walk in the woods"; only at the second meeting had Richard Perle, the undersecretary for defense, who had been absent from the first session, managed to put over the rejection—and he did so exclusively for reasons of national strategic interests, as he and Secretary of Defense Weinberger saw them. Today I believe that both Weinberger and Perle were determined to see the Pershing 2s and cruise missiles stationed in Europe. This reason aside, many people in the Reagan administration had become committed to stationing the weapons as a matter of prestige.

After the opportunity created by the "walk in the woods" had been frittered away, neither side made any further serious attempts at agreement during the Geneva INF negotiations; stationing the weapons in late 1983 thus became inevitable, in accordance with the second stage of the TNF resolution.

The Soviet leadership did hope that by employing a propaganda campaign waged at considerable expense and with great psychological skill, it could mobilize the Western European peace movements to prevent the deployment of the American Pershing 2s and cruise missiles at the last moment. The campaign failed, and the deployment that followed against all the Kremlin's expectations was without a doubt a crucial reason for Gorbachev's subsequent disarmament initiatives, especially the suggestion he made in Reykjavik in late 1986. Not the SDI program (which the Soviets, after all, are also developing, though under a different name) but the fact that Soviet targets were for the first time threatened by American ("Eurostrategic") nuclear weapons stationed in Europe brought Gorbachev to the point of placing serious arms limitation proposals on the table. Of course his hopes for his country's economic growth were an equally important motive.

No matter who occupies the presidency, Washington tends to unilateralism. As long as Western Europe cannot work its way to a joint design for overall strategy that it can unanimously uphold, the West will always

be confronted with American solo adventures. If we add the outrage of
the American media that the European governments, parliaments, and
public opinion do not instantly applaud and show approval, "anti-
American" feelings will arise rather often in Western Europe—and
the Americans are quite unable to understand these feelings because
they cannot see the extent to which they themselves are provoking
mistrust.

United States policies concerning the rest of the world are marked by
idealism, romanticism, and faith in America's own power and greatness.
If the rest of the world does not live up to the Americans' ideals and
their methods to turn them into reality, so much the worse for the rest
of the world! Historically this attitude has had two contrasting results:
Either the United States made up its mind to supply the world with a
better order, if necessary by using military intervention, in order to
abolish disorder, injustice, or oppression anywhere in the world; or it
decided to turn its back on the rest of the world and to concentrate on
its own immeasurably large and rich continent—that is, isolationism
and the Monroe Doctrine.

During the nineteenth century the isolationist tendency usually prevailed. The First World War brought out the country's missionary zeal
for the first time, but as early as 1919 Woodrow Wilson's altruistic
idealism was stopped, and the United States refused to join the League
of Nations he had helped to establish.

Hitler's crimes and his attempt to grasp world supremacy, and finally
the Japanese attack on Pearl Harbor, once again led the United States
to make an enormous effort to put the world in order. From 1937 on,
Franklin Delano Roosevelt did all he could to mobilize his country
morally, so as to make it ready to enter the war against Germany and
Japan if need be. But the people's isolationist spirit opposed any intervention in a distant war on a distant continent. Finally Berlin and
Tokyo, blinded by delusions of grandeur, took the decision away from
the American people.

The outcome of the Second World War, however, deeply changed
the world's political structure. In less than three years Uncle Joe, the
wartime ally, turned into Stalin, the dangerous enemy. During the last
forty years American policy toward the Soviet Union has gradually
arrived at the idea of "containment," a word coined by George Kennan
after the war. Beginning in the late 1940s, Americans saw the structure
of the world as a confrontation between two leading powers. The
American idealistic tendency to see everything in black-and-white terms
tempted many Americans to divide all other nations into two categories:

on the one hand, the "bad" ones, those willing to submit themselves to Soviet leadership; and on the other, the "good" ones, who are loyal to America. In both cases America is secretly persuaded of its own superiority, and at times this superiority, which is not only moral but also material, expresses itself publicly and dramatically.

The European peoples, who have been living cheek by jowl in limited space for centuries, have not forgotten the consequences of the wars they have waged against each other during that time. Though they seek a resolute defense against the superior power of the Soviet Union, they are appalled by a foreign policy that seems to accept the risk of renewed warfare. That is why disagreements continue to break out between the European allies and the United States, the dominant power in the alliance.

As long as the worldly wise East Coast establishment, which felt bound to Old Europe, was a significant factor in shaping American foreign policy (as it was during the time of Truman, Eisenhower, and Kennedy, and once again in the era of Nixon and Ford), such differences of opinion could always be limited and settled. No one needed to explain European ideas of parity to such a man as Henry Kissinger. Instead, his problem was explaining to his own people that a balance of power was not immoral and therefore contemptible but the only reasonable attitude if nuclear peace between the two giants were to be preserved. Other politicians—such as Dulles and later Brzezinski, Perle, Weinberger, and especially Carter and Reagan—found it difficult to keep their missionary impulses more or less under control. Since Western Europe has not the remotest intention of perforce participating in a worldwide mission, American contempt for the supposedly weak-kneed Europeans and conflicts with them will continue to be part of the scene in the foreseeable future. At such times it is only too easy for Washington to ignore its European allies, and the arrogance of supposedly superior morality is then easily joined by the arrogance of actual superior power.

Europe and its politicians would profit from understanding this attitude, so that in replying to such American behavior, they can avoid *both* conceivable extremes; for the Western European nations must not fall into the role of dependent wards, nor may they succumb to the anti-American delusion that the real danger emanates not from the Soviet Union but from the United States. Great efforts will be required if we Europeans are to continue to exert sufficient influence on the United States' international actions. In the European nations there is a need for constant explanations of and reasons for the alliance with the United

States, which the Europeans, in reality, need just as much as Americans do. In the United States the realization must grow that even the governments of the nations allied with them require successes in the pursuit of their interests from time to time—successes they can show off at home. A steady exchange with the Americans and a constant attempt to influence Washington are also required if we Europeans are to be safe from unilateral surprises on the part of Washington.

I witnessed a positive example of the ability to empathize with each other's interests when Reagan paid a visit to Bonn. His speech to the Bundestag of June 9, 1982, mentioned above, was a political and psychological masterpiece. He achieved what no German chancellor had ever been able to bring off: a long, standing ovation from both the right and the left for an address on foreign and security policy (only two unaffiliated and confused delegates failed to applaud at all). Although at this time there was considerable skepticism about Reagan in the Bundestag—and not merely on the left—he nevertheless managed, in a speech lasting half an hour or more, to win over the Bundestag, and its three party groups must have interrupted him twenty times with their collective applause.

Whoever conceived of this speech, which cleverly focused on German history, the German mentality, and the German desire for peace, and then helped write it could note with satisfaction that for the first time since Kennedy's famous speech in Berlin nineteen years earlier (*"Ich bin ein Berliner"*) an American president met with the approval of an overwhelming majority of Germans. The newspapers unanimously confirmed this triumph; in the *Neue Ruhr Zeitung* Hilde Purwin justifiably reduced it to the terse statement, "Reagan was persuasive." An anti-Reagan demonstration by hundreds of thousands, which took place simultaneously only a few kilometers away across the Rhine, could not change that.

Of course the everyday world of European-American divergence quickly emerged again, as did the dilettantism of Reagan's ideas on world politics. But he had given us Germans a new taste of the fundamental determination of the American nation to support the freedom and security of the Federal Republic of Germany and West Berlin. Like many American leaders before him and surely like many who will follow, Reagan had once again let us sense that generosity of the American nation that never ceases to fascinate me.

Most Americans are descended of ancestors who left Europe because here they had lived in oppression or poverty. To that extent de Gaulle was right when he called the United States a "daughter of Europe."

The decision to emigrate was also an act of self-liberation from oppressive European conditions that required great courage and great self-confidence. The will to freedom, courage, self-confidence, eagerness to work, and mutual helpfulness, as well as a certain tendency to despise Europe and an occasional inclination to self-justification in the purposes of self-defense have, on the basis of this collective experience, become elements of American political culture, which is marked by a basic attitude embodying both idealism and optimism.

In the foreign policy arena, this idealism has frequently appalled Europeans, who find it an unrealistic attitude, but in relation to the incomparable American willingness to help, it has done enormous service to the world. That help has ranged from America's contribution to the battle against Hitler's Germany through the private action of CARE packages to the help given by GARIOA (a German-American relief organization) and the Marshall Plan. These humanitarian actions also, and especially, benefited the war enemies who had only just been vanquished—the Germans and the Japanese. No other country in the world would have been able to bring this off. When anyone appeals to their helpfulness, Americans are the world's most generous nation.

When I came back from the prisoner-of-war camp, shabby and with my shoes in tatters, American Quakers gave me my first pair of serviceable boots; it is something I will never forget. Nor will I forget the Berlin airlift, or Leonard Bernstein's first concerts in Germany shortly after the end of the war, or the helpfulness of my relatives in Minnesota and the hospitality of countless anonymous Americans all through the country.

Of course Americans will also always serve their own interests—how could it be otherwise? Nevertheless, they must experience our affection; they require emotional reassurance, especially when we Europeans firmly assert our interests against them. But firmness is essential; it is the only thing that produces respect. And it is only through mutual respect that we can find workable compromises between diverging concepts and interests.

It's true that America's foreign policy is just as fallible as that of the European democracies. It's equally true that America's foreign policy can be just as ruthless as the foreign policy of the European nations was for hundreds of years. Nevertheless, my admiration for Americans' vitality and my affection for them remain undiminished. If ever I had to go live in another country, I would choose the United States.

But that possibility will not arise because the United States will stand by us, the European democracies. Because it will morally assume the

obligations it has taken on—just as Robert Frost's magnificent poem
puts it:

> The woods are lovely, dark and deep,
> But I have promises to keep,
> And miles to go before I sleep,
> And miles to go before I sleep.

III

***

China—
The
Third World
Power

I N October 1975 I paid my first official visit as chancellor to the People's Republic of China. At that time Mao Zedong told me in his lapidary way, "I know how the Soviet Union will proceed; there will be war." I disagreed with him; I was not willing to rule out the possibility of a third world war, but given the West's defense capability, I thought it unlikely. Mao, however, insisted on his theory of the inevitability of war, and Deng Xiaoping, who at the time was deputy prime minister, agreed with him.

Four years later, in October 1979, Hua Guofeng, successor to Mao Zedong and Zhou Enlai, came to Bonn and added some subtlety to the prophecy: "China is striving to delay the next war as much as possible."

In September and October 1984, almost ten years after my visit to Mao, I visited China again. This time Deng Xiaoping opened the conversation by recalling our conversation of years before. To my surprise he suddenly said quite candidly, "That time you disputed our assessment of the situation. And you were right."

Had I really been right? It is true that outwardly the history of that decade confirmed my judgment. But will I continue to be right in my belief that a third world war can be avoided? What must we do—in Beijing, Washington, Moscow, and Europe—to prevent a world war, and what must we leave undone? What conclusions must we draw from our analysis of the world situation if we want not only to maintain peace but also to stabilize it?

These are questions that are always raised when Europeans and Chinese talk together. Unlike Mao's contemporaries, today's Chinese are addressing these questions with far more pragmatism and much less dogmatism. There were and are no unresolved bilateral problems between Beijing and Bonn; successful cooperation has developed in many areas. The political exchange of views therefore was and is never devoted to bilateral conflicts of interest but always and ever to the same questions: How will the Soviet Union act? How strong is it? What does Moscow think it can afford to do? Are the United States and Europe a sufficient counterweight?

Uneasy at the presence of powerful Soviet forces along their common border, China has a marked interest in a strong Europe, and the Chinese make no effort to conceal this attitude but voice it openly. Europe, in turn, has an interest in the Chinese border because of the Soviet threat to Europe. Beijing looks to the West to ease Soviet pressure—especially to the United States, but to Europe as well. The West, conversely, knows the value of the restraint on Soviet power presented by China. Nixon was the first to draw strategic consequences from this situation and put an end to the twenty-year-long American enmity against the People's Republic of China.

By now the rise of the second large Communist nation to the status of world power seems inexorable, though its progress is very slow. The result could be a power triangle, a constellation possibly of greater stability than the bipolar world system of the last four decades. Among the most important questions in this context is: How will Asia develop? What, in particular, is the future of Southeast Asia and the Far East? What will be the role of China in this region of the world? What role will be assigned to Japan? What influences will impinge on the greater Asian Pacific region from Moscow and Washington?

The question about a stable power triangle is overshadowed by deep insecurity as to China's true domestic and international situation. The Americans, the Europeans, and the Russians are equally poorly informed about China and its internal trends. Will China be economically successful? Will consistency and reliability eventually take the place of ever new revolutionary, voluntaristic, or emotional campaigns? I always took the question of China's domestic and economic development as seriously as my Chinese counterparts took the questions of further changes in the European Community and Europe's unity.

This question began to concern me as early as 1969, when I became defense minister. In 1971 I urged Willy Brandt to establish diplomatic relations between Bonn and Beijing; in the fall of 1972, long before the United States took this step, we did so. After I was named chancellor, Zhou Enlai invited me to come to China; when I visited there in the fall of 1975, however, Zhou was already very ill, and I was not able to see him. His duties as host were assumed by the deputy prime minister, Deng Xiaoping.

Deng Xiaoping was waiting for me at the airport with a military honor guard and the obligatory troops of colorfully dressed, cheerfully shouting children waving little German flags. The girls wore large paper bows, blossoms, whole bunches of flowers, some had colorful pins in their hair—the remnants of Chinese traditions.

At the time the *Kölner Stadtanzeiger* wrote, "We think Deng capable of vigorously interrupting any negotiating partner who does not concentrate and deviates from the matter at hand. The chancellor will surely take a liking to this seemingly unassuming, powerful seventy-year-old." This opinion was true. I liked Deng Xiaoping from the first moment.

Our first impression of Beijing was unexpectedly "un-Chinese." The Jiangan, a large, enormously broad avenue from east to west, was clearly cut through old Peking in the postwar period. It separated the city into a northern and a southern half. The former Forbidden City is situated in the center of the city; this complex of imperial gardens, halls, and palaces is just north of the avenue; just across the road is the wide Tiananmen Square, the "Square of Heavenly Peace," which is loosely rimmed in by the Great Hall of the People on its west side and a museum building on the east.

The huge buildings of the ministries and other administrative offices, which are reminiscent of Stalinist architecture and hint only vaguely at traditional Chinese stylistic elements, are just as desolate as many postwar buildings in the capitals of other Communist states. But the unimaginably large number of people in the streets and the hundreds of thousands of bicycles—which are not lit even at night in the crowded commuter traffic—along with the willows and plane trees at the curbs and the countless flowerpots on the balconies of the apartment houses—all these made an image that was lively and homey, in spite of its foreign nature. Almost everyone wore fairly ugly blue or gray jumpsuits, but their faces were not as tight and remote as those of the people in Moscow.

After a few hours we noticed that in spite of the uniform manner of dress there were recognizable differences in rank. Thus Mao Zedong, for example, wore a medium-gray suit made of a fine wool-and-silk fabric, and the liveries of the high functionaries were also cut of better materials, at times clearly tailor-made. Though at that time the army uniforms were not provided with insignia of rank, officers were recognizable by the apparently obligatory ballpoint pen sticking out of the top-sewn breast pocket.

The uniform clothing of the women in the streets and the offices or factories was quite another matter. Almost without exception the women and girls wore ungainly blue cotton suits and sturdy shoes. Clearly lipstick and permanent waves were just as taboo as any other kind of makeup. But there must certainly have been lipstick for women in higher situations, since my wife found in her room a collection of at least two dozen in every conceivable shade, along with a variety of vials of perfume and toilet water, everything apparently of Chinese manufacture. Or had these actually been imported from Hong Kong?

During those days we must have seen thousands of women. Most of them wore their hair cut short; only a few of the very young ones sported a braid. At road construction and building sites women did some of the hardest pick-and-shovel work. Large woven straw and willow baskets, which were carried on the women's shoulders, were used to transport rubbish, sand, cement, and rocks. I remembered the phrase "blue ants." It was true: Now and then it seemed we were looking at streams of ants.

After the official talks were concluded, we had an opportunity to take a closer look at the Imperial Palace, an assemblage of many hall-like building complexes with broad stairs flanked by mythical animals. Most of the walls of the large buildings are painted Pompeii red; the curved, sweeping roofs are made of lush yellow tiles. Hundreds of little houses are grouped around intimate inner courtyards broken up by ponds, bridges, trees, and gardens.

We were shown two-thousand-year-old ink drawings from the hands of Chinese emperors; because of the climate, these ancient pictures can be brought out for only a few days in the autumn. The drawings depict many kinds of birds, finches, and golden pheasants, and especially plum and cherry branches thick with blossoms. The strongly abstracted waves and rings in the water reminded me of the work of the German expressionists. The Chinese architecture and gardening culture of past centuries left the impression of great evenness and cheerful harmony. What good luck, I thought, that Mao's wife, Jiang Qing, in her rage to destroy that had already claimed the sacrifice of so many priceless monuments, had spared the Imperial Palace and the Gate of Heavenly Peace—at least so far.

Of course during those days we also visited the Ming graves and the monumental Great Wall. The drive took us through a bare autumnal landscape. Our ascent to the top of the wall was exhausting, but the walk along the crest was worth the effort. The view was incomparable: following the hills and valleys, the grandiose structure wound through the landscape until it seemed to get lost somewhere in the foggy mist of the picturesque mountains. I was reminded of Chinese ink drawings in which the mountains are ranked in a similar way. The sight of the wall exceeded all my expectations and increased my awe of the four- or five-thousand-year-old Chinese culture. Years later, when I viewed the thousands of clay military figures in Xian, and when I once again visited the Buddhist temples around the western lake of Hangzhou, I was similarly overcome.

At the official banquet we were also made aware of the tradition-laden culture of the huge realm. We were seated at round tables with center-pieces of artificial flowers, bright blossoms and leaves in every color. The courses seemed arranged and served less according to culinary dictates than aesthetic ones; all were decorated with artfully carved ornaments, butterflies and birds made of radishes, red carrots, and red beets. A climax was a huge green melon that served as a salad bowl, its outer rind decorated with complicated incised patters that revealed the bright flesh. We were also impressed by an aquarium with live goldfish, which served as the heart of the centerpiece; if only for their long veil-shaped fins and tails, the splendid goldfish were a sight to behold. But we found the lip smacking and slurping, a Chinese custom, just as unusual.

We were served on small plates that were changed after every course; only the chopsticks remained the same throughout the meal. Of course we spurned the knives and forks that were offered to us and chose to eat with chopsticks, a skill we had already practiced a little during the plane flight. Deng Xiaoping took pleasure in correcting the way I held my fingers when I was being too clumsy. The hot napkins we were handed again and again were a delightful amenity. After the official toast, Deng went around the table to clink glasses with each guest—*"Gan bei"* ("Cheers"). We Europeans had to learn to get used to the smell of *mao-tai*, millet spirits. One of our security officers spilled a bottle of it inside a suitcase, and the strong odor spread; the poor guy was roundly ridiculed.

During the dinner a Chinese orchestra played German melodies; I have a vivid memory of "Brunnen vor dem Tore." The end of the banquet was announced over loudspeakers; the Chinese guests took the leftover sweets home to their families.

Of course we also went to great pains with the "counterbanquet" at the German Embassy; we had brought marzipan from Lübeck and German cut flowers for the centerpieces; these latter had suffered a great deal during the flight and had to be freshened in an embassy bathtub.

At the time, in 1975, Mao's Cultural Revolution was still far from over; my fear that the fanaticism of the radical zealots might further destroy the precious heritage of the millennia was great. We had heard and read a great deal about the absurdities and cruelties of recent years. I understood that Mao had brought about the Cultural Revolution of the 1960s to prevent the creation of new classes, to shatter the preeminence of the party apparatus, and to restore him, the great Chairman, to full power over party and nation. But aside from an opera in the Great Hall of the People—which seemed to me tacky rhetoric in its mixture of rhythmically accented music, balletic acrobatics, glaring scenery, and mechanical acting—we caught few glimpses of the consequences of the Cultural Revolution.

However, the dominance of Chairman Mao could not be ignored. Everyone I spoke with repeated what Mao had told me; all their discussions—including Deng Xiaoping's—not once involved individual thinking but concentrated entirely on explanations and elaborations based on Mao's schematically compact way of speech. Apparently all of them had promptly received a copy of the earlier talk between Mao and myself. Of course a similar procedure is customary in well-organized governments almost everywhere in the world; but with the exception of Shah Mohammed Reza Pahlevi and Nicolae Ceauşescu, I never saw such total conformity with the head of state.

This may be connected with the disputes among the factions and groups within the party at the time. Zhou Enlai's death was clearly imminent, and the death of Mao himself was obviously not far off. Perhaps my conversational partners covered themselves as a way of keeping their thoughts to themselves so they could not be accused or even punished if the impending power struggle had an outcome unfavorable to the given individual. Deng, however, was sent to Coventry by Mao himself in April 1976. It was, after all, still the time of the Little Red Book containing the sayings of Chairman Mao.

Mao Zedong

MAO'S home was in the outermost area of the Forbidden City. It was just as unassuming from the outside as it was inside: no pictures or picture scrolls on the walls, very businesslike furniture, office equipment, and a few armchairs in a semicircle—with antimacassars on the backs and armrests.

My first impression of this much-praised and often disdained man, who received us standing here and who unquestionably was and would remain a figure in world history, was frightening. His chin sagged, his mouth gaped open: a decayed face. Mao could not move toward us; he was, it seemed to me, showing the aftereffects of a serious stroke. We arranged ourselves for a "family photograph" including my wife, my colleague Kurt Gscheidle, Klaus Bölling, Marie Schlei, and Deng Xiaoping, as well as Mao's and my staff members, among them our ambassador, Rolf Pauls.

Once the pictures were taken, most of the retinue was asked to leave again. Chinese television had recorded Mao's welcome. When the pictures were broadcast that night, it seemed to me that the Chinese people were being prepared for the imminent end of their leader.

At first the reception seemed purely a polite gesture, since Mao was no longer able to carry on a conversation. He cawed and was unable to articulate properly; one of the three women around him seemed to be inventing his words of welcome but pretended to be translating them.

Nevertheless this altogether desolate impression was quite wrong. As soon as we sat down—Mao needed help to do so—lively chatter broke out. As unquestionable as it was that physically he was nothing more than a wreck, his intellectual presence and liveliness were just as undeniable. Unfortunately, he said as he took his seat, his legs would no longer serve him, and speaking caused him some difficulty. The three translators (one of whom was a deputy minister, another of whom headed the European department in the foreign ministry) conferred for a few seconds about what he might have meant to say before they gave a translation. This happened very often in the course of the conversation. At times they asked questions in return, and Mao would try to write his words on small pieces of paper kept at hand if they still could not understand him in spite of much repetition.

Clearly everyone had become accustomed to this procedure, since the mood was light and cheerful, at times punctuated by the women's laughter; no one was embarrassed, nor was there any display of the kind of deference practiced at royal courts. However, transferring his thoughts first into comprehensible Chinese and then into English was a very time-consuming process; clearly, articulating was very tiring for him. Both were good reasons why, in a deviation from his normal procedure, he concentrated on short sentences. He spoke plainly but not without wit.

The talk began with mutual compliments. Mao on Germany: "The Germans are good." Then, more precisely: "The West Germans are good." I spoke about the achievements of the Chinese people during the past twenty-five years under his leadership. I also mentioned Marie Schlei's appreciation of Mao's poetry. "My achievements are too small," Mao replied. "And by the way, I'm not good at writing poems. But I know how to wage wars and how to win them."

Thus we quickly arrived at one of the principal topics he had apparently planned for. We agreed to an exchange of views on the strategy of the Soviet Union and the proper strategy against Moscow. I decided to give a wider presentation in order to provoke a reaction: "It is my impression that a distinction has to be made between what the Soviet leadership says and what it actually does. Their actual foreign policy actions have shown much more restraint since the end of the Khrushchev era and since the abrupt end of the missile adventure in Cuba than can be found in the Soviet propaganda statements. We cannot, however, exclude the possibility that the Soviet Union could grow aggressive if situations that invite the misuse of power are tolerated. If any country allows its defenses to weaken, the Soviets might exploit the situation. As long as we maintain an adequate balance of power with the Soviet Union, we need not fear any such Soviet adventurism. That is why the nations of Western Europe and the United States are avoiding anything that might invite the Kremlin to attack. We have taken the warnings of the Chinese leaders seriously, but we are not afraid of a Soviet attack. Our common defense is strong enough to turn a Soviet attack or Soviet pressure through threats into a considerable risk for Moscow."

All well and good, Mao said, but the situation was sure to change in ten or twenty years. "Listen to me. There will be war with the Soviet Union. Your [that is, the Western] strategy of deterrence is purely hypothetical."

I contradicted him. "Our defense capability is not hypothetical. Our defense is very real and highly effective. It is this security that gives us freedom of action in relation to the Soviets; and on this we have built the other half of our strategy, which is to achieve a good-neighbor status, even cooperation, with Moscow and its allies."

He understood all this, Mao replied, but there would be war all the same. "It seems to me you are a Kantian. But idealism is not a good thing! I myself am a student of Marx, and I have learned a great deal from him. I do not think much of idealism; I am interested in Hegel, Feuerbach, and Haeckel. On our topic, Clausewitz was right."

These remarks were the occasion for a philosophical disquisition lasting ten minutes. I did not want to say more about Ernst Haeckel and his crudely materialistic "world enigmas," which I had found forty years earlier in my father's bookcase and had read at that time. On the subject of Hegel, I remarked only that he must bear a large share of the responsibility for much German mystification of the state. Of course, I made sure to mention my belief in Kant's theories. Then I brought the conversation around to Clausewitz: "Clausewitz was a genius, one of the few German officers with a talent for politics. Marx, Engels, and Lenin interpreted his famous statement to mean that war was not a special state but merely the continuation of politics by other means. I, however, prefer to read Clausewitz's aphorism as a lesson for the military, meaning that even in war precedence must be given to political leadership and not—as, for example, Ludendorff thought—military leadership. From this I conclude that war is only one of many alternative possibilities available to political leaders. We must never look to war as the only possibility."

Mao continued the thought. A defensive war, he said, was always better than an offensive one, because usually the attacker suffered defeat. Wilhelm II had had to learn this lesson just as thoroughly as Chiang Kai-shek had, and as the Americans had after their attack on Vietnam. "They sent five hundred thousand men to Vietnam. Fifty thousand of them died and a hundred thousand were wounded. Now they make a big to-do about it. America is too afraid of losing men."

"What do you think about the development of relations among the United States, the Soviet Union, and the People's Republic of China?" I asked.

"There will be war," answered Mao, who seemed obsessed by this idea. "Permanent peaceful coexistence is unthinkable. Europe especially is too soft. It is not unified, and besides, it lives in deadly fear of war—especially the Danes, the Dutch, the Belgians. At heart the Americans are just the same. Perhaps the Yugoslavs and the Germans are a little more willing to offer resistance. But if Europe continues in the next ten years to be unable to unite politically, economically, and militarily, it will have to pay the price. The Europeans must learn to rely on themselves and not on the United States. Why can't sixty million West Germans achieve the same end as the North Vietnamese?"

I did not react to this last comparison because I wanted to avoid any possibility of letting the rumor arise that the great Chairman and the German chancellor had talked about the mad idea of a West German offensive war for the purpose of German reunification. Instead I said, "Our army is among the best-trained and best-equipped fighting forces in the world; the same is true of its spirit. If need be, we can defend ourselves. But what interests me particularly is that you radically changed your mind. What turned your judgment of the Soviet Union around? Twenty years ago you spoke quite differently. What has happened since then in your relations with Moscow?"

"It is the Soviet Union that has fundamentally changed, not China," said Mao. "The men in the Kremlin today are no longer men such as Stalin. Today we are dealing with the Khrushchevs and Brezhnevs, and all of them are traitors to Lenin's cause."

But he himself, I objected, had supported the theory of permanent revolution. Did he consider it entirely unthinkable that subsequent generations of leaders in the Kremlin would find their way back to Lenin's principles, perhaps in the treatment of other states or national minorities or in regard to the primacy of political leadership over the bureaucracy?

Unexpectedly showing the fire of the old revolutionary, Mao interrupted me: "No, no, no! They will do none of that!" And when I asked him why not: "Because they have too much power, because they have too many nuclear weapons."

"But Moscow," I suggested, "is just as afraid of other nations' nuclear weapons."

To which Mao replied, "Both! But most important, they have four million soldiers!"

Whenever the Soviet Union was mentioned in the conversation, the serious trauma the "betrayal" by the Soviet Union in the late 1950s had meant for Mao raised its head. He had a deep distrust of the Soviet leadership; it was a primary factor of his world view. His picture of the rest of the world was painted entirely from this perspective. As he had tried to do with other Western visitors before me, Mao was eager to make the West suspicious as well and to persuade it to make strong efforts at an arms buildup. Ten years later, President Reagan and his simplistic Secretary Weinberger would have taken great pleasure in Mao's crude anti-Soviet picture.

At the time I saw it as my job to make Mao understand that he must not confuse Germany's will to peace with weakness, accommodation, or even submission to Moscow. The Federal Republic, I told him, was looking for a relaxation of tension only on the basis of undiminished security. We were striving not for a collaboration of numerous weak European states with a superior Soviet Union but for cooperation by a single, well-defended, and therefore politically strong Europe with an inevitably equally strong Soviet Union.

Mao seemed to take the gravity of this declaration seriously. Aside from his words about the Vietnam War, he avoided any disparaging remarks about the United States, but he left no doubt that he did not consider the United States capable of meeting all its strategic tasks and the obligations it had to its allies. Soon the conversation turned back to the subject of Europe. Mao repeated his statement that Europe was too degenerate and listless.

I raised a consideration: "The numerous nations and states of Europe are in part more than a thousand years old. Each has its individual history, its individual culture and language. To bring the twelve Western European states under a common roof after centuries of often conflicting evolution is a huge undertaking. It will take several generations. Should the unification of Europe come about more quickly than I now believe, Europe will appear very strong. If that happens, will the Soviet Union transfer its pressure to Central Asia or even the Far East?"

Mao was stony in his response: "It's conceivable. That is why we must arm against their coming." With this the conversation turned back to Asian territory, and I asked about Japan's role—what he, Mao, thought of Japan's dependence on the United States for its security.

Mao replied without hesitation, "Japan alone cannot achieve much. It has neither oil nor coal, neither iron nor enough food. Its population alone is not a sufficient factor. Tokyo needs the alliance with the United States; it has no choice but to rely on the United States."

Then he added, "The United States has overextended itself in its protection obligations. Besides Japan, it has entered into agreements to assist South Korea, Taiwan, the Philippines, India, Australia, New Zealand, and indirectly Thailand; to these are added the Middle East and finally Europe. It won't work. The Americans are trying to hold on to ten fleas with ten fingers. But that's beyond anyone's ability! You Europeans must rely on your own strength; it is a second-rate policy to entrust one's fate to others."

At the end of the hour-long conversation I thanked Mao, and while I was holding his limp hand, I told him that his thoughts were a valuable tile in the mosaic of my world view. Then I added, "Many Western statesmen before me have visited you. Others will follow and ask you for your assessment of the world situation. That is a responsibility for you. Your words carry great weight."

"Oh, you know," Mao replied soberly, "neither the French nor the Americans are willing to listen to me."

I quoted the saying about the constant drop of water that hollows out the stone.

"Yes—but I do not have enough water left. You must add your water to mine to hollow out the stone." The sentence was meant to have a double meaning, and all of us present, Germans and Chinese, laughed heartily.

That afternoon my wife was asked by the wife of the Chinese ambassador to Bonn whether she, too, had seen Mao. My wife said that she had and mentioned that she had shaken hands with the chairman. The diplomat's wife impulsively reached for my wife's hand, which had rested in Mao's so recently. It seemed to my wife that this gesture expressed pleasure, admiration, and envy all at once.

During the entire conversation between myself and Mao, Deng Xiaoping said not a word; for almost two hours he sat in an armchair without giving any sign of what he thought of the course of the talk. The following day he referred to Mao's remarks several times. Even before my visit to Mao, Deng and I had had a lengthy conversation; beyond that, we had met at one or two banquets. On those occasions

Deng had asked me to explain my view of the strategic and economic world situation; he was especially interested in my evaluation of European conditions.

Even during our first conversation Deng urged me on with repeated requests for further explanations and excursuses, so that I must have talked for an hour and a half. It seemed to me that Deng wanted to get an idea about me before he revealed his own views. I did not hesitate to go along with him; Deng would have to be all the more explicit in our second round of talks.

Later I understood that he had wanted to wait until my interview with Mao was over. When we met a few days later for our second exchange of views, it was up to him to take the initiative. And in fact Deng spoke for just as long as I had, and this time I was the one to interrupt with questions.

Deng did not go beyond citing Mao's utterances, and I was not sure whether they actually expressed his own opinions or if he was holding back and hiding behind Mao, as it were. Besides Deng, our foreign ministers and more than half a dozen Chinese functionaries were present, so that he had to assume that any deviation, no matter how subtle, would be reported to his opponents—the group that later made up the so-called Gang of Four.

Nevertheless Deng spoke firmly and with conviction. He chain-smoked one cigarette after the other and made artful use of the spittoon placed more than a yard away; this procedure was noisy and apparently pleasurable. The constant cigarette was not an expression of nervousness; obviously he was simply addicted to nicotine. I estimated his daily consumption to be at least three packs of cigarettes a day. I understood such things: I myself smoked just as much.

I have always liked it when people at the heads of states did not carry self-discipline so far that no human failings could be detected. Ten years later, when I met Deng again in Beijing in 1984, he was still smoking the same amount. He had not changed much in other ways, either; he only appeared more sovereign. But even earlier, in 1975, he was an imposing figure in spite of the fact that he was short.

Deng's speech, which lasted an hour and a half, was clear and well organized. He began by elaborating on Mao's remark on the inevitability of another war. It was rooted, he said, in the development of the "social imperialist social system" of the Soviet Union. The strong growth of its military and economic potential had aroused Moscow's covetousness and led to a struggle for world hegemony. Brezhnev's foreign policy was in reality more adventurous than Khrushchev's, especially as he controlled an immeasurably greater military potential than his predecessor.

When Deng finished, I replied that neither he nor Mao had to make us aware of such misgivings about the Soviet Union; Germans had not forgotten that it was the Soviet Union that had divided our country. Nevertheless, we were not afraid of an attack; NATO was standing in readiness to defend Europe, and its capability was impressive. After all, the Soviet Union knew what Mao had stated only yesterday: In the end it was seldom the aggressor who came away victorious, usually it was the defender.

We were unable to persuade each other of our assessments of the Soviet expansionistic drive, and neither of us tried very hard. Deng said the Chinese did not believe in maintaining an arms balance for one, two, or three decades. Through the nuclear test ban treaty in 1963, SALT in 1972, and Vladivostok in 1974 (Ford's meeting with Brezhnev to make detailed preparations for SALT II) Moscow had erased the United States' advantage; in some areas the Soviet Union was already superior. Only a few days earlier, Deng and Mao had said the same thing to Henry Kissinger, at that time secretary of state in the Ford administration. The arms race would continue, and there would not be balance. As Mao had emphatically said the previous day, whether war broke out in ten years or in thirty, the Soviet Union would always be the cause of the war.

Deng never deviated from Mao's line. What was interesting, however, was a passage on the kind of warfare to be expected. A war with conventional weapons, he said, was much more probable than the exchange of nuclear blows. This was the outcome, on the one hand, of the two superpowers' nuclear stalemate but more especially of the aims of the coming war: occupation of territory, dominion over peoples, and acquisition of raw materials. None of these could be reconciled with nuclear destruction. West Germany's conventional forces were therefore especially important.

In Deng's view of the situation the Soviet Pacific fleet apparently played a major part. He pointed out that it was already three times the strength of the United States Seventh Fleet. On the other hand, the political situation in Asia had developed along lines favorable to the United States since that nation had abandoned Vietnam. Japan, however, was still subject to Soviet pressure.

Deng talked in great detail about the Soviet threat to China. He had no fear of a direct Soviet attack on China, since the Soviets could occupy at most the large cities, not the entire huge country. No Russian would make Hitler's mistake. Instead, Moscow was trying to achieve political control over China. As early as 1958 the Kremlin had wanted to bring China's coastline under its control with the proposal of a joint Soviet-Chinese fleet; such a shared enterprise would also have meant that Soviet bases would be established on Chinese soil. Since that time relations between Moscow and Beijing had grown very much worse, partly because of the ideological confrontations that had broken out.

In any attempt to imagine theoretically possible operational objectives for the Soviet Union, the first one that came to mind was Manchuria, followed by northeast China, eventually Beijing itself, perhaps even the entire territory to the Yangtse River. The Soviet fighting forces along the border could be employed not only against China, of course, but also against Japan and other East Asian nations. Were they not also a threat to the American bases in East and Southeast Asia? And the Russian missiles were threatening the United States itself.

Without growing excited, quite without polemic, speaking matter-of-factly, Deng noted, "But China is not afraid of the Soviet Union. Our country is prepared. And after all, a million Soviet soldiers along a seven-thousand-kilometer border are not very many; to make an attack on China, the Soviet Union would have to bring at least two million more from the western part of the nation. Such a war would certainly last twenty years or more. We are not afraid."

When I asked him whether he thought a Soviet nuclear attack on China was likely, Deng answered very calmly, "That would not change anything important. China would survive even that."

As my visit continued, however, I could feel that many Chinese were seriously concerned about the possibility of nuclear war.

Toward the end of our talk Deng came back to the subject of the United States. He spoke once more about the excessive extent of its protection obligations. Then he addressed Washington's relations with Europe. Were we really sure, he wanted to know, that the United States would actually defend Europe? Even when it was a matter of "only" Yugoslavia or Scandinavia? It was, after all, conceivable that the Americans would behave as the British had done in 1940 at Dunkirk and leave their allies to their own devices.

Deng told me he had said the same thing to Kissinger; the secretary of state had replied that the United States' behavior would essentially depend on the Europeans' actions. Apparently that remark had made sense to Deng. There would have to be a stable partnership between Europe and the United States, he went on; that was why China had no objection to the presence of American fighting forces in Europe. But

China had some doubts about America's "policy of appeasement"; the example of the Helsinki Conference was very troubling. In any case, Western Europe would have to be prepared to defend itself if need be. And that was why Europe must unify politically.

I was relatively cool in my reply; I said that the unification of Europe was something Bonn had demanded and promoted at a time when Beijing, along with Moscow, had still strongly opposed it. But as far as a European defense capability was concerned, we Germans were making a military contribution to it that was highly valued, and not only by our friends. I added that because of its decades of experience with the Soviet Union, the Chinese leadership probably understood Moscow better than I did; but it was also important for them to know more about Europe, and therefore I would like to invite him to pay us a visit. However, I continued, Beijing should also cultivate closer contact with the United States. Gerald Ford and Henry Kissinger were strong and dependable men, and they could take criticism well.

Suddenly, almost without preamble and very tersely, Deng said, "We support the reunification of Germany." China, he went on, viewed the division of Germany from the point of view of the experiences of the divided countries in its own hemisphere; the desire for the reunification of Germany went along with the desire for the reunification of Vietnam, of Korea, and of China with Taiwan. All these problems of reunification could not be solved in five or ten years, but perhaps they would require less than a century. This perspective seemed realistic to me, and of course I liked Deng's initial sentence. I thanked him cordially for his unequivocal words.

Deng's remarks on the world economic situation were both extremely ideological and strikingly vague. In general he limited himself to the rhetorical reasons for the necessity of a "new world economic order" that was on the agenda of all the developing nations at the time. In the economic area Deng was merely a listener; what he had to say did not go beyond broad slogans. Even a decade later, when China became committed to domestic economic reform and to opening up to the international economy, his knowledge of economic conditions was obviously still very general, in no way comparable to his acuity on strategic questions.

Counting all the banquets, during which we could also talk at length, Deng and I exchanged views in a very personal way for eight or ten hours. I gained the impression that he, too, found this time very well spent.

To summarize my impressions of that visit, it seems to me that Mao's international picture was still fixed on Moscow, although China's rupture with Moscow had happened almost twenty years before. The Chinese leadership clearly had considerable worries as to the potential military threat from the north, but it concealed this concern behind pride, suspicion, and contempt. Since, conversely, I was aware of the Soviet fear of the growing human masses in China—the population of the two countries stood in a 1-to-4 relationship, as Brezhnev and Gromyko had repeatedly explained to me in concerned tones—the possibility of a war between the two giants could not be discounted altogether. However, such a war seemed to me highly unlikely. The talks in Beijing left me with the impression that at the moment the Chinese leadership had quite different worries; basically it was concentrating on domestic policies and not on foreign affairs. Nevertheless it did not for a moment neglect the grand strategies.

Mao and Deng seemed to have arrived at the belief that the strength of China alone was not enough effectively to counter Moscow's desire for world rule, of which they were truly convinced. That was why Beijing was counting on the United States and Europe. Their criticism of the United States was not that the Americans were too strong—quite the opposite; in China's eyes, they were not powerful enough.

Whenever China voiced slogans about the "hegemony" of the superpowers, it was almost meant to sound as if both the Soviet Union and the United States were meant. But this attitude was tailored to the masses in China and the Third World. In reality only the Soviet Union was the subject of these statements. Beijing's interest in Bonn was apparently based on the fact that it saw Western Europe as the crucial factor and that within Europe it assigned the Federal Republic of Germany the largest economic and military potential. Bonn was also credited with having greater political influence on Washington than did Paris, Rome, and London. That the Chinese would have liked to maneuver us into a sharper confrontation with Moscow was obvious, but the Chinese we spoke with probably understood that we would not play that game. Beijing unequivocally considered the Soviet Union the principal enemy for historical, geographic, military, and ideological reasons.

China's internal situation, on the other hand, remained obscure. The impressions we gathered during those days in Beijing were various and contradictory. The monotony with which "the thoughts of Chairman Mao" were parroted was overwhelming. This overwrought acclamation of the great leader just about provoked the questions: Why is this necessary? What are the people really thinking? In view of the thousands of years of Chinese history and culture, the flowering of philosophy,

science, and literature, it seemed inconceivable to me that the Chinese
had relinquished all of it in favor of a few black-and-white clichés that
were repeated formulaically.

Mao himself made a deep impression on me. When I sat across the
room from him, I was reminded that as the leader of the revolution,
his historical meaning for China's future was similar to Lenin's for the
Soviet Union. But the Russian leadership cadre with which Lenin dealt
had been small. Perhaps the educated class in China had not been any
broader, but because of the size of the huge and populous nation, it was
numerically very much larger. And Confucius, Lao-tse, and Buddhism
had been shedding their light on China for thousands of years.

Of course the imperial China of the nineteenth century had decayed,
run down by the colonial interventionist powers, but it seemed to me
altogether improbable that this empire would throw its history and
traditions overboard and trade them in for Mao's grand attempt to
create a "new man." Wasn't that oddly unhistorical? With reverent
respect I have always seen China as the only world culture that had
developed continuously and been preserved for thousands of years into
the present. Was this to be fundamentally changed by a "cultural revolution"?

I was shocked not only by the opera in Beijing but also by the
propaganda opera we were taken to see in Urumqi in the province of
Xinjiang (formerly transliterated Sinkiang). I disliked the style of the
dealings among the tens of thousands of people in the Red Star People's
Commune. I disliked the propaganda loudspeakers that showered the
people on the broad streets of Urumqi with political agitation. I disliked
the enforced uniformity of clothing, and I was shocked by the obviously
ruthless suppression of all individuality.

What my traveling companions Klaus Mehnert, C. F. von Weizsäcker, and Max Frisch reported to me about their private talks with
intellectuals in university circles gave me an equally desolate impression.
In the name of the Cultural Revolution millions of schoolchildren,
students, and artists had been sent to do forced labor in the peasant
communes, and the intellectuals had been humiliated, degraded, and
forced into self-criticism. Tens of thousands had been broken, thousands had died. Everyone was incessantly compelled to profess opinions
that were not his own; a whole people had been condemned to lying.
Those who had been allowed to return to the city and the university
found that their professional career depended—and probably depends
to this day—on their ideological attitude, and "the masses"—in reality,
of course, the so-called revolutionary committees—determined their

worth. Given such a widespread loss of humanity, I would not have wanted to live in the country of Mao and his Cultural Revolution at any price, I felt this very clearly. I felt sympathy for the millions and millions of people who were affected.

Only in one city did the people, both young and old, seem to me somewhat happier; this was Nanjing (Nanking), one of the many large Chinese cities that at one time or another had been the nation's capital. One could still sense a little of the former glory, even during a flying visit. Many of the people wore simple shirts and trousers, so they looked more colorful then the people elsewhere. One of us even saw a closely entwined young couple in Nanjing, while elsewhere we gained only an impression of puritanical severity; any flirtation, any recognizable sign of tenderness seemed to be suppressed.

Nanjing, a city of plane trees, seemed green all over; people seemed to deal with life in a more relaxed, easier way. Perhaps the climate had something to do with it. It is considerably warmer than in Beijing, and I was reminded of Naples over and over again. In all southern areas the government power clearly finds it harder to impose formal discipline; perhaps, I thought, this fact spells hope for the south.

My strongest memory is of the Yangtse River, on whose southern shore the city is situated. The banks are relatively flat, which is why the enormous yellow-gray stream, given to flooding, seems even broader than it is, two kilometers. The people were very proud of the great bridge the Soviets had left behind half-finished in 1960 after the break with China and which, like hundreds of other uncompleted projects, had been finished by the Chinese alone. After a short steamboat ride, the apparently obligatory group photo of the entire party was taken on the bridge; the narrow wooden ladders for this purpose are always at the ready.

A head of government's official visit allows little opportunity to gather impressions of a country and its people. Thus in 1975 I was able to see only one other city beside Beijing and Nanjing—Urumqi in Xinjiang, the Chinese part of Turkestan. The hours-long flight over the endless unpopulated wilderness, past the edges of the Gobi Desert and then along the foothills of the Tien Shan mountains, gave us a powerful impression of almost inexhaustible space that we would never forget. Somewhere down there had been the old silk road, with hundreds of kilometers of emptiness stretching between the larger oases and bases. Now and then I could glimpse the railroad that had taken the place of the caravan route. Somewhere down there, too, Buddhism had made its way eastward, and centuries later Marco Polo had wandered through this landscape. Over the centuries this endless wilderness had seen innumerable battles between Chinese and Mongols, Tibetans, and the Turkish peoples of Central Asia. Somewhere down there, in the deserts of Inner Mongolia, Genghis Khan had begun his expedition of conquest against China seven hundred and fifty years before. Inner Mongolia and Xinjiang give China a great additional potential for cultivation and settlement if enough water can be collected or brought to the surface. Though both under the czars and under the Communists Russia broke Outer Mongolia out of the Chinese realm, the Chinese will inexorably hold on to Xinjiang as well as Tibet and Manchuria.

The Tien Shan mountains, with their summits reaching 6,000–7,000 meters, divide Xinjiang into the southern Tarim basin and the northern Dzungaria. Its snowfields and glaciers gleamed in the sunlight as we flew along them. We could only guess at the summits in the north and northwest of the Dzungaria, but we knew that behind them lay the Soviet part of Turkestan, and still further behind were Kazakhstan and Kirghisia.

Our reception in Urumqi, the capital of Xinjiang province, was very different in its externals from the reception in Beijing. The people's faces, though Asiatic, were not Chinese. Everything was much more colorful. The women wore bright skirts, even when they were sweeping the streets with little twig brooms, the children's clothes were more colorful than in Beijing, and most of the men wore little embroidered caps. To welcome us, women soldiers in white gloves marched up, and there were groups of dancers in pretty local costumes.

The Uighurs speak quickly and vivaciously, and our Chinese companions had trouble understanding them. All the banners were printed in two languages: Chinese characters at the bottom, and above them— thus given precedence, as it were—Turkish writing, usually in Latin script. The Han Chinese were clearly a minority, the Uighurs predominated. They were interested and curious; probably there had hardly ever been an official Western visit to their part of the world. Proudly they told us that they could communicate without great difficulty with the Turks in faraway Turkey.

At a museum we gained an impression of a cultural mix that had grown over the centuries: marked on the one hand by the nomadic culture of the steppes and the oasis culture of the desert, on the other by the equestrian peoples of the Huns and the Mongols, who, coming from Mongolia, had set out from here to break through to the West.

The borders with the Soviet Union were not precisely defined, I was told by the constantly smiling leader, but they were practically impassable. They cannot always have been so impassable, I thought, since the Turks, Huns, and Mongols had managed to get through—to India, Persia, Asia Minor, and Europe. And both silk and porcelain had come all the way to Venice through what are today the Soviet cities of Tashkent and Samarkand. In the opposite direction Islam, which came from the Middle East, had also navigated the mountain passes.

Today Xinjiang is practically a Central Asian outpost of China, just as Kazakhstan and the other Islamic Soviet republics in areas the Russians did not conquer until the nineteenth century are outposts of the Soviet Union. The Uighurs not only showed pride in their uniqueness, they were also very candid: "We are not Chinese, and we don't want to be." "I surely will not marry a Chinese," a young girl assured my wife emphatically.

And yet the Uighurs seemed to me not a whit less loyal to their government than the Chinese—but who can be sure after such a short visit? In any case, our stop in Urumqi made me realize clearly how much empathy and sensitivity the leadership in Beijing must have and must go on having if the Chinese great power wants to keep its minorities in line. At times I doubted that the huge tasks of consolidation could be solved by the bureaucracy centralized in Beijing.

Though the Uighurs represent the largest contingent of the five or six Turkish peoples living within the People's Republic of China, the entire group consists of no more than ten million people or so. To these are added in other provinces the Tibetans, the Mongols, the Manchus, and all the other national minorities.

At a rough estimate, almost one tenth of the nation's population consists of countless linguistic, ethnic, and religious minorities. The so-called autonomous provinces, regions, districts, and villages are clearly being subjected to a steady process of "Sinization," in part through the immigration or planned settlement of Han Chinese, in part by the compulsory spread of the Han Chinese language, which in English is often confusingly called Mandarin. In Urumqi some of the Uighuric- and Han Chinese–speaking local functionaries appeared to require interpreters to talk with one another.

Our visit to Xinjiang confirmed my growing affection for China; on the other hand I felt an increase in my abhorrence of the Cultural Revolution, whose absurd effects we could feel even in this far distant province. Zhou Enlai was on his deathbed, Mao was obviously no longer able to lead the state, and who actually held the reins was unclear. Deng Xiaoping seemed to be the man who combined all the necessary qualities; but his ostentatious, almost importunate adherence to Mao's words made me doubt his freedom of action.

Six months after my visit, in April 1976, Deng Xiaoping was purged once more and—this time allegedly by Mao himself—sent to Coventry. From Bonn it looked as if the Cultural Revolution and the hate-filled zeal of Mao's wife, Jiang Qing, had after all triumphed over reason. I was saddened by the news—for one, because of my liking for China, and for another because I feared the repercussions on the West of the victorious Cultural Revolution. I had, after all, seen how students in my own country had been moved by infectious ideological hysteria to tear themselves away from their moral moorings and had been seduced into destructive voluntarism.

Interlude:
Hua Guofeng

MAO died in September 1976. After his death the Cultural Revolution rapidly came to an end. Mao's widow, Jiang Qing, and the leaders of her Cultural Revolution were arrested, and in June 1978 Deng Xiaoping was recalled to be deputy party chairman and deputy prime minister. Hua Guofeng occupied the top positions; after Deng's banishment Hua had been installed by Mao himself.

Hua was not able to hold on to his two top offices for long; he was overthrown in 1981. The power struggles within the Chinese Communist Party—not only during those years, but for more than fifty years since the beginning—would furnish ample material for an exciting historical novel. By the end of the 1970s the Chinese leadership was free of the compulsion of slavishly having to parrot Mao's every word. This situation also led to a differentiated picture of Chinese foreign policy. That picture holds true to this day, and I therefore want to give a detailed report of a conversation I had with Hua Guofeng in Bonn over the course of several days in October 1979.

Hua Guofeng, whom I had not known before, was accompanied by his foreign minister, Huang Hua, with whom I had met several times and with whom I have had numerous meetings since then. Huang Hua is an experienced, clever, and agreeable diplomat. As early as 1913, when he was a young man, he joined the Communist Party. During the 1930s he was Mao's interpreter and in the 1950s worked closely with Zhou Enlai. He had filled numerous ambassadorships and had become foreign minister in 1976. I valued my talks with this objective man very much. Today he is the head of the permanent parliamentary committee.

But in 1979 it was not so much he but his boss who was important. After three official talks, in which our foreign ministers had taken part as well, Hua Guofeng and I found ourselves so interested in each other that after one banquet we spontaneously retired to have a very private exchange of views. Before the Chinese delegation arrived in Bonn, I had spoken to Valéry Giscard d'Estaing on the telephone to learn what impression Hua had made in Paris; what Giscard had told me was already enough to make me curious.

Even during the talks of the official delegation, two interesting statements were made: First, after the Gang of Four was toppled, the theory of the class struggle became a thing of the past; China would need a long period of stability to carry out its internal reconstruction. And second, as far as foreign policy was concerned, it was summed up in two concepts—fighting the claim to hegemony and securing world peace; of course a peaceful and stable international situation could not be attained by prayer but had to be actively sought. The theory of the inevitability of war seemed to have been submerged and lost.

Our private talk dealt exclusively with the world situation and the position of the principal nations. Hua Guofeng asked about conditions in the United States, and I explained to him my view of American politics: "Both the war in Vietnam and Watergate have led to a considerable diminishment of the Americans' self-understanding, and they have also nibbled at the system's domestic stability. This state of affairs has not been entirely overcome yet. What is still lacking is the old homogeneity in the view of domestic and foreign affairs that will be needed in future as well. This is not only a problem for President Carter but even more a crisis of general political consciousness. But the American nation has a great vitality. With its help the United States will find its way back to its full powers during the 1980s. On the other hand, the Soviet Union has so far successfully exploited the United States' weakness in leadership in Angola, the Horn of Africa, Afghanistan, and many other places. It is nevertheless true that in Egypt, Somalia, and Iraq the Soviet Union has suffered considerable reverses. But how do matters stand," I asked my guest, "between the People's Republic of China and the Soviet Union?"

"We know," Hua Guofeng replied, "that the West has two conflicting concerns. For one, there is the fear that toward the end of the century Beijing and Moscow will form an alliance and together achieve dominance over the West. For another, some Western Europeans fear that the West could become involved in a war between China and the Soviet Union. We think the likelihood of war is small, even if the international situation should grow even more unstable and tension-laden. Some Anglo-American and Japanese research institutes do say that a third world war could break out in the mid-1980s because at that time the Soviet Union will have reached the apex of arms superiority. And of course there will be flashpoints in some of the Arab countries, in Southeast Asia, in parts of Africa, in the Caribbean, most critically in the Middle East.

"But in recent years China has normalized its relations with the United States. Our relations with Japan and Western Europe are well developed. The Soviet Union fears a war on two fronts. If China gains power in coming years, Moscow will not lightly march against Europe. To wage war against China, Moscow would have to increase its troops along the border from one million to five or six million; it would have to remove its most important, best-equipped troops from Europe. This is something the Soviets cannot do if they do not feel absolutely secure there. We have determined that the Soviet Union cannot help but fear a two-front war. That is why we do not believe it will launch a world war in the 1980s.

"Nevertheless," he continued, "the Soviets will make use of every opportunity for further expansion. That is clearly their strategy. They are intent on increasing the pressure on Western Europe and driving a wedge between the Europeans and the United States. It is equally clear to us that they want to strategically surround and—coming from the Near East, Africa, and the ocean—encircle Europe."

I asked whether there was unanimity in the leadership of the Chinese Communist Party on the idea that the Soviet Union could not afford a war on two fronts.

Yes, Hua Guofeng assured me, there was total agreement on this question, even though it might not be absolutely true. "If you in Europe intensify your defense efforts, if the Western European states become unified and keep up their relations with the United States, and if on the other side we Chinese remain allied with Japan and the United States, it would be in the Soviet Union's best interest to avoid a two-front war. Furthermore, Moscow is extremely worried about its own

Eastern European backyard. For these reasons we believe that a Soviet-Chinese world war will not break out in the 1980s."

A great deal of discernment was implicit in the thoughtful, serious manner of his discourse. Hua's analyses of the armed Chinese-Vietnamese conflict and the mutual Chinese-Soviet nuclear missile threat also impressed me. The Chinese-Vietnamese conflict, I was told, was a consequence of Vietnamese strivings for hegemony over Kampuchea. Vietnam had invaded that nation only after the Soviet-Vietnamese pact had been signed. There had also been numerous border violations and provocations of the People's Republic of China; China had had no choice but to defend itself. Finally, China's struggle against any form of hegemony was a serious matter: "If the battle is waged on China's doorstep, China cannot remain inactive."

Of course, he said, Beijing had not proceeded against Vietnam until carefully considering every alternative, and there had been no rash action. But if there had been no action at all, Thailand and Malaysia would have been the next victims; in that case the ASEAN nations could no longer have offered resistance. At that time the Soviet Union had won access to the Strait of Malacca and with it control over the crucial sea route between the Pacific and the Indian Ocean. This had consequences as far as the Persian Gulf and the Red Sea and had certainly affected the world's oil supplies.

"We therefore acted," he continued, "out of more than our own national interest. But of course, in our own interest, we first calculated all possible Soviet reactions. As I have said, we arrived at the conclusion that the Soviet Union was not prepared for a major war against China, so a major war was not likely. Of course we also considered the possibility of limited Soviet attacks on Xinjiang or northern China; we came to the conclusion that in such a case the Soviet Union was risking an escalation of military actions that it would not be able to control. Therefore we also decided that a limited attack was improbable. Finally, we had to consider the possibility of Soviet incursions and actions at the Chinese-Soviet border; we did not exclude this possibility but prepared for it before taking action against Vietnam."

China, he continued, had also consulted with the United States and Japan; the leaders of both, especially Carter, had been concerned and warned him about possible Soviet reactions. "But the actual events were as we had foreseen. Though on the first day the Soviets threatened us and demanded the withdrawal of our troops, when we did not respond, they initiated military maneuvers and sent naval units to the South China Sea. But that was all. They passed a stringent test [which meant they withstood a serious temptation] because they are afraid of war on two fronts. They are a great military power, but they cannot risk war on two fronts."

I will omit our conversation on Afghanistan, Iran, the Middle East, the supply of oil, the international situation in Laos and Kampuchea, the role of the ASEAN nations and Japan, and the role of the Third World and nonaligned nations. On all these subjects the Chinese party head and prime minister showed himself to be superbly informed. His geostrategic overview and his ability to present matters in simplified but by no means simplistic outlines was unusual, his frankness refreshing. In comparison to Mao's sweeping judgments four years earlier, which had assumed the guise of unassailable truths, this was all the more remarkable.

I had no doubt that Hua's statements could also be interpreted as an encompassing, deliberate attempt to win me—and other European leaders who heard him speak in a similar vein—over to exerting stronger Western pressure on the Soviet Union. For of course it is just as true in China as elsewhere that a third party is delighted to see two others quarrel. On the other hand, this was an improvised nighttime talk of considerable length that had originally not been included in the formally agreed upon program for the visit, a talk Hua Guofeng could not have prepared for until sometime during the dinner. If he nevertheless—acting on a psychological-tactical principle—was trying to influence me, he must have been a man of unusual competence.

I placed the personnel situation in Moscow and the resulting insecurity of the West at the center of my reply. I spoke about the situation in Europe, in the European Community and its member states, the results of the partition of Germany, the German-French alliance, the paramount position of Giscard, and the military capabilities of NATO and the Bundeswehr. And of course I also talked about the nuclear strategic situation, about SALT, about the new Soviet Eurostrategic missiles, the SS-20s, about the additional political vulnerability of Germany they represented, and about the NATO TNF resolution, which would be taken in eight weeks.

On this last point Hua Guofeng remarked, "The Soviet Union has deployed both intercontinental strategic nuclear weapons and intermediate-range missiles against us. We cannot object too much, for in view of the range of these missiles, they are far from our borders. . . . Our own nuclear missiles are far inferior to those of the Soviet Union and the United States. But if the Soviets launched a nuclear attack on China, they must count on our destroying Soviet cities, including Moscow.

Our nuclear weapons cannot possibly be destroyed by a Soviet first strike; they are concealed, as are our many armament factories, and they cannot be seen by the Soviet reconnaissance satellites. Besides, it is impossible to destroy our mobile system in one strike."

I do not wish to detail Hua's technical explanation here. He continued, "When Brezhnev was in the United States, he told Nixon he would like the two of them to destroy China's nuclear potential. Brezhnev asked, 'How long will it take China to have nuclear arms?' Nixon replied, 'Twenty years.' Brezhnev answered, '*Nyet, nyet*—not twenty, but ten years!' That is why in 1969 Moscow seriously considered eliminating the Chinese potential. But Brezhnev knows that by now the ten years have passed and it is too late. . . . The Soviets cannot run the risk of waging nuclear war against us."

I asked about the Chinese-Soviet negotiations. Hua Guofeng replied, "What is at stake is not an extension of the Chinese-Soviet friendship and mutual assistance pact; the previous one was directed against Japan, and since that time we have concluded a pact of friendship with Japan. Furthermore, the Soviet Union has long since trampled on our pact, although it is in force until April 1980. But we have not yet reached an agreement on procedure. The Soviet Union is trying for an accord on principles or a nonaggression pact. We, on the other hand, are eager to solve all open questions between both states and remove obstacles to normalization. This seems to be difficult for the Soviet Union. It could turn into a negotiation marathon; the talks on the border questions alone have lasted for ten years."

Answering another one of my questions, he said, "The northeastern frontier is especially in question. Russia has robbed us of a total of 1.6 million square kilometers of land. Although Lenin declared that the Soviets were eager to abolish all inequitable treaties and return these territories to us, China has not even raised this question. At the present time we are dealing only with a few small disputed border areas; Zhou Enlai and Kosygin had already come to an agreement on these, but after he returned to Moscow, Kosygin changed his mind. Today the Soviet Union is not prepared to admit that there are any disputed territories at all."

I asked about the significance of the Soviet troops along the border. This massing of troops, Hua Guofeng said, was a hostile act. Altogether there were forty-five divisions; Soviet troops were also stationed in the People's Republic of Mongolia, something that had not been true in Khrushchev's time. "There are three types of divisions. The first is at seventy to eighty percent capacity, each about ten thousand men; the other types consist of six to seven thousand and four thousand men, respectively. The Soviet tanks and airplanes are better than ours. If there is a war, it's possible the Soviet Union will penetrate deeply into our country and kill many people. But geographically China is composed quite differently from Europe; we have enough space and so many people—and the Soviet Union has a very long way to go to get here."

We then reverted to the subject of a Soviet two-front war. Once again I stressed my two strategic principles where Moscow was concerned: both security, if possible through West-East arms parity, and détente through cooperation, including cooperation in arms limitation by treaty. I noted, "In Paris, London, and Rome you will surely meet with similar positions. Because of what I have lived through, I am afraid of war. But I have no inferiority complex when it comes to the Soviet Union. Brezhnev has heard me say more than once that we Germans will make every effort to contribute to the preservation of military parity."

"I believe," Hua Guofeng replied, "that in any war the German forces would have the greatest fighting strength. In my opinion, the Soviets see it the same way. They are most afraid of the Germans. That is why they will oppose the reunification of Germany with every means at their disposal. . . . Though nowadays some people write that if Germany were to adopt a neutral position, the Soviets would agree to reunification, I consider that an unrealistic belief. . . .

"Therefore," he continued, "a long-term development of our relations with the Federal Republic is important to us. Even if West Germany grows strong, it will never attack China, and China will never pursue hegemonical tendencies and attack the Federal Republic. We are looking at things in a broad perspective. We want to learn from your advanced technology, and in return we can offer you raw materials and specific products." Hua stressed the fact that China fully understood the normalization of relations between the Federal Republic and the Soviet Union, since his nation approved of détente. No one, however, could reasonably expect everyone to speak the same language.

We parted long after midnight. The conversation had revealed a greater maturity and subtlety in Chinese strategic thought. My guest had behaved in an exemplary manner: candid and outspoken in private conversation and at the same time tactful and sensitive during public appearances.

At the time some circles in Moscow and East Berlin voiced a suspicion that West Germany and China were getting ready to act in concert against them. Thus the East German newspaper *Neues Deutschland,* under the headline "Playing with Fire," reported alleged statements by Hua Guofeng according to which "China supports the revanchist objectives of German imperialism directed at the German Democratic Republic." Conversely the West German CDU and especially the CSU opposition claimed that the West German government was neglecting China and Hua Guofeng—totally forgetting that for decades, in the face of our repeated exhortation to recognize reality, they had opted for Taiwan and against Beijing.

Even in the concluding press conference Hua Guofeng surmounted all conceivable hurdles. This conference ended with a satyr play: Rudi Dutschke infiltrated the group and provided a brief spectacle. This highly talented leader of the 1968 Berlin student revolt was physically handicapped as the result of a gunshot attack on his life. Hua Guofeng took it calmly. On this occasion, too, he radiated ease.

Subsequently he sent us two pandas as a thank-you for his visit. We gave them to the Berlin zoo, where they soon grew to be darlings of the Berlin public.

Soon thereafter, in 1981, Hua Guofeng was replaced; we also heard rumors of serious illness. His photograph disappeared from all Chinese offices. He had presumably been too deeply compromised by his closeness to Mao during the Cultural Revolution; besides, in view of the new reform line, he was probably too conservative. As far as I was concerned, he had given me many essential elements of my understanding of China's strategic position and the Chinese objectives arising from it.

China's
Strategic Position

A FTER a long and in part self-imposed isolation, China and its political leadership still lack adequate contact with the rest of the world. The tradition of Sinocentric, introverted thinking that has lasted two millenia plays an important part in this situation; "Mao Zedong thinking" was, after all, no more than a particular combination of the old world view with the standard inventory of Marxist and nationalist-revolutionary ideas. Such foreign policy and strategic dimensions as were incorporated into Mao's ideas were for a long time marked by every kind of negation: anti-imperialism, anticolonialism, anticapitalism. This way of mechanical thinking, so to speak, led to a rejection of the global division of labor that characterizes today's world economy. According to Mao's wishes, China was to develop as a Communist nation on its own strength. The break with Moscow strengthened this focus on national strength; the ideal was total independence from the rest of the world.

The Cultural Revolution beginning in the mid-1960s meant not only political isolation but also a dangerous weakening of the country's defense capability. China drove itself into a double confrontation with both the Soviet Union and the United States.

But since with the exception of North Korea, China had almost no friends and no allies in Asia and is not likely to gain any soon, the huge country's strategic position is particularly explosive, and the Beijing leadership gradually became aware of this. At Nixon's initiative, contacts with the United States were taken up, and after Nixon's 1972 visit détente and approaches to Washington were espoused. China's realistic fear of the neighboring expansionist Soviet Union had by now become much more important to Beijing than the merely ideological rejection of American capitalism. The sense that the United States represented a threat disappeared.

Today—and probably for the foreseeable future, at least to the end of the century—the Chinese see Soviet expansionism as the primary evil. Beijing considers the Soviet troop and missile deployment on its borders a military threat that it feels barely capable of withstanding; its nuclear strategic ideas resemble those of Charles de Gaulle in the 1960s. But beyond this, China feels increasingly encircled by the Soviet Union. In the south stand the battle-hardened troops of Vietnam, which is allied with the Soviet Union. In Vladivostok and Cam Ranh Bay in Vietnam there are the Soviet naval bases, and there may be others in Kampuchea in the near future. The strong Soviet submarine and deep-sea fleet cruises the Pacific; there is a growing Soviet presence in the Indian Ocean and the Malacca Strait, which unites these two oceans; and the fleet makes periodic guest appearances in Singapore. In this light the Soviet invasion of Afghanistan seemed like a step toward the eventual possession of a port on the Indian Ocean. Aside from the threat of the Soviet fleet cruising on all Asian seas and the Soviet missile bases, China must also take into account the Soviet air force, which is based in the northeast, the north, and the northwest, in Afghanistan— it is easy to forget that Afghanistan and the Chinese province of Xinjiang share a border—and in Da Nang in Vietnam.

Thus China feels encircled from both a political and a military point of view; at the same time Beijing sees very clearly—though it is never mentioned—that the way of the Chinese Communist Party is an ideological challenge to the Russian Communists' claim to leadership. They also have a different economic model, which in many respects is tempting to Moscow's satellites. In practical terms, then, the confrontation is occurring on several levels.

In the foreseeable future Beijing will be militarily too weak to incur the risk of war with the Soviet Union; it must hope that the major part of Soviet military forces remains committed elsewhere—meaning most of all along the western borders of the Soviet Union; that is the reason Beijing is urging Europeans to unite. In the extreme case the Chinese would act as the Russians did at the time of the invasions by Napoleon in 1812 and by Hitler in 1941: retreat to the interior in the expectation that superiority of numbers will, in the end, decide the battle. At present the Soviet Union represents a little less than 6 percent of the world's population, while the People's Republic of China has more than 20 percent. But such visions of war are a nightmare even for the Chinese revolutionaries, who are inured to terror. For these reasons, even if anti-Soviet propaganda continues in the guise of antihegemony, China will remain conscious of the risks of its policies toward Moscow. And that is why China will make every effort not to break off diplomatic ties with the Soviet Union—in fact the reverse is more likely to be the case.

It will be a long time before China can be a sea power of any consequence. For this reason alone Beijing must want the United States at least to maintain parity with the Soviet Union in the Pacific and Indian oceans; Beijing keeps a watchful eye on Soviet naval armament. Japan, which is industrially so powerful, cannot ease the situation, since Beijing is reluctant to allow Japan any weapons at all; memories of the Japanese conquests since 1930 and the ruthlessness of the Japanese occupation forces are still much too vivid.

Even outside its own area of the world, China needs the United States' globally effective strategic weight to counter that of the Soviet Union—and not only the United States' but also Europe's. Should China's relative security in relation to the Soviet Union, which is hampered by other potential confrontations and conflicts, appear assured, then a renewed development of at least partial cooperation with Moscow is entirely conceivable in future. In its talks with the Kremlin, which have never been entirely broken off, China has for some time quietly laid aside the demand for revision of the "inequitable treaties" and has instead limited its claims to three other preconditions for a normalization of Chinese-Soviet relations.

This so-called elimination of the three obstacles consists of, first, a reduction of the Soviet fighting forces along the border (and of the SS-20s east of the Urals?), second and most important, an end to the Soviet-supported Vietnamese occupation of Kampuchea, and finally, an end to the invasion of Afghanistan. I once jokingly said to the Chinese deputy foreign minister, Tsien Tsien, who was in charge of these talks, "It seems to me that your planning position is a lifetime job," and he replied, "Yes, for at least twenty years." Right now both a reduction of Chinese diplomatic pressure and consequently a partial reduction of the three demands, and the opposite—a renewed forward push of the Chinese claims concerning the "inequitable treaties"—are possible.

The crucial difference will be the extent to which the Soviet leadership takes Chinese interests and sensitivities into consideration or, seen in reverse, the degree to which Moscow can overcome its own resentments concerning the People's Republic of China. It is not altogether impossible that at one point or another in Chinese-Soviet relations there might be a parallel to the German policy of détente—in that in both cases the security interests of both parties take first place.

Of course the extent to which the American leadership respects Chinese interests and sensitivities also plays a role. In the foreseeable future there will be no great strategic conflict of interest between China and the United States. But since 1972 the American China policy has not always run a smooth course, especially on the subject of Taiwan, which is so sensitive for China; American arms deliveries to Taiwan are noted with particular criticism on the Chinese mainland. For Beijing, Taiwan is and will remain an internal Chinese affair; Washington occasionally realizes this, but in memory of its former ally, Chiang Kai-shek, the commandment of restraint is rather frequently violated, especially by the right wing in the Senate. China's pride is easily hurt, and the United States should include this pride in its calculations as a factor that will weigh heavily in the balance.

Aside from the problem of Taiwan, China sees the United States' strategic role to be an indispensable cornerstone in the global balance of power. Beijing knows that in time China will be a military world power, but it also knows that years will have to pass before that day, and at present the time is needed for economic reconstruction that is affected as little as possible by defense efforts. This plan requires American and European technological support, but even more, continuous economic cooperation with neighboring Japan. Japan, which is poor in raw materials but has great technical and industrial capabilities, is the ideal economic partner for China in the East and Southeast Asian region.

However, Beijing has no thought of alliances within the region; this, too, is included in the formula of "rejection of hegemony." The People's Republic of China does not see itself as a "superpower," although it absolutely believes itself to be a world power. As regards possible allies, China faces a Hobson's choice: even should China seek alliances, it would hardly find a willing partner in its own region. Like Germany, China has many neighbors; but unlike the Federal Republic, China has no friends among its neighbors—apart from North Korea—not even any who would be prepared to enter an alliance or other close relationship for reasons of common sense if not of empathy. The reason for this isolation is not only the overwhelming size of the country and its huge population; because the ASEAN nations have experienced the superior economic capabilities of the 16 million Chinese who live abroad, inferiority complexes and resentment are also involved. But most especially the Chinese form of communism is being rejected, and there is a fear of the infiltration of an ideology that has led to bloody wars in Korea and Vietnam. Finally, in many nations cultural traditions play a crucial part. Speaking of the Chinese-Vietnamese border war of 1979, an Asian politician once said to me, "Thank God; it will bring us twenty more years of uninterrupted peace." Today some Asian nations are not certain whether they are in greater danger from China or the Soviet Union.

The only exception at present is Prince Norodom Sihanouk's Kampuchean government-in-exile, whose survival depends on Chinese support against the Vietnamese occupation. Though the other Kampuchean leader, Pol Pot, is also relying on China in his struggle against the Vietnamese, the Kampucheans have had dreadful experiences with him.

And though North Korea is allied with China, it must act very carefully because of its geographic proximity to the Soviet Union. China verbally supports the reunification of Korea, but in actual fact sees the United States military presence in South Korea as a form of security. A reunited Korea under Soviet influence means a worsening of the strategic position not only of Japan but also of China. In regard to Korea, China is, in my opinion, a status quo power; changes on the Korean peninsula after the death of Kim Il Sung, who is considered a creature of Moscow, might lead to a change in China's assessment.

The enmity between China and Vietnam goes very deep on both sides; it is not only rooted in actual political grounds but is also based on historical backgrounds that were played down during the short phase of Chinese help to North Vietnam.

It is an ironic catch of communism in the Eastern Hemisphere that among all its neighbors in Asia, China—by far the most populous Communist state—has good relations only with North Korea—not with the Soviet Union, not with Mongolia, not with Communist Vietnam or the Communist governments in Phnom Penh and Vientiane. Quite the opposite: Everything that troubles China comes from Communist states, while Beijing's relations with the "capitalist" countries are almost entirely problem-free.

But from Beijing's viewpoint the situation is not at all bad. The only serious worry is Vietnamese imperialism, which China will never accept. The most urgent wish of the People's Republic remains reunification with Taiwan; China is even prepared to make concessions along the lines of the Hong Kong solution. And China may get Macao back any day. The return of these parts of the country, which today are outside the state authority, must—if only for reasons of self-respect—remain part of China's strategic objective.

In every other respect the current situation appears entirely acceptable to China. China recognizes the sovereignty and autonomy of the ASEAN states of Malaysia, Thailand, Singapore, Indonesia, and the Philippines, and in fact it respects their interests. In theory and worldwide, China pursues the basic principles of neutrality and nonalignment. I do not believe that this is merely an example of the fox and the sour grapes, as some in Southeast Asia fear. After the Bandung Conference of 1955 and the five principles of friendly coexistence as they were first formulated at the time by Zhou Enlai, China increasingly turned into the speaker for the nonaligned nations and the advocate of the interests of the Third World—that is, the developing countries. Today this is playing an important role in the international understanding of the People's Republic of China, since the developing countries represent a great majority of the world's nations. Though the nonaligned nations are no more of a homogeneous group than the developing nations are, there is no reason why China should give away this agreeable role.

China has a yearly per capita income of only $300 or so; objectively and quite correctly, the country thinks of itself as a developing nation and is resisting the temptation to take a leadership role such as Fidel Castro's Cuba, for example, tries to play now and again. Beijing is convinced that the striving for hegemony of the superpowers can be opposed most successfully by the Third World nations. The paradox of the situation is, of course, that China's economic interests call much more urgently for cooperation with the efficient industrial states of the Western world and with Japan. That is why China's support of the demand for a "new economic order" remains weak and merely verbal.

Only when it comes to India is it possible that an attempt at political "South-South cooperation" might be attempted. But it is entirely improbable that New Delhi has any such desire; India's political closeness to the Soviet Union is alone enough to prevent such a move. But India's cooperation with the Soviet Union will remain in force as long as the India-Pakistan conflict exists—probably well past the turn of the century. Because of this final factor, by the way, any Chinese-Soviet rapprochement would be a catastrophe for New Delhi.

All in all, for the rest of the century China's highest strategic objective will be as smooth an economic development as possible. The question remains whether the country's internal continuity will be sufficient to allow for it. And only then—and perhaps as early as the next century—will the real question surface: Will China resist the temptation to once again become the "Middle Kingdom" from which all other people and nations of the greater region are to take their direction?

From Revolution to Reform

I N October 1984, after the Chinese resolutions concerning economic reform, Western newspapers printed commentaries that were in part supercilious, in part euphoric. The *Economist,* for example, a periodical that is as knowledgeable as it is discerning, came out in December 1984 with the headline "China Has Decided: Marx is Dead." The paper mentioned a "counterrevolution." There were many such exaggerations. I was there to witness the final phase of preparations for the reform resolutions, and the impression I gained was quite different. It seemed to me that it was not communism that was being abandoned but merely the desperate attempt to convert economic utopias into literal reality. What was being introduced was not a counterrevolution but an attempt, after a successfully concluded revolution, to enter on a phase of pragmatic economic development.

Every economist with a degree knows that Marx never tried to supply formulas for a communist economic policy. Beijing knows that as well. If that fact is mentioned in passing there today, it does not mean Beijing is abjuring Marx; what is happening is that some foolish economic instruments and elements of the economics of a central administration, whose creators based their theories—largely mistakenly—on Marx are being put in mothballs. Marx, Engels, Lenin, Stalin: As revolutionary forefathers, their huge portraits continue to shine in splendor in Tiananmen Square. They will hold on to their status as great models for China, just as will China's own Mao Zedong, whose picture graces the center of the Gate of Heavenly Peace.

Of course, at present the early period of this man, who was most responsible for the success of the revolution, is emphatically being distinguished from his later phases. The subsequent catastrophic failures of the campaign of the Hundred Flowers, the Great Leap Forward, the Permanent Revolution, and the Cultural Revolution are not to be repeated and continued. All earlier attempts—by Deng Xiaoping, Liu Shaochi, Lin Biao, and especially Zhou Enlai—to restore order within the chaotic conditions created by Mao and his fanatic followers failed. The struggle within the Chinese Communist Party went back and forth for thirty years; many paid for it with their lives or were banished. But after Jiang Qing and her Gang of Four were arrested, after Deng Xiaoping was rehabilitated, there was an effort "to look for the truth in facts"—one of Deng's favorite Confucian sayings—and no longer in ideology. In 1978 the Central Committee declared that the doctrine of the alleged "key role of the class struggle" was incorrect because there were no longer any enemy classes in China. Hua Guofeng, as Mao's successor, had clung to the principle of the class struggle for a long time.

The 1981 party congress marked the end of China's revolutionary phase. The revolution had lasted for decades, even if it had won its definitive victory as early as 1949. I do want to note a clear reservation: Though it looks today as if the revolutionary phase had definitively and irrevocably come to an end by 1981, the intellectual, psychological, and political developments in the intellectual elites of the party are hard to predict; far too many have been forced to lie low for far too long. Are all of them telling the truth as they know it today?

Deng Xiaoping is surely being truthful to himself. He is the great engine that is driving China on to realism and pragmatism. He is unlikely to have changed much in this in recent years. His famous statement that it "does not matter whether a cat is black or white, as long as it catches mice" was coined in the 1950s. Zhao Ziyang and Hu Yaobang, whom he placed at the head of the party and the head of the government, respectively, are reformers like himself. Without a doubt the current majorities in the Politburo and in the Central Committee are on the side of reform.

Doubts nevertheless remain about the country's continuity. For example, the reformers were frightened by the great reverberation, which took on unanticipated dynamics, of the campaign "against spiritual environmental pollution," though they themselves had set it into motion; they stopped it again as soon as possible. In the same way the thousands of deprived "left" cadres have surely not been truly won back yet; more likely, they are waiting for their chance at rehabilitation and a renewed upward climb. To these problems is added the lethargy that resists reform in any bureaucracy. Most especially the question of the legitimacy of the dictatorship of a single postrevolutionary party will arise.

The further the decentralization of economic decision making progresses and the more the sole accountability of industrial and trade enterprises is strengthened, the greater will be the worry of those who owe their positions exclusively to the party—or, more precisely, to their adaptability to whatever tendency happens to be predominating in the party at any given time. An opportunistic grasping of progressive decentralization, however, will also mean accepting the loss of their own spheres of authority, which at one time were undisputed.

The second danger seems to me incomparably greater: If the assignment of economic decisions to local and regional authorities should actually lead to greater efficiency, could not a similar advantage be expected for political and intellectual decisions as well? Do we not have to take as a given the assumption that a process of protest against intellectual and political patronage will emerge? If experimentation in the economic area is permitted, then why not in the schools and universities as well? The creation of competition or even of a free market will probably give rise to a call for greater individual freedom in other areas as well. The student unrests of 1986 were a sign of the desire for pluralism; this desire is sure to return as economic reform continues.

However, as long as the masses of Chinese people continue to find themselves a little better off from one year to the next, it will be difficult to mobilize the population or even large segments of the young people against reform-minded party leadership. And in fact many Chinese, especially the peasants, are significantly better off today than they were a few years ago. The improvements are small, but they are clearly felt and consciously registered. In the cities, too, it is not possible to overlook the improved situation. When I returned to Beijing in 1984, the atmosphere in the capital had changed fundamentally. It had become more cheerful, brighter, more colorful, and altogether more humane; the pressure from above no longer lay on the people. Construction was going on all over the city; the blue or gray uniforms had been replaced with attractive dresses and suits. Many women were wearing high-heeled shoes and had put on moderate amounts of makeup, and some of them had permanent waves. The men were wearing colored shirts. At the dinner given by our ambassador, Günther Schödel, both sexes were overwhelmingly dressed in Western garb. Furthermore, the shops displayed many kinds of fruit and vegetables, and the streets were full of flower sellers. The contrast with 1975 was impressive: We felt relieved and were happy with and for the Chinese.

In 1984 the Chinese leadership invited me to deliver two lectures on the international political and economic situation. My lectures and the subsequent discussions were held at the International Institute, with Han Nianlong, its chairman, officiating. Both lectures took place in a small auditorium; in the audience were a few dozen leading officials from the ministries as well as leading party functionaries; in addition, a few ambassadors and a few high-ranking editors of Chinese newspapers attended.

For me, and probably for my hosts as well, the discussion of economics was by far the most interesting, if only because it related directly to what we had been shown in the real world—in the steelworks near Beijing, in Shanghai harbor, on an agricultural commune, and in the factories in Hangzhou, as well as in the everyday life of cities both large and small. The partial separation of agriculture from the constraints of central planning had not only brought the peasants greater income but had also supplied the cities with a greater supply of foodstuffs.

These changes could not be ignored, whether I was visiting industrial plants or workers' residential quarters. In Beijing I had been shown several huge apartment houses. By our standards most of the apartments were unimaginably overcrowded; though officially in Beijing and in Shanghai 4.5 square meters of living space were assigned to each person, we had the impression that this statistical average was in reality much too high. The average living space in the agricultural commune in Hung Chao near Shanghai, which was listed as 2.8 square meters, seemed more realistic. There too we had seen the insides of several residences; they were mostly houses that had been individually built except for the foundations.

The difference between the city and the country surrounding Shanghai, a city of 12 million people, was striking; it was immediately obvious why young people in the cities like to get married to someone from the country and move there. All the countryside apartments were furnished very modestly but had electricity and running water. There were radios, and everyone was saving up for a television set; where a television set was already present, it was covered in the daytime with a crocheted doily.

Nursery schools were clearly being vigorously promoted all over the country, and the number of nursery school teachers in proportion to the number of children seemed very high. Of course nursery schools are essential where both parents work, and as a result of the limitation on births, there are no older siblings to look after the younger ones. The ideal family promoted by the state consists of five people: one child, two parents, and two grandparents. Even in the ideal case, then, the new two-room apartments in the cities provide very close quarters.

In 1984 we stayed in the same guest house in Beijing where I had been lodged nine years earlier, when I was chancellor. Along with other such accommodations, it is situated in a large garden in the western part of the city that had originally been set up as the summer residence of an emperor. The public park nearby offered a unique show early in the morning. Huge crowds came there before going to work. While some took their singing birds on an outing—thousands carried their birdcages into the greenery on their bicycles—others practiced shadowboxing or did calisthenics, all the while uttering loud primal screams. Our ambassador's wife suggested that they were working off the aggressions that must inevitably arise, given the crowded living quarters. That made sense to us: the shortage of housing in the cities cannot help but have psychological consequences.

In the late afternoons, after work, the street scene was characterized by general strolling. Certainly there were many more people abroad than at the best of times on the Kurfürstendamm or Broadway. I suppose the decisive reason behind this custom of an evening stroll also lies in the crowded living conditions. I noticed that in the four major cities we visited—Xian, Shanghai, Hangzhou, and Guangzhou (Canton)—the street scene was considerably more colorful than in the capital. Peddlers hawked roast chickens, nuts, apples, beer, soup, and shashlik. The people wandered about, enjoying their peaceful existence and the dusk of approaching night. It was a cheerful picture.

We traveled to Xian to see the clay warriors that had recently been excavated—altogether apparently more than 7,000 figures that, concealed under an artificial hill, had been intended to guard the tomb of Qin Shi Huang Di, the "first emperor of China." To protect the horsemen and foot soldiers, only some of which have so far been excavated, against damage by the elements, a huge hall has been erected over them. Great parts of the large area from the third century B.C. and the burial mound itself are still waiting to be opened to the public, because the excavations are proceeding slowly and with scientific care. I could not help but compare the site with the majestic establishment of Hatshepsut at Luxor, though of course that installation follows a quite different plan: both are the awe-inspiring heritage of a thousand-year-old culture.

The plane that took us back to Beijing flew low enough for us to get a picture of how thickly the fertile land in the provinces of Shanxi and Hupei and the area around Beijing is populated. Only narrow strips of land separate the housing complexes of the individual villages from each other. Later, during the hours of the railroad journey from Shanghai to Hangzhou, we saw that in actual fact every square meter of soil was being used for agriculture. China has to feed one fifth of the world's population but has the use of only 7 percent of the world's arable land. Because the population keeps on growing and the cities need more land, the proportion of arable land to population decreases from year to year.

This is the reason for the rigorous restraint put on the birthrate. Europeans and Americans, Pope John Paul II and President Ronald Reagan at their head, may condemn the Chinese regulations of birth rates as a limitation of individual freedom or as un-Christian—but what other solution can the moralist put forward to quell the population explosion?

As far as I can see, China is the only developing nation that is making steady and successful efforts to prevent the uncontrolled population growth that is threatening not only China but the majority of humanity in the coming century. Only India has made similar attempts, at least from time to time, but the methods applied by Indira Gandhi's first son, which went so far as compulsory sterilization, were much more radical than China's. China's success so far has also ended the food shortages, which not many developing countries can say. Without approving all the details of the Chinese methods, I must call the Chinese objective sensible. In 1950 China's population was estimated to be 540 million; by now it has doubled. It is hoped that by the year 2000 the figure will not have risen beyond 1.2 billion. Some Western experts, however, believe that in spite of all family planning, by the turn of the century China will hold 1.5 billion (more than 60 percent of all Chinese today are under thirty years of age).

This has to be a nightmare—especially for the economists, but also for the leadership in general. How can both food and work be successfully found for such masses? Deng Xiaoping told me on one occasion, "If at least we can keep eighty percent of our people in the villages, as we do today, we may have solved eighty percent of our problem."

From Agrarian Reform to Industrial Reform

T HE successes of agrarian reform are obvious, and not only to the Chinese; any objective economist must be impressed by the spectacular rise in production figures since 1979. Basically this improvement is due to the partial change from a government-controlled economy and its replacement with a "self-responsibility system." Today, to an extent unimaginable until very recently, a commune, a group of agricultural households, and even a single agricultural household are free to make their own decisions on cultivation and sale of their products. However, there are still minimum delivery quotas, and the sales prices for these are centrally regulated.

Once these norms are met, the farmers are free to plant and sell additional products. The same rules apply to the agricultural communities, which are no longer government corporations but merely production associations, and to the state farms. Furthermore, every member of a collective owns a small garden or field, and he is free to sell its products at market prices. The farmers are also allowed to hire apprentices—that is, "employees."

All these measures together have led to a considerable increase in agricultural productivity, which goes hand in hand with increasing specialization. Agricultural incomes have risen steadily, offering additional lasting incentives for further achievements. Today, only a few years after the reforms were first implemented, China is self-sufficient in food production, needing no imports.

It was only logical to begin economic reform in the agrarian sector. Though it is much larger than all the other branches of the economy, it is also much less complicated and less subject to the division of labor. In the beneficial shade of agricultural success, model attempts were soon initiated in urban industries. These were to pave the way for subsequent general reform of economic policy. We visited one of these model enterprises, the iron-and-steel Shoudu Gangtil Gongsi collective, on the outskirts of Beijing.

At the time of our visit the collective consisted of 110,000 people and had its own schools, clubs, social institutions, sports arenas, parks, movie houses, and the like. In one of the refreshment gardens for the employees we saw a beautiful artificial waterfall that had the additional purpose of lowering the temperature of the plant's cooling water. The collective produced 3 million tons of pig iron and 2 million tons of crude steel a year, a truly modest accomplishment. Nevertheless, the young director was proud of his enterprise's achievement.

This collective was allowed to sell a specific percentage of its end products freely—even outside China—while the remainder was subject to centrally determined delivery norms at fixed prices. The collective was allowed to pay incentive bonuses of up to 20 percent of the workers' salaries and to award prizes. It was allowed to reinvest any profits above its target amount as it saw fit and in this way could modernize its production. The collective's general director was named by the Communist Party Central Committee, while the city of Beijing selected the deputy director. Otherwise the collective controlled its own personnel selection. In general some systems of responsibility had been created in the individual plants—with job descriptions for everyone—and the extent to which these were or were not met constituted the basis for awards as well as deductions from wages or salaries. Apparently the leadership of the party organization within the enterprise made the decisions.

By Western standards none of this was in any way remarkable, but by comparison with the usual almost mechanical steering of industry by the central bureaucracy—as in the Soviet model—this pilot enterprise enjoyed a number of advantages that resulted in annually increasing profit figures. I could see the difference in other factories in the provinces that did not have such privileges available to them.

At the previously mentioned discussion of economics at the International Institute I asked my hosts what the evaluation of these model experiments had revealed, and I inquired whether there was any intention of extending these freedoms. The professors, the gentlemen from the ministries, and the economic advisers to the Central Committee who were present appeared considerably more sure of themselves when they were dealing with abstract institutional questions than when they were asked about the significance of the overall economic control still in effect. As far as the institutional side was concerned, the necessity of reordering both the relationship between state and industry and the relations among the industrial management, the director, and the workers was clearly recognized. But even my questions on these topics received very vague answers.

Everything led to the same conclusion: The relationship between state and industry was gradually being modernized. For a year and a half now, only part of the profits—after the economic target set by whatever ministry was in charge had been met—was directly transferred to the government, the other part being collected in the form of taxes. Beginning in 1985, the transfer to the government was to occur entirely in the form of taxes; then the bonus, the "profit share" given to the workers, would also be subject to income tax. The firm's own capital funds would be transferred to government funds or foundations serving social purposes or technical progress.

In a second step management and government administration would be separated; however, yearly plans and five-year plans would remain in effect, though merely for the purpose of general orientation. The state would set the price of only a very few goods, for example, energy, cement, and steel. Many goods, on the other hand, would disappear from the government production catalog altogether, and their prices would be set entirely by the market, subject to industrial competition and possibly fluctuating widely.

I asked for details about overall economic control. Yes, of course the government would determine the exchange rate of the yuan, I was told; but otherwise balance would be brought about by a balanced budget and equalized balances of payments. It was not a question of monetary policy in the Western sense. So I asked straight out about this, pointing to the fact that China's budget was by no means balanced. Would the deficit be financed by private savings or the central bank? I was told bluntly that, no, the deficit would be met by credits of the industrial credit cooperative, on the basis of private deposits. This did not seem plausible to me; I therefore continued this line of questioning, asking how high the savings rate was. It did not, however, seem possible to obtain this information. In reality there had been considerable inflation for some time.

A few days later the same questions naturally arose in my talk with Premier Zhao Ziyang, since he was the man in charge of translating economic reform into reality. I called on him in a magnificent imperial reception hall, the "center of power," as he, only half joking, called it. The day we talked about his impending "reforms of the economic structure" was September 26. On October 20 they were accepted by the Central Committee.

I congratulated Zhao Ziyang on the enormous progress China had unmistakably made in the past nine years. Zhao mentioned the "great historical turning point" of 1979. When, a few months later, I studied the Central Committee's formal resolution, I saw that all the essentials had already been fixed in his mind.

He described the situation to me as follows: "The historical turning point began with an opening to the outside world. In the past we placed too much stress on relying on our own strength. Now we have put an end to our isolation. For another thing, we have made it our first objective to increase economic productivity and raise the standard of living. As long as there is no attack from outside on the People's Republic of China, we will stick to this plan. The structural economic reforms began with agriculture in 1979, and they were successful in that area. Now we will apply them to the urban economy. What we are striving for is socialism with Chinese specifics. Industry must be given greater freedom to make decisions. Of course, we begin with the law of excess value and apply it. We are not only hoping for success, we are sure of it."

It would be difficult, I noted, after so many years of total state control to accustom industrial management to greater independence and the party and government bureaucracy to greater restraint.

Zhao agreed. "These are precisely the problems that reform must solve. Allowing industry greater responsibility will give that sector greater latitude and therefore more vitality. . . . Either the managers are capable of it and their dynamism has in the past merely been held in check by the old structure, in which case they now have an opportunity to develop and prove themselves, or they will turn out to be incapable of independence, in which case they will have to go."

And what would happen then? "There are enough capable and ambitious people in industry; we simply have to place them in managerial positions. The need for capable managers will become apparent in every plant. Because if management is inadequate, the workers suffer. So the workers themselves will see to it that capable people rise to the top. We make every effort to train new leaders and managers who will be more than mere recipients of directives; we have already had considerable success in this area. You can be sure that progress will continue."

I asked whether and to what extent the government agencies would be affected by reform.

"Next month we will address the reform of the party and state bureaucracy. In future the government will intervene in industry to a lesser extent than heretofore. And what is especially important is that the party organs within the plants will no longer make up the plants' governing boards. The responsibility will soon be placed on management itself; though the party organs will continue to exercise certain functions of control, they will be responsible merely for ideological leadership and party work. The situation will no longer be one where the factory director can take responsibility only under the leadership of the party organization. Of course this reform will raise many problems, but these problems can be solved."

"Let me come back to the law of excess value you just mentioned," I interrupted. "Let me talk more simply about market price. To the extent that the price mechanism of the markets becomes more effective, indirect elements of control become appreciably more important. That is true of the government's budget policy, of monetary and credit provision policies, of the control of trade balances and the balance of payments altogether. Which leads to the question: How do you envisage the overall control of the Chinese economy?

"I've noticed, for example," I continued, "that your statistics show an accumulation of considerable reserves in foreign currencies because of steady trade surpluses. Presumably this relates to the fact that your central bank simultaneously carries on private banking transactions in foreign trade and has thus developed a leaning to profit."

What I was saying about the central bank was true, Zhao Ziyang admitted, and that was precisely why the decision had been made to distribute the separate functions to two different banks. "Of course the money and credit supply must be controlled by the central bank; but all credit business is to be left to the commercial banks. We will be forced to be cautious about our reserves of foreign currency. That is why we must prevent the increase in imports that has occurred in the past. We will have to concentrate on imports that help in the technical modernization of our industrial plants."

The first part of my analysis was also correct, he conceded. "Reforming the price system will become the key to structural reform of the economy and thus the success of reform. In other words, the new price system is the most important sign. Before, the structure was based on planning. Now we are introducing profit as the regulating principle. But profit depends on price. As a first step the prices of nonessential goods will be freed, they will be left entirely to the law of supply and demand. Of course the prices that will result will not necessarily coincide with our macroeconomic goals."

Zhao then asked me about the influences of the international economic system. I replied, "Your intentions for domestic economic reforms make sense to me; your basic aim is presumably an increase in production. There is also no question that your methods of control have so far helped to prevent what everyone had expected to happen—China's getting caught up in the consequences of the international economic recession. But to the degree to which you open your country and increase both imports and exports, you will naturally become more vulnerable to the ups and downs of international economic cycles and to undesirable trends in the world's financial and trade markets."

We then turned to the oil price explosion, the Latin American debt crisis, high interest rates, and the like. We discussed these subjects in detail, and Zhao proved to be astonishingly well informed. In the end he came back to the danger that China might find itself increasingly dependent on the international economy. "You see," he noted, "even the Soviet Union's economy is stagnating. But I wonder whether this has really been caused by the international recession or whether the principal reasons are to be found in the Soviet's excessive spending on defense and the rigidity of their planning system. After all, the Soviet Union's volume of foreign trade is not very high, and Soviet prices are completely isolated from the international market.

"In any case," he continued, "what is important to China is that we want to open up our country, but we want to avoid the mistakes made by so many other developing nations. Many developing nations assumed huge foreign credits to develop their processing industries, hoping to pay them back by exporting their products. Now they are in trouble because the international market is not buying their products. We too want credits to exploit our resources, but we will be cautious in accepting them. We will keep a careful watch to make sure that imports and exports remain in balance."

It was a long and, for me at least, a very informative talk. Today, as I read over the notes I made that same night, I wonder if they sound as if Zhao Ziyang had recited merely self-evident basic insights. But there are two arguments against that view: For one, given the fact that this man's whole life had been lived exclusively in a government-controlled economy, his instincts about a market economy were stupendous; I was amazed by his insight into the international economy, all of it learned within China. Second, except for Valéry Giscard d'Estaing and Raymond Barre, he is the only head of government I met in all the time I served as a minister and as chancellor who had such a sure, detailed, and feasible understanding of his country's economic situation.

Four days later, Zhao and I met again. This time I was the guest of honor at a banquet in the Great Hall of the People on the occasion of the thirty-fifth anniversary of the founding of the People's Republic of China. We managed a private conversation after the official speeches and toasts.

He began once more to speak about the impending economic reform. "We shall concentrate our efforts on developing our production, and you will see that we will succeed in steadily improving the people's material and cultural well-being. We shall never relinquish this determination, except in case of a major hostile invasion. You may be sure that China will never submit to foreign pressure."

I was impressed by this man, and I liked him. When we said good-bye, he called me an old friend of China, and I was pleased to be able to tell him, "German policy toward your country will remain unchanged under my successor in office."

That evening I exchanged impressions with my wife and my traveling companions—among them Theo Sommer, editor in chief of *Die Zeit,* and Gyula Trebitsch. All of us felt that the new leadership's goal of increasing agricultural and industrial production fourfold between 1980 and 2000 was entirely attainable, even if the structural reform of industry should turn out to be considerably more difficult than expected; the growth rates from 1979 on assured as much. If reform is fully implemented, the goal might even be surpassed.

But the country has shouldered an enormous task. The reforms China has embarked on are more complicated by far than Ludwig Erhard's statesmanlike action in 1948; at that time Erhard decided to change from a controlled economy to a market economy as a response to the supply of consumer goods that was beginning to occur as a result of the Marshall Plan and the limitation of monetary demand because of currency reform; he managed, in part against opposition in his own party, to implement and realize his plan astonishingly well. In the Germany of that time there were millions of employers, craftsmen, farmers, workers, politicians, and journalists who had had bad experi-

ences in a highly integrated market system and who therefore knew how
to agitate in favor of their own and the general advantage.

In today's China there are not very many people with such experience; Chinese people who have lived abroad for any length of time are
the exception. I doubt whether even the leading actors in the reform
movement fully comprehend the reasons, both obvious and hidden,
that lie behind the enormous economic success of the city-states of
Singapore and Hong Kong, both of which are run by the Chinese.
Where intelligence and industriousness are concerned, Zhao Ziyang
may be compared favorably with Harry Lee Kuan Yew, the uncommonly successful prime minister of Singapore. But Zhao must substitute
imagination for the international experience Lee and his people have
amassed and utilized with the help of their own inventiveness.

Zhao will encounter objective and subjective difficulties along the
way. For one, there are enormous economic differences within the
nation. The industrial northeast, with its great port of Dairen, is at
the top, as is the north, with its two metropolitan centers, Beijing and
Tianjin (Tientsin); these are followed by Shanghai in the Yangtse delta.
Even measured by real income, these are regions of relative affluence.
The bottom end of the scale is represented by Xinjiang and Tibet. In
between are many hundreds of millions of people who live in the
backward regions of the northwest and southwest. The country's transportation systems are highly inadequate; though the great seaport of
Shanghai is the primary domestic turntable, it can serve only the coasts
and the navigable part of the Yellow River.

Until now no general system of social security has been established;
the "iron rice bowl" with which industry provides for its old people is
a burden on the industrial balance sheet. It is therefore slated to be
abolished. There are enormous subsidies for food and rent; these alone
account for one third of the national budget. Consumer prices are far
below production and delivery costs. An economically reasonable system of industrial taxation is also lacking so far.

In addition to these hurdles, reform will create unavoidable new
problems—for example, a further extension of and increase in income
inequities, and not merely in the fourteen new "special economic development zones" that are being opened to foreign investment in the
coastal cities. The situation will be further complicated by the fact that
in the next few years China must unremittingly create new jobs because
of the once high birth rate and because of an increasing level of unemployment that is concentrated in particular regions.

How will reorientation of the bureaucracy from compulsory planning to future planning oriented to specific goals be managed? How much time will be required for the economic reeducation of the political leadership and its orientation to the magic square of the national economy—that is, price stability, high employment, growth, and foreign trade balance? Overall price stability will be the most difficult to preserve at first; at the same time it is the most vulnerable element of the process. Even now, inflation is probably considerably higher than the average 2 percent per year that is officially declared. The Central Committee's resolution on structural economic reform characteristically contains an appeal to industrial management concerning price policy, which reminds me of Ludwig Erhard's "soul massages."

Aside from all that, subjective resistance will emerge. It appears to me unthinkable that all of the strong Stalinist and Maoist groups will disappear from the party hierarchy, even taking into account the fact that the majority of current members did not join the party until after the beginning of the Cultural Revolution. Remnants of old doctrines surely also survive in the army, since from its revolutionary beginnings the army was inevitably deeply politicized. Today defense is given last place among the "four modernizations"; agriculture, industry, and science are ranked ahead of it. Will the party bureaucracy in the provinces, in the cities, and in the industrial plants survive its loss of power? Will factory and plant managements learn to make good use of the freedom they are being given? Will they develop the will to prevail?

I must leave all these questions open. Considering the little we Europeans know of Chinese history, we have the impression that since the disgraceful Opium War 150 years ago China has been unable to mobilize its own powers sufficiently to defend itself against foreign invaders. In China the stress seems to have been placed not on development or reform but on revolts—such as the Boxer Rebellion of 1900—and revolution—for example, Sun Yat-sen's in 1911 and finally Mao Zedong's. The persevering forces did not give way to the demand for reform; they had to be broken.

What Deng Xiaoping and Zhao Ziyang are undertaking today, however, is reform. It is intended to bring innovation and efficiency *within* Communism. It is a crude misunderstanding to interpret it as a desire to overcome Communism. It seems to me visionary foolishness for well-meaning Western politicians and commentators to count on events moving in the direction of Western concepts of freedom. The question of property is never raised in principle, and the supremacy of the party is certainly not going to be abandoned. The last thing the reformers have in mind are pluralistic democracy, general freedom of speech, and individual political freedom.

However, party despotism is slated to be abolished; after the confusion of the last few decades, justice and lawfulness are what are wanted. If reform is eventually to bring the masses something like affluence in the Chinese manner, it may lead to a great flowering even in the intellectual sphere. Perhaps then the cultural context of the thousands of years of Chinese history will return to full consciousness. It is a human need to be aware of one's own national and historical roots. Even Stalin understood this necessity and complied with it to strengthen the will to resist Hitler.

But for the moment China is still concentrating all its efforts on developing the national economy. And the success of reform crucially depends on Deng Xiaoping.

Deng Xiaoping

WHEN I visited China in 1984, all my private conversations, both in Beijing and especially outside the capital, made it almost oppressively obvious that there was one man on whom everyone pinned his hopes for improvements in living conditions: first, Deng; second, Deng; and third, Deng. He himself was not promoting a cult of personality; in fact, he probably despised such worship. But he did not need any such enhancement, since he is immeasurably popular. All expectations are fixed on him.

Deng received me in the Great Hall of the People, the same place we had met nine years before. A little while before, on August 28, he had turned eighty, but he looked to be physically and psychologically in excellent shape, vibrant and vital. He was quick-witted, humorous, competent and alert at every stage of our talks. For almost the entire time the two of us—along with a small group of Chinese and German guests, who had taken seats at other tables—were occupied with a lengthy luncheon. Only Deng's excellent English interpreter sat with us; she had to speak very loudly to Deng, which stood me in good stead.

After the introductory formulaic greetings, I thanked him for the invitation to China, which he had personally issued, and congratulated him on his special birthday and his obviously splendid health.

Deng reminded me of our talk of nine years earlier; then he returned to the topic of his birthday: "Oh, you know, as far as age goes, excessive old age has always been a problem for the Chinese leadership—for the Soviets too, by the way. But in ten or twenty years China will have younger leaders, and we can see very clearly that China's modernization requires younger and more dynamic leaders. There are some very complicated problems to be solved.

"So you remember our talk of 1975. It was not long after that I was cut down."

"But you came back," I replied, "fortunately for you and especially for China. How many times were you overthrown, anyway?"

Deng grinned. "That was the third time! But it will be the last."

Then he became serious and quickly came to the point. "Our foreign policy should focus even more seriously on gaining independence from the superpowers. That applies to your country as well. Of course we have no objection to Western Europe's being a part of the North Atlantic alliance, but you must not lose sight of an independent strategy for Germany. De Gaulle understood as much. Europe's relations with the United States should be based on absolute equality."

On this point, at any rate, Deng had not changed his views in the last decade. I admitted that international economic upheavals since 1974 had affected the European powers so deeply that the Europeans' integration process had suffered and consequently so had their independence from the United States.

Deng turned the conversation to the Soviet Union. "China is seeking to improve its relations with the Soviet Union, but there are hindrances that must first be removed. The course the Soviet Union has chosen is dangerous to China's security. What is the European situation?"

"For us, too," I replied, "relations with the Soviet Union have grown worse since 1976. In part this is related to the SS-20 missiles, which are aimed at Europe. But the invasion of Afghanistan also shocked Europe. There are additional reasons. But we hope for an improvement in relations with Moscow, and we advocate arms limitation."

Deng continued, "I assume the Soviet Union will make increasing difficulties as far as the removal of their missiles is concerned. But the Americans are not very reasonable, either. Their actions differ from their words.

"The Soviet Union is, like China, a socialist nation. Why did we have a falling-out? Because the Soviet Union never stopped trying to interfere in Chinese matters, because Moscow did all it could to control China. The Russians wanted to play Big Brother. When we objected, the

Kremlin simply tore up the treaties concluded by both countries. Finally the Soviet Union quite openly adopted an anti-China position. It tried to incite all the Southeast Asian nations against us."

I asked about the role of the Soviet Union in Vietnam. "You know," Deng replied, "for Moscow, Vietnam is an unsinkable aircraft carrier. The Soviet Union is pursuing the same strategy in Vietnam that the United States is in Taiwan. The Soviet Union is still called a socialist nation. But Soviet policy has little in common with socialist policy and Marxist principles."

"It seems to me," I said, "that as far as political objectives and geographic direction are concerned, Soviet foreign policy is guided less by socialist ideals than by the historically evolved Russian expansionist tradition."

"That's probably true," Deng agreed, "and that is why I do not yet believe that a change of personnel at the top will lead to changes in the basic principles of Soviet foreign policy. You see, China consistently supported Vietnam in its wars of independence—first against Japan, then against France, and finally against the United States. We furnished the Vietnamese people with goods to the value of twenty billion dollars—in prices of the time—and that was at a period when we ourselves needed every dollar we could get. But a few years later Vietnam, under Soviet influence, turned against China. Hundreds of thousands of Chinese were driven out of Vietnam. There was repeated aggression on the frontier with China.

"Finally the occupation of Kampuchea occurred, after Pol Pot had made huge mistakes in that country. This Vietnamese invasion was aimed at a greater Vietnam federation. China is not eager to see Vietnamese hegemony in this region. That is why, in 1979, we were forced to teach the Vietnamese a lesson. So as to be understood correctly, we repeated the lesson a few more times on a smaller scale. Should Vietnam continue to refuse to withdraw from Kampuchea, we reserve the right to teach Vietnam another lesson.

"And yet Vietnam enjoys complete Soviet support; that is why the Vietnamese occupation of Kampuchea is one of the three principal obstacles to normalization of our relations with the Soviet Union. Our relations with Vietnam could be normalized the day after Vietnamese withdrawal."

Next Deng turned to the subject of Laos, but he kept coming back to Kampuchea, which was clearly a particularly sore point for Beijing. I knew from Prince Sihanouk how much his role depended on China, and I questioned Deng on that point. He replied, "We advised Prince

Sihanouk that once Kampuchea was free of Vietnam, not to return to socialism. Let him build up a peaceful, nonaligned nation. Nor would we have any objection if Kampuchea were to join ASEAN."

When the conversation turned to Japan, I said, "To use your analogy, Japan, too, is an unsinkable aircraft carrier. And just because the Japanese know they are unable to defend themselves against the Soviet Union, their dependency on the United States can only increase. This in turn cannot help but disturb the Soviets. It seems to me that the Japanese are facing a long-term dilemma. On the one hand, they want to decrease their political dependence on America, but on the other hand, they do not want to carry this process too far, so as not to upset the other Asian nations with an arms buildup."

China, Deng said, had good relations with Japan; if there were any problems at all, it was only because some people in Japan wanted to turn economic strength into political and military power. "China isn't too disturbed at that, but you're right, other nations do worry."

I objected, "I've been to Japan frequently, but I never noticed any signs of a new militarism. If you really are in favor of Japan's greater independence from the United States, it follows that you would grant them somewhat greater independence in the defense area."

Deng contradicted me hotly. "No, no! If Japan wants to become a greater political factor in the world, that's all right; after all, it is already a significant economic factor. But should Japan try for greater significance in the military area, such an effort can cause nothing but uneasiness everywhere in Asia. In short: It would be better for Japan to be just a little more moderate." With all his objectivity and his thoroughly realistic assessment of the international situation, Deng's views were clearly still affected by the traumatic experience of Japanese occupation. Finally I asked Deng about China's position toward the United States.

"United States foreign policy has weaknesses similar to those of the Soviet Union's. The country's actual behavior often has nothing to do with what its lips are saying. Partnership without equality—how can that work? Differences of opinion about Taiwan form a barrier between China and the United States. Reagan once said Taiwan was a potential crisis. In the Shanghai Declaration, Washington recognized that Taiwan is a part of China. But American policy continues to vacillate. Congress has issued resolutions in a direction that differs sharply from the objectives of the Shanghai Declaration. In fact, they still recognize two Chinas, and they consider Taiwan to be part of their own sphere of interest. Besides, Washington thinks of Taiwan as one of its own bases; the United States clings to the policy of the 'four aircraft carriers,' " by which he meant Taiwan, Israel, Central America, and South Africa.

"Don't you think it's possible," I suggested, "that one day the way the Hong Kong problem is being handled now can serve as a model for solving the problem of Taiwan?"

"That is my hope," Deng replied tersely.

After an hour or more I brought the conversation around to the Chinese army and Deng's role as its leader. At the time he was chairman of the military commissions of both the Communist Party Central Committee and the government. Although he was not the highest party officeholder and was not a member of the government, he was the commander in chief of 4 million soldiers. At the time of our conversation the military was preparing for a huge parade to celebrate the thirty-fifth anniversary of the nation's founding.

The armed forces as such presented no problem, Deng stated. However, there were many superannuated military leaders. "But you see that the army needs an even older veteran such as myself to be commander in chief." He was nevertheless looking forward to giving up the office in a few years' time. He did not believe it a good idea for seventy-year-olds to hold key military positions and certainly not for the commander in chief to be eighty years old. Of course regimental commanders should really be no older than thirty, divisional commanders no more than forty.

These figures seemed very young to me. I suggested that I could easily imagine fifty-year-old divisional commanders. "No, under no circumstances," Deng objected. "After all, there are ranks higher than divisional commander, and that would make those who hold them too old. Even the commanders of army groups should be no older than fifty. But of course, achieving that aim is a slow process."

I asked about the political orientation of the generals. "The army is not looking for a new cultural revolution. . . . We want to modernize the army. But in the meantime we don't want to divert too many funds to it. Economic reform comes first; then we will look at the army. At present our nuclear armament is little more than symbolic—in any case, it doesn't amount to much. We can see how closely the Soviet Union's economic miseries are related to its wildly excessive military expenditures."

Although it seemed to me that calling Chinese nuclear forces symbolic was an understatement, the remark that the Soviet Union's economy was impaired by its arms buildup struck me as accurate. The statement allowed me to turn the conversation to the impending Chi-

nese resolutions about economic reform. I told Deng about my talk
with Zhao Ziyang; I said that he had given me a very impressive lecture
on the planned economic reforms. Where, I asked, had he acquired his
remarkable understanding of economics? He was better informed than
many Western statesmen.

"Everything Zhao knows, he learned during his work, based on
practical experience. He joined the revolution when he was only sixteen, and then he worked in the provinces for a long time. In 1975,
when Mao and Zhou were both so ill that for all practical purposes I
alone was responsible for the government and the party, Zhao was one
of my assistants. After that he went to the province of Sichuan for three
years, during a crisis; he overcame the famine there—by reforming
agrarian policy, by the way."

I remarked that such a career was surely possible only in exceptional
cases. How was China planning in general to train its younger economic
managers?

Deng said that of course schools and universities were what mattered
now. The important thing was to send capable young people abroad;
more than ten thousand were already studying in the United States,
about a thousand in West Germany. But the industries themselves were
also training young managers.

I pointed out that during my travels through the country I had been
struck by the youth of some of the executives I had met—they were
much younger than men in equivalent positions in Europe.

Deng confirmed my impression and added, "We should have placed
many more younger people in top-level positions! We must filter out
talented young people all over the country.

"At the time, during the third session of the Central Committee in
late 1978, we solved the problem of the agricultural economy with a
number of courageous resolutions. The new agrarian policy has been
in effect for six years now, and you can see the results. We are now
making an attempt to transfer these new, open economic policies from
the country to the cities. But of course the problems of the urban
economy are much more complex. . . .

"Of course China will have to continue to concentrate most of its
efforts on its rural areas. After all, that is where four fifths of our
population live. We must try to keep them from moving to the cities.
Though during the Cultural Revolution many young people were sent
from the cities to the country, there was no work for them there, so
they returned to the cities.

"If we were to adopt the capitalist system, we could not solve the problem of unemployment. Europe's unemployment crisis is nothing but a result of the capitalist system. China's population grows by seven or eight million people a year, and all these people need jobs. Unemployment is China's central problem. That is why we created new industries and thus new jobs, but for this same reason our economic structure will have to be made more flexible. That is why we have always encouraged industry to open new areas of production, as well as enterprises in collective or private ownership."

I thought about the magic square of economic policy that I had discussed with Zhao in detail. I therefore again asked the question about the danger of inflation in general and the current rate of inflation in particular.

Deng's reply was extremely optimistic. "I don't believe that there is inflation in China. But the forthcoming resolution concerning reform of the price system as well as wages and salaries may well end up by confronting us with some problems of inflation."

I pointed out that in the immediate future the Chinese leadership would be facing a number of still more difficult questions. "I hope you will be holding a lucky hand again! I congratulate you on your determination and on the courage with which you have tackled economic reform."

"I'm very well aware that I have only a very limited understanding of economics," Deng replied. "I simply made the very general suggestion that we enter on a more flexible policy. Others must take on the job of turning this into reality, but they have my full support for the reforms. I am convinced that reform is necessary. And the successes we have achieved so far in putting the new policies into practice prove me right. Most of all, they prove that those in charge can manage without me. I think in three years we will notice changes in the cities as well. Of course there are people who are disturbed by all this, who don't like the direction at all. China will need three years to dissipate their fears."

Finally Deng mentioned the upcoming military parade. It was the first one, he told me, in many years. The soldiers would be happy to have a chance to demonstrate the capacities of the Chinese army in public on the occasion of the anniversary of the founding of the state.

A few days later I myself saw the generals congratulating each other after their parade had gone off splendidly. Positioned on the reviewing stand, we could observe them embracing over to one side, invisible to the general audience.

In the course of my life I had seen all kinds of military parades, big ones and small ones, elaborate ones and simple ones. As a young soldier in the German Wehrmacht as well as three decades later as defense minister, I learned not to be overly impressed by a parade. But the spectacle on Tiananmen Square and along Jiangan Street was truly overwhelming. The televised opening ceremonies of the Los Angeles Olympics give some idea of the event in Beijing if the number of participants in the Los Angeles stadium is multiplied by a hundred. There were large and small flags in every color of the rainbow, many huge hot-air balloons in Pompeian red, and tens of thousands of tiny balloons all around the square, all this in addition to half a million people, colorfully dressed and dancing to the music in large circles.

Then silence. Deng Xiaoping, flanked by Zhao Ziyang and Hu Yaobang, has appeared on the balcony of the Gate of Heavenly Peace. He steps up to the microphone.

His speech states his political objectives concisely. He speaks for only seven or eight minutes; the English translation handed to us is all of sixty-three lines long. The goal of national reunification is mentioned in the very first sentence and is repeated and elaborated in the final three sentences. This goal, he says, is "deeply rooted in the hearts of all descendants of the Yellow Emperor." Zhao Ziyang used the same deliberately nationalistic formula yesterday, referring to a legendary figure in Chinese prehistory, an emperor who supposedly lived thousands of years before Christ.

Next Deng honors Mao Zedong as the founder of the nation. Mao is mentioned a second time, in connection with the "restoration" of his thoughts after elimination of the "perverse actions of the counterrevolutionary Gang of Four." Deng defines Mao's thinking as a "search for truth in the facts." No other names are mentioned. But across from Deng, at the center of the square, there is a huge portrait of Sun Yat-sen; this, too, is a sign of the national historical self-awareness. What is remarkable is Deng's concluding demand that education, knowledge, and the role of the intellectuals be recognized. All in all, Deng gives a self-confident and determined speech, powerfully delivered.

Following his speech Deng, standing in a car with an open or cutout roof, accepts the report of the commanding general. Then he drives along the front of the battalions lined up on Jiangan Street. He greets each one with a shout and receives thunderous replies. When he returns to the Gate of Heavenly Peace, the parade unfolds; no military organization in the world could perform it with greater precision.

On this October 1, 1984, in Beijing, the tanks and armored artillery are followed principally by rockets: air defense rockets; a CSS-NX 4 strategic submarine-based nuclear missile probably still in the developmental stage; an older CSS-2 intermediate-range missile with a range of about 2,000 kilometers, introduced in the early 1970s; a somewhat newer CSS-3 rocket with a range of about 6,000 kilometers; and finally the newest monster, a CSS-4 intercontinental ballistic missile, with a range of about 10,000 kilometers. The two trans-Siberian Soviet railroad lines—the second one is in the process of being completed—are 2,300 kilometers from Beijing, Moscow is 9,500 kilometers distant, and San Francisco is 10,000 kilometers away. The military attachés of the world's nations who are present see with their own eyes what they already know from their secret documents; the rest of the diplomats from many lands are clearly impressed—which, no doubt, is the intention of the commander in chief.

The military part of the performance is followed by a long, breathtakingly colorful, and casual parade of all the various delegations from every corner of the nation.

I admit that I, too, was impressed by this spectacle of China's self-representation. Deng Xiaoping is at the height of his career. He must feel satisfaction less at this fact than at the reality that after sixty years of ever-renewed struggles he can at last serve the cause of a unified Communist China, in great style and at its head. In foreign affairs, conciliation with Japan has been achieved; Hong Kong is being reunified with the mainland; relations with the United States have been normalized, Reagan has visited Beijing, Deng and Zhao have been to Washington. Domestically, Deng has helped Chinese Communism to achieve a state of rationalization and thus set it on the path to economic development.

There is no doubt that if Deng has his way, China will remain a Communist society in future—not a liberal one, not a democratic one on the Western pattern, but an authoritarian society in an authoritarian state.

Whether these reforms will run a stable and consistent course depends, in my view, on three factors:

1. How long will Deng Xiaoping and Zhao Ziyang remain alive, and how long will they be able energetically to control the nation?

2. How long will it be before tangible results, visible to the masses, will validate reform, and thus the leaders of the reform, in the eyes of the population and the party?

3. Will it be possible to keep the peace both with the Soviet Union and within the region? In other words, will China's policy of global

balance between the aggregated forces acting on East Asia and the Pacific be successful?

One cannot formulate a prognosis on the first question. But it does seem to me that Deng's assuming supreme command was a result of the fear that neither Zhao Ziyang nor (at the time) Hu Yaobang or anyone else possessed sufficient authority over the army. At the time Zhao and Hu had the reputation at least of an obvious difference in political temperament. Should Deng retire too soon, determining the succession might—as it has done in other Communist nations—cause a period of uncertainty. The process of reform may suffer failures and setbacks, especially in the economic area; compromises and corrections might also become unavoidable. But Deng's pragmatism, along with his authority, is at present the best guarantee for successful mastery of the difficult period of change. Since by Chinese standards Zhao Ziyang is still relatively young to head the economic reform policies (he was born in 1918), he will probably stay in office many more years to make good use of what he has learned so far. But economic reform represents the greatest experiment in all previous economic history, if only because of the number of people involved. It seems to me unlikely that greater and lasting successes will emerge soon. The destabilizing dangers of both unemployment and inflation could lead to challenging crises and setbacks. At least ten years will have to pass before the success of reform can be felt. Insofar as tangible improvement in the living standard of the billions of Chinese becomes pervasive, even an initial success can suffice to prevent a relapse into the old emotional voluntarism.

The third precondition for China's continuing stability, peace with the outside world, depends not only on the nation's own strategic actions but just as much on the stance of the other nations in the area, and most especially of the Soviet Union. Possibly the attitude of the West—both the United States and Europe—will be crucial.

The more successfully China's reforms run their course, the more Moscow may feel challenged, since a Chinese example of success could set a precedent for the Soviet Union's client states and elsewhere, particularly in the Third World countries living under dictatorships. But should one of the Soviet satellites be substantially more successful economically than Moscow, past experiences suggest that harsh reactions are more probable than a tolerance tantamount to a partial relinquishing of the claim to power. However flexible Gorbachev's generation may be, it will never accept a mutilation of the Soviet power sphere. So harsh reactions against China are also conceivable should the recent attempts at agreement with the Chinese leaders suggested by Gorbachev fail to meet with success.

In view of Gorbachev's very sweeping, seemingly almost boundless current overall strategy, we cannot exclude the possibility of a large-scale policy of détente with China. Even during Andropov's short era Moscow considered the idea, which had been raised cautiously and very timidly even under Brezhnev. The option open to the Soviets, however, has so far had no effect worth mentioning on Moscow's actual foreign policy. Instead, the Soviet leaders have unintentionally maneuvered almost all the East and Southeast Asian nations into adopting a hostile stance toward the Soviet Union.

Neighbors
But Not Friends

T HE larger region from Singapore or Manila to Urumqi and Beijing or Vladivostok is politically characterized by the almost complete isolation of large and important nations. China and the Soviet Union, Japan and Vietnam, North and South Korea—none has any real friends in the region. The military and economic presence of the United States is respected but does not generate friendship.

It is not only geography and history that impede mutual understanding; cultural multiplicity also stands in the way. Though the Chinese and Japanese have very similar forms of writing, they cannot understand each other's language. The Russians and Koreans have alphabets no one else can read. Jakarta is going to great lengths to introduce a uniform Indonesian language in its realm of thirteen thousand islands spread over almost fifty degrees of longitude; the Koran must, of course, be studied in Arabic—and Indonesia is the largest Islamic country in the world. The Filipinos are Catholic, and their parliamentary business in Manila is conducted in English.

Compared to North or South America, and even to Europe, this region is an enormously differentiated mosaic. Almost all of North America speaks a single language and follows Christianity almost unanimously; Latin America speaks two closely related languages and is characterized by Christianity throughout; though there are many languages in Europe, almost two thousand years of shared cultural development and a shared Christian religion have given the region a wide-reaching homogeneity. In Asia great religions, significant philosophies, and ideologies clash—Hinduism and Buddhism, Confucius, Jesus of Nazareth, and Mohammed, Shintoism, and Chinese or Russian Communism; totally different languages and cultures live cheek by jowl.

It is this multiplicity of separate developments that makes it difficult not only for Europeans but even more for Americans to gain a political understanding of the region that is casually summed up by the concept of the Pacific Rim. In reality the common traits of the Pacific Rim are hidden from the observer who looks at the region from the edge, whether from Los Angeles, Canberra, Beijing, or Tokyo. Conversely, the loose confederation of the five member nations of the Association of Southeast Asian Nations (ASEAN)—the Philippines, Indonesia, Singapore, Malaysia, Thailand—plays only a subordinate role.

Traveling to New Delhi, Singapore, Kuala Lumpur, Beijing, Seoul, Tokyo, Bangkok, Canberra, and Jakarta has taught me a little about the variety of the region. Many conversations with Harry Lee Kuan Yew, the Chinese prime minister of Singapore, and especially my numerous visits to Japan have done a great deal to enrich my understanding of China's role as a world power. Alongside this great neighbor, Japan will continue in the next decades to be limited to its role as an outstanding economic power. However, Japan's growth in foreign affairs cannot easily be predicted; there may be some surprises.

A phrase coined in the 1960s about the Federal Republic of Germany applies to Japan today: an economic giant, a political midget. There are several reasons why Japan plays a rather insignificant role in international affairs, and they supplement one another. There is, first, the insular mentality accreted over a thousand years, which grew acute during the 250-year reign of the Tokugawa Shogunate and did not significantly decrease after 1868, when the Meiji restoration opened Japan to the world. Not unrelated is the Russo-Japanese War of 1905, which ended in a victory by Japan and encouraged ruthless imperialism by the Japanese, who shortly thereafter seized Korea and Manchuria; Formosa (Taiwan) had already been conquered in the previous century. Japan never understood or worked through what these raids meant to its neighbor states.

Even before the outbreak of the Second World War, Japan had brutally subdued large sections of China; after 1941 it conquered the Philippines, today's Indonesia, Burma, today's Malaysia and Singapore, and more. By historical standards and measured against the earlier

imperialism of the European colonial powers, the United States, and
Russia, Japanese imperialism reigned for only a brief period. But it is
relatively recent, and the deep resentment it bred in the subjugated
peoples has not yet been overcome.

Only the Americans, with the generosity so characteristic of that
nation, have largely surmounted their anti-Japanese feelings (though
they are returning in response to the changing economic situation); the
United States' superpower position in the Pacific area has, of course,
made the psychological process much easier.

China, too, has overcome its hostility to the Japanese, at least outwardly; since it is by far the greatest power in Asia, China is not
burdened by inferiority complexes concerning Japan. Moscow's repeated attempts to sow the seeds of enmity between Beijing and Tokyo
have been unable to prevent the slow rapprochement of the two; good
relations are in China's economic interest and are essential to Japan
from the psychological point of view. In the autumn of 1972, when
Japan broke with Taiwan, diplomatic relations between the two countries resumed. Nevertheless, Chinese suspicion of the Japanese still
exists at a latent level; during the 1980s Yasuhiro Nakasone made some
statements expressing Japanese nationalism; he was quickly informed
that China interpreted them as a symptom of the old Japanese arrogance.

The Filipinos' suspicion of the Japanese is very much stronger. And
in the case of the Koreans—those who live in both the north and the
south of that divided peninsula—it is no longer a matter of mistrust but
actual enmity toward Japan and understandable hatred. The Thais of
course consider Vietnam the greatest danger, in view of the aggressive
Vietnamese imperialism in Laos and Kampuchea, both of which lie on
Thailand's borders. Otherwise almost all the people of the region are
equally afraid of Japan and China. The 16 million Chinese living
abroad, as well as the Communist parties and organizations in the
various countries, are seen as Beijing's fifth column; at the same time
memories of the Japanese occupation and Japan's economic superiority
prevent a rapprochement with Tokyo.

Furthermore, the Japanese—unlike the Germans—have done little
since 1945 to help their neighbors work off their resentments and
replace them with trust based on increasing cooperation. For many
Japanese, especially the right wing, who are essentially gathered in the
conservative Liberal Democratic Party, the balance sheet of the Second
World War was resolved by the destruction of Hiroshima and
Nagasaki—an error with grave consequences.

Japan's
Limited Role

D URING the 1960s the government in Tokyo began to try to bridge the political and psychological chasms between Japan and its neighbors. These had grown particularly deep after Japan's imperialist adventures, and until now Japan has had little success in mollifying the other nations. The principal cause is that the Japanese seem to lack any sense of guilt. As far as I can see, Takeo Fukuda—first foreign and finance minister under prime ministers Eisaku Sato, Kakuei Tanaka, and Takeo Miki, then prime minister from late 1976 to late 1978—was the one who did the most to create an image of a Japan considered friendly by all its neighbors. His most important successor, Yasuhiro Nakasone, who became prime minister in September 1982, after short terms by Masayoshi Ohira in 1979–1980 and Zenko Suzuki in 1980–1982, also made efforts to normalize relations with the other states of East and Southeast Asia. But since Nakasone also had to take into account the strongly nationalistic feeling of his people and his nation, he was less successful at normalization than Fukuda—although in the meantime another decade had passed since the war's end.

Fukuda and Nakasone are both members of the Liberal Democratic Party (LDP), which has been in power for more than thirty years. In matters of foreign affairs, each of them is on the far end of the spectrum formed by their party, which—not unlike Italy's Christian Democratic Party—is splintered into several factions; in 1986 Fukuda, at the age of eighty-one, relinquished the leadership of his faction.

I met both of them frequently during the last twenty years, and I have close ties of friendship with Fukuda. My meetings and experiences with these two statesmen seemed to me particularly suited to explaining the lack of flexibility in the overall Japanese strategy, which remains most characteristically limited by constraints that leave little freedom of choice and which may by the end of the century lead Japan into the dangerous temptation to break out.

The following pages will deal mainly with Fukuda and Nakasone, although I also came to know prime ministers Sato, Miko, Ohira, and Suzuki and their most important ministers.

I met Emperor Hirohito three times. The Japanese believe that his person, as well as the entire imperial family, embody the continuity of Japanese history. When I was first introduced to him, I had no idea of his national significance; today, after ten or twelve visits to Japan, my impressions on this point are still very vague. Of course I was familiar with the most important facts of his life. Hirohito was born in 1901 and became emperor in 1926. I knew that in the heyday of imperialism, beginning in the 1930s, the military seized most of the power; I nevertheless assumed that the emperor had participated in Japan's decision to attack Pearl Harbor and thus enter the Second World War and conquer huge territories in Asia and Polynesia. It was not until much later that I learned he had not concealed his disapproval from the military but had been unable to alter the decision. What I knew was that in 1945 he personally decided and announced that his country would capitulate; that neither General Douglas MacArthur nor the International Court of Justice had leveled any accusations at him; and that finally in 1947 he proclaimed a democratic constitution. He continued to head his nation through all these tremendously varied events, and for most Japanese he still represents an instance of the highest authority, even if they hardly ever have a chance to see him, since he is completely isolated from the public.

When I met the short, unassuming old gentleman in person, he seemed to me the incarnation of serenity and wisdom; the brutal political decisions in which he had participated remained an enigma to me in view of his quiet dignity.

Do the golden chrysanthemums, the coat of arms of the imperial house, still represent reality? They were visible everywhere: on the emperor's cards of invitation and on the silver vases that were handed out as gifts to his visitors; I exhibited the vases in glass cases in the chancellor's bungalow. Would the sword not have been a more honest symbol? I thought of the title of the well-known study by Ruth Benedict, *The Chrysanthemum and the Sword*. Could it be that by now the dualism in the Japanese people's nature that is expressed by these two symbols has been overlaid by other elements? Westernization and the overwhelming success of capitalism certainly suggest that it is more realistic to see modern Japan embodied in its worldwide industrial enterprises or in the multiplicity of television channels and microchips.

The imperial palace is located inside a park at the heart of the sprawling capital, which is crisscrossed by urban freeways on stilts or running through tunnels, carrying the traffic of millions of cars. The imperial enclosure is like an untouched islet in a churning sea. The palace combines traditional Japanese roofs and facades with contemporary, cleverly plain interior architecture. It is one of the most handsome buildings of the twentieth century, a persuasive synthesis of tradition and modernity. Has the entire Japanese nation found a similar synthesis? I do not believe so.

In Kyoto my wife and I visited the Rioan rock garden. It was moving to see not only middle-aged and elderly Japanese, but also young ones, lost in motionless contemplation of the artful arrangements. The park is a small garden without trees, hemmed in all around by wooden galleries as a still life is enclosed by a frame. Fifteen rocks and thousands upon thousands of small bits of gravel, carefully raked, give off a deep sense of peace, as they have done for five hundred years.

We had several experiences of this kind. For example, we observed a large crowd patiently waiting for the lighting of a pyre on the seashore across from the Golden Pavilion; the smoke was to rise to heaven through a starkly shaped old pine tree. We also watched the Japanese gathering colorful maple leaves in a moss garden, serenely meditating on their forms and colors. What an unbelievable contrast to the hectic activity in the factory halls!

Japan has not yet decided what road it will follow in the next decade and in the twenty-first century. The nation is not at all certain of its future; in this it resembles the Federal Republic of Germany, though for different reasons. While in the second half of the nineteenth century, under the Meiji emperor, Japan imitated German models in science, medicine, industry, and constitution, today American examples predominate; but in both cases the adaptation is only superficial. The Japanese are probably the most talented people when it comes to adopting the cultural, scientific, and technical developments of other nations and giving them a practical application. They have a great willingness to learn matters of science, technology, economics, and social organization from the West, and to adapt, refine, and surpass Western methods and technologies.

In prehistoric times they similarly adopted their script, their brush drawing, their art of horticulture, and especially their religion—Buddhism—from China and Korea and made them their own by modifying the originals. Japanese culture would be impossible without the five thousand years of China's cultural development. That is also probably the origin of the Japanese inferiority complex toward the Chinese, though eventually this contributed to the Japanese attempt at reconciliation with the neighboring people. In a very limited sense this policy can be seen as a Japanese parallel to Germany's *Ostpolitik,* separated in time by only a very few years. But at the same time there exists in Japan a widespread and for the most part carefully concealed arrogance, a feeling of superiority in comparison to almost all the neighboring nations. Japan's adaptability seems to be limited to people and cultures that are considered superior—China, the United States, and to a lesser degree, Europe.

The democratic parliamentary constitution imposed on the country by MacArthur and the consequent decision to give up military forces, also imposed from outside, have not caused the Japanese any great problems. Both acts, however, were quickly and characteristically modified to meet traditional Japanese social forms and Japanese needs. The parliamentary system did not abolish the traditional oligarchy of the conservatives and the principle of consensus among powerful groups and cliques; and instead of the military, interdicted by the constitution, there are now "self-defense forces" that encompass army, air force, and naval associations without meeting with any objections.

The annexation of the so-called Northern Islands—that is, the southernmost of the Kuril Islands—by the Soviets is in no way comparable to the partition of Germany; these islands are home to only a few thousand Japanese. On the other hand, the destruction caused by the war and the problems of economic reconstruction resemble those of Germany in many ways; they were overcome in a similar manner with the help of an enormously disciplined effort. Japan's rise to being the second-greatest economy in the world first astonished its neighbors as well as the Europeans and Americans and then frightened them. An American secretary of state once told me in Washington that the Japanese were plotting a new Pearl Harbor but this time by economic means. This interpretation, though considerably exaggerated, charac-

terizes the new hostility developed in the 1980s in the United States in
the face of the extremely uneven trade balance with Japan. The Americans and the European Community today look on Japan as a trade
competitor, even opponent, who uses allegedly unfair methods to best
the competition and who must therefore be forced into "voluntary
self-restriction"—even if unfairly.

After writing my thesis in economics on Japan's currency reform
immediately after the war, and also after my first visit to the country in
1961, I had quite a different view of Japan: I saw it as a nation that,
not unlike Germany, had been seduced by megalomaniacal imperialism
into energetic aggression and horrifying torment of its neighbors and
had been punished for these with total defeat and almost total destruction. Then I became aware of a country that after an interval of dull
shock entered with enormous energy on restructuring its cities and its
economy. A country whose policies after the war's end had been extensively determined by another nation but which, thanks to its own hard
work (in this, too, resembling Germany) seemed to find the way to a
new identity. Finally, I saw a people with a completely different cultural
tradition, completely alien at first glance but at the same time uncommonly attractive; its shrines and pagodas, its gardens and gates, its
colored woodcuts, its fine arts as a whole. In 1961 my friends Carlo
Schmid, Karl Wienand, and I were members of the same traveling
group; all three of us were impressed by these beauties—and Carlo was
enraptured by the women as well.

Since that time two unique parallels with Germany have become even
more evident, but so have fundamental differences. The great international success of Hitachi, Toyota, Fujitsu, and Sony on the one side,
and those of Mercedes, Bayer, and Siemens on the other, illustrate my
point. On the whole, the technological and economic successes of
Japan and the Federal Republic of Germany are not substantially different, despite German prejudices and misjudgments. It is true that on the
basis of their principle of leadership by consensus, Japanese management is on average somewhat more efficient than is German. There are
important chairmen and presidents in every Japanese enterprise, but
decisions are worked through and articulated by group discussions on
subordinate levels. The procedure in government ministries is similar.
Since those in charge do not rule by fiat, they have no subsequent need
to "motivate" their subordinates, since their subordinates already know
what they want. Though such a process is more time-consuming than
American or German management techniques, it is highly effective and
contributes crucially to the homogeneity of the plant's employees and

the ministries' bureaucrats. In Japan, by the way, salaries and fringe benefits are significantly lower than in Germany because of the social welfare system, which has not yet been adequately developed. Basic research and innovation are not yet very widespread. On the whole, Japanese exports are still somewhat less than Germany's—though Japan's population is twice that of the Federal Republic.

Today Japan has the most strongly egalitarian society of all the large industrial nations. The difference in living standards between rich and poor is comparatively slight; for an employer to live in a mansion with large grounds is a great exception. It is not the amassing of private property but the success of the company, the living standard of the workers, and the long-range survival of the firm that are the executive officers' guiding principles and at the same time the source of their social prestige. A similar attitude is pervasive not only among all managerial staff but among all employees. Thus the Japanese have attained a level of affluence that was unthinkable before the war.

But because all this is played out in the tightest of spaces, the Japanese feel that such concepts as discipline, hierarchy, and seniority are indispensable, and they continue to accept them.

It is true that this conservative tendency also has its very unlikable side: Women are still second-class citizens and often find compensation merely in the home. On this point Beijing and Nanjing seem much more progressive than Tokyo and Osaka. Many women in the younger generation, who have grown up under Western influence, suffer from their degradation; they comport themselves like Japanese among their compatriots, lighting the men's cigarettes and letting them walk ahead, while in Western company they behave freely and easily. To see the same woman in both situations in quick succession is confusing and charming all at the same time.

In view of the affluence and abundance, today's Japanese corporations can attract only some of the young people. At school and university, these adolescents cram in order later to get the better jobs in industry and administration and to work their way slowly up the ladder. But a large group is not at all tempted by these prospects; their frustration is expressed less in protests than in a tendency to enjoy life, especially as parents often provide financial support for a very long time. It is not only the older generation but also the middle group of forty-year-olds who are voicing concern about the youths' lack of direction. By now many Japanese suspect that economic growth alone cannot be a reason for existence and that the nation requires a renewal of its spiritual and political consciousness. The necessity of reform is seen not only by

intellectuals and socialists of the left but also by Prime Minister Nakasone and others on the right—even though there is little love lost
between the Socialist Party and the LDP.

Japan's reorientation is meeting with obstacles rooted in history. The
inevitable isolation of an island nation has already been mentioned, as
has the Japanese inability to feel national remorse, sorrow, and shame.
It is true that many political leaders are aware of the fact that Japan lacks
friends in the world and especially in its own region; and they would
like to make friends—but they don't know how to go about it. Their
neighbors' mistrust has been met with a lack of understanding.

The resulting caution is one of the reasons why after the end of the
war there was practically no Japanese foreign policy for a quarter of a
century. But at the same time Tokyo put unnecessary roadblocks in the
way of its neighbors' building up trust by believing it could get away
without a sign of regret about the Japanese invasions and atrocities. It
was not until a South Korean president visited Tokyo that Emperor
Hirohito and Prime Minister Nakasone, speaking for the nation, expressed shame and regret toward the Koreans—after almost forty years.
But to this day the children of Koreans deported to Japan during the
war are legally treated as second-class citizens, even though they were
born in Japan and grew up there.

A Japanese journalist once told me, "You Germans are fortunate in
that you have been forced by the families of the people you oppressed
who fled abroad—in particular the Jews in the United States—to con-
front your recent history and to tell your coming generations the truth
about it. We Japanese, on the other hand, are unlucky in that no
Chinese or Korean or Indonesian has alerted the world and thus forced
us to face the truth; and unfortunately we haven't sought it ourselves."
This is an imprecise judgment, to be sure. What is true is that some
Germans prattle about the "mercy of a late birth" and other Germans
occasionally commit the error of presenting their own history to young
people as a rogues' gallery; both these attitudes oversimplify guilt and
destiny into a black-and-white picture. The Japanese do something
different: As far as possible they suppress the dark pages of their history
during the 1930s and 1940s. This process has created dangers to the
development of Japanese ideology. Fukuda understood these dangers,
while Nakasone seems to underestimate them.

I first met Fukuda in 1971, when I made an official visit to Japan as
minister of defense. Later we met many times as finance ministers and
still later as heads of government. At present we see each other several
times a year because we are both members of the "Old Boys' Club"

founded by Fukuda. This club, also known as "Inter Action Council," is a loose association of about thirty women and men from every corner of the earth who at one time headed their states or governments.

My view of Fukuda is colored by our long friendship. Nevertheless I believe that everyone who knows him well will agree with me on two important points: One, he is one of the few internationalists among Japanese politicians, a man who makes an effort to transcend the interests of his country and recognize and respect the interests of other people and nations with a view to balance and preserving the peace. Second, he is one of the few Japanese politicians who, because of a comparatively clear way of putting things, can make themselves understood by foreign partners. Sato, Miki, Ohira, and Suzuki seemed to me exceedingly polite and courteous, but frequently I could not make out the meaning of their words, their judgments and views (the only person outside Japan with whom I had the same difficulty was Italy's Aldo Moro). Only Nakasone surpasses Fukuda in clarity—but the former's verbal precision, it seems to me, to a large degree obscures mental reservations.

In 1974, when he was minister of finance, Fukuda resigned from the cabinet of Kakuei Tanaka, who had been implicated in the Lockheed scandal; in late 1976 he became Miki's successor in the office of prime minister. At the economic summits in London in 1977 and in Bonn in 1978 we represented similar economic interests, especially in the area of energy policy. The effects of the first oil price shocks had hit both Japan and Germany hard, since both nations are dependent on imported oil. At the time Jimmy Carter urged us both to take on higher budget deficits and to accept higher inflation rates—but the United States was not prepared to contribute effectively to solving the energy crisis. In both Germany and Japan, economic recovery was the government's first priority. Almost equally important for us both, however, was the challenge of working off the foreign loans the Second World War had left behind.

For this purpose Fukuda traveled not only to the five countries of the ASEAN group and to Burma but also to Washington and the Middle East. He also sought mutual understanding in Southeast Asia, including Indonesia. "The Japanese government wants to share peace and prosperity with all of Southeast Asia," he said in a government statement in July 1977. He must have been the first, and so far the only, Japanese prime minister who recognized a moral obligation on the part of Japan toward the Third World and actually put it into practice with substantial increases in Japanese development aid. His greatest success was the conclusion of the peace and friendship treaty with the People's Republic of China in the summer of 1978; only a few years earlier, Beijing had repeatedly lodged harsh protests against Japan's alleged militarism. At the same time Fukuda resisted the pressures that were being exerted by Moscow because it interpreted the antihegemony clause contained in the treaty as directed against the Soviet Union. The Chinese-Japanese treaty was seen in East and Southeast Asia as a rebuff to the Soviet Union and infringed on Moscow's plans for an "Asian security system."

In the course of his public career Fukuda belonged to two of the three large social decision-making circles of Japan, which have alternately determined national policy since the end of the Second World War. They are, first, the top officials of the Ministry of International Trade and Industry (MITI), the Finance Ministry—from which Fukuda arose—the Foreign Ministry, and the Economic Planning Agency; second, the political leaders within the ruling LDP; and third, the leaders of private industry. None of these three groups recognizes a hierarchy in the European sense. Rather, the shaping of opinion occurs in a process, seemingly diffuse when viewed from the outside, of a mutual osmosis of opinions and interests that might deviate from each other completely even within the three complexes. The factions of the ruling party diverge as much as the various bodies of officials, with turf struggles similar to those in Germany. Though I am not competent to see through the internal structure of the entrepreneurial leadership class, I assume that here too interests collide in the same way but are brought into agreement through talking the same way the other areas are.

Unlike the leading politicians, the leading officials are retired at a relatively early age in order to make room for successor talents; many of them can be met again soon afterward in the upper levels of industry or politics. This is also the history of Fukuda, who was first an official and later became a politician.

As finance minister during the international currency crises of the early 1970s and the 1973–1974 international economic crisis resulting from the oil price shock, Fukuda not only gathered considerable international experience but also initiated friendly relations with important Western politicians. I, too, already knew Fukuda well before I officially visited him in his capacity of prime minister in October 1978. Thinking back to our talks in the autumn of 1978, I am overcome by memories of many earlier and even more numerous later conversations.

Like all his predecessors and successors, Fukuda had his office in the official residence, built by Frank Lloyd Wright. The building is a symbiosis of stylistic elements, in part derived from American 1920s modernism and in part echoing Japanese stylistic tradition—perhaps not entirely successful but interesting evidence of the fact that in the 120 years since the Meiji reformation Japan is now more, now less, open to Western influences.

In our general discussion of the political and economic situation Fukuda pointed out that the great fear—especially in the United States—that there would be major political breakdowns after the American departure from Vietnam had not been borne out in reality (he could not foresee the subsequent Vietnamese subjugation of Kampuchea). ASEAN had turned out to be one stabilizing factor; the Japanese-Chinese peace and friendship treaty would, he assured me, also have a stabilizing effect on the region.

Fukuda praised the ASEAN states; they had been promised further help, he noted, since Japan was aware that, given its economic potential, it was necessary to make an appropriate economic contribution. He mentioned the help given by Japan to Vietnam and Laos (at the time Kampuchea, under Pol Pot, was strongly in the orbit of China). Japan, he said, would have to take an interest in preventing overly harsh contrasts from arising between Australia and ASEAN on the one side and the nations of Indochina on the other. It seemed to me that Fukuda underestimated the significance of Moscow to Vietnam whenever he addressed Vietnamese independence efforts.

Fukuda saw Japan's future tasks as falling not so much in the political area as in the economic sphere. His eyes were open to the problems of the developing nations, and he was an advocate of the so-called North-South dialogue; he saw the economic triangle of United States, Western Europe, and Japan as the northern partner and regretted that within the triangle the two sides United States–Japan and United States–Europe were well developed, while the ties between Europe and Japan were still weak. On this point we were in agreement.

Fukuda felt less comfortable with my remarks about Japan's inevitably increasing role in the Asian Pacific region. The occasionally recurring propagandistic and political tensions between Tokyo and Moscow troubled and occupied him. "What can we Japanese do? How do you Germans manage to get along with the Soviet Union?"

I described the military situation and the overall strategies in divided Europe and spoke of the necessity of maintaining an overall strategic global balance; Germans would have to make their contribution both to the West's joint defense capability and to efforts at contractual arms limitation.

Fukuda was less interested in the military aspect and the arms limitation complex; he was more eager to learn precisely the methods by which German-Soviet economic exchange had been brought about and steadily increased. After the conclusion of the Japanese-Chinese treaty—which had much the same significance for Japan as, ten years earlier, the treaties with East Germany had had for the Federal Republic—he believed that now Japan could devote itself exclusively to building up international economic relations.

Although he was a very conservative politician, Fukuda was opposed to anything that could drive Japan into a military role. He was quite satisfied with the idea that in an emergency the United States would take over the defense of the area; in his view, Japan, in accordance with its constitution, did not require a large army, and its expenditures for defense should never be higher than 1 percent of the gross national product.

The fallacy of this idea of peace shared by many Japanese (the Socialist Party of Japan, headed by Takako Doi, goes even further—it wants unarmed neutrality) seems obvious to me: This well-intentioned concept would in the long run lead to Japan's permanent dependence on the United States for its overall strategy. The internal imbalance of the Japanese economy would produce more goods and services that are required within the country, resulting in a high balance of trade surplus. At the same time a very high savings rate, which is not even remotely affected by capital needs within the country, would lead to expanded Japanese capital exports, which Japan's trading partners would make use of to finance substantial amounts of their trade deficits. The United States, the European Community, and the rest of the world will not sit by forever while Japan thus becomes the largest creditor nation in the world.

For over a decade the United States has been leveling reproaches at Japan; as a rule these attacks have not been justified, since the United States' own undisciplined budget policy is responsible for the country's surplus purchasing power, its budget deficits, its structural balance of trade deficit, and its capital imports, which have been rising almost every year since the 1970s.

But the United States is Japan's most powerful trade partner by far. Since Japan has no other allies, it will continue step by step to give in to the pressure of the United States and the European Community. Tokyo will try to leave it at purely formal concessions; but if the West is not satisfied by these, Japan will in fact have to give in, which is what has happened up to this point. The present Japanese leadership generation often enough finds such concessions difficult; but because it has suffered the traumas of wartime and postwar events, it has so far always found solutions to current conflicts.

However, the position of the coming Japanese leadership generations remains an open question. They will inherit foreign and defense policies that are unilaterally directed at the United States, while at the same time they will be handed a state of permanent conflict with the United States. They will feel a growing American pressure to engage in substantially stronger defense efforts. But the Japanese people also have a strong dislike of arms buildups and of national military strength, which has been inculcated since 1945. To this is added the rejection of Japan as a military power by China, by all Japan's neighbors, and by the Soviet Union. Under these circumstances the inappropriate structure of the Japanese economy and its postwar abstinence in the area of defense may lead to impatient reactions and pressures on the part of the West, causing counterreactions in Japan that are hard to estimate now.

By the end of the century the counterreactions might also conjure up racist resentment; they might cause the domestic structure to be rejected and the LDP turned out. If such an eventuality occurs, a far-reaching alteration in the current foreign policy, guided entirely by Tokyo, would no longer be unthinkable. It might go as far as an attempt at regional association or—should this proposal fail—deliberate isolation through nonalignment. In 1975, when Giscard and I were thinking up the economic summits, we insisted from the outset that Tokyo be included precisely in order to guard against that nation's isolation. During the second half of the 1980s, however, the anti-Japanese attitude in the United States—especially among the unions, in industry, and in Congress—as well as in Brussels and the capitals of the other European Community nations has grown very much stronger. In general the Germans understand Japan's dilemma a bit better; after all, they usually sit with Tokyo in the international dock when it comes to matters of trade and economic policy. But so as not to arouse unfortunate memories of the last world war and the Berlin-Tokyo axis, every West German government will go to great lengths to keep any cooperation with Japan within the framework of European-Japanese cooperation and to present it as such.

During that same 1978 visit to Tokyo both Takeo Fukuda and I were aware of the necessity of minimizing any German-Japanese common cause; Jimmy Carter's demands to kindly "reflate" our economies, which were leveled at both of us during the economic summits of 1977 in London and 1978 in Bonn, had made us both feel that caution was desirable when publicly presenting our bilateral relations.

In general the media in both countries understood and respected the necessity of our reserve. There were a very few exceptions. Thus the *Frankfurter Allgemeine Zeitung* accused me of having been too soft on Moscow during my visit to Japan; this opinion was based on the concept that the rivalry between Moscow and Beijing was advantageous both to Germany and to Europe. Conversely, German national radio and the *Nürnberger Nachrichten* feared that my visit to Japan and my praise of the Chinese-Japanese treaty might have provoked the Kremlin. The Berlin *Tagesspiegel*, however, saw the matter correctly: "The Germans must deal with the Soviet Union, but they will prove their independence by not avoiding relations with China. Japan must deal with China but should nevertheless not avoid improving relations with Moscow. . . . Both Japan and Germany [are] not in a difficult position, provided that they are clever enough at manipulating the situation."

The Japanese press was less outspoken, but its reports were extremely detailed. And the papers in both countries printed pretty pictures, for example of the excursion to the great bronze Buddha that towers 50 meters into the sky of Kamakura, where it has been sitting since the thirteenth century. Another recorded Fukuda's attempt to try my snuff. My friend Hans-Jürgen Wischnewski had shown him my snuffbox; Fukuda shook a pinch out onto his palm and—licked it up with his tongue! "First rate!" he said. All of us laughed. Except for the proper use of snuff, the two heads of government got along very well politically and personally.

During my time in office I had no opportunity to get to know Prime Minister Nakasone more then slightly; it was only later that he and I met for longer conversation. When he became prime minister in 1982 (with Tanaka's help), he had already held a great many offices in a long political career. He was considered a "hawk" with strong nationalist tendencies. He had publicly advocated Japan's rearmament, and unlike most Japanese politicians, he had made no secret either of his service record in the navy or his respect for Japan's military achievements and his reverence for the war dead. For these reasons he would have been unacceptable to the United States (and most Japanese) as prime minister in the 1950s and 1960s; but in the 1980s, when Reagan was urging the Japanese to build up its defense system, Nakasone became Washington's favorite Japanese politician. His excellent knowledge of English and his flexible eloquence also stand him in good stead. Washington likes to believe in his pro-American sentiments, which are completely genuine—and yet are probably no more than the means to an end, which is to regain a position of power appropriate to the greatness and the historical tradition of Japan. Washington in part did not understand Nakasone's objective, in part put up with it, figuring that care could be taken to make sure that the dreams of Nakasone (and Japan as a whole) will not get out of hand. At the same time there were (and will continue to be) a plethora of trade policy pinpricks against Japan that could not help but injure Nakasone's national pride. But only once did he let his anger show.

Japan's foreign trade imbalance and its consequent ascent to the world's preeminent creditor nation—matching, conversely, the United States' fall to the position of most heavily indebted nation—will reverberate more and more strongly on Japan's isolation from the rest of the world. In the United States and other nations envy and fear of Japan will play an even greater role than they do today. It would therefore make sense for Japan to learn to apply its unusually high savings and capital formation to a far greater degree to domestic investments and at the same time to reduce them in favor of the general standard of living (improvement in social welfare!); in this way its balance of trade surpluses can be reduced except for a small remainder.

Occasionally there are some Japanese suggestions in this direction, as for example the 1986 Maekawa report, named for the former head of the Bank of Japan. However, these suggestions have so far run up against the traditional thinking of most of the politicians in the LDP (including Nakasone) and most especially of the bureaucracy in the Finance Ministry and MITI; and then there is the fact that Japan's development aid is so niggardly. The longer Japan can hold on to the enormous advantage—compared to the other industrial nations—of having to spend little more than 1 percent of its gross national product for military purposes, the more urgent the reconstruction of the Japanese economy becomes. The more, however, the Japanese defense budget is expanded, the more the neighbors' mistrust would grow—as would domestic political resistance. So a mixed strategy would be required, which in turn would require a deliberate, energetic, and very sensitive political leadership; neither is to be seen so far. None of the prime ministers to date has undertaken a large-scale attempt at a solution. As a result, in spite of the frequent change in top personnel, Japan's overall strategy vis-à-vis the rest of the world essentially continues to be marked by acquiescence and readiness to make concessions to the United States but not by imagination, a will to restructuring, or greater national freedom of action. Therefore the foreign policy positions of the prime ministers to date have differed less from each other as far as their results are concerned than they and almost all Japanese are prepared to believe.

Nakasone, like me born in 1918, is a man of many talents; he is athletic, he paints, and occasionally he writes poetry. On one occasion he sent me a slim volume of his haiku—the traditional short poem in which the first line consists of five syllables, the second of seven, and the third, concluding line again of five. The terse language of a haiku is intended to express a mood and awaken associations. It is therefore almost impossible to translate a haiku into a foreign language without sacrificing too much. A few years earlier, Nakasone and I had talked about the old capital of Berlin, about the Wall and the misery of partition. In the meantime he had visited Berlin, and he gave me two moving haiku:

> *Wind im grünen Mai;*
> *die Mauer in den Herzen*
> *bläst er nicht nieder.*

[Wind in the greening May; / it blows but cannot topple / the wall in the hearts.]

The second haiku referred to the Japanese plan, which he and I had discussed earlier, to rebuild the ruined embassy in the Berlin Tiergarten quarter and turn it into a cultural center:

> *Einschussnarben im*
> *Gemäuer, darunter grünt*
> *ein Rhododendron.*

[Scars of bullets in / the brickwork, below them blooms / a rhododendron.]

Japanese art has developed many extremely beautiful facets. I am always touched and often enchanted by the pavilions in Kyoto, by the ceramics, by the brush drawings and the colored woodcuts, by Japanese musicianship, by aspects of Japanese literature and by haiku. Many aspects of the Japanese, of their personality and their intellectual attitudes, seem to me unusually attractive—while others remain inscrutable to me. I am sure that, conversely, the Japanese feel the same way about Europeans. Lacking a knowledge of foreign policy and history, they have only a limited understanding of the world's political structure in general; they can also give themselves only an insufficient explanation of their own isolation and the concurrent small political role in the world.

The situation in East Asia and the Northwest Pacific area will continue to be dominated by China, the United States, and the Soviet Union. Neither the ASEAN states nor Australia, neither Japan nor any other nation will grow in importance in the region in the foreseeable future. Vietnam's drive to conquest can continue only with massive Soviet support, which strikes me as highly unlikely to occur. Beijing will tolerate Japan's economic preeminence because it hopes to profit by it, but China will prevent any steps by Japan toward becoming a military power. But of course for Beijing the Soviet Union will remain both the most important neighbor and the most dangerous power factor.

IV

Concluding
Observations
of a
European

T HE WEST must abandon bipolar thinking and learn to envisage a political triangle made up of the United States, the Soviet Union, and China, to take place as early as the 1990s. The United States will not find it as easy to accept this view as Europeans will, since Europe long ago arrived at the realization that an unaligned Third World is desirable. It is not very difficult to put this general attitude into practice when it comes to the People's Republic of China.

For Germans this should present no difficulties at all. On the contrary: Everything favors the idea that we Germans should contribute to satisfying China's enormous technical and economic needs according to our foreign trade abilities. Since Japan will in any case remain the most important economic partner of the People's Republic of China, probably followed by the United States, there is only a very slight danger—and this danger can be limited and compensated for—that Moscow will seriously misunderstand good economic and political relations between Bonn and Beijing as anti-Soviet provocations or effectively present them as such in propaganda. France, England, Italy, and the other nations of the European Community, as well as the nonaligned European nations, should not feel any hesitation about closer relations with China. It may therefore be assumed that Western Europe as a whole will develop better and closer ties with Beijing. Such an outcome is in both their interests and does not run into any ideological or other obstacles. It is only the Eastern European nations, under Soviet guardianship, that will have to exercise some caution in developing relations with Beijing.

The United States, on the other hand, will have to overcome numerous ideological obstacles arising from outraged rejection of the Chinese communist revolution, the defeat of Chiang Kai-shek, who was the United States' ally, and four decades of Taiwan policy. These internal hesitations will continue to play a role for some years in the Senate and among the public. Once, when I advised caution in supplying American military aid to Taiwan, Vice President George Bush pointed out to me, "You forget that we are talking about our oldest ally." Since 1979 there have been no formal treaty relations between the United States and the "Republic of China," and even in the United States the usage long current in Europe—"Taiwan" and "the officials in Taiwan"—is gaining ground. Nevertheless, the question of Taiwan remains a potential source of irritation.

And there are still other confusions, since the United States is so far lacking a clear China policy; Washington's behavior gives no clue as to an overall strategy on China. Nevertheless, if the Americans follow an exclusively objective strategic analysis, they cannot arrive at any conclusion other than the European one: Good relations with the People's Republic of China and support of its economic interests are in the Western interest. This interest could be endangered only if China, having changed leadership, should turn back to the Soviet Union— presupposing a willingness by Gorbachev or his successors to make very generous concessions—or if China itself should one day aspire to a hegemonical role in the East Asian region. Neither of these developments is likely within this century. Nevertheless, China will consider it expedient to keep a certain distance from the United States for the present.

There has been mention of an international political triangle the West must keep in sight: instead of the Washington-Moscow axis, the Moscow-Washington-Beijing conjunction. Presumably the Chinese will continue to reject this concept for a number of years. They like to give the impression of modesty, but in reality they will consider the concept of a triangle entirely appropriate.

It may seem strange to some that such a crude scheme of the division of power on the globe does not include any of the European states, India and the South and Southeast Asian nations, the two dozen Arabic states, Africa, Latin America, or the "Group of Seventy-seven" that on many occasions has represented more than one hundred developing countries. It nevertheless remains a fact that the United States, the Soviet Union, and China stand far above all other nations of the world not only geostrategically and by size but also on the basis of their centrally controlled political and military means of enforcing their power.

Not even the nuclear capability of England and France in the twenty-first century will basically change this situation, although at the present time it still seems substantially superior to China's. Other nations that are either on their way to acquiring nuclear weapons or who secretly already possess nuclear weapons, however, are already behind China.

The preeminence of the three world powers does not mean that each has a free hand in its respective region. They are constrained by moral considerations and by domestic and economic policy, as well as by the need to refrain from provoking possible hostile combinations or alliances of smaller nations or scaring away their own allies; finally, there is the concern that one of the two other world powers (or their allies) might exploit a precarious situation and intervene. This was why the Soviet Union could not force a success in Afghanistan simply by massing its power. For the same reason China could not forcefully end the war between Vietnam and Kampuchea and save Pol Pot. And these reasons keep both the Soviet Union and the United states from military intervention in the Mideast (Reagan's supplying Iran with arms is no more than a tactical game), although their own interests have repeatedly been at stake there. No American president can use military force to invade Cuba, Nicaragua, or any other nation of Central America or the Caribbean; Kennedy's serious error during the 1961 Bay of Pigs incident was an early confirmation of this rule.

An even clearer limitation on the international role of the three world powers is each one's objective, rational evaluation of the others' positions and the respect Washington, Moscow, and Beijing each has for the other two. These factors will keep each from approaching the interests and spheres of interest of the other two in ways that might endanger the peace. While suppressing the freedom fighters in Budapest in 1953, and again while building the Berlin Wall in 1961, Moscow carefully respected the geographic limits of the American power sphere, as it did in 1968, when invading Czechoslovakia. Conversely, Khrushchev's attempts in 1962 to install intermediate-range nuclear missiles on America's doorstep ended by being a major defeat for him as the result of Kennedy's readiness to go to war if necessary.

The most important reason for this mutual respect is that the three world powers are able to inflict unimaginable damage on one another with their world-spanning nuclear arsenals. This circumstance has increasingly been true of China for some years, although Beijing's nuclear missiles are still far inferior to those of Washington and Moscow in technical quality and number. According to Western estimates, in 1986 China had about 3 million active troops, along with 5.5 million reserves; China controls about 140 missiles with nuclear warheads, almost all of them in the intermediate range, less than one quarter of them based on submarines.

In the same year the Soviet Union had 5.1 million soldiers and 6.3 million reserves; its number of nuclear intermediate- and long-range missiles was roughly 3,000. Washington had armed forces of 2.2 million, plus an additional 1.7 million reserves; its stores included about 2,000 nuclear intermediate- and long-range missiles.

In addition, both the Soviet Union and the United States have huge air and sea forces; they are equipped with countless nuclear weapons, including some of great range. The land forces, furthermore, have the use of nuclear weapons that are played down by being called "tactical" or "battlefield" weapons. Altogether the Soviet Union and the United States probably have more than 20,000 warheads. Measured against this unimaginable destructive power, all other nations of the world would seem to belong to lesser power categories. This comparison is true as well for the naval forces of these two superpowers, with the American navy being far superior to that of the Soviet Union; the United States also has the use of naval bases all over the world.

Despite this accumulation of power, the two superpowers had good reason to consider themselves unable to use their nuclear weapons even once after Hiroshima and Nagasaki. The intimidating potential of nuclear armaments has always played an important role in the policies of the superpowers—usually indirectly, but very directly in the Cuban missile crisis of 1962. This potential could not, however, be exploited in Vietnam, Kampuchea, Afghanistan, Central America, or the Persian Gulf, not even to intimidate smaller or medium-sized nations, even though the intermediate-range nuclear missiles are specifically designed to menace small and medium-sized states in their own regions.

Nevertheless, the frequently cited hypothesis that the existence of nuclear weapons is what prevents war is deceptive; in fact, all three of the world powers have recently been involved in wars. The more limited statement that the possession of nuclear weapons prevents a direct war between the three world powers seems more justified. But even this notion is of dubious certainty.

In reality the two superpowers did not allow this idea to guide them in their armament efforts; rather, to this day they have allotted enormous funds—that is, sacrificed significant portions of their gross national products—to achieve advantages in the nuclear arms race. With the exception of France and England, all other nations of both Western and Eastern Europe have refused to participate in this race; the heads of the two alliances—the Soviet Union and the United States—would not have tolerated it. Instead the nonnuclear states of Europe have asked for limitations to the world powers' nuclear armaments, though their requests have generally been quite timid.

It was not, however, any third-party urging that caused Richard Nixon and, later, Jimmy Carter, to arrive at agreements with Leonid Brezhnev on limitation of long-range nuclear missiles (SALT I and SALT II); the treaties grew out of the insight of both world powers that it made sense to bring about a nuclear strategic balance and to stabilize it for a period of time.

The People's Republic of China took no part in the negotiations, nor has it been involved in the INF discussions, initiated in 1981, on limiting intermediate-range nuclear missiles or other efforts at disarmament. But considering China's huge population, relatively small per capita sacrifices might be enough to at least partially equalize China's arms disadvantage in comparison to the Soviet Union and the United States. It can therefore be assumed that in future both world powers will be interested in including China in arms control negotiations. Presumably in that eventuality the interest of the Soviet Union—as well as that of India and Vietnam—will be greater than that of the United States or Europe.

Western and Eastern Europeans have a common interest in keeping the peace on their continent, and this concern has given rise to their desire for balance, stability, cooperation, and consequently contractual arms limitation. The 1975 Helsinki Conference on Security and Cooperation in Europe, which brought all the European nations with the exception of Albania together with the Soviet Union, the United States, and Canada, gave a clear signal. Of course divergent opinions always make themselves heard among the European states as well as within each nation. The anomalous positions of France and Romania and the domestic confrontations in the Federal Republic, Holland, and Belgium concerning the TNF resolution and the zero solution are examples of such differences.

In Moscow, too, there are various opinions. It is inherent in the structure of the Soviet government that we can only guess at what happens behind the scenes, and it is only on rare occasions that we catch a glimpse of a corner of the diverging interpretations of the Soviets' security interests. It may be that even in this area the Gorbachev era will make matters somewhat more transparent; but that is by no means a certainty. The only thing that seems certain to me is that Gorbachev has understood how much his country's comparatively high expenditures for defense and the resulting sacrifices of goods and services handicap any economic reform. If any material success at all is to be made tangible within a very few years for the 290 million Soviet citizens, the objectives of Soviet economic reform require curtailment of the defense budget. But it seems that such cuts can win domestic approval only when there are treaties with the West that guarantee parity. As a consequence, economic reformers have an interest in disarmament negotiation and arms limitation treaties.

Because of the United States' democratic constitution and the important roles played by the Senate and House of Representatives as well as by the media, the process of opinion formation in the United States is almost transparent to any outsider. At times the United States seems to be negotiating more with itself than with the Soviet Union. The arguments and interests of others, even of its allies, seem to play a small part in this process, whether the subject under discussion is the development of SDI, INF negotiations, exports of nuclear power plants or pipes, the dollar exchange rate, or balance of trade deficits.

The American television audience hears and reads little about the opinions of other nations. Since it certainly reads no European newspapers, almost all the European editorials addressed to the United States miss their target. When an American administration nevertheless successfully makes the effort to be considerate of other nations' interests, it deserves praise. The tendency to egocentric and egotistical decisions—or "unilateralism"—increased substantially under Johnson, Carter, and especially Reagan. One of the reasons is the disappointment of many Americans that the concept of a worldwide "pax Americana" has long since become unrealistic; that the United Nations cannot remotely begin to accomplish all that had, idealistically, been hoped for it; and that the integration of Western Europe does not seem to be progressing.

I consider it probable that the thinking that goes on in Moscow and Beijing is no less egocentric, that decisions made in Moscow are even more strongly unilateral, and that the Soviet and Chinese masses are even less well informed about the interests of other nations than are most Americans. Most Chinese, for example, are likely to have little understanding of the fact that people in Singapore and the Philippines are afraid of China's power, just as most Soviet citizens fail to understand that Europeans and Asians living within the range of the Soviet Union fear the power of their nation.

Among the Europeans, the Germans are more afraid than the other nations; this is a result of the partition of Germany, the presence of foreign troops and weapons on German territory, and the absence of important freedoms in the restricted part of the nation. But other Europeans also experience fear in the areas of foreign and security policies. Many Europeans are made uneasy by their continent's dependence on the decisions in these areas by two superpowers. This is especially true of the politicians, from Warsaw to Paris and from Copenhagen and Oslo to Rome and Madrid. Nevertheless, they are even more unable today than they were in the 1950s to draw not only the theoretical but also the practical conclusions and work toward integrating Europe. Because during the early 1980s the Western European unification process came to a standstill, Europe's international importance has also shrunk. At the moment Europe cannot forcefully advocate its interest in a stable military balance through arms limitation treaties because even within Western Europe there are no shared objectives. Unless this situation changes, the superpowers will continue to dominate us.

If, after examining the military facts, we look at the economic situation, the power of the three world powers is far less impressive. The oil trade balances of the 1970s are a vivid example. The three world powers at first were little affected by the oil price shocks of 1973–1974 and 1980–1981, which were caused by OPEC. China's minimal foreign trade in oil and natural gas was—and continues to be—a negligible factor, the United States is to a large extent self-sufficient, while the Soviet Union is a net exporter of oil and natural gas (especially after the extensive restructuring of its electricity supply to nuclear power). Conversely, Japan, France, Germany, Italy, and the other highly industrialized nations with the exception of England were and are almost entirely dependent on oil and natural gas imports.

So it should have come as no surprise that the sudden twentyfold increase in the world market prices of crude oil (with gas prices generally following oil prices) would strongly favor the three world powers. But such was not the case. It is true that the highly industrialized states, as well as the many developing nations, were forced to accept considerable damage to their economy. Thus, for example, Germany's oil payments to foreign nations rose between 1972 and 1981 from 3 billion to 29 billion dollars; during the same period France's foreign payments for oil rose from 2.5 billion to 25 billion dollars. In that time OPEC's yearly income from oil exports rose from 25 billion to 260 billion dollars, and that of the Soviet Union from 1.5 billion to almost 43 billion dollars. This shock to the world economy had debilitating consequences for economies dependent on oil imports: a loss of buying power, higher budget and balance of trade deficits, the collapse of currencies, inflation in prices, in some cases high foreign indebtedness, and almost everywhere high unemployment. The developing nations have been as unable to recover from their high foreign indebtedness as the industrialized countries have been unable to overcome unemployment. The seismic shock to the world economy between 1972 and 1982 has caused pernicious economic structural changes in almost all the world's nations, and the consequences are not yet clear. Japan and the rapidly industrializing low-wage countries of East and Southeast Asia are the only exceptions worth mentioning.

However, the three world powers that were not primarily touched badly by the two oil price explosions—the Soviet Union even profited by a considerable expansion of its foreign trade sphere, with oil and natural gas today making up one half of Soviet export income—could not strengthen their economic position in comparison with the rest of the world. One reason is that the economic systems of China and the Soviet Union are generally cumbersome and inefficient; however, in the United States under Carter, and even more so under Reagan, some serious economic errors were made (at the outset the necessary cuts in oil consumption were artificially delayed by keeping domestic prices too low, and later the budget deficit was bloated to such an extent that it could not nearly be financed by domestic savings or capital formation). Another reason is that the foreign trade involvement of the three world powers is fairly insignificant, so that they could not profit a great deal from the international structural crisis. Of course eventually they too were affected by the indirect negative consequences.

The United States, which was responsible for more than 30 percent of the world's production in 1985, supplied only 11 percent of world exports (because of the fall in the value of the dollar, the percentage has decreased since that year); the Soviet Union accounted for 7 percent of world production, but its share of world exports amounted to only 4.5 percent; China's share of world production was 2.5 percent and its share of world export a mere 1 percent.

The figures for the European Community and Japan are quite different. The EC's share of world production was 19 percent and Japan's 10 percent, but their shares in world exports were 32 percent and 9 percent, respectively (because of the drop in the dollar exchange rate, these figures have since risen). Of course the high exports of the Economic Community and Japan are balanced by their equally high imports.

It is clear that Western Europe and Japan are much more deeply involved in the world economy than the world powers are; they therefore also have a much greater, a vital interest in the ability of an international economy based on division of labor to function. As opposed to these, the Soviet Union and China are so far merely onlookers in the world economy; until the beginning of their economic reforms the two Communist world powers therefore showed only slight interest in the workings of the world economy and its institutions.

Today, in the mid-1980s, the world power that is the United States—the greatest economy overall—has become the chief beneficiary of the functioning money and capital markets of the world economy. Although on the basis of per capita real income the United States is one of the richest nations in the world, it has become the greatest debtor nation (while Japan and West Germany have imprudently grown into the greatest creditor nations). Nevertheless the United States, the European Community, and Japan taken together are responsible for more than half of the world's production and more than half of the world's exports. The trade is predominantly in highly developed industrial products and capital goods. Without these three economic power centers, the other roughly 150 nations of the world would have to get by with a very much lower standard of living. It is not improper to speak of an economic triangle that largely controls the world economy: United States–European Community–Japan. Not only the trade in goods and services but also international capital trade and monetary policy are largely played out within the framework of this triangle of economic power.

The United States is the only one of the three world powers that is a keystone of both military and economic power structures; it is a corner of both triangles. This is the main reason for the United States' paramount position; the Soviet Union, China, Western Europe, and Japan are each components of only one of the two triangles.

Of course the situation need not remain the same in the twenty-first century. Though it seems unlikely, it is not entirely impossible that America's economic strength will continue to decline. Nor can we entirely reject the possibility that economic reform in the Soviet Union and China will lead to growth in the currently minor economic influence of these world powers. Finally, it is conceivable that the Western

European nations will gain both economic and military influence beyond their "common market"—a phrase that is merely optimistic so far—so that in the coming century the triangles will turn into squares.

History teaches us that power constellations have a limited lifetime; they cannot stop the dynamic of new powers, new ideas, and new leaders. The European pentarchy—the hegemony of Russia, Austria, Prussia, England, and France created by the Congress of Vienna—and its internal balance fell apart after only a few decades. The balance of five nations—the Soviet Union, the United States, China, England, and France—that was the aim at the founding of the United Nations, which charged them with having the final responsibility for war and peace through their veto power in the Security Council, never became a reality. The dual dominance of the United States and the Soviet Union that came about instead is more and more limited to Europe; internationally it will have to begin by including China, a nation that with its population of far more than a billion is more than four times as large as the United States and almost four times as large as the Soviet Union. China is followed by India, which so far is still struggling with great internal problems. And who can say with certainty that the many Islamic states will not one day make common cause?

From the point of view of the number of people involved, China is at present the site of the greatest economic experiment in history. This experiment involves the risk of great setbacks; but to make changes we must be willing to assume risks, even though they must be calculated and hedged. The risk Beijing is willing to assume in the area of power politics, that of moving military defense to fourth place in the national budget, seems slight on objective viewing. Deng Xiaoping's reforms and opening the nation to the outside world represent something qualitatively similar to that initiated by the Meiji emperor after 1868. Of course today China—unlike Japan, which was completely isolated after the 250 years of the Tokugawa Shogunate—can call on a number of entrepreneurial and foreign trade experiences; the many traders along the coasts from Tianjin through Shanghai to Guangzhou were not dispossessed until the 1950s, and they are flourishing in Hong Kong. China can also rely on the loyalty of many thousands who have had scientific training abroad and are willing to return and work with the nation.

Gorbachev's economic experiment has begun on a much higher level as regards both technical skill and the living standard of the masses. But Gorbachev cannot take the domestic risk of bumping the defense budget to fourth place. In Russia all entrepreneurial traditions were broken more than sixty years ago; the grandchildren of the Revolution no longer remember from their own experience how an enterprise is managed. Free market prices, the accumulation of profits, investment of profits in new technology, and an increase in the capacity of the enterprises—it would be an unheard-of innovation to have all these decided by individual managements. Even introducing them runs head-on into sluggishness and resistance.

The success of Soviet reform is in the European interest. But the Europeans cannot give more help than the Soviets are willing to pay for. We cannot financially secure the retreat of the huge military force that has established itself in our immediate vicinity and thus allow it to continue the tempo of its current buildup. But our situation would be quite different if treaties would guarantee arms reduction. In such a case Western Europe would have every reason to give economic assistance. Naturally the economic emancipation of the Soviet Union would also profit Poland, the German Democratic Republic, Hungary, and Czechoslovakia and diminish economic control by Moscow of the Warsaw Pact nations. Inevitably, too, the economic relations between Western and Eastern Europe, which have until now been slight when compared with Western European standards, would gradually increase, so that economic cooperation worthy of the name might come into being. People in both East and West would benefit by such a development, and the chances are good that in Eastern Europe not only would the standard of living increase but personal liberty and individual freedoms could also be expanded. All Europeans therefore have good reason to hope for success in the dual effort of international arms limitation and Soviet economic reform and in any case to contribute as much as possible to the former.

These are opportunities for Europe, but at the same time they are risks. Thus, through abstinence or the shortsighted insistence of some European states on the status quo, Europe could contribute to a possible failure of disarmament negotiations. Should the disarmament policies meet with great success, the risk will arise that the situation thus arrived at will represent purely bilateral decisions made over the heads of the Europeans; this situation could possibly, though not necessarily, once and for all freeze the division of Europe that has existed for forty years into American and Soviet spheres of influence. Another risk remains, which is that in the course of time an increasingly economically strong Soviet Union may try to reacquire a superiority in arms.

That is why the nations of Western Europe should concentrate their

interests in order jointly to become a politically, militarily, and economically effective subject of international politics. Here I have more in
mind than the creation of a United States of (Western) Europe, a goal
that seems utopian today; there should also be the close cooperation
envisaged by Churchill in 1946, de Gaulle in 1962, and Kennedy in
1963. Churchill's vision was ahead of its time; it failed because he was
unwilling to include his own country. De Gaulle's vision ran up against
the German Bundestag before it could be shattered by his own countrymen's fear of Germany, just as, eight years earlier, plans for a European
Defense Community (EDC) had failed. As an outsider, Kennedy would
probably have been unable to contribute substantially to the unification
of Europe, and his early, violent death robbed the United States of any
potential for positive influence.

Nevertheless, Kennedy's vision of an Atlantic community, to be supported by American and European pillars, is today more of a reality than
it was at the time the United States began to become enmeshed in the
Vietnam War. Today the necessary preconditions are in place: The
European Community is established; England is a member; French
reservations against Germany have largely made way for mutual trust;
since the beginning of the 1980s, the Council of Europe has repeatedly
proven its worth as the controlling institution of Europe, even creating
the principles of a European Monetary System; today the collective
economic power of the European Community members, especially
their international role, which overshadows that of all other nations
and alliances, has provided Europe with a unique political weight; and
finally, by now all quantitative preconditions for an independent and
sufficient defense of Western Europe (except nuclear weapons) have
been met.

Nevertheless Western Europe is about to throw its opportunity away.
Today it could become a subject of world history, determining its own
destiny—the fourth world power, if you will. Instead, the Western
European leaders are stuck in status quo ideology. England's leaders still
think that their "special relationship" with the United States is more
important, although by now the United States has pretty much forgotten about it; in American thinking the English Channel is wider than
the North Atlantic. France's leaders still have not realized that their
nuclear autonomy, which no one else covets or wishes to wrest from
them, could easily be combined with a military leadership role of the
joint conventional forces of Western Europe, all entirely within the
NATO framework. In spite of the above-average successful dynamic of
the Italian economy, Italy's political class is plagued by a latent inferior-

ity complex when it comes to foreign affairs; it exhausts its energies in domestic fun and games with political coalitions. After Hitler, Auschwitz, and the Potsdam Agreement, Germany is not in the running for leadership; furthermore, its largely undefined relationship with the German Democratic Republic and its somewhat exaggerated fear of the Soviet Union and communism still prevent it from having a constructive pan-European ideology.

Thus, at present, Western Europe lacks leadership and is therefore continuing its well-founded leaning toward the United States. But this also means that its dependence on the United States, the world power, continues. And just as on occasion we have complained about the leadership of Presidents Johnson, Carter, and Reagan in general and in foreign affairs specifically, we will surely go on complaining in future.

Japan is in a similar position. But unlike Japan, which is isolated in its region, the Western European nations have an alternative because Europe is united by more than a thousand years of common cultural evolution, forty years of military cooperation, and thirty years of economic collaboration and because today, unlike Japan in its region, the European nations have friendly relations with each other.

It is by no means impossible that in Western Europe we will neglect to draw the political conclusions pointing to the future from this historically unique situation. We might let slip the opportunity to clean up the Economic Community's agricultural policy, which has become nonsensical; to create a truly homogeneous common market; to replace the eleven currencies within the Economic Community step by step with a single European Currency Unit, so as gradually to achieve synchronized national budget and financial policies and create an integrated defense force. And we might forget to provide Western Europe with a shared overall strategic leadership.

If in Western Europe we continue as we are, the peoples of Eastern Europe will remain clients of Moscow while the peoples of Western Europe decline into clients of Washington—even if they are only occasionally, at critical moments, aware of the situation.

We Western Europeans are united with North America not only by the ideals and practices of democracy but also by the practice of a market economy and the contractual freedom of both consumers and producers, and especially by the ideal and practice of individual human rights. We have a great many areas of agreement and only a few disagreements. The North Atlantic alliance is an expression not only of geostrategic expedience but also of a great coincidence of basic values.

It is hard to tell the depth of the coincidence of basic values in the

two Communist world powers now or in the future. What is certain is
that we cannot expect either of them to agree with North America and
Europe on the fundamental values of democracy. That concept, which
is based on classical Greek ideals, was developed in the Western European and North American cultural area, and attempts to transplant it
to other cultures have not been very promising.

A separate question is whether the two Communist world powers can
discover and develop the basic value of personal freedom; the preconditions for it are greater among the Russians and the other European
peoples of the Soviet Union, because there is a greater common cultural
and historical grounding than there is among the Chinese and the
minorities in the People's Republic of China. But there is little reason
for us to consider ourselves superior and special on that account. The
culture of China grew over thousands of years while Europeans could
not read or write, and it developed its own values. The principle of
forced conversion, which was born in Western Europe, was a serious
breach of its own values even at the time of the Crusades.

But we Europeans do have a right to protect and defend ourselves
against any attempt to force foreign rule or dictatorial social and governmental forms on us. Our expectation of success would be greater if in
the twenty-first century there were not three but four world powers, if
through its own unification process Western Europe were to develop
into that fourth world power.

Even so, the preservation of our own freedom and our own peace
would still predominate. Manipulation of political, military, and economic power alone cannot fulfill these requirements. Farsighted-
ness, prudence, and an overall Western European strategy guided by
reason will also have to play their part. If we—far more than 300
million Western Europeans—can accomplish all this, our weight
would be placed in the world's scales. In this way we could attain self-
determination, as well as offer aid and support to the Europeans east
of the Elbe and the Danube. Their current constellation is not fixed for
all eternity, either.

An overall strategy guided by reason and directed at preserving the
peace of each world power and each nation requires diplomacy guided
by reason—that is, it requires a willingness to listen to each other and
to understand the other nations and their interests. Caution is an
essential quality, but the traditional ideas of the enemy can only do
harm.

Whoever the person is who sits on the other side of the negotiating
table, he is a human being, with human preferences and weaknesses that

are not so different from our own preferences and weaknesses. He represents interests that do not agree with ours. But he, too, is learning that peace and a dignified human existence are possible only if they are shared. All of us—Americans, Russians, Chinese, and Europeans—are beginning to learn that we share this world and that we must depend on each other. "One world" the American Wendell Willkie called it fifty years ago. The phrase "to give is to have" applies to each of us. In other words, if we wish to have peace in the world, we must be willing to give something up.

Index

About the Author

After holding the portfolios of defense minister and finance minister, HELMUT SCHMIDT was chancellor of the Federal Republic of Germany from 1974 to 1982. He currently lives near Hamburg.